AN IMPECCABLE SPY

ALSO BY OWEN MATTHEWS

Stalin's Children
Glorious Misadventures

AN IMPECCABLE SPY

Richard Sorge, Stalin's Master Agent

OWEN MATTHEWS

BLOOMSBURY PUBLISHING
LONDON • OXFORD • NEW YORK • NEW DELHI • SYDNEY

BLOOMSBURY PUBLISHING
Bloomsbury Publishing Plc
50 Bedford Square, London, WC1B 3DP, UK

BLOOMSBURY, BLOOMSBURY PUBLISHING and the Diana logo are trademarks of
Bloomsbury Publishing Plc

First published in Great Britain 2019

A catalogue record for this book is available from the British Library

Library of Congress Cataloguing-in-Publication data has been applied for

ISBN: HB: 978-1-4088-5778-6; TPB: 978-1-4088-5779-3; EBOOK: 978-1-4088-5780-9

6 8 10 9 7 5

Typeset by Newgen KnowledgeWorks Pvt. Ltd., Chennai, India
Printed and bound in Great Britain by CPI Group (UK) Ltd, Croydon CRO 4YY

To find out more about our authors and books visit www.bloomsbury.com
and sign up for our newsletters

Contents

Prologue
'Siberians!'

On a freezing morning in November 1941, Natalia Alexeyevna Kravchenko and her half-sister Lina buried their father's paintings in the garden of their dacha. The artists' village of Nikolina Gora, forty kilometres to the west of the Kremlin, had become the front line in the battle for Moscow. Days before, columns of smoke rising from the neighbouring village announced the arrival of the vanguard of the Wehrmacht, moving into position for their final strike on the Soviet capital. The dacha stood on a high, wooded bank of the Moscow River, and Red Army medics had commandeered it as a field hospital for the coming battle. The sisters had been told to evacuate immediately and hastily bundled their father's paintings and pre-revolutionary silverware into a large trunk which they buried in a hollow on the steep bank that descended to the river. They held out little hope that the handful of Soviet soldiers busily digging trenches at the edge of the village could hold off the imminent German attack for long. Natalia expected that night to be the last she would ever spend at the handsome country house her father had built.

Just before dawn, Natalia was woken by a low rumbling noise. She pulled on a sheepskin coat and felt boots and went to the gate to investigate. Lying by the roadside, huddled in their army greatcoats against the cold, hundreds of Soviet soldiers were snatching a few hours' sleep in the snowbanks by the side of the road. The rumble was the sound of their snoring. 'Siberians!' an officer told her, fresh off the train from the Soviet Far East: reinforcements come to defend Moscow.

Over the following days the Siberian boys died in their hundreds in the marshy ground between the villages of Nikolina Gora and Aksinino, alongside hundreds of thousands of other Soviet troops along a 600-kilometre front around Moscow. The huge draughtsman's desk specially made for Natalia's father was pressed into service as an operating table. But the Germans never advanced any further. Natalia Alexeyevna did return to the dacha; indeed, she lives there still. So does her granddaughter, who is my wife. This book was partly written there. The paintings are back on the walls. Even the pit that the girls dug in the hillside is still visible when the undergrowth dies back in autumn. The old steel trunk stands rusting behind the house.

The tide of the Second World War turned outside Moscow that month, thanks largely to those Siberian reinforcements. They might not have been there without the efforts of a German communist spy operating on the far side of the world – an agent who penetrated the innermost secrets of both the Japanese and the German high command, yet was distrusted by his own spymasters in Moscow. Victory, of course, has many fathers, especially one as bloody and momentous as the Soviet victory in the Second World War. But Richard Sorge's brilliant work played a crucial role in saving the Soviet Union from disaster in 1941 and enabled Stalin's eventual victory in 1945.

Introduction

Richard Sorge was a bad man who became a great spy – indeed one of the greatest spies who ever lived. The espionage network that he built in pre-war Tokyo put him at just one degree of separation from the highest echelons of power in Germany, Japan and the Soviet Union. Sorge's best friend, employer and unwitting informant Eugen Ott, German ambassador to Japan, spoke regularly to Hitler. Sorge's top Japanese agent Hotsumi Ozaki was a member of the cabinet's inner advisory council and regularly talked to Prime Minister Prince Konoe. And in Moscow, Sorge's immediate bosses were constant visitors to Stalin's Kremlin study. Sorge survived as an undetected Soviet spymaster for nearly nine years in Tokyo, even as Japan was swept by hysterical spy mania and the police constantly hunted for the source of his regular, coded radio transmissions. And yet he managed to steal the most closely kept military and political secrets of both Germany and Japan while hiding in plain sight.

Sorge was both an idealistic communist and a cynical liar. He saw himself as a soldier of the revolution, a member of an exalted class of secret party cadres entrusted with the sacred task of penetrating the citadels of the USSR's imperialist enemies. But at the same time he was a pedant, a drunk, and a womaniser. He was addicted to risk, a braggart, often wildly indisciplined. On his frequent alcoholic binges, he crashed cars and motorcycles, drunkenly confessed his love for Stalin and the Soviet Union to audiences of Nazis, and recklessly seduced the wives of his most valuable agents and closest colleagues.

Sorge often spoke of himself as a romantic hero, a robber-knight from German Romantic poetry. In truth he was one of the lonely deciders who haunt the fringes of the political desert, a man always destined to carry the burden of superior knowledge and higher motives than the lesser humans who surrounded him. A self-professed champion of the working masses, he was a raging intellectual snob whose natural milieu was the casinos, whorehouses and dance halls of pre-war Shanghai and Tokyo.

Above all he was a professional dissembler. Like most who reached greatness in his profession, Sorge was driven by a profound compulsion to deceive. Deception was both Sorge's skill and his fatal addiction. For most of his life Sorge lied to all those around him – his many lovers and friends, his colleagues and his masters. Perhaps he even lied to himself.

One of the most extraordinary things about the Sorge story is the realisation that he moved in a world of shifting international alliances and infinite possibility. To the nation-state players at the time, even the most cast-iron certainties of hindsight were still malleable – even such apparently immutable matters as which nation would be on which side in the Second World War. For much of Richard Sorge's career, the Soviet Union and Germany, while ideological opponents, were in fact covert allies. Throughout the 1920s the German Army sent thousands of troops for training on the plains of Belorussia, under the terms of a secret agreement between Moscow and Berlin. In 1939 Stalin struck a deal with Hitler to divide up Europe, from the Baltics to the Balkans via Poland. Soviet and Nazi troops, victorious against their common Polish enemy, staged joint victory parades in Brest and other occupied cities. As late as February 1941, Hitler was offering Stalin membership of the Axis powers – albeit while simultaneously preparing to invade the USSR – and urging that Germany, Italy, Japan and the Soviet Union divide the world between the great dictatorships of the age. Stalin, while wary, was certainly tempted. Until the night of 22 June 1941, Hitler and Stalin were allies and the latter apparently believed that he would remain so. Even more strangely, we now know – as Richard Sorge did not – that from September 1940 Stalin had also laid his own contingency plans for invading Germany, known as Operation Groza. Even as he sent Germany vast supplies of corn, oil and steel to fuel the Nazi war effort under the terms of the 1939 non-aggression pact with Berlin, the Soviet dictator had his own opportunistic scheme in place for double-crossing Hitler should the opportunity arise.

Japan's role in the world war was even more mutable. It was clear from the moment that a group of renegade Japanese officers provoked an invasion of Chinese Manchuria in 1931 that Tokyo's military had expansionist dreams in Asia – ambitions that would, in time, swamp the protests of the civilian government at home. But Japan's attitude to Russia was deeply ambiguous. The Japanese Army lobbied forcefully for an invasion of the Soviet Union – an invasion which would have utterly destroyed Stalin's efforts to fight the Germans after the Nazi invasion of Russia in 1941. The Japanese Navy was equally adamant that the nation's imperial destiny lay to the south, in seizing control of the rice fields of Indochina and the oil wells of the Dutch East Indies. Thus the survival of the USSR hung on the intricate power plays inside the Imperial Japanese General Staff in 1941. Could Stalin afford to denude the Soviet Far East of troops in order to defend Moscow? It depended on knowing whether or not Japan's 1941 invasion plan for the USSR was going to be put into action. And it was their master agent, Sorge, who could tell them.

Nor was Japan's collision course with America by any means certain, even as late as October 1941, just weeks before the Japanese Navy's surprise attack on Pearl Harbor. On the contrary, Prime Minister Konoye had spent years desperately trying to forge a deal with Washington to avoid war in the Pacific. His envoy, Admiral Nomura, Japan's ambassador in the United States, came tantalisingly close to negotiating a non-aggression pact with US president Franklin Roosevelt in the summer of 1941.

Sorge's world was one where alliances even between such natural enemies as Hitler and Stalin, Stalin and the Japanese militarists, were made and broken. Unlike most spies of the twentieth century, Sorge's espionage was not merely a matter of betrayed agents and blown secret operations; it had a terrifyingly direct bearing on the fate of nations and the course of the entire war.

Among the stranger aspects of the Sorge story is that unlike many other tales from the shadow world of espionage, it is extraordinarily well documented. After their arrest by the Japanese authorities in October 1941, every member of the Sorge spy ring – with the honourable exception of Kawai, one of Sorge's junior agents – sang like canaries. All confessed because of a basic desire to survive. But the various members of the group all had different motivations for their cooperation. Sorge himself had been misunderstood and unappreciated for years by his Moscow masters, and wrote a long prison confession that boasted about his own espionage prowess, his professionalism and integrity. We know, but Sorge did not, that he was also frankly distrusted by his controllers in Moscow who thought he could be a double agent. Sorge hoped, until the very end, that the Soviet Union would save him; therefore Sorge confessed nothing of his doubts about communism, his plans for flight, his secret bank account in Shanghai – these we now know about from other sources.

The spy ring's long-serving radio man, Max Clausen, had the opposite message for the Japanese. He freely admitted to losing his communist faith and even boasted about systematically sabotaging his boss's espionage efforts by regularly ripping up or severely truncating the cables that Sorge had given him to send. Clausen evidently hoped for mercy from his captors, which he received. Sorge's star agent, Hotsumi Ozaki, an idealistic young journalist who later rose to the position of trusted adviser to the Japanese cabinet, was keen to prove that his apparent treachery was a species of patriotism. Ozaki told his captors that he had been working for the cause of international peace and had his nation's best interests at heart, as he strove to avoid a war between Japan and Russia.

Whatever their various reasons, the prisoners gave their Japanese interrogators a gigantic trove of detailed information on their lives and espionage careers stretching back as far as the early 1920s. More, the Japanese secret police had been intercepting and transcribing the ring's encoded radio messages from almost the first moment that Clausen had begun transmitting the secret reports from Tokyo to Moscow. Despite strenuous efforts, the Japanese had never been able to locate the transmitter, nor decipher the messages. But once Clausen surrendered the book code that he had used to encrypt his telegrams, Japanese military intelligence was able to read almost every word of Sorge's secret correspondence with his masters in Moscow. The confessions and the transcripts, which fill two thick volumes of testimony, were published in full after the war. This evidence was later cited at length by McCarthy-era anti-communists in the United States as a lurid blueprint of how Soviet intelligence could penetrate the highest levels of a government.

Two things are missing in the vast trove of confessions and decrypts gathered by the Japanese police, as well as from the hundred-odd books that have been written about Sorge, mostly by Japanese historians, since his execution in Sugamo prison in Tokyo in November 1944. The most important omission is the Soviet side of the story. No Western historian has accessed the Sorge files in the archives of the Communist International in Moscow or the Soviet military intelligence archives in Podolsk – or cited the important recent work by Russian historians based on parts of the military archive that have been closed to foreign researchers since 2000. The story of Sorge's turbulent career as an agent for the Communist International, his apparent disgrace as that organisation was ruthlessly purged of all but the most slavishly loyal non-Russians under Stalin, of Sorge's recruitment by Soviet military intelligence and the subsequent cycles of distrust and paranoia that led to Sorge's gold-standard intelligence being dismissed as enemy disinformation, is told here for the first time. So is the inside story of Sorge's desperate attempts to warn Stalin of the coming German invasion of the Soviet Union in July 1941 – a warning that was systematically suppressed by the top brass of the Red Army, terrified of contradicting Stalin's fixed idea that Hitler would never attack him.

The other missing piece from the Japanese version of events is any sense of Sorge's inner life: his doubts and fears. As John le Carré observed, spies make for tremendously unreliable narrators because they have so often invented and reinvented themselves. For most of his adult life Sorge lived in a world where the risk of arrest and betrayal followed him like a shadow. During his years in Japan he had nobody but his immediate subordinates with whom he could share his secrets. Even his closest Japanese agents, Ozaki and Miyagi, never became personal friends.

Sorge was, like many spies, an indefatigable ladies' man. The talents of spy and serial seducer are deeply intertwined. American intelligence estimated that he had affairs with at least thirty women over the course of his residence in Tokyo. But even Sorge's lovers were, to a greater or lesser extent, pawns that he deployed in his spy games. He thrilled and terrified them with wild motorcycle rides through the night. To a few, he revealed a megalomaniacal side as he danced about his house, waving a samurai sword and ranting drunkenly about how he was going to slay Hitler and become a god. Even in his most private moments, he was play-acting at being someone greater than himself. He frequently complained to his lovers of his loneliness, but allowed none of them to share the burden of the secrets he carried within himself. All the same, the testimonies of the women in Sorge's life give us a valuable side view of the man he wanted to be. And the Soviet archives reveal many more insights into his private world in the form of his letters to his Russian wife, and in the memoirs and correspondence of his Moscow friends and colleagues, cited here in English for the first time.

Sorge presents an unusual challenge for a biographer. He lived most of his life in a shadow world where his life depended on secrecy. Yet he was also an extrovert and, in many ways, an exhibitionist. Once the game was up, in the loneliness of a Japanese prison, Sorge busied himself with spinning an idealised version of himself for his interrogators, and perhaps for posterity. In his extensive correspondence with Moscow, his letters to his wife, Katya, his journalism and scholarship and his confessions, he left a vast written record. However, like many apparently gregarious people, he kept his inner self a closely guarded secret. He was a man with three faces. One face was of Sorge the social lion, the outrageously indiscreet life of the party, adored by women and friends. His second, secret, face was turned to his masters in Moscow. And the third, the private man of high principles and base appetites living in a world of lies, he kept almost entirely to himself.

Sorge had a talent for situations, which served him well throughout his erratic and changeable life. The ease with which he was able to move from one milieu to another, from one place, woman, friend, to another, was staggering. Men and women alike found his self-destructive charisma irresistible. He could be savagely elemental, temperamental, capricious, often as selfish as a child. His story reminds one of a man constantly trying out a series of savage caricatures of himself on the world, adopting slightly new variants of his social persona. And as with many lonely people, he had a burning desire to be loved, and to be fabulous, but loved from afar. And that was his paradox; the more fabulous and successful he became, the more impossible it became for him to be loved for himself.

He was a man of many friends, but could confide in almost none of them. He spent most evenings out carousing at parties, bars and restaurants – yet he lied to and used almost every one of his wide circle of acquaintances. Indeed, it was his magic facility for putting people at their ease that was his greatest life skill. Sorge's charm also kept him alive. When the brutal Gestapo Colonel Joseph Meisinger, nicknamed the 'Butcher of Warsaw', was sent to Tokyo to investigate him, Sorge took him out carousing in the fleshpots of Ginza and quickly made a bottle-mate of his deadliest enemy.

Sorge was also brave. Whether it was snatching photographs of secret documents when left alone for a few minutes in the German ambassador's study, or lying terribly injured in hospital after a drunken motorcycle wreck, but fighting to hold on to consciousness until a friend could arrive to recover incriminating documents from his jacket pocket, Sorge maintained an almost supernatural cool. He always thought of himself as a soldier, from his teenage years in the service of the Kaiser in the trenches of the First World War to his last moments on the gallows, when he stood to attention and saluted the Red Army and the Soviet Communist Party. For all his drunken indiscretions, he always lived a life of furious activity, rising early and spending hours every day writing, reading and spying. He was an officer and a professional, even when drunk, even in despair. And in some ways he was also a gentleman. In prison he refused to discuss the women in his life and never mentioned his long-standing Japanese mistress to his interrogators. The prosecutor who questioned him described Sorge as 'the greatest man I have ever met'.

Sorge was also an intellectual of sorts. He certainly had at least a robust and competent intelligence. He wrote in his prison memoir that in peaceful times he would have been a scholar. He lived his life as the principal actor in a one-man show whose real audience was unknown to its physical spectators – his nearly always remote spymasters in the Fourth Directorate of the Red Army's General Staff. It was Sorge's tragedy that for the most crucial part of his career they doubted his loyalty and thought him a traitor – though he himself mercifully never knew that the brilliant intelligence that he supplied was often scorned and discounted.

The last word, before we embark on the story of Sorge's extraordinary life, belongs to John le Carré, who wrote a brilliant review of the first book to appear in Britain on the Sorge case in 1966.[1] Le Carré, who had spent time among the denizens of the shadow world, understood Sorge better than most. 'He was a comedian in the sense of Graham Greene, an artist in the sense of Thomas Mann,' wrote le Carré:

Like Spinell in Thomas Mann's *Tristan* he is always working at
an unfinished book. It was at his bedside, together with an open
volume of 11th-century Japanese verse, at the time of his arrest.
He played the Bohemian, keeping a pet owl in a cage in his room,

drinking and whoring his way to triumph. He was an entertainer; people (even his victims) loved him; soldiers warmed to him immediately. He was a man's man, and like most self-appointed romantics, had no use for women outside the bedroom. He was an exhibitionist, I suspect, and the audience was always of his own sex. He had courage, great courage, and a romantic's sense of mission: when his colleagues were arrested he lay in bed drinking sake, waiting for the end. He wanted to train as a singer; he is not the first spy to be recruited from the ranks of failed artists. A French journalist describes him as possessing a 'strange combination of charm and brutality'. At times, he undoubtedly betrayed the symptoms of an alcoholic. These then are the characteristics he brought to spying. What did spying give to him? A stage I think; a ship to sail upon his own romantic seas; a string to tie together a bundle of middle-range talents; a fool's bladder with which to beat society; and a Marxist whip with which to scourge himself. This sensual priest had found his real métier; he was born wonderfully in his own century. Only his Gods were out of date.[2]

I

'From the Schoolhouse to the Slaughter Block'

'They integrated you with imperial ambitions and then let you
loose into the world with a sense of elitism – but with your heart
frozen. When you've become that frozen child, but you're an
outwardly functioning, charming chap, there is a lot of wasteland
inside you that is waiting to be cultivated'[1]

John le Carré

Richard Sorge was born in 1895 in Baku, the Russian Empire's wealthiest,
most corrupt and most violent city. For centuries oil and gas had been
bubbling naturally up from the ground in the marshy lowlands along
the Caspian Sea, busting spontaneously into flame and inspiring
fear and worship. But it was a couple of Swedish brothers, Ludwig
and Robert Nobel, who transformed this acrid-smelling backwater
into a great oil boomtown when their drills hit Baku's first gusher in
1879. The resulting fountain of wealth drew workers, architects and
merchants from all over Russia – as well as a boomtown's compliment of
prostitutes, revolutionaries and chancers. Baku, in the words of one of
its most famous residents, Iosif Stalin, fast became a city of 'debauchery,
despotism and extravagance' for the wealthy.[2] For the working class
who toiled in the notoriously unhealthy oil-company shanties, it was a
twilight zone of 'smoke and gloom'.[3] Baku's own governor called it 'the
most dangerous place in Russia'. For the firebrand young writer Maxim
Gorky, 'the oil wells of Baku left the impression of a painting of hell'.[4]

Hell it may have been, but Baku was an infernal region that spouted
money. Foreign oilmen, attracted by high wages and lucrative stakes

in the fast-proliferating oil companies, flocked to the smoky Caspian city.[5] One of them was Wilhelm Richard Sorge, a drilling engineer from the small Saxon town of Wettin am Saale. He arrived in Baku in 1882 at the age of thirty-one, having spent several years in the oilfields of Pennsylvania. Sorge was hired by the Caucasian Oil Company, a Nobel subsidiary.[6] Another fortune seeker was the merchant Semyon Kobolev, who relocated from Kiev to take advantage of Baku's burgeoning business opportunities. His daughter Nina was born in Baku.[7] In 1885, at the age of eighteen, she met and married Wilhelm Sorge.[8] Their union of oil and commerce was a match made in a particularly capitalist inferno.

Baku's backstreets, where the workers of the Nobel and Rothschild companies lived, were 'littered with decaying rubbish, disembowelled dogs, rotten meat, faeces'.[9] The city literally choked on its own effluent. 'The oil seeped everywhere,' recalled Anna Alliluyeva, who lived there a decade later with her revolutionary son-in-law Iosif Stalin. 'Trees couldn't grow in this poisonous atmosphere.'[10] However the Sorge family, like well-to-do expatriates of later generations, managed to stay well clear of the filth, violence and nascent revolutionary fervour of Moscow's German residents. They rented a handsome two-storey brick villa in the prosperous suburb of Sabunçi, to the north-west of the city. Downtown Baku may have been, as the novelist Essad Bey wrote, 'not unlike the Wild West, teeming with bandits and robbers'.[11] But Sabunçi was a haven of middle-class respectability, with wide acacia-lined streets that were soon to boast the town's first electric tram line. The Sorges' house still stands, now a dilapidated slum inhabited by ten refugee families. The grounds are now a maze of jerry-built shacks housing dismembered motorcycles and noisy chickens.

A group photograph taken in 1896 shows the Sorges as an ideal bourgeois German family. Paterfamilias Wilhelm Sorge, bearded and frock-coated, leans magisterially on a bannister. His five surviving children (five more died in infancy[12]) are arranged in matching dark suits on steps leading down to a garden where rugs have been laid out on the lawn for the occasion. The eight-month-old Richard is perched on a wooden flower-pot stand, steadied from behind by his mother and surrounded by a huddle of servant women in plain frocks.

Sorge made no mention of his mother in an autobiographical confession written in a Japanese prison in 1942, except to note her Russian nationality. Certainly, it seems that Nina Sorge spoke to her sons in German rather than her native Russian, making young Richard twice a stranger – secluded from both the teeming oriental life of Azeri-speaking Baku and from the Russian colonial elite of the city. When Sorge later moved to Moscow he had to learn his Russian mother tongue from scratch.[13]

Wilhelm Sorge was 'unmistakably a nationalist and imperialist ... unable to shake off the impression made upon his youth by the building of the German Empire during the War of 1870–71', Sorge wrote in his prison memoir. 'He was strongly conscious of the property he had amassed and the social position he had achieved abroad.'[14]

Yet despite Wilhelm's stern Prussian patriotism, a spirit of rebellion seems to have run strong in the Sorge family. Richard's paternal great-uncle, Friedrich Adolf Sorge, had joined an armed rebellion against the Saxon authorities in 1848, and in the wake of the revolution's failure emigrated to America in 1852.[15] He became a passionate communist and served as secretary general of the International Workingmen's Association – better known as the First International – when it moved to New York in the 1870s. He also corresponded extensively with his fellow German exiles in London, Karl Marx and Friedrich Engels.[16]

For the Sorge children growing up in Baku, 'home' was a Germany which they had never seen. Perhaps it was Sorge's insular expatriate upbringing that helped to sow a lifetime's sense of otherness in him. Wilhelm Sorge moved the family back to Berlin when Richard was four years old. A Russian connection remained, as Sorge senior worked in a German bank involved in the import of Caspian naphtha from Baku. But Richard clearly never felt fully at home in his new fatherland. 'What made my life different from the average was a strong awareness of the fact that I had been born in the southern Caucasus,' he wrote in his prison confession. 'Our home also differed immensely in many respects from that of the average bourgeois family in Berlin.' The Sorge family's half-foreignness and the 'peculiarities' of their expatriate past made 'all my brothers and sisters slightly different from the average school child'.[17]

The Sorges settled in the prosperous Berlin suburb of Lichterfelde 'amid the comparative calm common to the wealthy bourgeois class'.[18] By his own account, at school Richard was a difficult but brilliant pupil who 'defied the school's regulations, was obstinate and wilful and rarely opened my mouth'.[19] He told his Japanese interrogators that he had been 'far above the rest of the class ... in history, literature, philosophy, political science' and boasted of his athletic prowess. He dreamed, he told his captors, of becoming an Olympic high-jumper. By the age of fifteen the young Sorge had developed an avid interest in Goethe, Schiller, Dante, Kant 'and other difficult authors'. In later life Sorge would often speak of himself as a 'gypsy-scholar' or a 'robber-baron', both characters from German Romantic poetry. Schiller's *The Robbers*, the tale of a Robin Hood-like hero who robs the rich and protects the poor, was a particular favourite.[20]

On his death in 1911 Wilhelm Sorge left all his children with comfortable private incomes. 'Economic worries had no place' in the Sorge home.[21] Young Richard grew more serious, taking a particular interest in history and politics. 'I knew Germany's current problems better than the average grown-up,' he explained to the Japanese. 'At school I was known as "Prime Minister".' It says something about his self-regard that Sorge, even in middle age, apparently saw no possible irony in his schoolboy nickname. His teachers found him talented but lazy, and a show-off.[22] He joined the Wandervögel – 'The Travelling Bird' – a patriotic, sentimental youth group that organised camping and hiking holidays for clean-living young men and women of the German Empire – though Sorge would later describe it as 'a workers' athletic association'. It was while on a Wandervögel camping trip to Sweden in August 1914 that the news broke that Germany was at war.

The boys, in a fervour to come to their country's call, hurried to catch the last steamer home. On 11 August, without consulting his mother, reporting back to school or taking his final high-school graduation exam, Sorge presented himself at a Berlin recruiting office and signed up for the German Imperial Army as a private soldier. 'I was impelled to make this decision by a strong urge to seek new experiences, a desire to liberate myself from school studies and what I considered the whole meaningless and purposeless pattern of living of an 18-year-old,' he wrote – adding, perhaps more honestly, that he had been caught up in the 'general outburst of excitement created by the war'.[23] The shadow of his late father's stern patriotism must also have played a part.

Sorge was assigned to the student battalion of the Third Guards Field Artillery Regiment,[24] and was given, again by his own account, 'a completely inadequate six-week training course at a drill ground in the outskirts of Berlin'. At the end of September, he and his ill-trained fellows were shipped out to the River Yser in Belgium, where they faced British and Belgian regulars stubbornly holding prepared positions. Glowing with naive enthusiasm, Sorge's student battalion went over the top for the first time on 11 November at Dixmude, south of Ypres, and was massacred. Any illusions Sorge may have had about the romance of war were shredded along with most of his comrades on his first day of action. 'This period may be described as "from the schoolhouse to the slaughter block",'[25] Sorge later recalled with palpable bitterness.

The German survivors of that angry and deluded generation of 1914 would later describe the bloodshed of the Western front as the *Kindermord* – the massacre of the innocents. The experience 'stirred up the first and most serious psychological unrest in the hearts of my comrades and myself ... after our thirst for battle and adventure had been glutted, several months of silent and pensive emptiness began'.[26]

Like many of his class and generation, Sorge's experience of war was profoundly formative, and shocking. Sorge, the bright young contrarian, found his reason beginning to rebel against the pointlessness of the conflict. 'I mused over my knowledge of history and realised ... how meaningless these oft-repeated wars were. My political curiosity led me to wonder what motives under lay this new war of aggression. Whose desire was it to capture this objective at the sacrifice of life?'[27]

For the first time in his young life, the gymnasium student and banker's son Sorge found himself side by side with genuine members of the proletariat. But to his apparent surprise, his 'simple soldier friends' seemed to have no interest in examining the root causes of the conflict in which they found themselves the fodder for cannons. 'Nobody knew the real purpose of the war, not to speak of its deep-seated significance. None of them even understood the meaning of our efforts. Most of the soldiers were middle-aged men, workers, and handicraftsmen by trade. Almost all of them belonged to industrial unions, and many were Social Democrats.' He found only one 'real leftist, an old stonemason from Hamburg, who refused to talk to anybody about his political beliefs'.[28] They became close friends. Perhaps Sorge found in him an alternative father figure. The older mason told his young protégé of his life in Hamburg and of the persecution and unemployment he had suffered. Growing up in a world of unquestioning patriotism, this was the first pacifist Sorge had ever met. Their friendship was cut short when the old socialist was killed in action in early 1915.

A few months later it was Sorge's turn to stop enemy steel. His unit had been transferred to Galicia, on the border of Russia and the Austro-Hungarian Empire, in June 1915. For the first time he found himself fighting for his fatherland against his motherland. In July, Sorge caught a piece of Russian shrapnel in his right leg. He was sent to recover in the Lazarett Lankwitz military hospital in Berlin. A photograph taken at the time shows Sorge standing arm-in-arm with a young bespectacled cousin and friend, Erich Correns (later a distinguished chemist and East German politician). Sorge holds a cigar in his right hand and turns to his comrade, as Correns grins. Despite the Iron Cross medal ribbon on the breast of Correns's tunic, the two of them look like the young schoolboys that they so recently were.[29]

Sorge used his convalescence at Lazarett Lankwitz finally to take his school leaving certificate. He passed with top marks. He also enrolled in Berlin University's department of medicine and began attending lectures. But the Germany to which he had returned was very different from the one he had left. 'Money could buy anything on the black market. The poor were irate. The initial excitement and spirit of sacrifice apparently no longer existed. Wartime profiteering and surreptitious buying and selling were beginning to appear, and the lofty ideals underlying the war were receding farther and farther into the background. In contrast, the material objectives of the struggle were gaining increasing prominence, and a thoroughly imperialistic goal, the elimination of war in Europe through the establishment of German hegemony, was being publicised.'[30]

Sorge was 'not very happy in Germany and at a loss as to what to do'.[31] Alienated from the corruption of civilian life, he chose to return to the only adult world he had ever felt comfortable in – the comradeship of the trenches. He volunteered to rejoin his unit before his official convalescence period was up. German-led offensives in Gorlice-Tarnów in Galicia – the borderlands between the Austro-Hungarian and Russian empires – and in the Masurian Lakes in East Prussia in the summer of 1915 had pushed the Russian Army back hundreds of miles behind the pre-war border. However, when Sorge returned to his regiment he found that most of his old friends had paid for the advance with their lives. Those who survived were deeply war-weary. 'All the men dreamed of peace in their spare moments. The fact that, although we had already pierced deep into the heart of Russia, there was still no end in sight, made some of them begin to fear that the war would go on forever.'[32]

Wounded again in early 1916, Sorge found Berlin slipping ever deeper into the grip of 'reaction and imperialism'. He 'became convinced that Germany was unable to provide the world with … new ideas'. But though his revolutionary consciousness may have been awakened, the twenty-one-year-old Sorge nonetheless volunteered to return once more to his regiment on the Eastern front. 'I felt that I would be better off fighting in a foreign land than sinking deeper into the mud at home.'[33]

Fighting deep inside the territory of the Russian Empire, Sorge met some true communists for the first time – two soldiers who were in contact with radical political groups in Germany who frequently talked of the radical German leftist leaders, Rosa Luxemburg and Karl Liebknecht. Socialism, they told Sorge, offered a way to 'eliminate the causes of all this meaningless self-destruction and endless repetition of war … What was important to us was a broad solution, a permanent answer on an international scale.'[34]

Three weeks after his return to the front near Baranovichi, south-west of Minsk, in March 1916 Sorge was wounded for a third time. This time his injuries were nearly fatal. Both his legs were shattered by shrapnel and three fingers partially amputated. His injuries left him with a pronounced limp for the rest of his life. After an agonising journey across occupied Russia he was brought to the university hospital in Königsberg, the historic capital of East Prussia recently recaptured from the tsar. He was promoted to the rank of corporal, received the Iron Cross second class and a medical discharge from the army. He also learned that two of his bothers had been killed in combat.[35]

The Russian shell that shattered Sorge's legs and his military career also destroyed his last illusions. 'I was plunged into an intense confusion of the soul,' he wrote. A powerful revulsion for 'claims of spirituality and idealism trumpeted forth by nations at war' grew in him, as well as 'the notion … that a violent political change was the only way of extricating our selves from this quagmire'.[36]

Like many of his contemporaries, Sorge had undergone a violent rebirth. It isolated him in an inner world divorced from his family and class and placed in doubt the very foundations of the society in which he had grown up.[37] Another German infantry corporal who was also recovering from his wounds in the military hospital of Beelitz-Heilstätten near Berlin at the same time was similarly tormented. 'There followed terrible days and even worse nights. In those nights hatred grew in me hatred for those responsible,' wrote Adolf Hitler in his 1925 memoir *Mein Kampf*. 'In the days that followed, my own fate became known to me ... I for my part decided to go into politics.'[38] The anger and revulsion which drove a generation of young war veterans into radical politics on both left and right had an identical wellspring.

Immobile and in traction in his hospital bed, Sorge began to read his way towards truth. A 'very cultured and intelligent nurse' in the Königsberg hospital brought him books that were the building blocks of his socialism – Karl Marx's *Das Kapital*, Friedrich Engels's *Anti-Dühring*, Rudolf Hilferding's 1910 tract *Finance Capital*. Her father, a doctor, gave Sorge his first 'detailed account of the state of the revolutionary movement in Germany, of the various parties, factions, and groups that had been established, and of international phenomena in the revolutionary movement. For the first time I heard of Lenin and of his activities in Switzerland ... Already, I regarded myself as an apostle of the revolutionary labour movement.'[39] Sorge also devoured Kant and Schopenhauer, the ancient Greek philosophers and Hegel – 'a ladder to Marxism'. For the first time in many years, and 'despite the seriousness of my injuries and the excruciating pain involved in their treatment, I was happy'.[40]

After weeks learning to walk again, Sorge was able to move back to Berlin with his mother in the late summer of 1916. In October he enrolled in the economics faculty of Berlin University. As he studied, Germany's war effort and economy began to fall apart. 'The highly vaunted German economic machine crumbled in ruins; I myself, like countless other members of the proletariat [sic] felt the collapse through hunger and constant food shortages. Capitalism had disintegrated into its component parts: anarchism and unscrupulous merchants. I saw the downfall of the German Empire, whose political machinery had been termed indestructible. The members of Germany's ruling class, shaking their heads in helpless despair over these developments, split morally and politically. Culturally and ideologically, the nation fell back on empty talk of the heritage of the past or turned to anti-Semitism or Roman Catholicism.'[41]

News of the Bolshevik coup in Russia in November 1917 cemented Sorge's growing socialist convictions. 'I decided not only to support the movement theoretically and ideologically but to become an actual part of it.'[42] A lifetime later, in a Japanese prison as a convicted communist spy, he remained convinced that 'my decision of some 25 years ago was correct ... the only fresh and effective ideology was supported and fought for by the revolutionary labour movement. This most difficult, daring, and noble ideology strove to eliminate the causes, economic and political, of this war and any future ones by means of internal revolution.'[43]

The British journalist Murray Sayle noted a striking similarity between Sorge and another great Soviet spy, Kim Philby, whom he had interviewed in Moscow in 1967. Though of different generations, Philby and Sorge were 'psychic twins', wrote Sayle, 'two textbook examples of the rare species we might call *Homo undercoverus* – those who find the dull, unclassified lives that the rest of us lead simply not worth living. The parallels between the two are eerie. Both were born to peripatetic parents, far from what was to pass for home ... Both enjoyed privileged educations which turned them, at least outwardly, into convincing representatives of their respective upper classes ... Both became Communists as impressionable students, both at times when Communism was high fashion among young intellectuals. The decisive influence in each case was war.'[44]

Sorge was formally discharged from the army in January 1918. He immediately headed for Kiel, headquarters of the German Imperial Navy and a known hotbed of socialism. By luck or judgement, he found himself at the epicentre of Germany's brewing revolution.

2

Among the Revolutionaries

'To betray, you must first belong. I never belonged'[1]

Kim Philby

Karl Marx had always believed that Western Europe, not backward Russia, would be the birthplace of socialist revolution.[2] Russia was a country 'surrounded by a more or less solid intellectual Chinese Wall, erected by despotism', wrote his friend and supporter Engels.[3] Yet in November 1917 it had been Russia that showed the world the path to revolution. Germany would soon follow.

Both Russia and Germany's revolutions were led by mutinous sailors. Battleships, with their harsh discipline and stark class divisions, proved a fertile breeding ground for resentment and revolutionary violence. In June 1905 the crew of the battleship *Potemkin* rebelled against their officers and murdered eight of them. In November 1917, Bolshevik sailors of the cruiser *Aurora* fired a blank round across the Neva River that signalled the storming of the Winter Palace. In August of the same year an abortive revolt of 350 crewmen of the German dreadnought *Prinzregent Luitpold* had ended in two executions and the imprisonment of the revolutionary ringleaders. But the mutiny also spurred the formation of secret sailors' councils on a number of the capital ships of the Imperial German fleet, and sowed the dragon's teeth of future rebellion.[4]

Soon after arriving in Kiel in late summer of 1918, Sorge joined the Independent Social Democratic Party, a newly formed and far more radical offshoot of Germany's official leftist opposition, the Social

Democratic Party of Germany, or SPD. He established a student section of the party with two or three others, acting 'as head of the training group in the district where I lived', and working as an 'agitator, party recruiter, and instructor in Marxist dogma'.[5] We know from later accounts that Sorge was a charismatic and convincing speaker; he evidently honed his skills addressing audiences of revolutionary sailors in Kiel. 'One of these lectures I can recall even today,' he wrote in 1942. 'I was called for early one morning, secretly led away to an unknown destination, which proved to be sailors' underground barracks and there asked to conduct a secret meeting behind closed doors.'[6]

These back-room lectures on Marxist theory burst spectacularly into real-life revolution in the autumn of 1918. On 24 October, as Germany's land forces were crumbling into mutiny and retreat, Admiral Franz von Hipper ordered the German Imperial Navy to sea for a final battle against the Royal Navy in the English Channel. In the Schillig Roads off Wilhelmshaven, where the fleet had formed up for battle, sailors on three ships from the Third Navy Squadron refused to weigh anchor while the crews of the battleships SMS *Thüringen* and *Helgoland* declared outright mutiny. The revolt was temporarily checked when the squadron commander ordered torpedo boats to train their cannon on the rebels. But by 1 November several hundred sailors gathered in the Union House in Kiel under the auspices of the Independent Social Democratic Party. Sorge was one of the young volunteers on hand to distribute revolutionary leaflets. Two days later, despite attempts by the Kiel police to arrest the ringleaders, the movement had grown to thousands, who gathered on Kiel's Grosser Exerzierplatz under the slogan '*Frieden und Brot*' – peace and bread. A squad of soldiers ordered to disperse the demonstrators opened fire, killing seven and seriously injuring twenty-nine. The enraged sailors beat the commander of the loyal soldiers nearly to death.[7] Fresh troops brought in to quell the growing mutiny refused to obey orders. By the evening of 4 November, Kiel was firmly in the hands of 40,000 rebellious sailors, soldiers and workers. They issued a fourteen-point manifesto demanding the freeing of prisoners, freedom of speech, the end of censorship, and the establishment of workers' councils.[8]

The revolt quickly spread as delegations of sailors from Kiel dispersed to all of the major cities in the Reich. By 7 November, the first anniversary of the Bolshevik coup in Russia, revolutionaries had seized all Germany's large coastal cities as well as Hanover, Brunswick and Frankfurt am Main. In Munich, a workers' and soldiers' council forced the last King of Bavaria, Ludwig III, to abdicate. Bavaria was declared a *Räterepublik* – 'Council Republic' – and the hereditary rulers of Germany's principalities all resigned, leaving only Kaiser Wilhelm II as the final symbol of the old order.

The German Empire was crumbling – but was this to be a bourgeois revolution or a radical Bolshevik one? Friedrich Ebert, leader of the moderate Social Democratic Party, demanded the chancellorship for himself – as well as the abdication of the Kaiser. If the Kaiser remained, warned Ebert, 'social revolution is unavoidable. But I do not want it, indeed I hate it like sin.'[9]

On the afternoon of 9 November, the Kaiser abdicated. But it was not enough for the leaders of the Spartacist League, a radical socialist movement re-founded just a day before by its leader Karl Liebknecht, recently released from prison. From a balcony at the Berlin City Palace, Liebknecht proclaimed a German Socialist Republic. Yet Germany's newly hatched provisional government, led by the centrist socialists of the SPD, did not fall – despite signing a humiliating capitulation to Allied forces on 11 November, 1918. Ebert promised elections, and was supported by key elements of the regular army. Liebknecht's socialist revolution had temporarily stalled.

It was during these febrile days in Kiel that Sorge met Dr Kurt Gerlach, a professor of political science at the city's College of Technology. Gerlach was both a communist and a very wealthy man, and held salons for radical students at his comfortable home. 'Painters were talking about new art, poets were breaking with all the traditions,' recalled Gerlach's wife, Christiane. 'A young student of my husband sat silently among the guests: Richard Sorge ... It was soon clear that my husband favoured him over all the others. A friendship developed between the two of them; we called Sorge by his nickname Ika.' Christiane was immediately attracted to the handsome, brooding young man. 'In his clear, sharp eyes there lay infinite distance, and loneliness, everybody could feel that.'[10]

After two months of desperate jockeying for power between the SPD and the Spartacists, Liebknecht and his partner in revolution, Rosa Luxemburg, made their move. Once more, sailors from Kiel – many of whom would have listened to Sorge's speeches – played a central role.

In the first days of revolution in early November, Ebert's provisional government had ordered a newly created People's Navy Division – Volksmarinedivision – from Kiel to Berlin for its own protection. By Christmas it became evident that this had been a grave mistake. The radical Kiel sailors showed clear signs of Spartacist sympathies. After Ebert attempted to suspend their pay, they occupied the former Imperial Chancellery, cut the phone lines and put the Council of People's Representatives under house arrest.

Seizing the moment, the Spartacists formally renounced all ties to the SPD and Ebert's moderates. On 31 December 1918, Rosa Luxemburg drew up the founding programme of the revolutionary Spartacus League – though she vowed that her new party 'will never take over governmental power in any other way than through the clear, unambiguous will of the great majority of the proletarian masses'.

The revolution quickly ran out of the control of its instigators. Over Luxemburg's objections, the majority of the new party members rejected participation in the coming elections and favoured gaining power – like the Bolsheviks before them – via 'pressure from the streets'.[11] Luxemburg and Liebknecht warned that the workers were unprepared to take on the forces of the German state. Nonetheless Spartacist hotheads assembled at Berlin's police headquarters to elect an interim revolutionary committee that called for a general strike and mass uprising. Half a million demonstrators answered the call, coming out onto the streets of Berlin with placards calling on loyal troops not to fire on their countrymen.

It was a fatal miscalculation. The Volksmarinedivision, whose threatened disbandment had triggered the Christmas crisis, refused to join the rebellion. The demonstrators were met by regular troops – one unit even deploying a captured British Mark IV tank – as well as irregulars of the newly formed right-wing paramilitary militias. Known as Freikorps, these units had been recruited by reactionary officers who were passionately opposed to Germany's capitulation in the war and to Bolshevism. They were to become both the future Weimar government's most implacable enemies and the core of Hitler's Nazi Party.[12] Despite their ideological differences, the provisional government, fighting for its life, was quick to make a pact with the Freikorps. Deputy SPD leader Gustav Noske, who until recently had styled himself 'People's Representative for Army and Navy', accepted executive command of the reactionary paramilitaries. 'If you like, someone has to be the bloodhound,' he said.[13]

In Kiel, Sorge and a group of his friends gathered arms – presumably easily concealed pistols – and hastened to Berlin to join the fight. They arrived too late. The Freikorps, deploying artillery, brutally cleared several buildings occupied by the revolutionaries and killed 156 of them. 'The party needed assistance, but it was already too late to do anything when I arrived in Berlin,' Sorge would later tell his Japanese interrogators. 'We were forced to halt at the station and searched for arms but fortunately my weapon was not discovered. Any person who carried a weapon and refused to turn it over was shot. After being detained for several days inside the station, my comrades and I were sent back to Kiel. One could hardly call it a triumphant return.'[14]

While Sorge and his companions sat under arrest in Berlin-Hauptbahnhof, the Spartacist ringleaders went into hiding. On 15 January, Rosa Luxemburg and Karl Liebknecht were discovered sheltering in an apartment of the Wilmersdorf district of Berlin. They were immediately arrested and handed over to the largest Freikorps, the Garde-Kavallerie-Schützen-Division. That night, both prisoners were beaten unconscious with rifle butts and shot in the head. Luxemburg's body was thrown into the Landwehr Canal, while Liebknecht's body was dumped anonymously in a city morgue.[15]

The German revolution was over – for the time being. Kiel had become too dangerous for Sorge, so he moved to Hamburg to study for a doctorate in political science. There he organised a socialist student group, and formally joined the German Communist Party. The party recognised the young Sorge's skill as an agitator by appointing him 'training chief of the party's Hamburg area organisation guidance department'.[16] During this period, he also began to write for the local Communist Party paper – a journalistic career which he would maintain, both as a cover and in practice, for the next twenty-three years.

It is not clear whether it was Kurt Gerlach or his wife Christiane who drew Sorge to Aachen, a city in western Germany, in early summer 1919. Gerlach, like Sorge, had moved away from possible police scrutiny in Kiel to teach at Aachen University, and had invited Sorge to follow him. Nonetheless, his arrival on the doorstep of the Gerlachs' new home was clearly unexpected.

'The doorbell rang one evening and I went to see who was there,' recalled Christiane. 'Outside stood Ika. It was as if a stroke of lightning ran through me. In one second something awoke in me that had slumbered until now, something dangerous, dark, inescapable. Ika never pushed. He did not need to court people, they rushed to him, both men and women. He had more subtle means of bending them to his will.'[17] Christiane, like many other women to come, was taken by Sorge's good looks and dark charisma. 'Ika, tall, well built, with a full head of hair, gave an impression of strength,' wrote another contemporary. 'His features, although sallow, were attractive, with a strong, prominent forehead, which made his eyes seem very deep-set.'[18] When she was interviewed in 1989, the ninety-one-year-old Babette Gross, widow of Willi Muenzenberg (one of the other extraordinary communist underground operatives of the inter-war period), sighed winsomely when she recalled that she had known Richard Sorge 'when he was young and beautiful'.[19]

Gerlach secured his old protégé a teaching position at the higher school in Aachen. He also resigned himself to the budding romance between his wife and Sorge. This would prove to be another leitmotif of Sorge's life: people loved him, even his victims, even men he had cuckolded and whose confidence he had betrayed.[20]

Communism certainly appealed to a didactic streak in Sorge; all his life he enjoyed lecturing and haranguing people. He also saw himself as a man of action, a leader, a teacher, an organiser. Sorge had arrived too late to fight in the Spartacist uprising of 1919. But when on 13 March 1920, right-wing officers Wolfgang Kapp and Walter von Lüttwitz attempted to overthrow the government by staging a military coup in Berlin, he was ready.

The first call for a general strike to resist the Kapp Putsch came from the SPD-led government. But in the industrial Ruhr the communists saw the general strike as an opportunity to complete the Spartacists' unfinished revolution. In Aachen, Sorge sat on the general strike committee that brought thousands of miners onto the streets. Around 50,000 former and serving soldiers across the industrial Rhineland were organised into a 'Ruhr Red Army' and prepared to 'win political power by the dictatorship of the proletariat'. There is evidence that Sorge also belonged to the party's military committee in the Ruhr, which rallied physically fit young followers to do battle in the streets with the counter-revolutionaries. In the words of a friend, Sorge was 'quite incapable of staying out of a fight others had joined'.[21]

It was at this time that the German Communist Party formed its secret military wing, known as the M-Apparat, whose purpose was to prepare for the civil war the communists believed was impending in Germany, and to liquidate opponents and informers who might have infiltrated the party.[22] It is not clear how closely Sorge was affiliated with these fighting communists – though he would later boast to friends in Moscow about his running battles with reactionaries on the streets of Aachen and Solingen. In his later prison statement, he would change his tune, casting himself as an intellectual and organiser rather than a fighter and brawler.

The right-wing Kapp Putsch soon collapsed under the pressure of the general strike, which was supported by some twelve million workers across Germany. The Ruhr Red Army occupied Dortmund, Essen and Hagen by force, disarming government troops and declaring the sovereignty of workers' committees. By the end of March the entire Ruhr was in the hands of the rebels – though the uprising had no common leadership nor a common political programme. The restored SPD government, confronted with an armed uprising in Germany's heartland far larger than the Spartacist revolt had ever been, resorted to the same tactics as Noske had employed in 1919. Both the regular army and the Freikorps were mobilised to crush the communists, summarily executing rebels. By 5 April 1920, over a thousand socialists had been killed and the remnants of the Ruhr Red Army fled across the Rhine into the area occupied by French troops since the Armistice.[23]

The failure of the revolution left Sorge desperate and rootless. 'I have almost totally cut myself off from everyone in Germany, which is not something I would call sad in the usual sense,' Sorge wrote from Aachen to his cousin and friend Erich Correns. 'For a vagabond such as I, who cannot keep anything in his hands, this seems the only possible state. I am so completely up in the air, so completely homeless that the road is my preferred place and path.'[24]

It was not only Sorge who had lost hope and direction. Germany's communists, too, descended into the kind of infighting and bickering to which they had been pathologically prone since the days of Sorge's great-uncle Adolf, Karl Marx's friend, forty years before. In the wake of the German revolution's failure, the German Communist Party split into two, then three, rival factions. Though Sorge, from his lowly vantage point of a local labour organiser, could not have known it at the time, the struggles of the German party were a clear reflection of a larger power grab by Moscow.

Vladimir Lenin had always envisioned himself the undisputed leader of world revolution. Yet the Spartacists and their successors had always remained infuriatingly independent of the Russian Bolsheviks' party line. Now, with German communism temporarily crushed and many of its leaders murdered or imprisoned, Moscow's men were moving in to take control of the German party. In due course, they would also take personal control of Richard Sorge.

Sorge continued teaching at the higher school in Aachen while at the same time editing a local communist party newspaper, *The Voice of the People*. Kurt Gerlach agreed to an amicable divorce, and Sorge and Christiane moved in together in the nearby steel town of Solingen. It soon became evident that the police were keeping a close watch on Sorge, and were looking for an excuse to chase him out of town as a dangerous radical. A couple living in sin provided the excuse the authorities needed. To stay out of trouble Sorge, the wanderer, would have to contemplate entering what he called the 'bourgeois curse' of marriage. 'Because the police naturally want to throw me out of Solingen, but had no grounds to do so, they will try to use the pretext that [our cohabiting] is creating a public scandal,' Sorge explained in a letter to Correns on 19 April 1921. 'To the bourgeois, living together constitutes a scandal. It annoys both of us, but we will have to bite the sour apple.'[25] In an earlier letter to Correns he had vowed that 'not even internally, do I need another person to be able to live; I mean really to live, not simply vegetate'.[26] Nonetheless in May 1921, he and Christiane were officially registered as man and wife.

It was during this period of domesticity that Sorge also made his first forays into Marxist polemics, penning a pamphlet on 'The Accumulation of Capital and Rosa Luxemburg', a critical study of the theories of the dead Spartacist leader. It is an extraordinarily dull work. Even Sorge later admitted it was 'clumsy and immature, and I hope that the Nazis burned every last copy'[27] – though it's more likely that his politically incorrect praise for Luxemburg's respect for parliamentary democracy made the monograph an embarrassment to his later communist orthodoxy. But if Sorge had hopes for a career as a Marxist academic, they were disrupted at the end of 1922 when he was expelled from the higher school at Aachen for 'engaging in a heated political controversy'.²⁸ The party, in any case, had different plans for him. The Ruhr was a solidly proletarian region demonstrably ripe for revolution – but the labour movement was dominated by moderate Catholic trades unions that were, in the party's view, in need of urgent conversion to communism. The local branch of the German Communist Party, correctly valuing Sorge more as a doer than a thinker, therefore suggested that he become a miner and – literally – an underground agitator.

Unskilled but physically strong, Sorge found a job at a coal mine near Aachen, where he organised a socialist cell before moving on to do the same at another pit. 'Life in the mines was tough and dangerous,' he would later tell his Japanese captors, especially hard because his war wounds still brought on spasms of pain. 'But I never regretted the decision. The experience as a miner was no less valuable than the experience of the battlefield, and my new vocation was equally significant to the party.'²⁹

An effort to do similar work for the party in the coal-mining district of Holland in the Netherlands failed. Sorge was immediately identified as a troublemaker, expelled from the mine, and deported from the country. The Aachen mine-owners had also become alert to the threat of communist agitation, and Sorge found himself unable to find another job back in the Ruhr.

Becoming a party cadre remained as the obvious career choice – though Sorge, perhaps hedging his bets at this nadir of communist fortunes, continued to harbour hopes of becoming a serious academic. These scholarly aspirations would continue until the end of his life. He would always insist on being addressed as Herr (or Kamerad) Doktor Sorge, and contributed to academic journals. When he was arrested by the Japanese the secret police found an unfinished scholarly study of Japan in his bedside table.

Sorge was offered a salaried position in the party's Guidance Department. He refused, choosing instead a post offered to him by Kurt Gerlach – who clearly bore no grudges towards his wife's new spouse – at the newly founded Institute for Social Studies in Frankfurt of which Gerlach had recently been appointed director.³⁰ Christiane created a tasteful home that quickly became a lively leftist salon. One guest was Hedwig Tune, an attractive, slender actress of Austrian Jewish background and the wife of Gerhard Eisler, editor of the communist newspaper *Die Rote Fahne*. Inclined to schoolgirl crushes on people and causes, Hedwig – later to become famous under her second married name of Hede Massing – admired Sorge extravagantly.[31]

'He did not fit the general pattern of the German communist, neither did Christiane. They displayed better taste and more gusto than was customary in communist circles,' she wrote of the Sorges. 'Their home was the centre of social life within this group. I remember how quaint it looked, with its antique furnishings carried over from Christiane's past as a rich bourgeois professor's wife. There was a fine collection of modern paintings and rare old lithographs. I was impressed by the easy atmosphere and grace with which the household was run. I liked the combination of serious talk and lust for living.'[32] Massing cheerfully admitted that she moved 'only among the upper crust of the communists' – and described their circle's 'rather snobbish attitude' to people who were not as bright as they were.[33] Hede would nonetheless soon become a legendary Soviet spy.[34]

Sorge combined teaching with part-time party work, lecturing and editing as he had in Aachen. But he soon he found himself pulled into the clandestine world. With the police keeping close watch on the better-known leaders of the Frankfurt party, Sorge was tasked with handling 'all the secret liaison between the Central Committee in Berlin and the organisation in Frankfurt'. He hid the party funds and propaganda material in his study at the university, also concealing 'large bundles in the coal bin in the classroom' of the social science library. By October 1923 galloping inflation saw the value of the Reichsmark decline to 60 million to the dollar. In Saxony the party took advantage of mass protests to launch yet another armed rebellion and declare a workers' republic. During the brief rebellion Sorge was chosen to maintain 'constant secret communication' with the rebel leadership, travelling 'frequently on special missions to deliver essential political and organisational reports and directives' from Frankfurt and Berlin.[35]

The Saxon uprising was crushed, as was a similar communist rebellion in Hamburg and, soon after, an abortive right-wing putsch in Munich organised by the young firebrand Adolf Hitler. But Sorge had proved his worth as a clandestine operative. When a communist convention was organised in Frankfurt for April 1924, Sorge was a natural choice to provide security for the Soviet guests. Specifically, they were delegates of the Communist International, better known as the Comintern, an organisation that would soon gather Sorge into its embrace.

Karl Marx had declared in his *Communist Manifesto* that 'the working class has no country' and called for proletarians of all countries to unite.[36] In his 1902 tract *What is to Be Done?* Lenin laid out the idea that communist parties should be established across the world to aid the international proletarian cause – and founded the Comintern as the 'General Staff of the World Revolution'.[37] In practice, after taking power in Russia, Lenin saw himself as the unequivocal chief of that General Staff. He insisted that the Russian Bolsheviks, as the only group in the world that has actually brought revolution into being, should assume leadership of revolution around the world too.[38] The Comintern was in many ways the quintessential Leninist institution, shaped by the Russian leader's twin passions: an obsession with secrecy and a preoccupation with absolute power. Its aims were never remotely democratic.[39] Thus, from its very beginning in 1919, the Communist International was founded on a deception. Ostensibly, its role was to foster communism all over the world. Its true function was to gather all foreign radicals into one grand network under the control of Moscow, and to act as a front for Soviet propaganda and intelligence-gathering.[40]

The First Congress of the Comintern, held in a crowded little hall near the Moscow Courts of Justice in March 1919, set the tone of fake ecumenicalism. It ostensibly hosted fifty-two delegates from thirty-seven international communist parties. In practice, however, the English 'delegate' was a Russian émigré who had worked as a tailor in England and now served as secretary to the Soviet foreign minister, while the Japanese were represented by a Comrade Rutgers who had only once visited Japan. Lenin penned an editorial in *Pravda*, the official party paper, boldly declaring that 'the Soviets have conquered throughout the whole world'. There was, according to one English witness, 'a make-believe side to whole affair'.[41]

Germany was, from the very beginning, world revolution's key prize. Germany, as Lenin often said, was the 'powder keg of Europe'. And he proposed to make the keg blow with a spark sent sizzling through the Comintern's invisible incendiary network, a fuse that ran from Lenin's office at the Kremlin straight to that unexploded bomb that was the German proletariat's revolutionary consciousness.[42]

By the time Richard Sorge encountered the Comintern delegation at Frankfurt in 1924, the organisation had acquired a formidable apparatus and was led by Lenin's trusted lieutenant Grigory Zinoviev. It had also successfully backed a series of very real and violent revolutionary actions. One was the abortive Hungarian Soviet Republic in 1919, which had been supported by Moscow's gold and several hundred Russian fighters who styled themselves the 'Terror Group of the Revolutionary Council of the Government'. The Comintern also played a leading role in a failed coup in Estonia by the local Communist Party. And soon after French troops occupied the Ruhr valley in 1921 – after a dispute over unpaid compensation payments stipulated in the Treaty of Versailles – a Soviet sabotage cell was dispatched to Germany to try to spark a fresh wave of revolutionary violence. The team of Russian saboteurs and their German accomplices attempted to dynamite an express train from Halle to Leipzig as part of a wider 'March Action' of locally organised rebellions intended to kick-start a fresh nationwide uprising.[43] The Soviet Army was even mobilised on the newly drawn Russian-Polish border to intervene in this latest attempt at a German revolution. But, like the Spartacist rising, the Red Ruhr and the Saxon People's Republic before it, the March Action of 1921 ended in failure.

The Comintern's ideology may have been undeniably Marxist. But its primary tactical consideration, as laid out in Lenin's 'Twenty-one Conditions' of August 1921, was that communist parties worldwide should never acknowledge the legality of the bourgeois state and refuse to participate in bourgeois democracy. In practice that led to a fundamental clash with the German Communist Party, whose moderate leader Paul Levi found himself expelled from the party under pressure from Moscow for condemning the March Action – as well as for proving insufficiently hostile to participation in elections.[44] In short, the Russians who attended the 1924 Communist Party congress in Frankfurt were not so much delegates as the unacknowledged puppet masters of the German party.

Sorge's job was to 'look after the security of these important delegates, to see to their quarters, and decide upon the activities in which they might safely engage'.[45] Heading the delegation was Osip Pyatnitsky – born Iosif Aronovich Tarshis – head of the Comintern's International Department. The son of a Jewish carpenter from Lithuania, Pyatnitsky had trained as a tailor's apprentice before going into revolutionary politics and rising to become a member of the Soviet Party's Central Committee. He was personally close to Lenin and had smuggled clandestine correspondence from Lenin in Zurich into Russia during the abortive 1905 revolution. His deputy was Dmitry – born Dmitro – Manuilsky, a grinning, heavily moustachioed son of a Ukrainian priest. Another member of the Comintern Executive Committee was Otto Kuusinen, a Finnish communist who went on to found the Scandinavian branch of Soviet military intelligence, personifying the blurred line between the Comintern and the USSR's spying activities (he would later be appointed head of a puppet regime set up by Stalin in his homeland).[46] The fourth key delegate was Solomon Lozovsky, general secretary of the Red International of Labour Unions, or Profintern, set up by Lenin as a separate institution to the Comintern but with the parallel aim of bringing international trades unions under Moscow's control. Not one of the senior Soviet delegates to the German congress was, in fact, an ethnic Russian.

Sorge, by his own account, 'fulfilled this far from simple mission to the satisfaction of all concerned'.[47] Though all the Russian delegates were in Germany illegally, none were arrested or harassed. Their confidential communications remained so, and they evidently found their quarters comfortable. In short, they were impressed by their sternly efficient twenty-eight-year-old German protector.

Unbeknown to Sorge, Pyatnitsky's mission was less a friendly gesture of solidarity to the fraternal German Communist Party than a calculated headhunting mission. Lenin had died in January 1924. In the wake of the failures of communist uprisings in Germany, Estonia, Hungary and Italy – where the Fascist *squadristi* broke up strikes that gave their leader Benito Mussolini the excuse to assume power following a march on Rome in 1922 – the Comintern's focus was shifting decisively from the immediate activity of world revolution towards helping to defend the Soviet state. More importantly still, the party's rising star Iosif Stalin was advocating 'socialism in one country'. As Stalin was soon to make clear: 'an internationalist is one who is ready to defend the USSR without reservation, without wavering, unconditionally; for the USSR it is the base of the world revolutionary movement, and this revolutionary movement cannot be defended and promoted without defending the USSR'.[48]

So in Frankfurt Pyatnitsky and his comrades were in fact scouting out which German communists were willing to support the USSR over and above their own local party interests – and would therefore be earmarked for future leadership roles – and which were not. They were also on the lookout for bright young recruits who would be useful to the Soviet intelligence network.

'My relations with the Comintern delegates were very intimate, and we grew more friendly every day,' recalled Sorge.[49] Both sides, evidently, had succeeded in charming the other. The same cannot be said for Christiane, who was appalled by the revolutionaries' table manners when her husband brought the delegates to the apartment that she had tastefully furnished. 'I see them sitting on my violet sofa, eating peanuts which they had brought with them,' she recalled in a short memoir published in 1964 in a Swiss newspaper. 'They simply threw the shells on the carpet.'[50]

Ignoring Christiane's dubiously bourgeois sensibilities, Pyatnitsky made Sorge an offer. 'At the close of the session, they asked me to come to Comintern headquarters in Moscow that year to work for them.' Specifically, the Soviet comrades had asked Sorge 'to have me set up an intelligence bureau for the Comintern'.[51]

Sorge may have been waiting for the call for some time. Christiane wrote that the couple had already talked about moving to Moscow as early as their arrival in Frankfurt in 1922.[52] A visiting high priest of Marxism, David Ryazanov, excited by Sorge's great-uncle's connection to Karl Marx, had invited Sorge to join his fledgling Institute of Marxist-Leninism.[53] The German party chose not to let him go. But by 1924 such defiance of Moscow's requests was becoming politically impossible. This time Berlin approved Sorge's application to join Comintern headquarters. In October 1924, leaving Christiane to await confirmation of her future job as a librarian at the Institute of Marxist-Leninism, Sorge boarded a train for Moscow.

3

'A Fanatic Riff-Raff from a Ruined Century'

'Sorge's ghost has marched to glory, but behind him in wretched procession come the lost intellectuals, the lost patriots, the lost priests, defending countries and religions of which our children may never hear, a fanatic riff-raff from a ruined century'[1]

John le Carré

The Comintern lodged Sorge at the Hotel Lux on Tverskaya Street 36, Moscow's central thoroughfare.[2] Built in 1911 as the Hotel de France, the property had been one of pre-revolutionary Moscow's smartest addresses. Taken over by the Bolsheviks and renamed – curiously – the Hotel de Lux, the place had quickly gone downhill. The guests were soon complaining of the rats.[3] Nonetheless, it was convenient for the party's newly formed security services to have foreign visitors where they could keep an eye on them. It was also a handy ten-minute walk from the Kremlin.

By 1924 the Lux was run by the Communist International and inhabited by a community of displaced dreamers. Socialists from around the world – from the future Chinese premier Zhou Enlai to Yugoslav leader Josip Broz Tito – mingled over the meagre breakfast buffet. According to the Soviet newspaper *Sovietskaya Rossiya*, these idealists had been drawn to the world capital of socialism from among the 'millions of people in all corners of the world who had said to themselves "this is my revolution" ... a new young generation which listened with hope and belief to every word from Moscow'.[4] The self-selected champions of the proletariat pose stern and unsmiling in group photographs of the period. Soberly dressed, peering through angry little glasses, they resemble indignant librarians more than tough street fighters. In a world of physically diminutive Jewish intellectuals, the tall, Aryan, war-wounded Sorge literally stood out from the crowd.

The atmosphere at the Hotel Lux was a strange mixture of revolutionary fervour and paranoia. 'Everybody calls everybody a spy,' recalled American radical Agnes Smedley after a visit in 1921. 'Everybody is under surveillance. You never feel safe.'[5] The Soviet government did not trust its foreign guests and kept close watch on what they were doing and saying.[6]

Rats and spies notwithstanding, Sorge was in his element. He told his Japanese interrogators that his first job was in the Comintern's Department of Information, 'compiling reports on the labour movements and on economic and political conditions in Germany and other countries'.[7] This was only partly true. Osip Pyatnitsky, who had personally recruited Sorge in Frankfurt, had been charged by Lenin in 1922 with establishing a clandestine organisation under the aegis of the Comintern that would run all illegal activity abroad, including running underground revolutionary cells.[8] This espionage centre was innocuously named the International Communications Section, or OMS.[9] It is clear from the Comintern archives that Sorge had extensive contact with OMS from the earliest days in Moscow and formally joined the network by 1927. Pyatnitsky, for his part, would remain Sorge's patron and protector until the old spymaster fell from grace during Stalin's Great Purge of the party in 1937 – at which point he would become a fatal liability to Sorge's reputation.

Christiane joined Sorge in Moscow in March 1925.[10] Her 'first impression of Russia: infinitely melancholy!'[11] The couple, speaking no Russian, mingled almost exclusively with other German communists. The centre of the community was the German Club, a dingy place which contained a small library of German books but offered little else by way of entertainment. Sorge, soon elected its president, livened the club up a little by setting up a Young Pioneers Group for the children of the city's German residents. Though she shared a small room in the Lux with her husband, Christiane felt desperately alone: 'No one, ever, could violate the inner solitude, it was this which gave him his complete independence.'[12] Hede Massing, who saw a lot of Christiane in Moscow, formed the impression that 'she did not like the Russians'.[13]

The feeling was apparently mutual. Contemporaries recalled that Christiane's nickname was '*burzhuika*' – the bourgeoise.[14]

Sorge, on the other hand, 'saw everything in black and white', noted a friend, and would brook no criticism of the workers' paradise.[15] Leaving Christiane alone at the Lux with increasing frequency, he would attend soirées at the homes of top Bolsheviks. The son of Grigory Smoliansky, sometime head of the All-Russian Central Executive Committee, remembered Sorge's magnetic presence at his father's dinner table at their apartment in a building on Granatny Lane, reserved for the senior party elite. Sorge 'wore a rough wool sweater and yellow corduroy jacket and looked like a foreigner', recalled Vladimir Smoliansky. The German guest's 'intelligence and willpower made him stand out. Tall, strong, fair-haired, his direct gaze could be somewhat grim, but not self-absorbed. He listened to you with all signs of sympathy.'[16] There are strong hints in Christiane's memoir that Sorge was already using his strong, silent presence to attract other women. Bolshevism had, in its early years, gone hand in hand with sexual liberation. Sorge, like the feminist revolutionary Alexandra Kollontai,[17] considered himself an advocate of free love. Any woman who for whatever legal, moral, or social reason did not follow her physical urges he stigmatised as a 'bourgeois goose'.[18]

In the summer of 1926, Sorge and Christiane holidayed separately. He travelled to his home town of Baku, now the capital of the Azerbaijan Soviet Socialist Republic, where he found his old family home in Sabunçi converted into a convalescent home.[19] Christiane took the train to the Black Sea resort of Sochi with a female friend. Sorge briefly joined them in Sochi, but their relationship was clearly on the rocks. 'A tormenting anxiety came over me,' wrote Christiane. 'I could sense ever more clearly that our paths were moving apart through the same providence that once had made us collide with one another.' By autumn, fed up with the miserable life at the misnamed Hotel Lux and her husband's philandering and constant absences, she left for Berlin. As they parted on a cold Moscow railway platform late at night, Sorge 'acted as if we would meet again soon. But as the train moved off, I could not stop the flood of tears. I knew it was the end of our life together, and he must have known it too.'[20]

If Sorge was upset by Christiane's departure, none of his friends or acquaintances noticed. Comintern official Pavel Kananov recalled often running into Sorge, happy and absorbed in Moscow bookshops. 'He was a passionate bibliophile, you can tell by how a person holds a book in their hands.' Another colleague, A. Z. Zusmanovich, frequently saw Sorge in the library of the German Club, 'buried in books'. Zusmanovich also attended lectures given by Sorge at the club, which showed a 'very organised and analytical mind ... he gave the impression of an outstanding person and I thought he would become a great scholar'.[21]

During this period, Sorge the scholar produced a series of learned, didactic articles and books,[22] mostly about Germany's social problems and the risk of renewed imperialism. As early as 1926, Sorge warned that 'Germany, more than any other country, is inclined to pursue a policy of inflaming new imperialist conflicts and therefore German politics, with its conflictual nature, is inclined towards creating future wars'.[23] His prescience had its limits, however. Sorge – writing in 1928 under the pseudonym of 'R. Sonter' in *Inprecorr*, the official journal of the Comintern – firmly predicted that the German working class would eventually revolt against the 'dictatorship of capitalist interests devoted to crushing them'.[24] Sorge, like most other socialists, completely failed to anticipate that German workers would become the most avid backers of fascism.[25] He wrote two books during the time: *The Economic Provisions of the Versailles Peace Treaty* and *The International Labour Class*; both were published in Germany and translated into Russian.[26]

Sorge the apparatchik, meanwhile, was charging up the Comintern's career ladder. At the end of June 1925 he was already writing to the leadership to request a transfer to 'more active work' in the agitation and propaganda department. By April 1926 he had been promoted to the secretariat of the Comintern's Executive Committee (known as the IKKI).[27] The following May he sat on an important IKKI committee, charged with drawing up instructions for overseas communist parties in the event of a new war.[28] His special subject was the rising problem of fascism.[29] On at least three occasions Sorge attended meetings of the presidium where the party's rising star, Iosif Stalin, was present.[30] Conversation between the two, if there was any, must have been limited. Sorge still spoke little Russian, while Stalin's German was non-existent and his English basic.[31]

As for Sorge the spy, his own deliberate reticence about his activities in the 1920s and the breathless evidence of his admirer Hede Massing have given the impression of a secret and exciting career as a secret agent. 'He took to conspiracy like a fish to water,' recalled Massing. 'He would flash an amused smile at you, his eyebrows raised in disdain for being unable to tell you where it was that he had spent his last year.' She 'did not have the slightest doubt that what he did was of the utmost importance':

So indoctrinated was I with communist behaviour that it seemed absolutely proper and right for me not to know and never to ask what he did, where he went, and for how long. Throughout the years that I knew him, he would turn up, call me and say, 'What are you up to?' I would cry out with joy and ask, 'But how did you find me?' And he would laugh. And I was pleased. It is he who instilled in me the feeling that there was simply nothing an apparatchik could not find out or do if he wanted to or had to. It was he who told me how lonely and ascetic the life of an apparatchik must be, with no attachments, no strings, no sentimentalities. I saw him as the hero of the revolution, the real hero, the quiet one, about whom nobody knew ... To me he was the man of whom Rilke spoke in his poetry, '*Ich bin der Eine*' [I am the lonely one] ...[32]

Sorge would indeed go on to do work of the utmost importance – in China and Japan. But the reality of Sorge's first forays into secret work in Europe seems to have been rather less exalted than Massing imagined. For a start, despite Sorge's own apparent enthusiasm for a foreign assignment, his superiors in the Department of Agitation and Propaganda seem to have had their doubts as to his suitability for secret work. 'Re: Sorge. He cannot sit still and his work here isn't working out,' wrote a Comrade 'Mikhail' to Comrade 'Osvald' in April 1927. 'He wants to leave as soon as possible and we are having difficulty sending him out for independent work because he has hardly any experience of practical work.'[33] Nonetheless, Sorge's persistent lobbying paid off. German police records show a Richard Sorge visiting Frankfurt from August to October 1927. He seems to have had contact with Yakov Mirov-Abramov, nominally the press attaché at the Soviet embassy in Berlin, who in reality headed Pyatnitsky's secret OMS network in Berlin. It is not clear what Sorge was up to in Frankfurt – though the Berlin OMS bureau would become his main covert line of communication to his Comintern spymasters in Moscow.[34]

In December 1927, Sorge was in Stockholm on his first clandestine mission outside Germany, under the codename Johann.[35] It did not get off to a good start. 'I arrived 17.12 at S[tockholm]. I have had no news from Oswald,' Sorge wrote plaintively in a coded telegram dispatched to Comintern headquarters via Mirov-Abramov in Berlin. 'Our friends here knew nothing about my arrival or what tasks I should undertake. I fear it will be the same in Kop [Copenhagen].'[36] Sorge's role seems to have been one of a government inspector, reporting on the 'organisation of work in the [local party] apparat, the work of the departments, the question of leadership in general of unions and agitation and propaganda'. He also told his superiors that he intended to address 'the question of factory newspapers and preparation for a likely coming strike in the paper industry at the end of January'.[37] The picture of the Comintern that emerges from Sorge's correspondence with his OMS chiefs in Moscow is of a chaotic organisation, obsessed with control while at the same time little able to organise its own agents.

Nonetheless, Sorge impressed local communists with his intelligence and common touch. Kai Moltke, a member of the Danish Communist Party, wrote that as far as he knew, Sorge's 'mission had nothing to do with intelligence service or espionage'. Instead, Sorge gave lectures to party cells and advised Danish comrades to team up with radical trades unions. 'His sense for detailed organisation was extraordinary. His behaviour was not at all illegal or conspiratorial. In his visits to the tough areas of the ports and the factories of Copenhagen he had to show that he would guzzle as many beers as a sailor, docker or cement worker or show his physical prowess as a wrestler.'[38]

Back in Moscow, Sorge described the mission to the adoring Massing in mysterious, even bizarre, terms. 'Ika's first assignment was to some Nordic country (he never said which) where he lived "high in the mountains", and where his company were "sheep, mostly". He would ramble on about the human qualities of sheep once one got to know them.'[39] In the altogether more serious setting of a Japanese prison, he told his interrogators that he had 'assumed a position of active leadership alongside the other party heads'. Of his boozing and wrestling with the tough guys down at the docks, he admitted that he had done 'intelligence work on Denmark's economic and political problems, discussing my observations and findings with party representatives'.[40]

On 9 December 1927, Sorge formally resigned from the IKKI secretariat to take up a full-time post as an *OrgInsktruktor* – organisational instructor – at the OMS, the heart of the Comintern intelligence apparatus.[41] His old recruiter from Frankfurt, Dmitry Manuilsky, personally recommended him as a suitable member of the world revolution's most secret club, and he was seconded by Grigory Smoliansky, his old host on Granatny Lane.

The next year Sorge was back in Scandinavia, reporting on the party networks in Sweden and Norway and squabbling with the accountants back at head office over his expenses (an irritation that has persisted for foreign correspondents and, doubtless, spies ever since).[42] In Oslo, as he told the Japanese, Sorge ran into 'party problems of various descriptions that seriously impeded intelligence work'.[43] The sources are silent on the exact nature of the squabble – but it is clear that some in Moscow were again growing frustrated by the waywardness of their man in Scandinavia. 'There is no cause for you to fret as much as you have been,' scolded one 'Comrade Leonard' in July 1928.[44] The same apparatchik also wrote to OMS boss Pyatnitsky, strongly opposing an apparent plan to send Sorge on a secret mission to Britain. 'Concerning the suggestion that he travel to A[nglia – England] I will express myself against. He is too weak for A and he cannot resist getting involved in political affairs. For A this is absolutely unacceptable.'[45]

Despite his immediate bosses' carping, Sorge still had powerful friends at the top levels of the Comintern. Manuilsky had enough confidence in his German protégé to appoint Sorge personal secretary to Nikolai Bukharin, the head of the Comintern, during its summer congress in Moscow in July 1928. At those meetings, Sorge later boasted, he: 'participated in discussions concerning Trotsky, Zinoviev and Kamenev' – all senior anti-Stalin Bolsheviks whose fate would have been the subject of extremely sensitive discussions.[46] At the end of the congress Bukharin, almost certainly acting on Stalin's orders, formally excluded those three old Bolsheviks from the Comintern. It would be the beginning of a fall from grace that would end, for Zinoviev and Kamenev, in show trials and the execution cellars of the Lubyanka, and for Trotsky with an ice pick in the head in Mexico City. In other words, in 1928 Sorge had loyally stood with Bukharin against the 'rightist deviationists' and supported Stalin, the 'Kremlin mountaineer',[47] in his inexorable climb to the summit of power.

Back in Moscow, Sorge began taking Russian lessons from a young aspiring actress,[48] Ekaterina 'Katya' Maximova. Friends described Katya as 'calm and restrained ... but she could take unusual decisions'.[49] The most unusual – and ultimately fatal – such decision was to fall in love with Richard Sorge. One of Katya's artist friends remembered Sorge as 'a broad-shouldered guy in a blue sweater who sat in silence'. His expression was 'calm and kind and open ... an expression not captured in photographs'.[50] The friend recalled that Sorge would jestingly describe himself in company as an *Azerbaijanets* (an Azeri) but could not speak a word of the language (this appears to be one of Sorge's few recorded jokes).

At gatherings at Katya Maximova's tiny room in a communal apartment on Nizhny Kislovsky Lane the guests 'didn't drink wine – it was not done'. The clean-living young people drank tea with yellow sugar, sang songs, argued about the plays of Konstantin Stanislavsky and Vsevolod Meyerhold, about the music of Beethoven and Scriabin, and about socialist art.[51] Katya taught Sorge poems by Alexandr Blok, which he would recite by heart – and though he was 'a good storyteller, he often waved his hands when stuck for words and looked at Vera Izbotskaya, who knew French, to translate a word. But more often he would look to Katya.' He liked to quote a poem by Vladimir Mayakovsky:

> In our veins is blood not water
> We go forward through the bark of revolvers
> In order that as we die
> We transform
> Into ships
> Into shipping lines
> And other long-lived things.[52]

The poem was written as a tribute to Theodor Nette, a Soviet diplomatic courier killed in Latvia in 1926 while defending a package of diplomatic post, who had a ship of the Black Sea fleet named after him. (Sorge would, after his own martyrdom for the revolution, also have a ship named after him – as well as streets, schools and planes.)

Sorge's image of himself as a hero-poet from Schiller, formed in his schoolboy days, had only been strengthened by war and revolution. 'He

was always a little romantic,' recalled Dorothea von During, a friend
from Berlin. 'Richard was a strong-willed, open, determined young
man. We all loved Ika ... I have somewhere a poem he wrote: "Forever
a wanderer, condemning himself forever never to know peace".'[53]
Nonetheless, this wanderer parked his cross-country skis and books in
the corner of Katya's room and, by the end of 1928, he had moved in
with her.

The young couple's revolutionary idyll was short-lived. Katya may
have dreamed of the stage, but her teacher at the Leningrad Institute
of Theatrical Arts thought her no more than a 'competent actress'.[54] At
the beginning of 1929, Katya shelved her life's ambition and instead
went to work in the newly opened Bolshevichka* men's clothing factory
in northern Moscow as a machine operator. She would claim in later
letters to Sorge to be very happy among real proletarian workers – but
one cannot help thinking that Katya protested too much in denying her
regret over the compromises she had made.[55]

More seriously for Sorge, the political winds in the Comintern were
turning against the very idea of world revolution. Over the last decade,
multiple communist risings all over Europe had failed. Treacherous
socialists all over the Continent were making common cause with
moderate social democrats, the Comintern's arch-enemy. At the same
time the equally fickle working classes were becoming worryingly
enamoured with fascism. Mussolini was already in power in Rome.
Hitler's political fortunes were on the rise in Berlin.

To Moscow – and particularly to Stalin – the message was clear. At
the Comintern's annual congress in 1928, Stalin finally pushed through
his long-held belief in a 'new course of socialism in one country'.[56]
Hopes of 'imminent world revolution were put aside', Sorge would
later explain to the Japanese. 'There occurred in fact a shift in the centre
of gravity ... Pyatnitsky believed that imminent world revolution was
an illusion and that we must concentrate on the Defence of the Soviet
Union.'[57]

All the same, in the spring of 1929, Sorge returned to Norway
for what was to be the last time. Moscow's hand was tightening
over foreign communist parties – and over the Comintern's agent

---

*'Woman-Bolshevik' – an odd name for a menswear factory.

network. If previously Sorge had sent many of his day-to-day reports via a local party, by 1929 he was forced to travel personally to the OMS headquarters in Berlin for transmission. 'In other words, I had absolutely no independent means of communication.'[58] Worse, when he returned to Moscow in April 1929 he found that his reports had not even been read. 'The Comintern had no interest in my political information.'[59]

Foreign communists were also being systematically squeezed out of the Comintern's central apparat. Swiss socialist and leading Comintern hierarch Jules Humbert-Droz complained to Italian Communist Party leader Palmiro Togliatti that almost no non-Soviets were left at headquarters, with most of the remainder preparing to be reassigned abroad. Otto Kuusinen, one of the last remaining foreigners at the top of the organisation, was withdrawing into 'regional and editorial work'. The Comintern's head, Bukharin, was officially 'busy with Russian affairs'.[60] In fact Bukharin was fighting for his political life. In addition to purging the Comintern of unreliable foreigners, Stalin was also purging the Soviet party itself, systematically removing every top Bolshevik who could challenge him for supreme leadership. Having used Bukharin to oust Trotsky, Kamenev and Zinoviev, Stalin was now preparing to destroy Bukharin himself.

Sorge found himself bounced from one job to another. Though he would be later accused of being a 'Bukharinite-rightist', the beginning of Sorge's fall from grace pre-dated Bukharin's removal from the leadership of the Comintern and from the editorship of *Pravda* in late April 1929. In the new political climate Sorge's foreignness certainly counted against him. But perhaps more important was his independent-mindedness, even cussedness, with relation to his Comintern colleagues that is evident from their streams of bickering telegrams carping at his expenses and refusal to follow instructions.[61]

In May, Sorge was moved into the Comintern's economic commission, then briefly became personal secretary to his old patron Manuilsky.[62] He attempted to reverse his downward mobility, appealing to Pyatnitsky to be allowed to engage in pure intelligence-gathering, without the impediment of involvement in local party politics: 'I believed that espionage work, which I liked, and for which I think I am well fitted, would be impossible with the narrow framework of party activities ... my character, tastes and strong preferences all lead me towards political, economic and military intelligence and away from the field of party controversies'.[63]

On 18 June, a day before the start of the Tenth Plenum of the Comintern Executive Committee, Sorge left Russia on his most ambitious foreign assignment yet – to England and Ireland. It is not clear from the archives how he overcame his superiors' objections to the mission. But the timing of his departure is significant. It is possible that Sorge's remaining friends in the Comintern wanted to get him out of Moscow before the congress in order to save his skin from a coming purge. More likely, his enemies wanted him out of the way as they moved to destroy him.

True to his own advice to Pyatnitsky – but also perhaps because of the unseemly party squabbles in Oslo the previous year – Sorge was under 'instructions to remain strictly aloof from internal party disputes'.[64] He was also, tellingly, warned to live in seclusion and avoid 'slim, long-legged English girls', or so he later told the Japanese.[65] His OMS bosses were already well aware of Sorge's weakness for wine and women.

Britain in 1929 was a far more challenging environment for a Soviet spy to work in than Scandinavia had ever been. For years the popular press – in particular the *Daily Mail* – had been sounding alarmist warnings to their working-class readers of the dangers of foreign subversives in their midst. In 1924 the paper published the sensational Zinoviev letter, a document purporting to be a directive from the Comintern to the Communist Party of Great Britain ordering them to hasten the radicalisation of British workers. The letter was in fact a forgery, but it sowed anti-communist hysteria and helped to instil a deep aversion in the Parliamentary Labour Party to compromising contacts with Moscow that would last until the end of the Cold War.[66] In May 1927 police raids on the Soviet Trade Mission operating out of a building at 49 Moorgate, London, had revealed an extensive espionage network that caused Prime Minister Stanley Baldwin to break off diplomatic relations with the USSR. The records of British police's Special Branch and the Security Service, MI5, list hundreds of suspected Soviet sympathisers and agents who were being kept under rigorous surveillance.[67]

So by the time Sorge arrived by ship in July 1929, Britain was thoroughly hostile territory for a Soviet spy. He remained for ten weeks. By his own account his 'purpose was to study British politics and economics – but since the Depression had thrown so many people out of work ... I also undertook investigations to see whether a general strike might develop'.[68]

Stalin had made clear in the previous year's Comintern plenum that he had his hopes of an English revolution, and that the British Labour Party could be drawn into Moscow's orbit. Neither aspiration had much ground in reality, as Sorge soon discovered. The British Communist Party numbered only 3,500 members, compared to some 300,000 in Germany.[69] The party was also, as Special Branch records show, riddled with informers – a fact of which Moscow Centre seems to have been aware, instructing Sorge to strictly avoid contact with known British communists.

So if he was not organising party work – his Scandinavian speciality – what exactly was Sorge up to? He told the Japanese that he travelled to 'mining areas' and saw for himself 'how deep the crisis was'. But he was lying. The Wall Street Crash would not come until October of that year, long after Sorge had left Britain, so the Great Depression that he referred to in his confession to the Japanese in fact still lay in the future. It seems that Sorge's true mission in England was – at least in part – to collect sensitive information from a top Soviet spy. Christiane, still on good terms with her husband despite their separation, joined him in London. She later reported that the purpose of their trip was to meet a 'very important agent'. The couple went together to the rendezvous on a London street corner. While the two men talked, Christiane kept her distance and a watch for signs of danger.[70]

Who Sorge's contact may have been was a mystery that worried British spycatchers for decades to come – notably Peter Wright, the Australian-born head of MI5 counter-intelligence. Wright's theory was that Sorge's agent was Charles 'Dickie' Ellis, another Australian who began his career in military intelligence in Constantinople in 1922 and was recruited by the Secret Intelligence Service, or SIS, the following year while serving as British vice-consul in Berlin. Dickie Ellis went on to work in Vienna, Geneva, Australia and New Zealand under the cover of a foreign correspondent for the *Morning Post*. Ellis would later work alongside Kim Philby in SIS and come under suspicion after maintaining contact with Philby after the latter's departure from British intelligence under a cloud of suspicion following the defection of Guy

Burgess and Donald Maclean in 1957.[71] Wright came to believe that Ellis, like Philby, was a Soviet spy, and that he had also passed secrets to the Germans.[72] In 1964, Christiane – by then living in retirement, improbably enough, in a convent in New York – was questioned by a colleague of Wright's and shown photographs of possible suspects. Christiane tentatively identified Ellis as the man she had seen in London – 'this man looks familiar' she told her MI5 interviewer – but could not say with certainty.[73]

Given Sorge's perilous position in the Comintern and his relative inexperience of running secret agents – as opposed to his extensive expertise in corralling fractious communist cadres – it seems odd that he would be given such a sensitive task as contacting a top Soviet spy inside the British establishment. Handling such agents would normally have been the province of David Petrovsky, alias A. J. Bennett, who served as Soviet consul in London and was the official liaison between the British Communist Party and Moscow. Moreover, by 1929 the USSR's foreign intelligence was being increasingly run not by the Comintern but by the GPU – the Soviet secret police later known as the NKVD and still later as the KGB – and by the Red Army's fledging military intelligence unit, the Fourth Directorate of the General Staff. In any case, whether the contact was indeed Ellis or someone else, Sorge warned Christiane that the mission was extremely risky – and later told the Japanese that he had faced twelve years' imprisonment if he had been caught.

In fact, Sorge *was* caught, though it was not for the clandestine meetings with any Soviet agents.[74] Sometime towards the end of his visit Sorge was arrested by the British police, though it is not clear exactly when and why. Almost certainly this was not by the Bolshevik-hunters of Scotland Yard's Special Branch, since there is no mention in their meticulous records of Sorge, unless it is under a hitherto unknown alias. He was not charged. Perhaps he had been drinking with the same rough docker types that he had fraternised with in Copenhagen and got into a spot of bother with the law. Nonetheless, Sorge had, in the parlance of Soviet espionage, *provalilsya* – literally 'fallen through' – in the sense of being rumbled by the authorities.[75]

In the event, it did not matter. Sorge's career in the Comintern had, unbeknown to him, already come to an abrupt end. On 16 August 1929, Pyatnitsky and the Comintern's Executive Committee (IKKI) resolved to 'exclude comrades Sorge and [head of the Comintern's Anglo-American Secretariat Ivan] Mingulin from the lists of the workers of the IKKI'.[76] Sorge and three other Germans were to be 'transferred to the direction of the Central Committee of the [Soviet] Party and to the Central Committee of the German Communist Party'.[77] Eight days later the German four were mentioned as having been 'purged' as a group of 'active Bukharinites'.[78] In November Bukharin himself, having already been removed from the leadership of the Comintern earlier that year, would also lose his seat on the Politburo.[79]

Sorge was understandably furious when he learned what his fate would be, probably on his return to Berlin after his London mission. 'Those swine, how I hate them,' he railed to a friend. 'This disregard for human suffering and feeling … And they have not paid me for months.'[80] The Soviet betrayal ran deep. For one, it was clear that his old protector, Pyatnitsky, had turned against him. Worse, he was not even allowed to return to Moscow. Sorge was now, in the words of a German party comrade, *kaltgestellt* – jargon for a party member who had been put 'on ice'.[81]

On 9 September 1929, Sorge had been, according to a secret telegram dispatched from the head of Soviet military intelligence in Berlin, waiting for nearly a month 'without any instructions about his future. He is also without money.'[82] A week later, according to the same source, Sorge received a telegram from the Comintern 'allowing' him to return to Moscow for talks – 'however he must pay for his return ticket himself'.[83]

The Berlin spymaster who was sending reports on Sorge's fate was Konstantin Mikhailovich Basov. Born Jan Abeltiijs in Latvia,[84] Basov had joined Lenin's first secret police, the Cheka, in 1919, but soon moved on to the Registration Directorate of the Red Army – the Soviet Union's first military intelligence organ. From 1927, Basov had been the chief Soviet spy in Berlin, eclipsing and annexing both the existing Comintern apparatus and the local German Communist Party's spy network.[85] Basov had been introduced to Sorge by Christiane in London a couple of months before.[86] During Sorge's miserable *kaltgestellt* Berlin days, the two men had met and spoken about the newly unemployed spy's future. Basov evidently saw a man he could work with. Sorge most likely saw a potential saviour.

Sorge was 'a rather well-known colleague who needs no introduction', Basov telegraphed his superiors at military intelligence headquarters in Moscow on 9 September. 'Speaks Germ., Engl., Fr., Russ. Education: doctor of econom.' The Berlin bureau chief had even formed a precise idea of Sorge's possible place in the Soviet military intelligence apparat that he was building. 'He will be best suited for China. He can obtain commissions from publications over here to write scientific articles.' Sorge – perhaps understandably for a man with a very specific skill set and no current employer – was 'very seriously set on coming to work for us'.[87]

By the time Sorge got permission to return to Moscow, Basov's background check of Sorge was complete. 'His bosses evidently want to fire him,' Basov wrote to his chief in Moscow Centre, the headquarters of the Red Army's military intelligence network. 'I have made enquiries as to why the Comintern made such a decision. I received some hints that he was involved in the Rightist opposition. But in any case, all the comrades who know him speak highly of him … he will come and see you and discuss the question of moving over to us.'[88]

Back in Moscow by mid-October, Sorge addressed his old comrades, friends and enemies on the Comintern Executive Committee for the last time. The minutes make moving reading. Contrite, for once, Sorge admitted to occasional 'wavering' but insisted that he 'actively fought against Trotskyites in the German Club'.[89] He listed all the fallen factions of which he was not a member – the heretics of the Ruth Fischer circle, the deviationist Samuelsohn, the wrong-headed Everta. It was Sorge's futile attempt at self-justification – but more poignantly, a sad list of all the once-idealistic men and women who had been jettisoned as the Comintern devoured itself.

In public, Sorge's fall looked like a disgrace. On 31 October the IKKI, headed by Pyatnitsky, formally and unanimously voted to exclude Comrade Sorge from the Comintern, the organisation to which he had devoted half his adult life.

The real story was different. Eleven days before Sorge's expulsion, a secret meeting of the IKKI confirmed that he had successfully passed through the 'purging' process (*proshel chistku*) – and could count himself 'positively vetted' (*proveren*).[90] Sorge had 'conversations with Pyatnitsky and Kuusinen in personal terms about the project' of his future career. Pyatnitsky, for his part, had also spoken about Sorge to his friend, General Jan Karlovich Berzin, head of the secretive Fourth Directorate of the Red Army's General Staff.[91] To the world, Sorge had suffered an ignominious downfall. In reality, he had been recruited by Berzin, the man who would set Sorge onto his new, brilliant and ultimately fatal career path, penetrating the secrets of the USSR's enemies in the Far East.

4

Shanghai Days

'His work was impeccable'

Kim Philby on Sorge

The headquarters of the Fourth Directorate of the General Staff of the Workers' and Peasants' Red Army – more familiarly known as the Fourth Department – were housed on a quiet side street behind the Pushkin Museum of Fine Arts in a handsome two-storey Italianate pre-revolutionary mansion. From the outside the only concession to the Bolshevik order was a new pair of heavy wooden front doors – decorated with carved revolutionary stars and, oddly, the Saint George-slaying-the-dragon coat of arms of the city of Moscow – which remain in place to this day. Today the building has been expensively renovated and the windows facing the street are all fitted with mirrored glass. Unlike other government offices there is no sign announcing to which department the building belongs, though the steel garage gates bear the double-headed eagle insignia of the modern Russian Ministry of Defence.

When Sorge pulled on the long, ornate brass door handle for the first time in late October 1929, Jan Berzin was well on the way to becoming the chief architect of all the Soviet Union's foreign intelligence operations. True, Berzin's newly formed Fourth Department was just one of six Soviet spy agencies operating abroad. Berzin's chief rivals were the Comintern's OMS spy network and the overseas agents of the GPU secret police. The OMS was mired in amateurishness and squabbling; the GPU was, at this early stage, more concerned with hunting down enemies at home and abroad than in systematically gathering serious political information. Both would soon be outclassed in gathering foreign intelligence by Berzin's ruthlessness and professionalism.

Jan Karlovich Berzin was born Pēteris Ķuzis, the son of a poor Latvian farmer. He began his revolutionary career at the age of sixteen, when he led a guerrilla detachment during the 1905 revolution. The young Berzin was wounded, captured and sentenced to death, but was spared execution because of his youth. After two years in a tsarist prison he was deported to Siberia, whence he escaped twice. During the First World War he served as a private with the Imperial Russian Army before deserting in 1916 to join the Bolsheviks.[1] By the spring of 1919 civil war had broken out all over Russia. Berzin was appointed commander of a division of Bolshevik Latvian riflemen against the counter-revolutionary White forces near Petrograd.[2] Berzin devised a system of taking and shooting hostages to recover deserters and to put down peasant rebellions in areas seized by the Red Army from the retreating Whites. In September of that year, two months before his thirtieth birthday, Berzin's ruthlessness earned him the post of Minister of Internal Affairs of the newly formed Soviet Socialist Republic of Latvia. The following November he was transferred to Moscow to found the Soviet state's first military intelligence bureau. When Russian sailors at the Kronstadt naval base revolted against Bolshevik authority in March 1921, it was Berzin who pursued, arrested and liquidated the survivors.[3]

Clearly, Berzin was a very different kind of man from the well-meaning, idealistic comrades who led the Comintern. Official photographs show a fit man with piercing eyes and crew-cut hair. He has the air of one born to wear a uniform with commander's stars on the collar. Berzin's instincts were those of a partisan commander and a merciless revolutionary, ready to execute civilians and prisoners of war if expediency demanded. The first generation of Soviet spies had been a motley cast of gentlemen amateurs, *demi-mondain* chancers, opportunists and naive conspirators. Berzin's outfit, by contrast, was to be an intelligence service for a new world – disciplined, ruthless, systematic and professional.

In this ambition Berzin was a true disciple of Count Felix Dzerzhinsky, architect of the Red Terror that followed the Bolshevik coup of 1917, and founder of the All-Russian Extraordinary Commission, or Cheka, the first Soviet secret police and predecessor to the GPU. Dzerzhinsky said that 'only a saint or a scoundrel' could serve in his ruthless new force. The Cheka's agents were the revolution's avenging angels invested with the prestige of a righteous elect. If the Comintern was a community of bickering dreamers, Berzin sought to create a cadre formed of a steely new clerisy, 'a puritan high-priesthood, devout in its atheism. Here were the avengers of all the ancient evils; here were the enforcers of new heaven, new earth.'[4]

Sorge, even before his recruitment by Berzin, certainly had no doubt about the need to apply violence and guile in the service of the revolution. 'The proletariat does not like to turn the other cheek,' Sorge told friends, quoting *Pravda*.[5] Like his contemporaries, Whittaker Chambers – a young American socialist who also became a spy – and the poet Isaac Babel, Sorge was mesmerised by the secret world's mixture of bloody ruthlessness and high ideals. 'Once a person ... had fully identified with the apparatus, he would justify anything, even criminal acts, according to the law which he no longer recognised,' wrote Hede Massing, who also saw herself as a 'trusted soldier of the revolution' and became a Soviet spy at around this time. She described 'the elation, the self-denial, and often the self-abasement involved' in secret work. 'Once he is incorporated and a functionary of the quasi-religious brotherhood, he lives in what seemed to be an elevated world. The rules are strict.'[6] Lenin called the Soviet Union's secret services 'the decisive weapon against the countless plots and countless attempts to destroy Soviet power from the side of people who were infinitely stronger than us'. Massing, and Sorge, saw themselves as front-line soldiers in that secret army.

In Sorge, Berzin saw a promising recruit. Sorge was no pigeon-chested, bespectacled Comintern bookworm. He was a former soldier, a strong, tough man who had shovelled coal and brawled with reactionary thugs in Aachen. Sorge would later call Berzin 'a friend, like-minded comrade in arms'.[7] General Berzin's secretary, N. V. Zvonareva, recalled that 'they had good, warm relations – they understood each other'.[8] The two men – both tall, strong and stern-faced – even resembled each other physically.

On the practical side, Sorge had established academic and journalistic credentials that would serve as a perfect ready-made cover for foreign assignments. He was not Russian, and therefore free of the most obvious taint of association with Soviet espionage. Sorge had proved too independent-minded for the Comintern's taste. But Berzin was on the lookout precisely for men able to work on their own. The Red Army needed good agents, and fast. From the collapsing hen house of the Comintern's intelligence network, Berzin and his agents hoped to pluck out a few tough, experienced operatives who might suit their purposes.

Berzin and Sorge seem to have struck an immediate deal at their first meeting. 'Our talk centred on the question of how far the Fourth Bureau as a military organisation was concerned with political espionage, for Berzin had heard from Pyatnitsky that I was interested in this kind of work,' Sorge told his Japanese interrogators, who were naturally intensely interested in learning the inner workings of Soviet military intelligence.[9]

The Red Army needed detailed political information on China, Berzin bluntly informed his latest recruit. As the prospect of revolution in Europe faded, the Far East was becoming more of a priority for the Kremlin, both as an opportunity and a danger. A successful communist revolution in China could spread though Asia and destroy the supremacy of the Western capitalist powers by overthrowing their colonial empires. A nudge from the Soviet Union might, therefore, turn the whole Orient Red and shift the balance of power in the entire world in Moscow's favour.[10] Or Asia could go the other way and become a mortal threat to the Soviet Union. China could fall under the control of nationalists backed by US capital, avowed enemies of Soviet power. Japan was industrialising and arming at an alarming rate – and its fragile democratic government was becoming increasingly dominated by aggressive military factions.

What Berzin perhaps did not admit was that the Far East was a blind spot for the Soviet military. Up until 1928 most intelligence on China had been gathered by the Comintern using a highly insecure network of Soviet officials, diplomats, Chinese communists and paid informers. This mixture of professionals and amateurs, officials and illegal spies, proved a security nightmare. The memory of the single police raid on the Soviet Trade Mission in Moorgate, London, in 1927 that had smashed almost the entire Soviet espionage apparatus in England at a single stroke must have been still fresh in Berzin's mind. And unfortunately – for the Soviets – it was the British who ran the most effective counter-intelligence and anti-communist operations in its colonial outposts in Shanghai, Hong Kong and Singapore. Moscow had sensibly decided that its diplomatic quarters abroad were no longer safe centres from which to control agents. More, doubts were also accumulating about the basic competence of the Comintern as a spy agency.[11]

Berzin's task, therefore, was to create an entirely new network of illegal agents run by a variety of undercover espionage officers posing as journalists, brokers, merchants and academics. The main principle was that the Fourth Department's men and women should not be connected in any obvious way to the Soviet Union, that they should operate their communications and finances independently of the Soviet embassy and of local communist parties, and that they would have watertight cover. That, at least, was the theory. The practice, as Sorge was to find out to his cost, would prove rather different.

Berzin's energy and ambition is witnessed by the gigantic volume of correspondence that issued from his desk on a daily basis, now carefully filed in the basement of the Ministry of Defence archive in Podolsk, near Moscow. At the time he met Sorge, the archives show that Berzin was also busy preparing fully fledged *rezidenturas* – illegal spy centres – in New York, Paris, Marseilles, Le Havre, Rouen, Prague, Warsaw, Danzig, Vilnius, Brailovo, Kishinev and Helsinki as well as in the Chinese cities of Harbin, Shanghai, Mukden and Canton. Sixteen commercial companies – including general stores in Romanian Bessarabia, nut and raisin merchants in Samsun and Constantinople, and a corned beef dealership in Mongolia – were bought or set up in a dozen countries at Berzin's command in order to give funding and cover to his new agent network.[12] The Fourth Department's new Shanghai team, as assembled by Berzin, would consist of four men: bureau chief Alexander Ulanovsky, radio operator Sepp Weingarten, an officer with the alias of 'Vetlin' (code-named 'Koreets', or the Korean) whose real identity remains unknown – and the newest addition, Richard Sorge.

Berzin's reasons for choosing Ulanovsky as *rezident* remain something of a mystery, given that his career before Shanghai was a litany of failure – and continued in the same disastrous fashion during and after his spell in China. In 1921, Ulanovsky had been sent by Dzerzhinsky's Cheka to spy in Germany. But his orders were so vague that Ulanovsky had to call in at the Soviet embassy in Berlin to ask for more precise instructions. Berlin telegraphed Moscow for guidance, only to be told by the Cheka that they had never heard of Ulanovsky and advised the embassy to chase him away as a provocateur. Ulanovsky's only experience of China had been a visit in 1927 as a member of an official Soviet delegation of trade union representatives, where he addressed large audiences of Chinese communists and met scores of Soviet and local officials using his own name. It was scarcely a promising prelude to a career as an underground operative under cover of a new identity.

Perhaps the secret of Ulanovsky's remarkable, Teflon-coated career was his combination of charm and ruthless fervour.[13] 'There was something monkey-like in the droop of his arms, the roll of his walk and the look in his brown eyes, alternatively mischievous and wistful,' recalled Whittaker Chambers, who worked with Ulanovsky in the USA in 1931–34. 'He was deeply kind-hearted and very ironic. He was a modest man … but had huge life experience and a wonderful understanding of people, with that rare capacity of seeing things through the eyes of another person. His favourite phrase was "I would strike you". I never doubted that if necessary he would do so – that he would shoot me to protect the case in hand, or if he had been ordered to.'[14]

Just days after his recruitment by Berzin in late October 1929, Sorge and his new boss Ulanovsky were sent to Berlin. Their contact was to be Konstantin Basov – codename 'Richard' – the man who had talent-spotted Sorge and one of the most experienced agent trainers of his generation. Basov's job was to orchestrate the building of the two men's cover stories, stitching their fake new identities into the fabric of reality like an expert tailor, invisibly patching over their Soviet past. He had already procured a Czech passport under the name of 'Kirschner' for Ulanovsky. His plan was to set the fictional Herr Kirschner up as a businessman representing a legitimate German or European company in China. To that end he had Ulanovsky place classified advertisements in the *Berliner Tageblatt* and *Berliner Zeitung* newspapers advertising himself as an independent metals salesman en route to China and offering his services as a trade representative.[15]

The scheme worked a little too well. To Basov's surprise the Schelder-Consortium, a company specialising in the export of German arms based in the Netherlands port of Rotterdam, responded within days to offer Kirschner the position of their official agent in China, on generous terms. There was just one hitch: arms exports from Germany to China were currently banned by both the Treaty of Versailles and the League of Nations. The Schelder-Consortium breezily suggested that the ban could be easily circumvented thanks to the company's excellent contacts with both the Belgian and French members of the Allied Commission of the Rhine, who were meant to monitor Germany's rearmament. These corrupt officials could be prevailed upon to provide false export certificates for shipments of German arms to non-existent customers in India and Indo-China, though the weapons would ultimately be diverted to China.

The Schelder-Consortium's proposal was clearly grossly illegal, and as such – one might have thought – not the most obviously discreet cover for an active Soviet spy. Nonetheless, Basov judged that a position as an international arms smuggler would help Ulanovsky make contacts in Chinese military circles. The Fourth Department quickly gave its blessing.

Sorge's cover, by contrast, was to be hardly covert at all. In Germany and Moscow he was already known as an academic and journalist, albeit one with socialist leanings. In China, Basov judged, Sorge should simply seek work as a foreign correspondent and freelance commentator, hiding in plain sight under his real name. In order to do so Sorge would have to establish himself as a China expert, ingratiate himself with journalistic, academic and business circles in Berlin, and procure the necessary letters of introduction. He had approximately four weeks to get the job done.

Undaunted by the tight deadline, Sorge took an apartment on Reichskanzlerplatz in the bourgeois Berlin district of Charlottenburg and began seeking out old friends and comrades. A university chum, Karl August Wittfogel, put Sorge in touch with Richard Wilhelm, scholar and founder of the influential China Institute. Wilhelm, despite Sorge's complete lack of any previous experience or expertise on China, agreed to furnish him with an official letter commissioning him to collect 'scientific materials' on 'social and political' subjects in China.

Armed with this letter, Sorge headed to the Getreide-Kreditbank – the Grain Credit Bank – Germany's largest agricultural financier. Crucially, the bank also published an important trade paper, the *Deutsche Getreide Zeitung* (*German Grain News*), that carried reports on harvests around the world. Would they accept articles from Dr Sorge on China's soy, rice and bean harvests – on a strictly freelance basis, no retainer required? Of course they would. The editor quickly drew up an official letter of recommendation for the attention of the German consul generals in Shanghai and other Chinese cities, dispatched via the German Foreign Ministry's official channels, asking for the *Deutsche Getreide Zeitung's* new correspondent to be afforded all possible assistance in his studies of the Chinese agrarian sector.

Sorge's chutzpah did not end with the agricultural press. A well-known Berlin publisher accepted his offer to write a monograph on China, supplying him with several more letters of introduction to prominent foreigners and intellectuals in Shanghai. Sorge also got himself hired to write a report on the development of the Chinese banking system for an influential consortium of German businesses with interests in China, who again furnished him with an impressive contract, written in both Chinese and German. The final fillip of this networking tour de force was to procure press accreditation from two German photo agencies for his boss Ulanovsky.[16]

On 29 November, Basov cabled Moscow Centre that his team was ready for departure – despite the fact that Weingarten the radio operator had arrived too late in Berlin for any kind of cover to be prepared.[17] On 7 December the three Soviet spies departed on the same ship from Marseilles, bound for Shanghai. It was a risk to send them all together, explained Basov to Centre, but such was the urgency of their assignment that he did not want to risk waiting two or three weeks for the next transport.

The Fourth Department team had an agreeable voyage. Rather too much so, as it turned out. At a boozy New Year's Eve party somewhere in the South China Sea, Ulanovsky had got drunk with a group of friendly Britishers. 'Kirschner' had introduced himself as a representative of the Schelder-Consortium – and later, as the bonhomie flowed, confided to his new friends his plans to sell arms to the lucrative Chinese market. Unfortunately for Ulanovsky – and unbeknown to him, as they were better at holding their tongues when drunk than he – his Hogmanay companions were British officers from the Criminal Investigation Department of the Shanghai Municipal Police, returning to China after leave. Ulanovsky had jeopardised his own cover even before arriving in his new post.

The port of Shanghai, the great commercial entrepôt of China, was neither exactly a colony nor a sovereign Chinese city. In the wake of the the Opium Wars of 1842 the tottering Imperial government in Peking had ceded large pieces of territory along the banks of the Yangtze river to various foreigners – first to the British, then the French and the

Americans. Known as 'concessions', these were self-ruling enclaves beyond the authority of the Chinese government. The largest was the International Settlement, covering nine square miles of prime waterfront and in 1929 home to 1.2 million people – nearly half the city's population. Some 3 per cent of the Settlement's residents were foreigners, mostly British and Americans, and it was run by a municipal council elected by the enclave's mostly foreign property owners. It also had its own 50,000-strong police force, commanded by British officers and staffed by Chinese, Indian and Russian constables, as well as law courts, newspapers and an efficient postal service.

The Settlement was the commercial heartland of Shanghai, where the largest banks of the world had branches and where commodities such as rice, tea, oils, grain, cotton and tobacco were traded from a row of modern skyscrapers that lined a broad waterfront boulevard known as the Bund. Behind lay a dense warren of factories and workshops – including glass foundries, soap works, silk-spinning sweatshops and over sixty textile mills – as well as workers' tenements.

To the south was the smaller French Concession, centred around the smart offices and banks of the Avenue Joffre. A largely residential area favoured by wealthy foreigners and Chinese, it had a separate police force under the authority of the French consul general. The French Concession was also – naturally – known for its restaurants, pleasure gardens and whorehouses. Shanghai boasted some three thousand bordellos, most of them operating around the clock and segregated for Chinese and foreigners, as well as around two hundred dance halls and thousands of legal and illegal casinos catering to every social caste. Du-Yuesheng's three-storey gambling house on the Avenue Foch, for example, was famous for providing high rollers with limousines, the best wines, girls, cigars, and opium, as well as a special 'service' shop next door where less fortunate clients could pawn everything from fur coats to underwear.[18]

Shanghai was 'the Whore of the Orient', a city of nightclubs that never closed and hotels that supplied heroin by room service, where gangsters and warlords mixed with bankers and journalists in the cabarets and at the racecourse.[19] It was also, by the late 1920s, Asia's espionage capital. In the 1920s Shanghai hosted many of the great Soviet illegals of the age – Arnold Deutsch (who went on to recruit Kim Philby), Theodore Maly (later controller of the Cambridge Five), Alexander Rado (one of the many agents who would later warn Stalin of Nazi plans to invade the Soviet Union), Otto Katz (one of the most effective recruiters of fellow-travellers to the Soviet cause from Paris to Hollywood), Leopold Trepper (founder of the Rote Kapelle spy ring inside Germany before the Second World War), as well as legendary Fourth Department illegals Ignace Poretsky and Walter Krivitsky, Ruth Werner and Wilhelm Pieck. It was also teeming with idealistic young Westerners sympathetic to the communist cause.[20]

Shanghai offered unrivalled opportunities for secret work. No residence permit was required for foreigners, and the only official requirement for most Europeans was the need to register at their respective consulates. Most foreign citizens enjoyed extraterritoriality from Chinese justice and could be tried only by the concessions' own courts. An important exception was the German community – some 1,500 strong in 1929 – after the Weimar government had voluntarily waived extraterritoriality in a bid to sign a trade deal with China in 1921.

The city's three police forces – International, French and Chinese – distrusted one another and rarely shared information. A large community of foreign speculators, swindlers, crooks and 'persons of no declared profession' offered a rich pool of informers and couriers. Ferries along the Yangtze linked Shanghai with cities 1,700 kilometres into the Chinese interior, as well as up and down the coast to Canton and Hong Kong to the south and Hangkow to the north. It boasted China's most modern telephone and telegraph systems, a concentration of international news bureaus, and a cacophony of private short-wave radio transmitters that made interception all but impossible.

Most important of all for Moscow, Shanghai had also become the headquarters of Chinese communism. By 1929 an uneasy alliance between the Chinese Communist Party (CCP) and the ruling Nationalist government of the Kuomintang Party, led by Generalissimo Chiang Kai-shek and headquartered in the inland city of Nanking, had broken down. Members of the CCP were on the run. Communists from all over China hid from the Kuomintang police in the relative protection of the city's concessions. Shanghai was also China's most industrialised city, with the country's largest urban proletariat. Therefore, by Marxist theory – if not, as it turned out, in practice – it should have been the ripest ground for revolution. By 1930 there were 250,000 factory workers in the city, as well as 700–800,000 coolies, rickshaw men and unskilled labourers.

By 1930, Shanghai's economy was in deep crisis. Tea, cotton and wool prices had collapsed after the Wall Street Crash of the previous year. Several parallel civil wars in the Chinese hinterland had wrecked irrigation systems and hindered harvests, resulting in a 30–70 per cent shortfall in grain the previous year. A famine had killed hundreds of thousands in nearby Shanxi province and hunger riots were common across the countryside. Unemployment in Shanghai had tripled to 300,000, and inflation had made food unaffordable and driven thousands of peasants from the countryside into the cities to earn, beg or steal food.[21] Behind the luxurious facades of the Bund's palaces of capitalism, the backstreets of the city seethed in revolutionary anger.

Sorge and his party docked in the port of Shanghai on 10 January 1930 and checked into the Plaza Hotel. This was perhaps not the most discreet choice of accommodation as, of all the dozens of hotels in the city, the Plaza was known to be the favoured haunt of Comintern officials and senior Bolsheviks. Four days after their arrival the incumbent Fourth Department bureau chief, Lieutenant Colonel Alexander Gurvich (alias Gorin, codename 'Jim'), received an encrypted telegram from Moscow Centre informing him that his replacements were waiting for him to make contact. This came as news to Gorin, who had no plans to leave Shanghai before spring. Nonetheless, he presented himself at Room 420 of the Plaza the following morning.

'Hello from August,' said Gorin – the coded greeting provided by Centre by which he was to identify his surprise successor. 'I know his wife,' replied Ulanovsky.[22]

The meeting was not a happy one. Ulanovsky had instructions from Centre to take charge of the bureau's cover businesses and funds, to avoid contact with any of its agents and staff, and to start a brand-new agent network essentially from scratch. Gorin had no such instructions.[23] It seems that Berzin believed that Gorin's cover had been blown and his networks compromised. Hence Centre's haste to dispatch the new team with only the most peremptory preparation – and their instructions to Ulanovsky to stay clear of Gorin's compromised networks. Berzin's suspicions were founded on his debriefing of one of Gorin's deputies, one Zussman (alias Decross, codename 'Inostranets'), on his return to Moscow from Shanghai the previous October. For reasons that are not clear from the archives, Berzin seems to have concluded that Zussman was either a double agent or had been rumbled by the authorities. Gorin strongly disagreed, and his strenuous protestations to Centre occupied his correspondence for months. More, he refused to hand over any money and insisted on continuing to run his networks as before. For the first three months of Sorge's mission to Shanghai, there were effectively two rival Fourth Department *rezidenturas* operating in the city.

Thus Ulanovsky's main occupation in his first weeks in Shanghai was wrangling with his predecessor. Sorge, on the other hand, got on with what he did best – befriending men and charming women. His first targets were the German military advisers who had been drafted in by the Chinese Nationalist government to turn the Kuomintang Army into a modern military machine. The letters of introduction from Berlin established his bona fides with the German consul general, and with his help Sorge joined the Shanghai Rotary Club, the German Club and the International House. From Berlin, Sorge had also gleaned personal information on the key military advisers who might be best informed about Chinese affairs. Gorin's old radio man, Max Clausen – who would play a key role in the Sorge story – was immediately impressed by the new arrival's ruthless charm. Sorge quickly struck up 'friendly conversation' with the German officers, recalled Clausen, 'filled his interlocutors with wine to loosen their tongues ... and "gutted them like a fat Christmas goose", as he told us several times'.[24]

Sorge was obviously a natural dissimulator of rare talent. The officers whom he befriended were men he naturally despised. The German instructors were 'all Fascists, very anti-Soviet', reported Sorge. 'They all have dreams of attacking Siberia with the support of local warlords. They are mostly linked to industrial magnates in Germany and help them to get military orders.'[25] Yet it was compatriots like these – Nazis, militarists and cynics ready to enrich themselves on the suffering of the proletariat – who would, for the rest of his career, become Sorge's most valuable informers and closest supposed friends.

It was in the company of these well-paid swells that Sorge discovered, and quickly developed a taste for, the high life of Shanghai. In his previous career among rough and earnest communists, proletarians and intellectuals, Sorge had little opportunity to drink cocktails, dance with elegant women and eat in the finest restaurants. But his new job practically obliged him – at least in his own interpretation – to consume imported whisky and swap war stories with his new German friends in the salons of Shanghai's swankiest clubs. To cover his true background as a communist, Sorge had to play the debauched bourgeois expatriate. He found the role entirely to his liking.

Clausen also soon fell under Sorge's spell. 'He was an extremely charming man, and an excellent bottle-companion,' the radio man wrote in a post-war memoir. 'It was not surprising that many were keen to spend time with a well-known journalist and no less well-known social lion. I cannot say that this style of life was distasteful to Richard himself. He went to many restaurants, drank a lot, talked a lot. To be fair to him he was never indiscreet, though from time to time got into drunken fights and occasionally allowed himself some more desperate adventures.'[26]

On 26 January, after just a fortnight in Shanghai, Ulanovsky reported to Centre that 'agent Ramsay' – Sorge's new codename – had achieved 'excellent integration into the top circles of the German colony'. Citing 'a friendly conversation between Ramsay and German Generals', the *rezident* reported that Chiang Kai-shek was strongly opposed by commercial circles in Shanghai because they hated the nationalists' requisitions and forced nationalisation of strategic businesses.[27] Days later, he informed Centre that Ramsay had been told by the German consul that the nationalists were attempting a reconciliation with some of their warlord enemies in order to form a united front against the communists. Berzin marked the information 'valuable' and passed it directly to the Soviet People's Commissar for War. Sorge, a newly minted agent in a strange country, was already turning up intelligence gold.

Chinese circles proved harder to crack. Ulanovsky and Sorge both joined the Shanghai Christian Youth Union in an attempt to meet influential young Chinese. They failed, possibly because earnest Christian tea parties may not have been Sorge's natural milieu. Sorge had more luck with Shanghai's community of foreign communists and fellow-travellers. Already in Berlin he had been advised to contact one of the most fearless and outspoken foreign correspondents in Shanghai, an American socialist who worked for the *Frankfurter Zeitung* – Germany's most prestigious daily newspaper – named Agnes Smedley.[28]

Smedley was thirty-eight when she met Sorge. Born into a poor family of coal miners in Osgood, Missouri, she had witnessed police violence against striking colliers as a child. After leaving school she worked for a spell as a rural teacher before supporting herself through Tempe Normal School in Arizona. Having suffering a nervous breakdown, she was befriended by two neighbours, Thorberg and Ernest Brundin. Both were enthusiastic members of the Socialist Party of America and inspired Smedley with their devotion to the cause of justice for the oppressed. In 1917 Smedley moved to New York and became involved with Indian nationalists fighting British colonial rule in India, who recruited her to operate a front office for the group and publish anti-British propaganda. Most of these activities were covertly funded by Germany and Smedley changed addresses frequently to avoid surveillance by American and British military intelligence. Between May 1917 and March 1918 she moved ten times. Despite her precautions, in March 1918, Smedley was arrested by the US Naval Intelligence Bureau, indicted for violations of the Espionage Act and sentenced to two months in jail.

After her release, by now a committed communist, Smedley moved to Berlin where she became the lover of Indian revolutionary Virendranath Chattopadhyaya. She visited Moscow for the Comintern congress of 1921 and again in 1929.[29] It was in Berlin that she met Yakov Mirov-Abramov, the Comintern's top spy in Europe. Smedley's relationship with the Comintern and the Soviet Communist Party would always be deliberately ambiguous. She consistently denied working as a spy and never formally joined the party. But it is clear that Mirov-Abramov enlisted her to his network as a helpful sympathiser, at the very least.

In 1928 Smedley published *Daughter of Earth*, an autobiographical novel that established her fame as a crusading socialist and humanist, passionately devoted to relieving exploitation and poverty. Sorge read the book in Moscow. The following year she left Chattopadhyaya and – perhaps with the encouragement of Mirov-Abramov – moved to Shanghai as a correspondent for the liberal *Frankfurter Zeitung*.

Smedley was disgusted by Shanghai's decadence. 'In the big cities, and especially Shanghai, life follows its normal carefree pattern. There are opulent official receptions and balls, new banks opening, the establishment of great financial groupings and alliances, gambling on the stock exchange, opium smuggling and mutual insults by foreigners and Chinese under the aegis of extra-territoriality,' she wrote in February 1930. 'And there are the night clubs, the brothels, gambling clubs, and tennis courts and so on. And there are actually people who call this the beginning of a new era, the birth of a new nation. That may be true for a certain class of Chinese: for the merchants, bankers and racketeers. But for the Chinese peasantry, that is for 85 percent of the Chinese people, all this is like a life-destroying plague.'[30]

Soon after her arrival in Shanghai, Smedley made contact with the innocuously named Cultural Committee of the Chinese Communist Party (CCP). This was in fact a key branch of the party's central propaganda directorate whose task was to recruit Chinese intellectuals to the cause. Smedley, a well-connected foreigner with no formal ties to the party, was a godsend to the beleaguered left-wing Chinese whose lives, even in the concessions, were in constant danger. Radical literature was strictly banned, and communications and meetings were fraught with risk. Smedley's foreign passport and status as a respected international journalist was the perfect cover for mail drops and liaison between party members. She also offered her home for meetings and set about winning over China's pre-eminent short-story writer, Lu Hsun, to the cause. Smedley also set up a League of Left-Wing Writers, whose mail communications became a valuable covert conduit between the CCP and the rest of the world. In return, the party put Smedley in touch with Chinese and foreign communists, passed her the reports of the CCP's Central Committee and even provided a secretary – a young leftist intellectual – who translated reports and newspapers for her. By early 1930 Smedley was the only Western journalist in China receiving information directly from CCP sources.

Shortly after moving from the Plaza to the more modest Foreign YMCA on Bubbling Well Road, probably sometime in late January 1930, Sorge called on Smedley at her home in the French Concession. Introducing himself as 'Johnson', a supposedly American journalist,* Sorge presented her with a letter from someone he referred to in his prison statement as 'a mutual acquaintance in Berlin'. Most likely it came from Basov or one of his proxies. In any case, it seems that Sorge's intention from the outset was to recruit Smedley into his new Fourth Department network. He told the Japanese that he had been 'authorised to recruit personnel' and had 'heard of Smedley in Europe, and felt I could depend on her'. Soon after their first meeting, by Sorge's

*It is unlikely that Sorge expected the American Smedley to genuinely believe that he was her fellow-countryman, further proof that Smedley had already been signed up by the OMS.

account, he asked Smedley to help 'in establishing an intelligence-gathering group in Shanghai'. She immediately agreed.[31]

Their relationship quickly progressed beyond the strictly comradely. Soon after they began working together, Smedley and Sorge became lovers. It is hard to imagine that Sorge's motives were anything other than cynical: six years Sorge's senior, short and muscular with cropped hair, Agnes was far from Sorge's usual type. Ursula Kuczynski, a future love rival, described her as 'an intelligent working woman in appearance, in no sense pretty, but a well-proportioned face. When she strokes her hair back, one sees the great dome of the forehead.'[32] And Sorge himself would later uncharitably describe Agnes as 'a mannish woman'. Her earnest disapproval of the decadent luxuries of Shanghai could not have sat well with Sorge's penchant for restaurants, bars, fast motorcycles and women. Yet in one important sense this mismatched couple were kindred spirits. Both were passionately committed communists; both fiery characters who wanted to change the world.

By early spring, Smedley was frequently spotted riding behind Sorge – or 'Sorgie', as she took to calling him – on his powerful motorbike, speeding down the Nanking Road feeling 'grand and glorious'. She was obviously smitten with her rugged younger lover. 'I'm married, child, so to speak, just sort of married, you know,' Smedley wrote to her friend Florence Sanger. 'But it's a he-man also and it's 50–50 all along the line with he helping me and I him and we working together in every way. I do not know how long it will last; that does not depend on us. I fear not long. But these days will be the best in my life.'[33]

Sorge made clear that their relationship was a 'friendship' which he insisted precluded such bourgeois sentiments as monogamy. Smedley, an early public advocate of birth control and women's rights, also tried to convince herself that she too had transcended such conventional morality. 'It is a rare husband that wears well,' Smedley wrote to Sanger. 'I never expect one to wear so well – that is perhaps because I myself do not.' Monogamous relationships, as she had experienced them, were 'senseless, dependent, and cruel'.[34] But a few months into her affair with Sorge, Smedley confided to Sanger that she had at long last found that 'rare, rare person' who could give her 'everything I wanted and more'.[35]

Smedley introduced Sorge to her circle of Chinese communist intellectuals. More, she was able to give him first-hand information about the rapidly developing CCP-orchestrated insurgency that was taking over the Chinese interior. In March 1930, Smedley went on the first of several investigative trips up the Yangtze valley to Shaanxi province, where Chiang Kai-shek had his power base, as well as other more remote cities. She travelled with Chinese comrades who took her to the homes of peasants who had been forced to sell their land because of usurious government taxes and greedy landowners.[36] She reported in the *Modern Review* that a 'social revolution has broken out in earnest'. Mao Tse-tung's group of communist insurgents numbered over fifty thousand hungry, illiterate peasants and government soldiers who had defected into more than a dozen openly Red armies across central and southern China. In the communist-controlled 'Soviet areas', Mao's fledgling Red Guards were confiscating property from landowners and redistributing it to peasants. Kuomintang officials were replaced with local 'soviets', or workers' councils, that banned prostitution, gambling, and opium dens and closed temples and churches. Representatives of the 'former classes' such as missionaries, wealthy peasants, gentry, and officials, were executed after summary trials by people's courts.

Chiang Kai-shek's German-trained army enjoyed superior weaponry and discipline. But for the moment they were distracted by infighting between provincial regimes that until recently had been part of the Nationalist coalition. Smedley reported that the bands of armed communist partisans fighting government forces were poorly equipped, with a single rifle to every five to ten men and their ammunition limited to what they could capture from the enemy. Sorge passed on Smedley's reports of the weakness of these communist irregulars to Moscow Centre. He also reported that, according to his German officer contacts, Chiang Kai-shek was training a force of 20,000 model troops in Nanking, bribing opponents and preparing for a major offensive against the communists once he had crushed all Nationalist opposition closer to home.

Nonetheless, in Shanghai the chairman of the Chinese Communist Party's Politburo, Li Li-san, saw a chance to press their advantage while the Nationalists fought their private civil war. Moscow and the Comintern, insisting that China's revolution would be hatched in the cities and not, as Mao believed, by holding the countryside, officially encouraged Li Li-san to try to seize a major urban centre. The target was to be Canton (modern Guangzhou), capital of Kwangtung

(Guangdong) province, close to Mao's power base and a large industrial city apparently ripe for a Bolshevik-style coup.

On 9 May 1930, Sorge set off for Canton with Gorin's radio man, Max Clausen. Smedley followed them a week later. Chen Han-seng, the young communist who worked as Smedley's translator, wrote a memoir written half a century later in which he loyally repeated their cover story: the couple travelled south 'to celebrate their honeymoon in Hong Kong'.[37] In truth, of course, Sorge went to Canton on orders from Ulanovsky and in the company of Clausen in order to establish covert radio contact between this new cradle of revolution and Shanghai and Vladivostok.

Clausen had been a member of Gorin's Fourth Department team in Shanghai since the autumn of 1928. According to Berzin's original instructions to the Ulanovsky-Sorge group – to break off all contact with the old, supposedly compromised bureau – Clausen should have been sent home. Instead, like so many of Centre's sensible intentions, security was put aside in favour of operational convenience. Sepp Weingarten was, quite simply, proving an incompetent radio operator. Clausen was an excellent one.

Max Christiansen-Clausen – codenamed 'Hans', following the Fourth Department's quaint but insecure practice of giving all German agents German nicknames – was born in 1899 into the family of a poor bricklayer on the tiny Frisian island of Nordstrand. He joined the German Imperial Army in 1917 and trained as an electrical engineer, erecting radio masts across northern Germany. The following year he became a field radio operator and was deployed to the defence of Metz and Compiègne before succumbing to a botched German gas attack at Château-Thierry that left him coughing blood for a month. Like Sorge, Clausen's lifelong socialism was born of his profound anger at the waste and horror of the war. Clausen attempted to desert but was arrested and spent time in a military brig. In the aftermath of the Armistice in November 1918, Clausen and a friend made their way to Hamburg, where he got a job in the Merchant Navy. By 1922 Clausen had become a prominent activist in the German Seaman's Union, was briefly imprisoned for organising a seamen's strike in Stettin, and on his release joined the German Communist Party's Red Army organisation.

Clausen first visited the USSR in 1924 aboard a German sailing ship that was being delivered to the Soviet government at the Arctic port of Murmansk. He spent a week at the International Seamen's Club in Petrograd and liked what he saw of the workers' paradise. On his return to Hamburg, Karl Lesse, officially head of the International Seamen's Trade Union but in fact a Comintern operative, recruited Clausen to smuggle revolutionary literature on board merchant vessels.[38] His skill at this clandestine work earned Max an invitation to Moscow in September 1928 – just as Sorge had been headhunted from the German party three years previously. But, unlike his future boss, Clausen was not destined for the intellectual salons of Moscow. The Fourth Department sent Clausen for training in constructing and operating short-wave radios at the Fourth Department's Technical School in suburban Moscow, where he studied alongside Weingarten. In October 1928 he was sent to join Gorin's apparat in Shanghai.[39]

Under the cover name of 'Willi Lehmann', Clausen set up a household goods shop in the International Settlement using the Fourth Department's money. Clausen may have been a dedicated communist, but he was to show a natural flair for business that would later become a fatal conflict of interest with his masters in Moscow. Demonstrating impressive technical skill, he constructed a portable radio set with a tiny 7.5-watt transmitter capable of making contact with Vladivostok – codename 'Wiesbaden' – which he carried around Shanghai in a leather suitcase.

Gorin had been pleased with his new radio man's talents, but less so with Clausen's relationship with Anna Zhdankova, a White Russian émigré he had met in Shanghai. Anna was born in Novonikolaevsk (now Novosibirsk) in 1897 into the family of a tanner. At the age of eighteen she married Eduard Wallenius, a Finnish leather workshop owner, who later bought a flour mill in Seimapaltinsk in the Kazakh steppes. The Walleniuses lived a comfortable bourgeois life before the Bolshevik revolution of 1917 forced them into exile. The couple emigrated to Shanghai along with tens of thousands of other refugees, fleeing the Bolsheviks with nothing more than they could carry in their suitcases. After her husband died in 1927, Anna found work as a nurse. By the time she met Clausen in 1929 – she had placed a classified advertisement to let out her attic, which Max answered – Anna Wallenius had developed a deep loathing of communists. She had no idea that her new lodger, and future husband, was a Soviet spy.

Centre disapproved of the relationship on the entirely sensible grounds that no agent could be expected to maintain the secret of his double life in his own home. The fact that the Shanghai apparat's main secret transmitter was concealed in her attic without Anna's knowledge was also a major security risk. But Clausen stood firm. After his arrival in Shanghai, Sorge – in contrast to his later habit of putting his colleagues' personal lives second to the needs of the apparat – also defied Centre by backing the talented radio operator. Sorge had met and liked Anna Wallenius and believed that she could be talked into sympathy for the cause. It would be six years before Moscow gave its blessing for Clausen officially to marry, and ten before Sorge would be proved disastrously wrong about where Anna's true loyalties lay.

So the Fourth Department apparat that assembled in Canton in May 1930 was a curious group. Sorge himself was posing as Richard Johnson, an American journalist. His lover Agnes Smedley was a conspirator posing as a neutral reporter. Clausen was under cover as a businessman, and Anna Wallenius was an innocent unaware of her lover's role as a secret agent. Also accompanying the team was Konstantin Mishin, a White Russian who had been recruited as an additional radio operator by Gorin and whom Centre had declared politically unreliable – but was brought along anyway for want of any other qualified personnel.

The group rented several properties around Canton. Clausen leased two houses from the British consulate in the city's British Concession for himself and Sorge, while Smedley rented an apartment at her own expense in the Chinese area of Tungshan. Smedley's flat was modest in size but had sufficient space for a darkroom. This was for Sorge, who would need such a space to photograph documents, prepare microfilms, and establish the wireless station that was the key mission of his trip.[40]

Smedley clearly hoped that her little apartment would become a kind of home for her and her dashing lover. 'You may think the two chairs express a hope or a reality,' she wrote to her friend Karin Michaelis. 'Oh well – far be it from me to contradict a woman who knows so much about women as you do.'[41] She tried to hide her desire for a more exclusive attachment with brash statements like 'no man will ever get his hooks in me again'. But her need for a deep and lasting love, as she confessed in her letters to Michaelis, remained.[42] (Clausen never thought much of her: 'the only impression I have of [Smedley] is that she was a hysterical, conceited woman', he recalled.)[43]

By late summer Clausen had succeeded in establishing radio contact between Canton and Vladivostok – albeit with a much more powerful, and therefore less portable and therefore more vulnerable, 50-watt transmitter.[44] Smedley undertook arduous reporting trips into the Chinese interior, visiting villages of impoverished silk workers whose worldly possessions consisted of just 'a clay stove, narrow bench, table, and a few cooking utensils and cocoon frames'. She wrote movingly in the *Modern Review* on the usurious interest rates peasants paid to moneylenders that sometimes led to families selling their children into servitude. Meanwhile Sorge was making good use of Smedley's contacts to recruit a network of Chinese helpers. Her secretary, Chen Han-seng, introduced him to a 'Mrs Etui', a Kwangtung native, and another Cantonese comrade, who both began providing Sorge with military and political reports on the situation in south China.

Sorge, a trained spy with solid cover, was able to stay under the radar screen of the British police in Canton. The famous socialist Smedley, however, had a harder time maintaining a low profile. She discovered in July that the Chinese authorities in Shanghai had warned officials in Canton to keep an eye on her, on suspicion that she was engaging in communist propaganda. A censor was assigned to monitor her mail. 'This is a warning for future letters,' she instructed Florence Sanger on 19 July 1930. 'George and Mary' – Smedley's nickname for the British police – 'are again hot on the trail of my letters. Refer no more to lovers and revolutions, etc.'. She headed to the American consulate general in Canton to renew her American passport and seek the protection of the consul general, Douglas Jenkins. Smedley protested her surveillance by Chinese police, and warned a startled Jenkins (as he reported to Washington) that she was 'afraid of being shot in the back'.[45] As soon as Smedley had left his office, Jenkins cabled a request to the US Secretary of State to ascertain at once whether she was indeed a communist agent, as local authorities claimed.

Three days later, as police in Canton cracked down in anticipation of a widespread communist uprising, Smedley once again appeared at Jenkins's office to report that her apartment had been invaded and rifled by armed police who had seized various papers. She insisted that Jenkins return home with her. Finding two policemen still there, the diplomat ordered them to leave. The search had unearthed nothing more compromising than a parcel full of the current issue of the *League of Left-Wing Writers' Journal.* Smedley was not an official member of the apparat and – fortunately for Sorge – no confidential material had been kept at her apartment. Nonetheless, quite apart from personal considerations, Sorge's lover was too valuable an asset, and knew too much, for Sorge to allow her to be arrested and interrogated by the notoriously brutal Chinese police.

Sorge's solution was ingenious, a tribute both to the efficiency of Canton's radio communications and the respect in which Agent Ramsay was then held in Moscow. On 7 August, by Sorge's request, an article by no less a luminary than Karl Radek, head of the International Information Bureau of the Russian Communist Party's Central Committee, appeared in the official party newspaper *Izvestia*. Radek denounced Smedley as 'the bourgeois correspondent of an imperialist newspaper' and attacked her for spreading erroneous stories about outrages that China's Red armies were perpetrating upon the country's poor in order to 'create sympathy for its landowners, usurers, merchants, and officials'.[46] The charge was quite false. But the deliberate libel helped Smedley distance herself from any links to Moscow.

The day before the *Izvestia* article, Smedley had signed an affidavit at the American consulate to the effect that she was neither a communist (which was clearly not true), nor a member of the communist party nor any other political party (which was). She also swore that she was not in any way connected with the Communist International, and denied any involvement in communist agitation, Bolshevik propaganda, or any subversive activity directed against the Nanking government – which was all, again, a lie.[47] We know from the correspondence of the Comintern's Far Eastern Bureau that Smedley had declared to its chief, Ignatii Rylsky, as early as 20 March that her 'journalistic accreditation was just a cover and she was in reality a representative of the anti-Imperialist league and has money to give to Chinese Communists for this work'.[48] The only other part of her statement that was, surprisingly enough, perfectly correct was Smedley's avowal that she had not been paid a dime either by the USSR or the Comintern for her efforts.[49]

Despite this upset, Sorge's Canton mission continued to produce impressive results. With the help of Smedley's friends, Sorge reported to Moscow on troop movements, military manoeuvres, command structures, the creation of an eight-aircraft strong Nationalist air force in Canton, the whereabouts of German instructors, and the progress of the communist-led peasant insurgency. On 1 August 1930 the communist leader Li Li-sang finally seized a major city – Changsha in Hunan province – just as Moscow had encouraged him to do – and declared a Soviet government there. Just as Mao predicted, it proved a fatal mistake. Within a fortnight Nationalist gunboats, backed by the British and Americans, had destroyed the Red forces and summarily executed over two thousand communists. Sorge reported to Moscow; Smedley wrote for the *Frankfurter Zeitung*. Both were in their element. Smedley, at least, was blissfully happy.

'Never have I known such good days, never have I known such a healthy life, mentally, physically, psychically,' Smedley wrote to a friend. 'I consider this completion, and when it is ended, I'll be lonelier than all the love in the magazines could never make me.'[50] But Sorgie and Smedley's romantic Canton idyll would soon be shattered – precisely as she had predicted – just weeks after she wrote her heart-breaking letter. On 3 September, Sorge was urgently called back to Shanghai. Ulanovsky's cover had been blown. The bureau chief was fleeing for his life.

5

The Manchurian Incident

'I was in ecstasy from this ride and shouted to him to ride faster'
Ursula Kuczynski (alias Ruth Werner)

Ulanovsky's tenure as head of the Shanghai apparat had not begun well when the genial Brits to whom he had boasted of his arms-dealing mission on the boat from Marseilles turned out to be British policemen. But in truth his mission was doomed long before he ever boarded the ship.

A time bomb was ticking under Ulanovsky's career in China. It had been laid in 1927, when Ulanovsky had visited the northern Chinese port of Hankow as part of an official Soviet delegation of the Pacific Secretariat of Trade Unions. While in Hankow, Ulanovsky had not exactly hung back from the limelight. Using his own name, he had chatted with dozens of comrades, Soviet and Chinese, and had given a speech to a packed conference at U-Hang alongside Solomon Lozovsky, secretary of the Trades Unions International. It was only a matter of time, therefore, that an old acquaintance from Hankow days would run into the man posing as the Czech citizen 'Kirschner' on the streets of Shanghai and recognise him as a Soviet official.

Precisely that happened with tragicomic immediacy on one of Ulanovsky's first forays into Shanghai's nightlife, a couple of weeks after his arrival. In the Arcadia nightclub the hapless *rezident* bumped into a German merchant who remembered him well.[1] Ulanovsky could scarcely claim mistaken identity, as he and the German had shared a train compartment on the seven-day trip from Moscow to Vladivostok back in 1927. The businessman had even attended his Hankow speech. Ulanovsky reported sheepishly to Centre that this unfortunate meeting had rendered his Czech 'boot' – the Soviet spies' jargon for a false identity – a liability. He suggested avoiding the German community as a precaution. Sadly for Ulanovsky's career, this was his chief source of information. He was forced to fall back to scouring independent Chinese newspapers like the left-wing *Gemin Jibao* for information. But even this meagre resource was cut off when a new wave of censorship shut down most of the non-official press in early summer, 1930. Foreigners were also placed under close police watch, Ulanovsky reported to Centre; all post was examined and mass searches and arrests made spying extremely difficult. While Sorge was hobnobbing with German officers and senior Chinese communists, Ulanovsky had become a lame duck almost from the outset of his tour.

Worse was to come. On another ill-advised sortie outside his front door, Ulanovsky was immediately spotted by another old acquaintance from Hankow, a man currently styling himself Captain Evgeny Pik. Also known by at least a dozen aliases, Pik – born Evgeny Kozhevnikov – had already distinguished himself in a city filled with unscrupulous adventurers as a one-man *opéra bouffe* of skulduggery.

The son of an Astrakhan merchant, Kozhevnikov had been taken prisoner during the First World War and joined the Red Army on his return from German captivity to Russia in 1918. Thereafter he pursued an unusual combination of careers, studying at the GPU secret police academy while at same time putting in time at a Moscow theatre school under the pseudonym of Khovansky. As a newly commissioned GPU officer he spent time in Turkestan, and later policed the Ukraine–Polish–Romanian border, a notorious hotbed of smuggling and corruption. He served on a special Soviet mission to Turkey and Afghanistan, and in 1925 travelled to China with a top-level Soviet delegation to the government of Sun Yat-sen, led by General Vasiliy Blyukher and senior Comintern executive Mikhail Borodin.

Kozhevnikov's career as an international double agent and *macher* – wheeler-dealer – began in China when he stole Borodin's diary and papers and sold them to the French consul in Hankow. With the help of the British police he escaped to Shanghai, where he published a series of sensational articles on communist penetration of China, under his Evgeny Pik pseudonym. He sent the Shanghai International Settlement police an anonymous letter – later traced back to him – exposing sixty-two supposed Comintern agents in the city. Simultaneously, the energetic Kozhevnikov found time to keep up his acting career, establishing himself as a popular character actor and theatre director and starring in Russian-language productions at local Shanghai music halls. A contemporary publicity photograph shows Kozhevnikov posing in a Tatar skullcap with a fake scar across his foxy face.

Finding that neither his parallel careers as a professional informer nor as a theatrical impresario could keep him in the style to which he aspired, Kozhevnikov/Pik turned his hand to extortion. In 1928 he teamed up with two other actors to extract bribes from a wealthy Chinese casino owner. Pik posed as the head of the Criminal Department of the Shanghai Municipal Police (no less) and his accomplices played members of the US consulate staff. This protection racket netted him £15,000, with which he fled to the northern Chinese city of Mukden. When the money ran out the following year he returned to Shanghai and was promptly arrested for extortion and forgery of US and British consular documents. After spending some months in jail, Pik quickly re-established himself in the graces of the British and French police, as well as the Chinese government, as a recruiter of agents and informers in the White Russian community. The agents Pik enlisted, as it turned out, were registered with all three agencies.

On the side he also re-formed his old gang of actors to attempt another confidence trick. This time Pik and his associates posed as German officers 'Captain Kurt Kluge' and 'Major Levitz' and began negotiations to buy contraband weapons for the Chinese government to the tune of $2 million – ironically, enough, exactly the game that Ulanovsky was supposed to be in had he not been rumbled at the outset by British police – but with the added twist of soliciting kickbacks from corrupt arms dealers to secure the non-existent contract. Pik succeeded in extracting some $70,000 from a Chinese merchant before being unveiled. He was once again briefly arrested.

In short, Pik was trouble. Yet on his release from custody in the wake of the Kluge caper, Pik turned up at Ulanovsky's house in search of more money. With chutzpah bordering on the maniacal, he proposed a deal. Claiming to be an agent for Chinese and French counter-intelligence, Pik offered to save Ulanovsky's star (and indeed only) agent, a shyster and petty criminal by the name of 'Kurgan', from jail.

In early spring a desperate Ulanovsky, under pressure from Moscow to provide some hard intelligence, had recruited a single agent. His name was Rafail 'Folya' Kurgan, an old comrade of Ulanovsky's from their days fighting in the Bolshevik underground in White-held Crimea during the Russian civil war. Kurgan – later codenamed 'Kur', surely one of the least secure pseudonyms in the history of intelligence – was a penniless émigré when Ulanovsky ran into him on a Shanghai street. Kur began to recruit a series of extremely expensive and, it turned out, mostly unreliable agents into Ulanovsky's new network. Among these was one Maravsky, a former member of the White government of Siberia who was providing Chiang Kai-shek's German instructors with intelligence on how to invade the Soviet Union. Maravsky demanded a thousand silver dollars a month for his services but, as Centre discovered, he was also working for Japanese intelligence. Another of Kur's less-than-stellar informants was the playboy son of a wealthy Chinese casino owner who demanded cash in exchange for 'contacts' in high society.[2]

Kur's one real success was in recruiting a technical secretary to the Nanking government who agreed to hand over the monthly audits of all Chinese Army arsenals, as well as all contracts with foreign companies, for a one-off payment of 5,000 Mexican silver dollars. Ulanovsky gladly handed over the money and received photos of the documents – the one real intelligence coup of his Shanghai days.

Unfortunately, the prospect of pocketing a similar sum proved too much for Kur. Inventing details of a second cache of documents from this valuable agent, Kur instead took over a thousand dollars of Soviet silver from Ulanovsky and disappeared for three weeks. He made contact with Ulanovsky again on 12 June 1930, claiming that Maravsky had betrayed him and made off with the cash. Kur also asked for even more money – which Ulanovsky, improbably enough, handed over. This was perhaps not so much naivety as desperation. Kur knew the address and real names of Ulanovsky and his wife Sharlotta. He also knew the identity of every informer that he himself had recruited. It was easier for Ulanovsky to hand over money than risk his entire Shanghai network being blown. Ulanovsky at first claimed in his telegrams to Moscow that Kur had a gambling habit that had caused him to lose apparat money. But on 16 July he was eventually forced to admit to Centre that he was being blackmailed.

In early August, Kur showed up once more at Ulanovsky's house demanding $1,200 to go to South America. When the station chief demurred, Kur hysterically threatened to shoot himself. At another meeting a few days later Sharlotta Ulanovskaya attempted to persuade Kur and his wife to take the train to Harbin and offered them 300 Mexican dollars for the tickets. Kur took the money and, to the *rezident's* undoubted relief, disappeared once more.

It was at this point that the latest unwelcome guest materialised at the Ulanovsky residence in the person of the newly released Eugene Pik. The former secret policeman-turned-actor-turned-double-agent bore alarming news. Pik told Ulanovsky that Kur had not left for Harbin but remained in Shanghai. Worse, Kur was under arrest for the forgery of bonds. But Pik proposed a solution. He could use his contacts with the Chinese and French police to release the unfortunate agent before he could spill the beans. All Ulanovsky had to do was pay the (unrecorded) sum of Kur's forged promissory note and all would be well. As an additional bonus, Pik also offered his own services as an agent to the Ulanovsky spy ring.[3]

It is highly likely that Pik's offer was made in collaboration with the elusive Kur. At any rate, this latest démarche was too much even for Ulanovsky's elastic credulity. Pik was 'put outside the door', Ulanovsky reported to Centre, and the two men never saw each other again – though Kozhevnikov/Pik went on to a spectacular career in crime and espionage for the Japanese and later the Americans.[4] It was equally clear, however, that the game was up for the Ulanovskys. Too many of Shanghai's shysters knew their identities, and they would have to leave in a hurry before one of them sold them out to the authorities. Ulanovsky urgently telegraphed Centre to warn them that he had been busted. He also recommended Sorge as his replacement.

Days later the Ulanovskys were on a boat to Hong Kong. From the relative safety of the British colony, on 23 August the departing chief shared with Sorge his wisdom for the future of the Shanghai *rezidentura*. In the opinion of Ulanovsky, agents should be taught dancing, golf, tennis and bridge – 'as essential as a reliable passport' in order to give 'a good foundation for small talk'.[5] More substantively, he warned Sorge of the heightened counter-intelligence measures now in place in Shanghai, including news that British police agents were conducting morning rounds of popular brothels in order to debrief the prostitutes on the previous evening's conversations, and instruct them on what questions to ask their patrons. Understandably, given his experiences, Ulanovsky also warned that all White Russian groups were riddled with informers and crooks.

Agnes Smedley followed Sorge back to Shanghai in early September. Through the League of Left-Wing Writers, she had met and befriended several young foreign communists. One was Irene Wiedemeyer, a handsome young German woman of Jewish heritage with freckled skin, milk-blue eyes and unmanageable red hair. While living in Berlin, Wiedemeyer had become involved with the propaganda apparatus of the formidable Comintern *macher*, Willi Muenzenberg, whose forte was persuading left-wing intellectuals to support the Soviet cause via a series of supposedly non-communist front organisations such as the Anti-Fascist League. After a spell in Moscow studying Asian revolutionary movements, Wiedemeyer had turned up in Shanghai to run a branch of the Zeitgeist bookstore on the banks of Foochow Creek. The Zeitgeist stocked radical German, English and French literature, much of it produced by Muenzenberg's publishing syndicate. It was also used by the Comintern as a rendezvous and recruiting station, where messages and information were conveyed to agents on sheets of paper slipped between the pages of designated books.[6]

It was during this time that Smedley was befriended by Ursula Maria Hamburger, née Kuczynski. A slim, twenty-three-year-old, dark-haired Berliner from a prominent leftist family, Ursula had previously worked as an agitation and propaganda leader for the German Communist Party. Ursula would, in the course of several marriages and a stellar career as a Soviet spy, accumulate several pseudonyms, including Ruth Werner and the codename 'Sonja'. But when she sought out the great author of *Daughter of Earth* she went by her married name of Ursula Hamburger, the wife of Rudolf Hamburger, a successful young architect who had moved to Shanghai in July of 1930.[7] The two women met on 7 November 1930, the anniversary of the Russian Revolution and a favoured time for leftist gatherings, at the cafe of Shanghai's Cathay Hotel. Ursula confided to Smedley that she had come to China hoping to be put to work for the communist cause.

Smedley invited Ursula to meet with her Chinese comrades – among them the writer Lu Hsun and her assistant Chen Han-seng – and also gave her work writing for the League of Left-Wing Writers' banned paper. Most fatefully, she introduced Kuczynski to Richard Sorge.

Ursula's infatuation with the journalist she knew as Johnson was immediate. She found Sorge 'charming and handsome' with a 'long face, thick curly hair and deep-set, bright blue eyes'.[8] Soon Sorge had persuaded Ursula to offer her spacious house on the Avenue Joffre in the French Concession for meetings, unbeknown to her husband. The house was surrounded on three sides by a large garden and had a separate servants' staircase allowing discreet access to the drawing rooms on the second floor. Chinese guests – in fact senior Chinese Communist Party members – were passed off to the Hamburgers' seven servants as language teachers. Sorge would always arrive first and leave last. By spring the Hamburger house had become such an obvious hotbed of clandestine activity that the English landlords complained about 'too many Chinese' coming to their property.[9]

Ursula did not care. Despite being a young mother – or maybe because of it – she was profoundly excited by the risk and glamour of her secret life as a conspirator that took her out of the domestic world of the nursery and into a large new one of jeopardy and high ideals. Sorge personified both the danger and the romance. 'In the first week of spring, when my boy was two months old, Richard asked me if I wished to ride with him on his motorcycle,' recalled Ursula in her bestselling 1958 memoir, *Sonja's Rapport*. 'It was the first time in my life I had ever been on a motorcycle … I was in ecstasy from this ride and shouted to him to ride faster. He was racing the bike as fast as it could go. When we stopped I felt as though I had been born again. Maybe he used this ride to check my bravery and endurance.'[10]

Ursula may have begun her involvement with the communist underground as a naive and infatuated hero-worshipper of first Smedley, then Sorge. But she soon showed herself to be a talented and disciplined agent, whom Sorge formally recruited. Ursula and her husband cultivated some of the most influential expatriates in Shanghai, including the German consul general, the head of the chamber of commerce and the head of the Trans-Oceanic news service, as well as a scattering of professors and correspondents. The table talk reported by Ursula – or 'Sonja', as Sorge codenamed her – began appearing regularly in his cables to Centre. Rudolf Hamburger, though a leftist, remained in the dark about his wife's secret activities.

Sorge would later pay a strange kind of tribute to the women in his network by insisting to his Japanese interrogators that 'women are utterly unsuited to espionage work ... They have no understanding of political and other affairs and I have never received satisfactory information from them.'[11] He was covering up for them. In reality, women – including Smedley, Ursula, and at least two Chinese agents, recruited with Smedley's help, as well as dozens of women during his Tokyo career – would play a central role in Sorge's intelligence work.

Another potential recruit was a young British executive of British American Tobacco (BAT) named Roger Hollis.[12] After a flirtation with communism at Oxford, Hollis had dropped out of university in 1927 and travelled to China to try his hand at freelance journalism before joining BAT. He spent time in Shanghai and Peking and moved in leftist circles – though he and Ursula Hamburger later denied having met. He certainly met Comintern recruiter Arthur Ewert and Smedley, though 'Ramsay' himself made no mention of any contact with Hollis in his detailed dispatches to Centre.[13]

Hollis went on to join MI5 and was appointed director general of Britain's internal security service in 1956. In 1986 Hollis was accused by author Chapman Pincher of being 'Elli', an alleged Russian military intelligence mole in MI5 during the war mentioned by Soviet defector Igor Gouzenko. The case against Hollis rests largely on the fact that Hollis repeatedly, and inexplicably, quashed surveillance of Ursula Kuczynski after she moved to London in 1938. Divorced from Hamburger, Ursula had become a professionally trained Fourth Department spy. Her mission in England was to act as the controller of Klaus Fuchs, the nuclear physicist who acted as liaison between the Manhattan Project and Britain's own atomic research network. Despite MI5 suspicions that a covert transmitter was operating in north Oxford – where Kuczynski moved after MI5 was relocated to nearby Blenheim Palace during the war – 'Sonja' was never caught or even questioned.

Had Hollis been recruited by the Soviets while in China? According to Hollis's British flatmate in Peking, Smedley came to visit him there in 1931 in the company of Arthur Ewert, the head of the Comintern's intelligence in China. Hollis also knew the Soviet spy Karl Rimm, who was to replace Sorge as Fourth Department Shanghai station chief in 1932. He also possibly had an affair with Rimm's wife Luise. Hollis also visited Moscow in 1934 and again in 1936 on the way back to London, then obfuscated about these visits during his vetting process.[14] But if the Soviets did recruit Hollis in China, it was not Sorge who bagged him. Neither Sorge nor Rimm made any mention of such a promising recruitment in their correspondence with Centre in the files of the Shanghai *rezidentura* at the Defence Ministry archive in Podolsk.[15]

In any case, in the late autumn of 1930 Smedley produced a far more immediately promising catch than the idealistic young tobacco executive Hollis. Hotsumi Ozaki was a special correspondent for Japan's most respected newspaper, the Osaka *Asahi Shimbun*.[16] Born in Shirakawa, Gifu Prefecture, in 1901, Ozaki was the descendant of a samurai family. He had become inspired by communism while studying law at Tokyo's Imperial University, but never formally joined the party. In November 1928 Ozaki was posted to Shanghai by the *Asahi Shimbun*, and became a regular at meetings at the Zeitgeist bookshop. Like Ursula Kuczynski, he asked Wiedemeyer to introduce him to the 'famous American authoress'.

Smedley's first conversations with Ozaki were coy. They earnestly discussed what could be done to help the newly formed Chinese branch of International Red Aid – a Muenzenberg-style front organisation designed to rally leftist humanitarians – and how to mobilise a worldwide protest movement against the Chinese Nationalist government's anti-communist terror. She also 'suggested that they exchange information on contemporary social issues', Ozaki told his Japanese interrogators a decade later. Soon they were discussing more politically sensitive subjects including the inner workings of the Nationalist government. Smedley was 'so perceptive that her questions sometimes frightened me', confessed Ozaki.[17]

Smedley introduced Sorge as an American newspaperman – though Ozaki, whose English was just as fluent as Sorge's, said he never believed the 'Johnson' alias. What Ozaki did believe was that Mr Johnson was affiliated with International Red Aid, the same Comintern front for which Smedley also worked. It was only some months after he agreed to share information with Johnson that Ozaki decided that his American friend was in fact a senior member of the Comintern's OMS intelligence.[18] It seems that Ozaki continued to believe that he was working for the Comintern, rather than for Soviet military intelligence, right up until his execution for espionage on Revolution Day 1944.

Sorge and Ozaki had plenty in common. Both were 'good bottle-men'. And though Ozaki was married with a young daughter when he met 'Johnson', he was an incorrigible *enpuka* – a ladies' man – and was described by a friend as a 'hormone tank'.[19] Ozaki's entanglements with women had begun at university when he moved in with a married woman who was a family friend. In 1927 he wed Eiko, the divorced wife of his elder brother, which also shocked traditional-minded Japanese. Ozaki and Sorge's cooperation was also based on a shared respect for each other's intellect, and a deep and genuine ideological commitment to communism. In many ways, the relationship would become an exploitative one. Sorge would use Ozaki ruthlessly and even, at the end, recklessly put him in danger. But Ozaki saw the role of spy that Sorge invented for him as his fate. 'If I reflect deeply, I can say that I was destined to meet Agnes Smedley and Richard Sorge,' Ozaki told the Japanese police. 'It was my encounter with these people that finally determined my narrow path from then on.'[20]

Ozaki had excellent contacts with the Japanese consulate general in Shanghai, as well as with Japanese businessmen in the city, and with officials of the Chinese Nationalist government and the ruling Kuomintang Party. By December 1930, when Chiang Kai-shek unleashed 350,000 Nationalist troops into Red Army-held areas of Shaanxi province, Ozaki was already assisting Smedley with her extra-legal activities for International Red Aid and keeping Sorge informed of developments. Soon Ozaki would recruit two other young Japanese for Sorge's network: Mizuno Shigeru, a student agitator, and Teikichi Kawai, a freelance journalist.

The risks that Sorge, Smedley, Ursula Kuczynski and Ozaki were running became terrifying clear in the new year of 1931. In late January, twenty-four CCP members, including five young leaders of the League of Left-Wing Writers, were arrested in Shanghai and turned over to Kuomintang authorities. It later emerged that they had actually been betrayed by the incoming Chinese Communist Party leader, Wang Ming, a Moscow loyalist, who had informed the Shanghai Municipal Police that some of his dissenting comrades were conducting a secret meeting. Ruthless infighting of this kind made security among the Chinese comrades poor. Equally slim were the chances that arrested comrades would withstand brutal interrogation.

In the wake of the arrests, Sorge urged Smedley to lie low in Nanking, where she met up with Ozaki. They travelled together to Manila, where they attended the founding congress of the Philippine Communist Party conference organised by Earl Browder, head of the Communist Party of America. While the Sorge group kept a low profile, Nationalist death squads roamed the Shaanxi countryside. Five of Smedley's Chinese comrades from the Writers' League were executed, reportedly by being buried alive.[21]

With Smedley away in the Philippines, Sorge embarked on an affair with Ursula Kuczynski. Using his tried-and-tested seduction technique, he took her on thrilling motorcycle rides. 'If he thought this would bring us closer together then he was right,' she wrote in her memoir. 'After this ride I was no longer scared and our chats became more frank.'[22] When in March Smedley returned to Shanghai, she took the news of her best friend's affair with her lover badly. Too proud to confront the younger woman directly, they bickered fiercely over ideological questions. 'Agnes would storm off, enraged,' according to Ursula. Then, a few hours later, she 'would telephone as if nothing had happened' and resume their friendship. Smedley, prone to night terrors and bouts of depression, would regularly call Ursula at three in the morning, asking her to come over and hold her hand.

While his two mistresses vied for dominance, Sorge attempted to contain the damage caused by the Kuomintang's relentless round-up of communist activists. His major problem was that Centre's instructions to cut off all ties with the previous Fourth Department networks – and also to steer clear of the multifarious Comintern networks in Shanghai – were impossible to follow in practice. In Moscow, Comintern intelligence and Soviet military intelligence could operate as separate, and even rival, entities. In the chaotic Shanghai underground, the lives of the two sets of Soviet spies were hopelessly and inextricably tangled.

In the late spring of 1931, Shanghai was host to a bewildering collection of Soviet organisations, all partly or wholly engaged in espionage. There was a secret Comintern OMS *rezidentura*; the clandestine representative office of the Comintern's Far Eastern Bureau (Dalburo); representatives of the International Organisation of Unions (MOP); the Pacific Secretariat of Unions; the Communist Youth International (KIM); as well as the official Soviet consulate general and Soviet military commission. The Dalburo alone had a permanent staff of nine, kept fifteen apartments around the city for secret meetings and received a budget of $120–150,000 a year from the Comintern's Western European bureau in Berlin in order to train and support communist cadres across Asia.[23] All these Soviet comrades had legitimate covers; all of them met both overtly and covertly with Chinese trade unionists, members of the Chinese Communist Party, leftist writers, visiting foreign communists – and of course the fellow-travelling Europeans of the Zeitgeist bookshop circle. To complicate things still further, the OMS had failed to establish proper radio communications with Centre. That meant that much of the secret radio correspondence between the OMS and Dalburo actually went through Sorge, who had to personally encode it and pass it to his radio man for painstaking transmission in Morse code to Vladivostok.

The whole edifice was staggeringly insecure, as was proved when Chinese police arrested Huan Dihun, a Moscow-trained Comintern agent known by the codename Kalugin, in Canton in March 1931. Under torture, Huan soon began naming other communists. More arrests quickly followed. By mid-April, five CCP couriers and eight Central Committee members had been arrested. One CCP Politburo candidate member, Gu Shun Jian, was arrested in Hankow where he had been posing as a street juggler (which had in fact been his genuine pre-party profession). Gu knew every clandestine meeting place in Shanghai and had met most of the Soviet cadres in the city, albeit under flimsy codenames. Within days, Gu had confessed all he knew. (Gu's treachery not only did not save his own life, but condemned thirty members of Gu's extended family to being murdered by communist partisans who spared only his twelve-year-old son from the massacre.[24]) The CCP organisation in Shanghai was utterly destroyed. By the end of June over three thousand Chinese party members had been arrested and many of them shot.

The Comintern suffered another disastrous security breach when courier Joseph Ducroux Lefranc, alias Dupont, was arrested by British police in Singapore on 1 June 1931. Police found two sheets of paper on his person bearing a Shanghai post-office box number and a telegram address. The Shanghai Municipal Police quickly traced the addresses to one Hilaire Noulens, allegedly a professor of French and German. His real name was Yakov Rudnik, and he was in charge of the Dalburo's communications, security and accommodation in Shanghai. After a week of surveillance, police arrested Rudnik and his wife Tatyana Moseyenko at a Comintern apartment at 235 Sichuan Road. In Rudnik's pocket were the keys to apartment 30C at 49 Nanking Road, where police discovered a trove of secret documents relating to a variety of Comintern front organisations in the city. Many were coded. But unfortunately for the Profintern, the Dalburo and all the rest, a sheet listing the keys to the cipher had been left folded in copies of the Bible and the *Three Principles* (by the early Chinese socialist leader Sun Yat-sen) found in the same apartment.

From Moscow, Berzin telegraphed that the '*khozain*' – literally, the master, Centre's codename for Stalin himself – had ordered that the Dalburo close all its extensive Shanghai operations and evacuate its staff immediately. A large gaggle of Comintern personnel fled for their lives. Sorge was left alone as the sole senior Soviet intelligence officer in the city.

Centre's strict instructions to Sorge to avoid contact with the CCP and the Comintern turned out to have been well founded. Unfortunately for the Fourth Department and for Sorge himself, Centre then proceeded to ignore its own good advice. On 23 June, OMS chief Yakov Mirov-Abramov appealed to Berzin to ask Sorge to do everything possible to free the Rudniks. Unwisely, but given little choice, Berzin agreed. For the next few months Sorge would handle what came to be known as the Noulens affair, hiring lawyers, coordinating publicity and investigating which Chinese officials could be bribed to secure their release.

The Rudniks' flimsy aliases had been concocted hurriedly by the OMS and quickly collapsed under police interrogation. At first the 'Noulens' couple claimed to be Belgian citizens in order to take advantage of Belgium's extra-territorial rights in the International Settlement. When the Belgian Foreign Ministry refused to confirm their citizenship, the Rudniks were handed over to the Chinese court in Shanghai. On 4 August, Rudnik changed his story, claiming to be Xavier Alois Beuret, born on 30 April 1899 in St Leger, Switzerland. Again the Swiss consul general was not prepared to confirm Noulens's new identity without specific directions from Berne – and indeed the real Xavier Beuret was soon found to be alive and well and living in Brussels.

With increasing desperation – and decreasing credibility – the Comintern persuaded another Swiss comrade living in Moscow to lend his identity to the unfortunate 'patients' languishing in Chinese jail. In late August, Rudnik became Paul Christian, a Swiss wallpaperer and agricultural labourer. Weeks later Centre changed its mind once more and Rudnik now claimed to be yet another Swiss national, a mechanic called Paul Ruegg. All the while the prisoner stretched the credulity of the Chinese court by continuing to maintain that he was not a secret communist agent – despite the fact that Chinese police had leaked large sections of the secret documents discovered at the Nanking Road apartment to the press.

Meanwhile the Comintern had mobilised an international campaign to protest the 'Noulenses'' incarceration. From Berlin the master propagandist Willi Muenzenberg formed the International Noulens/Ruegg Defence Committee and roped in such luminaries as Albert Einstein, H. G. Wells, Madame Sun Yat-sen and Henri Barbusse to support the cause. The case was discussed in both the British House of Commons and the United States Senate.[25]

Clearly, the glare of publicity surrounding the Noulens case was hardly the best place for a secret agent to hide. Nonetheless with blithe – or reckless – disregard for its bureau chief's security, Centre continued to insist that Sorge negotiate with defence lawyers, handle large sums of cash bribes[26] and deal with a number of Comintern operatives dispatched to Shanghai with various schemes to free the couple. The extraordinary effort made to free Rudnik – the money spent, the international resources mobilised, the risk taken by the USSR's secret workers – would make a bitter contrast to the total lack of interest Moscow would later show in getting Sorge out of Japanese incarceration.

Centre's obsession with the imprisoned Noulens couple became even more absurd in the wake of Japan's increasingly aggressive advances in the northern Chinese region of Manchuria, a far more pressing concern for Soviet national security. Japan's influence in Manchuria – which bordered Japanese-ruled Korea, Chinese Mongolia and the Soviet Far East – had been growing for decades. Manchuria was a key source of raw materials, such as coal and iron ore, for the booming Japanese industrial economy. By 1931, 203,000 Japanese citizens lived in northeast China and Japan accounted for 73 per cent of foreign investments in the region. The South Manchuria Railway that linked the port of Dalian to the Manchurian interior – and ultimately the Russian Trans-Siberian line – was Japanese owned and staffed, and Japan had controlled a swathe of territory along the length of the railway since its victory in the Russo-Japanese war of 1904–05. Crucially, the Japanese-run Railway Zone was protected by a 15,000-strong force of troops from the Kwangtung Army, a semi-independent branch of the Imperial Japanese armed forces based on the Chinese mainland.[27]

Nominally, Manchuria was part of the Republic of China. In practice the region had been ruled by the anti-Japanese warlord Zhang Zuolin since 1916. In 1928 the Japanese assassinated Zhang with a bomb, hoping that his opium-addicted, womanising son Zhang Xueliang would prove more amenable to Tokyo's interests. They were wrong. By April 1931, Zhang Xueliang – nicknamed the 'Young Marshal' – pledged loyalty to the Nationalist government of Chiang Kai-shek, continued his father's policies of harassing Japanese and Korean citizens, and began negotiating with American companies to open Manchuria to Western businesses.

The plan to overthrow the troublesome Young Marshal and establish Japanese control over all of Manchuria was hatched by two officers of the Kwangtung Army behind the back of Japan's civilian government. However, recent research has shown that the senior Japanese Army command in fact gave the scheme its covert blessing.[28] On 1 August 1931, all seventeen divisional commanders of the regular Imperial Japanese Army were invited to a secret meeting at the Imperial Palace in Tokyo, where it was agreed that their comrades in the Kwangtung Army would expand their zone of control to defend the interests of Japanese citizens all over Manchuria.

The operation began on the night of 18 September 1931, when a small explosive charge placed by a Japanese platoon went off under the tracks of the South Manchuria Railway just north of Mukden.[29] The railway was undamaged (a local train from Chen Chung to Shenyang passed by the site of the explosion ten minutes later). But the Kwangtung Army blamed Chinese extremists and immediately attacked a nearby Chinese military barracks, killing 450, followed by a full-scale assault on Zhang Xueliang's forces across Manchuria.

Zhang had previously been instructed by the Chinese government in Nanking to offer no resistance to possible Japanese provocations. Despite the outrageous provocation represented by the Manchurian incident, Chinese president Chiang Kai-shek continued to insist on appeasing the Japanese rather than fighting them. This was partly because Manchuria was not in any case under his direct control, and partly because Chiang Kai-shek feared that a major northern campaign against Japan would encourage new communist uprisings in Canton and across south-central China. 'The Japanese are a disease of the skin,' Chiang Kai-shek told his generals, 'the communists are a disease of the heart.'[30] As a result many units of Zhang's quarter of a million-strong Northeastern Army had been ordered to store their weapons and remain in their barracks. And though numerous and well equipped, Zhang's troops were under-trained, poorly led, and suffered from low morale. The Northeastern Army he commanded was also full of secret agents put in place by the Japanese military advisers who had created the force for Zhang's father.[31] Within six weeks of the 'Mukden incident', the 11,000-strong expeditionary force of Japan's Kwangtung Army had overrun the whole of Manchuria. Zhang was ridiculed as 'General Non-Resistance'.[32]

Japan's aggression was a matter of the most urgent concern for Sorge's masters in Moscow. Would the Japanese, fresh from their easy victory in Manchuria, now turn north and invade the USSR's sparsely populated and scantily defended Far Eastern provinces? The question would be central to Sorge's mission for the next decade. And just as central would be the Japanese to whom Sorge turned for urgent information on his country's intentions – the young journalist Hotsumi Ozaki.

Ozaki was 'my first and most important associate', Sorge would tell his Japanese captors. Since his arrival in Shanghai in 1928, Ozaki had not only developed unrivalled contacts among the Japanese diplomatic and business community in Shanghai and the Kuomintang authorities but also, secretly, with the Chinese Communist Party. One of Ozaki's major sources of contacts and gossip was the East Asia Common Script School, a university set up in Shanghai by the liberal-minded Japanese statesman Prince Konoe to promote Japan–China understanding. Ozaki would frequently lecture there on Asian politics. The school was a centre for left-leaning young Chinese, many of whom went on to senior positions in the government of Nationalist China. Ozaki also spoke often to Smedley's circle of communist sympathisers who brought reports from beleaguered CCP-held areas of the Chinese interior. And Ozaki was also in frequent contact with pro-Japanese elements in the Nanking government.

Sorge quickly recruited Ozaki – though as we have seen, under the false flag of the Comintern. Soon they were meeting frequently in restaurants and teahouses to exchange information and political gossip. Ozaki had also signed up an informant of his own, his colleague and friend the Japanese journalist Teikichi Kawai of the *Shanghai Weekly*. Kawai, like Ozaki, sympathised with communism but was not a party member. Soon Kawai was travelling to Manchuria at Sorge's request to report on the progress of Japan's puppet state, on the preparedness of the Kwangtung Army and the political news of the White Russian, Muslim and Mongolian minorities on China's northern border. 'Take your work step by step. Do not rush things,' Sorge told Kawai at their first meeting in a restaurant on the Shanghai's Nanking Road. The young Japanese was intensely impressed. 'One meets one like him only once in a lifetime,' Kawai recalled after the war. 'Sorge's words lived with me. I think I am alive today because I followed Sorge's advice.'[33]

Another important aspect of Sorge's personality also crystallised in September 1931: his love of physical danger tipped into near-suicidal recklessness. Riding his motorcycle at full speed down the Nanking Road, Sorge lost control of the machine and crashed. His already damaged right leg was once again broken. In hospital, where he was visited by both the devoted Ursula and Smedley, he joked that his 'body was already so battered' by the wounds of war, 'what difference did another scar make?'.[34]

Laid up at home with his leg in plaster, Sorge reported to Centre on 21 September 1931 that according to the Japanese military attaché – information almost certainly provided by Ozaki – the invasion of Manchuria was 'not of an active anti-Soviet character'.[35] In Moscow, the Central Committee were relieved and agreed with Stalin that 'it is good that the Imperialists are quarrelling'.[36]

The autumn brought worse news for the Chinese government, however. Sorge's German military advisers reported that the Japanese were pushing beyond Manchuria to the railhead and entrepôt of Harbin and preparing seaborne troops to attack Shanghai itself. Three Japanese cruisers appeared on the Yangtze river, in full view of the Bund. Sorge's agents in Canton sent urgent word that the Japanese had offered the local warlords a $5 million bribe not to make peace with Chiang Kai-shek, keeping potential Chinese resistance weak and divided. Most alarming of all for Moscow, Kawai brought word from Mukden that the cossack Ataman Grigory Semyonov,[37] a fiercely anti-Bolshevik White Russian general who was now living under Japanese protection in Manchuria, was negotiating an alliance with local warlords and the Kwangtung Army. Semyonov planned to gather a mixed force of Chinese, Japanese and White Russian troops to invade the USSR.[38]

On 1 January 1932 Japanese marines attacked Chinese Army barracks just outside Shanghai's International Zone. The fighting raged for thirty-four days. Sorge visited the front lines almost daily. 'I saw the Chinese defensive positions and I saw Japanese aircraft and Marines in action,' he wrote in his prison confession. 'The Chinese soldiers were very young but their discipline was very good, although most of them were equipped only with grenades.'[39] Within weeks the Chinese section of the city had been reduced to rubble. Japanese were unable to walk its streets in safety, so Sorge would meet Ozaki and Kawai in the dead of night at the boundary of the Japanese Concession and escort them by car to Smedley's home in the French Concession where he would debrief them. In the absence of any backup from the now-dissolved Dalburo, Sorge had become the Soviet Union's only eyes and ears in the heart of the unfolding crisis.

'My work became much more important during the Shanghai Incident,' Sorge wrote. 'I had to try to discover Japan's true purpose and to study in detail the fighting methods of the Japanese Army ... Of course at the time we did not definitively know whether the [fighting] was simply a skirmish or whether it represented a Japanese effort to conquer China following the acquisition of Manchuria. It was likewise impossible to tell whether Japan would push northwards towards Siberia or southwards into China.'[40] Sorge would spend the rest of his career – and ultimately give his life – trying to answer precisely that question.

In February 1932, shortly after the Japanese forces finally withdrew from Shanghai, Ozaki was recalled to Osaka by his newspaper. Sorge tried to persuade him to quit his job and stay in China – but Ozaki insisted that the *Asahi Shimbun* was too prestigious a career to abandon.[41] The next month the Fourth Department also finally sent Sorge some of the backup that he had been urgently requesting since the Noulens-related exodus. Karl Rimm, alias Klaas Zelman, codename 'Paul', an Estonian-born Fourth Department officer, arrived in Shanghai to act as Sorge's deputy.[42] Clausen was also recalled from a posting in Hankow to take charge of communications after the death of a stand-in radio man from tuberculosis. A Polish communist codenamed 'John' also joined the team, encrypting telegrams and letters and photographing documents in the back room of a photographic shop on the North Szechuan Road.

Sorge was finally free to travel. On a trip to Nanking in the summer of 1932, according to a story he told his Japanese interrogators, he seduced 'a beautiful Chinese girl' and persuaded her to give him blueprints of a Chinese military arsenal which he photographed and sent to Moscow.[43] There is no mention of this dangerous liaison in Sorge's telegrams to Moscow.

Sorge had promised Berzin to spend two years in Shanghai. He ended up staying three. Though Sorge did not know it, the danger to him was growing. Chief Detective Inspector Thomas 'Pat' Givens of the Shanghai Municipal Police was compiling a list of suspected Soviet agents, based on various confessions of arrested communists.[44] By May 1933 the grimly efficient Ulsterman had come up with six names of key communist cadres in the city. One was Sorge's (whom Givens mistakenly suspected of being a member of the Soviet-backed Pacific Trade Union Council). Another name on the police's list was Smedley's.[45] Sorge was living on borrowed time.

By the late autumn of 1932, Sorge judged that Rimm was ready to handle the Shanghai apparat on his own. Clausen and his radio set were installed in Japanese-occupied Harbin, where he posed as a general trader. Smedley and Kawai were working well with Rimm. Only Sorge's personal friendship with the German liaison officers could not be passed on to other operatives. In December 1931, Sorge handed over his *rezidentura* and boarded a ship to Vladivostok.

6

Have You Considered Tokyo?

'The question of whether or not Japan was planning to attack the Soviet Union … was the sole object of my mission'[1]

Richard Sorge

General Berzin gave Sorge a 'warm welcome' – by Sorge's own account – on his return to Moscow in January 1933. His Shanghai mission had been a success, certainly in comparison to his bumbling colleagues in the Comintern. He had managed not to blow his cover; none of his Chinese comrades had been arrested and shot. Sorge had left the Shanghai *rezidentura* with more agents, more radios and better informers than he had found when he arrived. Best of all, from Centre's point of view, Sorge's alias as a respected German journalist had emerged untainted by any hint of communist sympathy, despite his reluctant involvement in the mess of the Noulens affair.

Katya Maximova, too, had waited eagerly for her lover's return. Sorge soon moved into her small basement apartment on Nizhny Kislovsky Lane, round the corner from the Fourth Department HQ. After a dangerous and debauched mission in Shanghai, Sorge now convinced himself that all he wanted was to settle into the quiet life of a scholar. He began work on a soporific book on Chinese agriculture, using the less-than-riveting reports he had filed for the soybean trader readership of the *Deutsche Getreide Zeitung* as his main source material.

Sorge's ambition to be taken seriously as an academic often surfaces in his correspondence with Katya, and in his prison memoir. 'Had I lived under peaceful social conditions and in a peaceful environment of political development, I should perhaps have been a scholar – certainly not an espionage agent,' he wrote in his jailhouse autobiography. After his arrest he insisted that his captors see him as a scholar, not a mere spy. 'I am sure that I had access to much more material than the average foreigner,' Sorge boasted, listing the highlights of his collection of 'between 800 and 1,000 books' on Japan.[2]

Yet all of Sorge's attempts to actually settle into the academic world – in Hamburg, Berlin and Aachen in the 1920s and in Moscow in 1933 – were inevitably interrupted by the call of party agitation and espionage work. Doubtless a part of Sorge sincerely yearned for a life with the dutiful Katya pouring tea at the earnest parties where strong drink was frowned upon and spending his days in Moscow libraries. But the more powerful part of his personality always, in the end, chose the world of action, women, restaurants, fast motorcycles and unrelenting risk.

Sorge could not have been very surprised – and was perhaps even a little relived – when Berzin summoned him to the Fourth Department headquarters on 19 Bolshoi Znamensky Lane in April 1933 and informed him that his book leave would have to be cut short. Soviet military intelligence clearly saw Agent Ramsay as a man of action rather than of letters. Berzin and his new deputy, General Semyon Petrovitch Uritsky, had a worldwide intelligence service to build: Agent Ramsay's agricultural treatise would have to wait. Berzin asked Sorge where he would like to be posted next. 'I jokingly suggested Tokyo as a possible destination,' wrote Sorge. While in Shanghai he had visited Tokyo on a holiday and spent three days at the Imperial Hotel that left him 'favourably impressed with Japan'.[3]

Perhaps Sorge exaggerated his own agency in Berzin's decision to dispatch him to Tokyo. In any case neither man was under any illusions about how difficult and dangerous establishing a *rezidentura* in Japan would be. Unlike Shanghai, which teemed with so many spies that they had to make conscious efforts to avoid running into each other, no Soviet 'illegals' had ever succeeded in settling in Tokyo. The Japanese were known to be intensely suspicious of all outsiders, and the formal and informal surveillance of foreigners was constant.

Nonetheless, Sorge set about preparing for the challenge with his usual thoroughness. Berzin gave him permission to consult his old Comintern colleagues Pyatnitsky, Manuilsky, and Kuusinen, on his Japan mission. Their talks, 'although they touched on political problems of a general nature, were purely personal and friendly'. They were, in Sorge's words, 'quite proud of their protégé'. He claimed that Pyatnitsky in particular 'was extremely worried about the hardships I would face but delighted with my enterprising spirit'.[4] He also met with Karl Radek (born Karol Sobelsohn), one of the original founders of the Comintern. Radek had been closely involved with the early Comintern's attempts to turn the East Red, and had headed the Sun Yat-sen military university in Moscow that had been set up to train Communist cadres from all over Asia.[5] Radek had been briefly disgraced for criticising Stalin and backing Stalin's arch-rival Leon Trotsky, but by 1932 he had been reinstated as a Central Committee member and by 1933 headed its International Information Bureau. Sorge also met with Radek's deputy, Colonel Alexander Borovich (real name Lev Rosenthal), another veteran of the Sun Yat-sen university.[6] All shared the latest Soviet thinking on Asian politics with Sorge and advised him on his new mission. But they were all also marked men. As we will see, Stalin distrusted the Comintern as dangerously independent and fundamentally disloyal and was already carefully laying plans for its destruction. Sorge's meeting with these future enemies of the people would leave a taint of treachery by association that would have fatal consequences for his future.

Japan's intentions towards the USSR were certainly of the most urgent concern to the Kremlin in the wake of the invasion of Manchuria. They would become more and more vital as the Second World War approached. Sorge's main role, as he later told the Japanese, was 'to observe most closely ... the question of whether or not Japan was planning to attack the Soviet Union. It would not be far wrong to say that it was the sole object of my mission in Japan.'[7]

Fear of imminent encirclement and attack by Russia's enemies had been a touchstone of the Kremlin's strategic thinking from the very earliest days of Soviet power. The entire vector of Soviet foreign policy, long before the rise of Hitler and of Japanese militarism, was to confuse and undermine the USSR's enemies and encourage them to fight among themselves wherever possible. Through the 1920s the senior Soviet leadership feared that Imperial Russia's First World War allies Britain, France and America, would attempt to 'strangle Bolshevism in its cradle', as Winston Churchill had put it when arguing for an Allied expeditionary force to Murmansk in 1919.

That fear extended in particular to Japan, which had invaded Russian territory no fewer than three times in living memory. In 1905 the Japanese had seized the Russian Far Eastern stronghold of Port Arthur and sunk the Russian Baltic fleet at the Battle of the Tsushima Straits. Then in 1910, Japan annexed Korea, shaving more pieces off the Russian Empire. The most recent and most extensive Japanese incursion had come in 1918. In the aftermath of the tsar's overthrow and the collapse of Russia's war effort, Japanese troops occupied swathes of Russia's Pacific coast, sent troops deep into Siberia as far as Lake Baikal, and seized the island of Sakhalin. After the Armistice, Japan was eventually persuaded by the Allies to relinquish most of the Russian territory they had taken – apart from the island of southern Sakhalin – but as a consolation prize received mandates over former German possessions in the North Pacific and generous oil concessions in North Sakhalin. In short, Japan was no phantom menace. Tokyo had repeatedly proved itself both greedy for Russian land and ruthlessly efficient at seizing it. With Japan again expanding on the Chinese mainland, getting secret Soviet eyes and ears into place in Tokyo was a matter of the highest urgency.

The Fourth Department decided that Sorge should once more hide in plain sight, working as the now-respected German journalist and Asia expert. They drilled him in the latest cipher codes, based on page and line numbers of the 1933 edition of the German Statistical Yearbook. They again warned Sorge against contact with local Japanese communists, who were hopelessly infiltrated with police informers. He was also to avoid officials of the Soviet embassy in Tokyo, who were kept under constant watch. All that remained was to establish Dr Sorge's bona fides with a fresh set of German journalistic accreditations and letters of introduction to top German and Japanese officials in Tokyo.

What of Katya Maximova? We know much more about Sorge's feelings towards Maximova after his departure for Tokyo because he regularly included personal letters, photographed on microfilm, among the secret dispatches that he couriered to Moscow. These were enlarged and printed for Katya, with copies duly filed in the archives. Of their life together in Moscow we know much less. Sorge told his Japanese interrogators little about her – except to claim that he was 'not married'. Only a few clues survive to give us an idea of their relationship during the few months they spent together in 1933. Chief among these is a marriage certificate dated 8 August 1933, five months after Sorge left for Berlin, en route to his new posting.

We have already heard of Sorge's contempt for the bourgeois institution of marriage in his letters to his cousin Correns, when he and Christiane were forced to tie the knot so as not to outrage the local authorities of Solingen. His second marriage, to Katya, may have had similarly practical motivations. In later correspondence he fretted about whether she was receiving the payments due to the wife of a Red Army officer serving in the field. In 1930s Moscow such things were important for the allocation of ration cards, holidays and, most vitally of all, accommodation. 'The apartment question has spoiled us all,' wrote Mikhail Bulgakov in his 1940 novel *The Master and Margarita*; it is quite possible that Sorge once again forced himself to go through the formalities of marriage for the prosaic, and indeed bourgeois, if understandable, reason that she wanted a better flat.

There remains the mystery of the long delay between Sorge's departure and the finalisation of his marriage to Katya. One problem may be that he was still married to Christiane. The couple had not seen each other since their brief time together in London in 1929; the first time they could have met in person to sign the papers of their amicable divorce would have been when Sorge arrived in Berlin in May 1933. But since there is no trace of any request from Sorge for official help in his new marriage – nor of his divorce – it is more likely that he simply married (or in the jargon of the day, 'signed with') Katya bigamously before he left, with the formal paperwork coming through only later, in August. Sorge seems to have been sincere, however, in his intention to return to Moscow – and to Katya – as soon as reasonably possible. He agreed with Berzin, again by his own account, that his mission to Japan would last only two years. In the event, he stayed for eleven, the last three of which he spent in Tokyo's Sugamo prison.

Sorge found the Berlin of 1933 much changed from the chaotic, communist-leaning city he had last seen in 1929. The Nazi Party had become the largest parliamentary faction of the Weimar Republic government in November 1932. Adolf Hitler had been appointed as Chancellor of Germany on 30 January 1933. The burning of the Reichstag (Germany's parliament building) by a Dutch communist on 27 February had given Hitler a pretext for suppressing his political

opponents. The following day he persuaded the Reich's president Paul
von Hindenburg to issue the 'Reichstag Fire Decree' suspending most
civil liberties. On 23 March, parliament passed an Enabling Act that
gave Hitler's cabinet the right to pass laws without its own further
consent, effectively giving the Chancellor dictatorial powers. By the
time Sorge arrived at Berlin's Ostbahnhof on 16 May,[8] the Nazis had
abolished labour unions and other political parties, and had started
rounding up their political opponents – including hundreds of
communists.

Sorge's main Soviet contact in Berlin was Yakov Bronin (born
Yankel Liechtenstein), whom Sorge knew as Comrade Oscar.[9] After
a distinguished espionage career, which included a spell as Fourth
Department *rezident* in Shanghai from 1934–35 and six years in the
Gulag, Bronin wrote a memoir entitled *I Knew Sorge*. Writing under
the pseudonym 'Ya. Gorev', Bronin recalled that Sorge struck him as
'confident, thorough and brave' and was impressed by Sorge's 'sense of
purpose of a Soviet military intelligence officer'.[10]

Bronin briefed the new arrival on the dangers he faced in Berlin as
Sorge sought to renew his German passport and obtain a newspaper
correspondent's card. All Germans returning from abroad would be
subjected to a background check by the newly formed state secret police,
the Geheime Staatspolizei – commonly known as the Gestapo – before
issuing a new passport. In Bronin's opinion it was unlikely that Sorge's
communist past – his brawling on the streets of Kiel, his reputation as a
dangerous socialist agitator in the pits of the Ruhr, or his role as a party
courier and fixer in Frankfurt – would be unearthed by the Gestapo,
formed less than a month before Sorge's arrival. Nonetheless, Bronin
admired the 'calculated risk' taken by Berzin, a 'master of the dialectics
of intelligence' in sending Sorge into such danger.

Sorge was clearly aware of the risks he was running in returning to
his old stamping grounds. On 9 June he telegraphed Berzin that 'the
situation is not very attractive for me here, and I will be glad when
I can disappear from this place'. Three weeks later he wrote again to
warn that 'with things livening up in these parts interest in my person
may become much more intensive'.[11] Sorge was so concerned that he
might give himself away during beer-fuelled sessions with his new Nazi
acquaintances that he actually gave up drinking for the duration of his
Berlin sojourn. 'That was the bravest thing I ever did,' he joked to Hede

Massing when they met in New York in 1935. 'Never will I be able to drink enough to make up for this time.'[12]

Despite the danger of exposure, Sorge was working his impressive charm to lever his niche reputation as China correspondent of the *Deutsche Getreide Zeitung* into something far greater. He called at the offices of the *Zeitschrift für Geopolitik* ('Journal of Geopolitics'), an influential magazine much read in Nazi circles. Its editor, Kurt Vowinckel, a well-known publisher and ardent Nazi had, by an improbable chance, read and been impressed by Sorge's essays on China in the agricultural press. Vowinckel asked Sorge to contribute to his magazine and furnished him with an open letter of introduction to the German embassy in Tokyo, as well as personal introductions to embassy secretaries Josef Knoll and Hasso von Etzdorff.

With characteristic chutzpah, Sorge then travelled to Munich to pay his respects to *Zeitschrift für Geopolitik*'s legendary founder, General Dr Karl Haushofer.[13] A professor at the University of Munich and director of the Institute for Geopolitics, Haushofer had a considerable reputation as Germany's leading expert on Japan – as well as being the originator of the doctrine of German territorial expansion known as Lebensraum. Before the First World War, Haushofer had travelled to Japan as an officer of the German Army and had written extensively about the country. By the 1930s he came to believe that the Japanese were the Asian equivalent of the Aryan master race, destined to rule all Asia. Haushofer had connections with the highest levels of the Nazi Party (despite having a Jewish wife) and had been a friend of deputy führer Rudolf Hess, since the latter's student days at Munich in 1918.[14]

Hess and Haushofer had co-authored a book entitled *Japan and Espionage* where they advocated a programme of total espionage modelled on that of the Japanese, who counted on every citizen living and travelling overseas to provide a full account of all they had seen and heard to the state as a matter of course. Following this principle, Hess even established a special card index in the Foreign Department of the Nazi Party which held details of every Nazi Party member based abroad. Every man, and a very few women, were expected to act as spies for the Third Reich.[15] As Albrecht Haushofer, Karl's son, noted in his own study of Japan: 'every Japanese abroad considers himself a spy, and when at home takes upon himself the role of spy catcher'.[16]

Sorge was able to convince Haushofer that he was an ardent national socialist, an able young recruit to the cause. He wrote Sorge a personal letter of introduction to the German ambassador to Japan and another to the Japanese ambassador to the United States.[17] He also assured Sorge that he looked forward to reading his contributions to his influential journal.

Not content with making friends with senior Nazis like Haushofer and Vowinckel, Sorge returned to Berlin to collect yet more accreditations. The *Tägliche Rundschau* was a moderately anti-Nazi daily that was already under pressure from the authorities (and was destined to close soon after Sorge's arrival in Japan). Nonetheless, its editor-in-chief, Dr Eduard Zeller, also knew Sorge's work and was happy to accept articles from Tokyo. Zeller made out a contract on the spot and gave Sorge a 'To Whom It May Concern' letter of introduction to the German embassy. More fatefully for all concerned, Zeller also wrote a letter to a personal friend from wartime days, one Lieutenant Colonel Ott, who was serving as an officer with a Japanese artillery regiment at Nagoya as part of a German–Japanese military exchange. Zeller, succumbing to Sorge's charm, asked Ott to trust his new friend 'in everything that is, politically, personally and otherwise'. Neither man realised at the time quite how valuable this introduction was to prove. Later Sorge was to tell the Japanese that this letter would provide him with 'my first opportunity ... to get closely acquainted with Colonel Ott and to win his confidence'.[18]

Membership of the Nazi Party was not yet a necessity in order to work for a major German newspaper. However it was clear that Sorge would have to make a convincing pretence of being a part of the new order. Sorge had read *Mein Kampf* in Moscow, in addition to studying Nazi phraseology and ideology. Bronin, after quizzing Sorge, passed him as 'ideologically qualified' for his new role as a keen national socialist. In late summer 1933, Sorge decided to take another calculated risk and submitted an application for membership of the Nazi Party – despite the more thorough Gestapo checks into his background that this would entail. His two Nazi seconders were the editor-in-chiefs of the Berlin newspaper *Pozendai Zeitung* and of the monthly magazine *Heidelberg Geopolitik*, to whom Sorge had contributed articles during his Shanghai days.

Did Sorge decide on this bold step because he knew that a Soviet agent would 'clean' his police files before they were checked by party officials? When Brigadeführer Walter Schellenberg, deputy head of the SS intelligence service, examined Sorge's files in 1940 he found that the police record, 'if it did not exactly prove him to be a member of the German Communist Party, one could not help coming to the conclusion that he was at least a sympathiser. He had been in close contact with a large number of people who were known to our intelligence service as Comintern agents – but he had close ties with people in influential circles and had always been protected against rumours of this sort.'[19]

Hede Massing – not always a reliable source – also later claimed that Sorge had a German guardian angel, 'another Soviet agent who had been planted in the Gestapo. Sorge never knew his name, although he knew of his existence. At the crucial moment [of Sorge's Nazi Party application], this agent had been able, temporarily, to remove all the incriminating evidence from the file on Sorge.'[20] But if Schellenberg was able to easily find the compromising material in the files in 1940 it is also possible that it was there in 1933 – but that the Gestapo simply failed to look. The story of Sorge's secret protector remains unsubstantiated, particularly since neither the Fourth Department archives nor later Soviet histories make any mention of a Soviet agent in the Gestapo. In any case Sorge's application was accepted, though his Nazi Party membership card did not catch up with him until October 1934 in Tokyo.[21]

Sorge's last task in Berlin was to rendezvous with his new radio operator, Bruno Wendt, alias Bernhardt, a former member of the German Communist Party and, like Sorge's Shanghai radio men Clausen and Weingarten, a graduate of the Fourth Department's Moscow Technical School. The two men agreed to meet at the Imperial Hotel in Tokyo.

'I cannot claim to have achieved one hundred percent but it was simply impossible to do more – and it would be pointless to stay on here in order to obtain representation agreements with other newspapers,' Sorge reported to Moscow Centre on 30 July 1933. 'I am sick of being idle. At present I can only say that the prerequisites for my return to work have been more or less created.'[22] He took a train to Cherbourg, France, in order to avoid the stringent customs controls at German ports and boarded a liner to New York.

Sorge, no ascetic, spent eight days at the Lincoln Hotel on 8th Avenue, which was then the tallest and most modern hotel in Manhattan.

That year aspiring jazzmen Count Basie and Fats Waller played at the Lincoln's Blue Room nightclub. But since Prohibition was still in place (it would not be repealed until December), Sorge would have had to seek more discreet speakeasies to make up for his lost months of drinking in Berlin. In New York, he made contact with a Soviet agent who worked at the *Washington Post* – whose identity has never been revealed – who would help him establish contact with Sorge's new Japanese assistant.[23] They agreed to meet at the Chicago World's Fair for the handover of recognition codes.

Sorge then proceeded to Washington, where he presented his letter from Haushofer to Katsuji Debuchi, Japanese ambassador to the United States. Debuchi duly furnished Sorge with another valuable letter of introduction, this time to Amaha Temba, head of the Information Department of the Japanese Foreign Ministry. After three days in the capital Sorge headed back north to Chicago to meet his *Washington Post* contact, who passed on instructions from Centre. On arrival in Tokyo, Sorge was to place an advertisement in the *Japan Advertiser*, a Tokyo English-language newspaper, indicating a desire to purchase *ukiyo-e* – a style of Japanese woodcuts and paintings – and provide a post-office box for a reply.[24] His Japanese assistant, who was en route to Tokyo from California, would check the paper and reply as soon as he saw the advertisement.

His arrangements finalised, Sorge caught the *Empire Builder* transcontinental express train to Seattle, changing for Vancouver. There he took the Canadian steamer *Empress of Russia* for the ten-day voyage to Yokohama.[25]

7

The Spy Ring Forms

'The 20th Century has been the century of espionage, and Richard Sorge was probably its most fascinating exemplar – a spy of unparalleled charm, nonchalance, courage, impudence, and brilliance'[1]

Arthur M. Schlesinger

September is the season of typhoons in Japan. The heat of late summer turns damp and clammy, the choppy waters of Yokohama harbour become grey and monsoon clouds gather low and black over Tokyo Bay. The *Empress of Russia* docked at Yokohama on 13 September 1933. The name of 'R. Sorge' duly appeared on the passenger lists published regularly in the *Japan Advertiser* and eagerly read by Tokyo's small European community.

Tokyo was a world away from the cosmopolitan, thoroughly Westernised world of Shanghai that Sorge had left nine months before. Until 1853, when US Commodore Matthew Perry had sailed his warship into the same port demanding trading privileges at gunpoint, Japan had spent over three centuries closed off from the outside world. In 1933 the entire foreign community in Japan numbered just 8,000. Of them, 1,118 were German. Japan's profound suspicion of outsiders and spies had its roots in centuries of isolation. One of the first news items Sorge would have read in the *Advertiser* was a report of a police raid on an antique shop in Tokyo where eighteenth-century prints of Nagasaki harbour had been confiscated as a potential source of information for saboteurs.

Sorge checked into the Sanno Hotel, a grim box-like building offering European-style amenities. During his first walks around the city, Sorge was impressed by seeing crowds of Japanese travellers bowing deeply in reverence to the Imperial Palace as they emerged from Tokyo train station in Marunouchi. Three days later Sorge paid his first call to the German embassy, a two-storey brick-built confection of Wilhelmine neoclassical facades and Japanese windows standing on a rise near the Imperial Palace.* Sorge respectfully presented his credentials to Counsellor Otto Bernard von Erdmannsdorff, since the new ambassador was not due to arrive until December. He also presented his personal letters from *Zeitschrift für Geopolitik*'s editor, Kurt Vowinckel, to First Secretary Hasso von Etzdorff and Commercial Secretary Josef Knoll.[2] Both men had, like Sorge, served as privates in the First World War. Sorge's months of preparation in Berlin stood him in good stead with his new acquaintances. 'The German embassy asked me if I knew anyone in the Foreign Ministry and I was told I could be given an introduction to officials there,' recalled Sorge in his prison memoir. 'I said rather proudly that with my letter to Temba Amaha [head of the Information Department of the Foreign Ministry] their introduction ... was unnecessary.'[3]

The following day Sorge presented his letter from Ambassador Debuchi to Temba, who greeted him 'cordially', introduced him 'to many Japanese and foreign journalists' – including the influential government spokesman – and gave him a number of valuable tips concerning travel in Japan.[4] One of these new acquaintances was Aritomi Mitsukado, a correspondent for the *Jiji Shimpo* newspaper, who recommended the cheaper Meguro Hotel and later helped Sorge find his own house in Azabu district. Aritomi also introduced him to a socialist friend who spoke to Sorge in Russian, which he affected not to understand. Sorge was convinced that Aritomi was working for the Metropolitan Police Board. The new arrival was being quietly, but thoroughly, vetted.[5]

Not all was unfamiliar. There were several modern buildings in central Tokyo, including the Frank Lloyd Wright-designed Imperial Hotel, which was built in the style of a Mayan altar inspired by the pyramids of Yucatán. The Imperial boasted an underground bar and shopping arcade and a bookshop that stocked foreign newspapers.

---

*The site is now occupied by the Library of Japan's National Parliament.

There was a German Club five minutes' walk from the embassy that shared a modest building with a Japanese curving roof, a pond and bamboo garden with the German East Asia Society. The library and reading room held volumes of English and German works on Japan, as well as anthropological studies illustrated with photographs of naked Japanese women.[6] Across the courtyard was a bar and restaurant which was the venue for Nazi Party meetings. In the nightlife district of Ginza was Lohmeyer's, a German restaurant known for its roast pigs' trotters and wurst, as well as the Das Rheingold and Die Fledermaus German beer halls. There was a German bakery in Yurakucho that sold strudel and Black Forest gateau.

Sorge quickly found that, despite the outward appearance of an intensely stable and regulated society, the Japan of 1933 was in reality as stormy as the September weather. Just as in Germany, a brief experiment with liberal democracy had recently floundered. In 1932 the prime minister and finance minister, as well as several leading industrialists, had been assassinated by fanatical young army officers (the killers also, eccentrically, planned to murder the visiting Charlie Chaplin in the hope of sparking a war with America). Japan's post-First World War political order was being convulsed by economic forces beyond the government's control. The Great Depression caused American and European silk demand to collapse, bringing much of the Japanese countryside to the edge of destitution. In the winter of 1932–33 many small farmers had been forced into prostituting their daughters – sold to travelling representatives of teahouses and brothels so their families might eke out an existence. The economic crisis was compounded by a disastrous crop failure in 1932 across northern Japan. Many young officers and soldiers came from peasant backgrounds and had seen the suffering of their communities at first hand. A large former rural population had also recently moved to the cities to work in shipyards, mines and factories, as well as a vast network of small workshops who relied for their work on orders for the *zaibatsu*, Japan's great financial-industrial concerns. These workers, too, had suffered in the Depression – and like the people in Germany's industrial heartlands, were turning to extreme nationalist rather than socialist politicians to rescue them from destitution.

The leader of the militarist party was General Araki Sadao, Minister of War, who was a radical advocate of *kodo-ha* – 'the Imperial Way' – a mystical belief in the direct rule of the emperor and Japan's heaven-sent mission to extend her empire. Again, like national socialism in Germany, *kodo-ha* had a strong anti-capitalist streak. Ultra-nationalists such as Araki believed that major enterprises and agricultural land should be 'restored' to the emperor. The Kodo doctrine had a powerful appeal to young army officers who, as a result of the recent economic crisis, had come to despise the great capitalist conglomerates of Japan and the democratic politicians who often spoke for them. It also attracted many former socialists and communists, who supported Kodo because it reconciled revolutionary action with loyalty to the Imperial house and Shinto piety which enshrined loyalty to the emperor as a national religion. Uncomfortably for a Soviet agent hoping to set up an espionage network, almost all Japanese politicians were united in a vivid fear of Marxism and communism, represented by the Comintern and the USSR, as an existential threat to the hierarchical Japanese way of life.

That fear also represented a direct threat to the USSR's security. In a speech shortly after Sorge's arrival, Araki contended that war with Russia was 'inevitable'. The US ambassador Joseph Grew noted in his diary on 7 September 1933 that 'the [Japanese] Army has complete confidence in its ability to take Vladivostok and [Russia's] maritime provinces and probably all territory to Lake Baikal'.[7] Grew also predicted that a new Russo-Japanese war was 'absolutely inevitable' by the spring of 1936.

On a practical level, the Communist Party of Japan had been outlawed in 1925 under a Peace Preservation Law that was intended to control subversion against *kokutai* – Japan's 'emperor system'. By 1933 all potential subversives – including liberals, socialists, Christians, pacifists, feminists, birth-control advocates and Esperanto enthusiasts – were deemed to have committed thought crime or *shisohan*. All were subject to summary arrest and detention. Communists were threatened with the confiscation of their family's property unless they sincerely recanted and offered proof of their apostasy, a throwback to the days of the first shogunate of the seventeenth century when recanting Christians were forced to trample a crucifix.[8]

In 1933, the hothead advocates of *kodo-ha* were still a political insurgency rather than a military one – alarming, but containable, in the opinion of the old courtiers who still retained ultimate control of the empire. The Emperor Hirohito himself – thirty-two years old when Sorge arrived in Japan – was a scholar devoted to his personal hobby of marine biology. On his rare public appearances at the annual review of the Imperial guards' battalions at Yoyogi parade ground, Hirohito was magnificent on his white charger. In reality the 124th Emperor of Japan was short-sighted, shy and bookish and easily dominated by the forceful advisers who surrounded him.[9]

The emperor's closest courtiers, Count Makino and Prince Saionji Kinmochi – a fifty-year veteran of the Imperial governing council and one of the last surviving *Gen-ro*, or 'original leaders' of Meiji-dynasty Japan[10] – believed that the excesses of the Nationalists could be contained. 'Everything will be all right as long as we old men are here to put on the brakes,' another member of the old guard, Prime Minister Admiral Makoto Saito, told the editor of the *Japan Advertiser* in 1933. By law, criticism of the emperor was blasphemy. But in practice the invasion of Manchuria in 1931, unauthorised by the emperor, had clearly demonstrated to all clear-eyed observers of Japanese politics that the army was no longer under the old courtiers' control. Another sign that real power had slipped decisively away from the palace was another officers' plot to assassinate the entire cabinet, including Premier Saito and other conservative courtiers, uncovered in spring 1933. Yet for the time being a majority of senior officials and army officers – known as the *tosei-ha*, or Control Faction – considered the expansive adventures in Manchuria tacitly condoned by Araki were impulsive and dangerous. They also believed it unwise to pick a fight with Russia.

Sorge's central question – whether Japan would attack the Soviet Union – was, therefore, closely bound up with the question of who was really in charge in Tokyo. The riddle consisted of how to parse a state ruled by a god-emperor who could barely exercise authority, governed in practice by a centralised bureaucracy which was obliged to follow the course settled upon by the army, and of a society famous for its self-discipline but which was regularly prone to unrest and murderous political violence.[11]

In early October Sorge set off to the industrial city of Nagoya, four hours' south-west of Tokyo, to meet the last and (as it would turn out) most important of his German contacts.

Nagoya was, and remains, a grim place full of porcelain and textile factories. Lieutenant Colonel Eugen Ott had recently been posted there as a liaison officer to the Japanese Third Artillery Regiment. Ott and his family lived in spartan quarters in the regimental barracks with no other Germans for company. If Sorge had come into Ott's life at any other point their relationship might have been different. As it was, the lonely officer was delighted to welcome the charming, self-confident journalist as a friend – especially since the new arrival bore a letter from Ott's old friend Zeller in Berlin assuring him of Sorge's political and personal trustworthiness.

The two men had much in common. They quickly established that they had served in the same division on the Eastern front – another example of the *kampfkameraderie,* or battle-comradeship, that would bond Sorge with so many Germans of his generation. Sorge was thirty-nine when they met, Ott forty-four. Both enjoyed chess and shared a fascination with Japan.[12] Though Sorge was ruthlessly to exploit his relationship with Ott, their friendship had a genuine core. 'Ott was a man of fine character ... shrewd, able, politically realistic,' Sorge wrote in his prison memoir. Both shared a scepticism of the Nazis – though Ott would soon overcome his qualms and become a loyal servant of the Reich, to Sorge's disgust. Ott, in Sorge's estimation, 'thought me to be a man of rare progressive views, neither a Nazi nor a Communist, a somewhat eccentric person with no partisan commitments'.[13]

Ott had served a stint on the front lines of the First World War as an artillery officer, where career officers of the old school had snubbed him. 'Ott is a little Swabian who wanted to play Grand Prussian,' said General Walter von Reisenau, Ott's one-time immediate superior. 'But after all he was only a pale copy of a Prussian sergeant, not an officer.'[14] Ott's true talent was indeed in the underhand and decidedly ungentlemanly skills of espionage and black operations. After his spell at the front Ott was talent-spotted by Colonel Walter Nicolai, chief of the German high command's intelligence service, who put him to work gathering military intelligence.

It was in the aftermath of Germany's defeat in 1918 that Ott's career had taken a decisive turn into the clandestine world. General Kurt von Schleicher, a ruthless anti-communist who had been one of the founders of the Freikorps in 1919, recruited the intelligent young officer for his own covert purposes. Schleicher was forming a secret group within the army, Sondergruppe R (for 'Russland'), which was devoted to rebuilding covertly the German Army in defiance of the Treaty of Versailles. This secret rearmament meant dealing with Bolshevik

Russia, under a confidential deal negotiated between Schleicher and Soviet Central Committee member Leonid Krasin in 1921.[15] The funds for Germany's covert military build-up were supplied by a network of dummy corporations created by Schleicher – notably the GEFU, or Company for the Promotion of Industrial Enterprise, that funnelled 75 million Reichsmarks into the Soviet arms industry. Between 1921 and 1933, when the deal was terminated by a Soviet leadership nervous of the rise of Hitler, these clandestine arms contracts provided the USSR with much-needed foreign currency and ensured that Germany did not fall behind in military technology in the 1920s, despite being officially disarmed by the victorious Allies.

Eugen Ott served as the head of Schleicher's Political Department. He also acted as liaison with the so-called 'Black Reichswehr'. Headed by Major Bruno Ernst Buchrucker, this was an army of *arbeits-kommandos* – 'work commandos' – which claimed to be a civilian labour corps but was, in reality, a paramilitary force. This fiction allowed Germany to exceed the limits on troop strength set by Versailles. Buchrucker's Black Reichswehr, just like the old Freikorps from which many of its members were drawn, was also infamous for murdering Germans it suspected of working as informers for the Allied Control Commission, the organisation charged with policing the terms of the peace treaty. Victims were assassinated after being convicted of treason by secret military courts known as *femegerichte*. The *femegerichte* murders were a clear challenge to the authority of the Weimar government – and proof that the German Army had effectively become a state within a state, contemptuous of the weak civilian government and pursuing a policy of rearmament behind the back of the democratically elected authorities.

Ott would have understood very well the dynamics of the Japanese Army's rise to power in the 1930s. He had been part of the same process in his own homeland. Ott, as this story unfolds, may appear as a naive dupe thoroughly taken in by his wily friend Sorge. But it is worth remembering that in the formative years of his career, Ott was a professional dissembler himself, active not only in Germany's secret rearmament deal with communist Russia but also in a clandestine organisation responsible for a spate of political murders.

In December 1932, after a stint as Minister of Defence, Schleicher became briefly Chancellor of Germany. He sent Ott as his emissary to Adolf Hitler to offer the rising Nazi star a cabinet post. Hitler refused, holding out for the supreme power that he quickly achieved on 30 January 1933. After Hitler took over as chancellor, Ott's superiors in the high command arranged to have Ott, the trusted lieutenant of the fallen Schleicher regime, removed out of sight and mind to distant Japan. The move probably saved Ott's life. Schleicher himself was murdered on 30 June 1934 during the Night of the Long Knives, Hitler's bloody purge of his enemies inside the Nazi Party and possible rivals outside it.[16]

Ott's lonely posting to Nagoya was, then, a species of political exile. His career abruptly stalled, he faced an uncertain future. Sorge's dynamism and intellect must have come as a welcome distraction not only to Ott but also to his family. A few days after their first meeting, the Otts were on a weekend motoring trip through the countryside outside Nagoya when they came across Sorge hiking through the rice paddies. Sorge greeted Ott's wife Helma courteously and chatted to the couple's two children, Podwick and Ulli, then aged eleven and seven. Before long the children would be addressing him as 'Uncle Richard'.

Sorge returned to Tokyo delighted with his new contact. His social career at the German community launched, it was time to move on to assembling his underground network. En route to Japan, Sorge had learned at a brief meeting with an unnamed operative at the Hotel Noailles in Paris that one other member of his prospective team – 'a certain Vukelić' – was already in Tokyo and waiting for contact. Proceeding with extreme caution, Sorge waited for Bruno Wendt, the Moscow-trained radio man and the one member of the new *rezidentura* that he had actually met, before making any attempt to contact the mysterious Vukelić.

Wendt and his wife arrived by ship in mid-October. They met up with Sorge in the lobby of the Imperial Hotel, as agreed. For security reasons the new radio man had arrived without any actual radio parts. Wendt's first task would therefore be to buy the necessary components and assemble from scratch a set powerful enough to reach Vladivostok. He would also have to create a plausible cover that would allow him to travel and buy the transformers, radio valves and so on. Using Fourth Department money, Wendt duly set up a small company supplying samples of Japanese products to foreign firms. But for reasons lost to history he established it in Yokohama instead of Tokyo, meaning an hour-long train ride whenever Sorge wanted to make a transmission. Perhaps Wendt believed that Yokohama, with its heavy traffic of commercial shipping radio, would be a less conspicuous location for a covert radio transmitter. Or he may have thought that police surveillance would be less comprehensive outside the heart of the capital. Soon Sorge would be complaining to Centre that Wendt was 'extremely timid and does not send half the messages I give him'.[17] He would not be the last uncooperative radio man to let down the Tokyo spy ring by failing to transmit his comrades' hard-won information.

Either because of Wendt's 'timidity' or Sorge's caution, it was not until November 1933 that Wendt finally got round to telephoning Vukelić at the Bunka Apartments, a once-grand nineteenth-century residential block facing the Ochanomizu River.[18] 'Do you known Johnson?' Wendt asked, quoting the pre-arranged recognition code supplied by Centre. 'I know him,' answered Vukelić, beside himself with relief that the call had finally come. 'I myself am not Schmidt, but I was sent by him,' Wendt concluded.[19] A meeting was set for the following day.

Branko Vukelić was a tall, heavyset Yugoslav with a receding hairline and a military bearing. Sorge – or Schmidt, as he introduced himself – found his new agent in 'a pitiful state ... ill, homesick and broke'.[20] It emerged that Vukelić and his family had been waiting in Tokyo for Sorge to make contact since February, without money, instructions or any way to contact Centre.

Exactly why Centre chose Vukelić as a member of Sorge's Tokyo spy ring remains something of a mystery. He had not been trained as a spy, had no knowledge of military affairs or of Japan. He was not even a particularly enthusiastic communist. Born in Osijek, in modern-day Croatia, in 1904, Vukelić was the son of an officer in the Austro-Hungarian Imperial Army. He spent his childhood in garrison towns and discovered socialism while a high-school student in Zagreb. His mother, Vilma, recalled Branko being much moved when in 1922 the young communist assassin who shot Yugoslavia's interior minister was executed. Vukelić laid carnations at the Red martyr's grave.[21] He enrolled in the Fine Arts Academy in Zagreb, joined the Marxist student club and was arrested by police after street brawls with nationalists. After two terms, Vukelić left the academy and transferred to the architecture faculty of the University of Brno in Moravia. In 1926 his mother, now widowed, took her son to Paris where he enrolled in the law faculty of the Sorbonne.[22]

Vukelić's communist past followed him to France in the concrete form of his Yugoslav police dossier, which was requested by Paris police after he was twice arrested for participating in socialist-fomented unrest. In 1929 Vukelić's mother recorded in her diary that her son had taken her to see Sergei Eisenstein's propaganda classic about the 1905 Russian revolution, *Battleship Potemkin*. 'My son held my arm as we walked silently. Suddenly he said, "See, mother, this wonderful, truthful film! Do you like all that the Soviet Union has achieved in the name of the future of humanity?" "Yes, son, because it is your world," I answered. "But the Soviet Union is surrounded on all sides by enemies," continued Branko. "The whole world is in arms against the young proletarian state. To defend the USSR today is to defend yourself and your own country."'[23]

Despite his romantic notions of defending the revolution, on graduating in 1929, Vukelić joined the petit-bourgeois ranks of clerks at Paris' Compagnie Générale d'Electricité. He had a baby with his Danish girlfriend, Edith Olsen, a maid in the household of a Danish family living in Paris, and then married Edith despite his mother's objections. The necessity of putting food on the table had temporarily trumped his Marxist enthusiasm.[24]

Vukelić only came to the attention of the Communist Party's underground in 1932. He had just returned to France from a four-month spell in his native Yugoslavia, where he had belatedly been doing his national service in the army. He was by now unemployed, supporting his young family by freelance journalism and photography. On a Paris street he ran into two old friends from a Marxist student group in Zagreb, Hugo Klein and Milo Budak.[25] Vukelić had lost all contact with the party. His two comrades certainly had not. Before long they had persuaded Vukelić to write a personal report on the political and social state of the Yugoslav Army, based on his recent experiences, to be published in the Comintern magazine *Inprecorr* (to which Sorge had also been a contributor). 'A man who can write such a report is always in demand, so you needn't worry about getting a job,' Klein told Vukelić flatteringly. 'This report is useful to the Movement.'[26]

And so the recruitment began. Vukelić was reluctant at first, claiming (by his own detailed account to Japanese interrogators in 1942) that he was no longer a convinced communist.[27] Klein talked him round. 'Let us give a chance to Soviet Russia to establish socialism by maintaining peace for another several years,' he urged. In March 1932 another, more senior, Soviet operative took over the seduction. She was a tall, beautiful woman with a heavy Baltic accent (or so it sounded to Vukelić) and a passion for skiing, who called herself 'Olga'. (It is possible that Olga was Lydia Chekalova, also known as Baroness Stahl, a courier and photographer for Soviet intelligence working for the Paris headquarters of the Fourth Department.[28] Or she may have been the sister of Alfred Tilden, a senior OMS operative stationed in Paris at the time.[29])

'Our task is to protect Soviet Russia,' Olga explained to the young recruit. 'This is the duty of all good communists, but our special duty is to collect information.'[30] Vukelić protested that he had no experience of secret work, nor any knowledge of military matters. 'We won't expect you to crack safes, but we will expect you to use your experience as a journalist,' she assured him. 'You will have to utilise your observational and analytical ability as a Marxist. No matter what country you go to, there will be experienced comrades who will guide you and sympathisers who will cooperate with us in our work.'[31] Like many other agents recruited by the Fourth Department in this period, Olga allowed Vukelić to believe that he was signing up for covert Comintern work – the 'cause of international peace', in Willi Muenzenberg's formulation – rather than Soviet military intelligence. Her final question of the interview was a melodramatic one: 'Do you have sharp sensitivities or not? This is the most important condition for this kind of work.' 'No', was Vukelić's frank answer.[32]

Inexperienced and lacking in self-belief, Vukelić – or rather 'de Voukelitch' as he had begun to style himself in imitation of French aristocracy – may not have been the most promising of recruits. However he spoke eight languages, was a skilled amateur photographer – a talent very useful to an espionage ring – and had a real, if modest, track record as a freelance reporter. More importantly, he had not been a party member since his youth, and his police record was also far in the past. At their next meeting Olga brought Vukelić some papers to translate and 3,000 francs for living expenses, along with instructions that he was to develop his cover career as a journalist.[33] By October 1932, after going through several vettings by mysterious and nameless Eastern European men, Vukelić was told that he had been selected to go to Japan.[34] 'I envy you for going to such a beautiful country,' Olga told him. His assignment would last two years, she said, after which he hoped to be 'allowed to go to Soviet Russia as a compensation for my effort and enjoy the peaceful and cultured life in the paradise of socialism'.[35] His wife Edith was a qualified instructor in Danish Gymnastics – a type of callisthenics very popular in Japan at the time – and this would give her a cover story of sorts for her presence in Tokyo.

Vukelić was recovering from appendicitis but nonetheless dragged himself across Paris to apply for a Japanese visa and offer his services to French newspapers and magazines. By happy chance, the pictorial weekly *Vue* was preparing a special number on the Far East and agreed to consider his photographs. The Yugoslav *Politika* newspaper also agreed to take his articles on a freelance basis. On 30 December 1932, the Vukelić family – Branko, Edith, and their three-year-old son Paul – boarded an Italian ship sailing from Marseilles to Yokohama. They had only the flimsiest of cover stories, no training in covert work, and no instructions on what to do on arrival, other than wait at the Bunka Apartments for someone to contact them with the prearranged code.

The Soviet archives reveal that the likely reason for Centre's haste in dispatching the ill-prepared Vukelić – while Sorge was still in Shanghai – was fear that the French Sûreté Nationale police were on his trail. In June 1932, Izaia Bir, a senior Soviet spy, had been arrested along with six associates in Paris. The French Communist Party leader Jacques Duclos had already fled France for fear of what Bir would reveal. An intensive hunt for communists was under way in France, hence Centre's haste in deploying their fledgling agent across the world to the as yet non-existent Fourth Department *rezidentura* before he could be caught and betray his recruiters.

Vukelić may have escaped arrest by the Sûreté, but what he did not realise until it was too late was that France's thrifty communists had radically miscalculated the cost of living in Japan. The budget they provided for Vukelić and his family was just 1,800 yen for the first six months, or ten yen a day. This covered only rent and the most basic meals at the Bunka (its motto in its final days as a low-rent flophouse in the 1990s remained, with endearingly Japanese frankness: 'No luxury but every comfort'). He was told that his new boss would make contact in August. In fact, Sorge only got in touch in November.

During their first, long-awaited rendezvous, Sorge gave Vukelić cash and advised him to 'to rent a house, move there with his wife and child, and begin to work in earnest as a reporter'.[36] Before their meeting, Sorge had cabled to Moscow that he planned to use Vukelić as a spy in the British, French, and American communities, to act as the ring's photographer, and to use his home as a radio site. But it seems that Sorge immediately clocked his new associate as a dud, untrained amateur. Vukelić, for his part, told Japanese police that his first impression of Sorge 'was not very good'. He suspected – probably correctly – that Sorge considered him 'not the serious kind', and he later discovered that his boss thought of him 'as an outsider and could not get out of this feeling until the last day of our cooperative work'.[37]

Nonetheless, Sorge and Vukelić began meeting regularly at the Florida Kitchen restaurant in Ginza. Sorge soon dropped the Schmidt pseudonym, since as reporters working under their real names he and Vukelić would be sure to meet at the Japanese press agency Domei and at official press conferences.[38] Nonetheless Sorge was careful that his new friends at the German embassy should not know of their meetings, as he feared that Vukelić 'was on the other side of the ideological fence from them'.[39] Vukelić duly moved into a house at Sanai Cho 22 in Ushigome-ku, which Sorge would indeed later use as a radio post.[40] Vukelić augmented his income by giving language lessons at home while Edith taught gymnastics at the Tamagawa Gakuen school.[41]

Vukelić's first mission, on 6 December, was to place an advertisement – at five sen a word – in the *Japan Advertiser*. 'UKIYOE prints by old masters', it read. 'Also English books on the same subject. Urgently needed. Give details, titles, authors, prices to Artist, c/o The Japan Advertiser, Tokyo.'[42] The telephone number for replies was that of an advertising agency in Tokyo's Kanda district.[43]

The secret signal was intended for Yotoku Miyagi, a young painter who had arrived in Yokohama on 24 October 1933. Miyagi was born in 1903 on Okinawa, the southernmost of Japan's home islands. He was the second son of a peasant family. When he was two years old his parents emigrated, eventually settling in California, leaving him in the care of his maternal grandfather. The old man sowed the seeds of Miyagi's idealism. 'When I was a little boy, my grandfather's discipline was: "Do not maltreat the weak and be conscientious,"' Miyagi would tell his captors in 1942.[44] Miyagi attended the village school and the Okinawa

Prefecture Normal School, but did not graduate because he developed the first symptoms of tuberculosis at the age of sixteen. In the hope of improving his health – and fulfilling his dream of studying art – he joined his father on his small farm in Brawley, California in June 1919.

Miyagi enrolled in the San Diego Public School of Art. A year in the dry Californian air of the Imperial Valley healed his lungs, and he moved to Los Angeles's Little Tokyo neighbourhood, where he established himself as an artist and joined three Japanese friends to open a small restaurant called 'The Owl'. All his young life Miyagi had suffered from discrimination, first as an Okinawan – considered second-class citizens by the Japanese of the period – and again in America – not only from whites but also from fellow Japanese of the second generation who looked down on new immigrants. It is no coincidence that many prominent Japanese communists – including Kyuichi Tokuda, their most famous leader – were of Okinawan origin, just as many Bolsheviks came from the oppressed ranks of Russian Jews. When Miyagi met socialists in America, he was immediately drawn to their egalitarian doctrine. He became a communist, Miyagi explained to his interrogators, because of the 'inhuman discrimination practiced against the Asiatic races in the United States'.[45]

Miyagi and his partners in the Owl restaurant established a Marxist study group, which was quickly spotted and supported by the Communist Party of the United States. But his personal conversion was not immediate. When the group – now a club with the name Romei Kai, or 'Society of the Dawn' – split into communist and non-communist factions, Miyagi stayed with the latter, largely because of his deep dislike of the 'mainland' Japanese who mixed their communist ideals with a strand of nationalism that he strongly distrusted.[46] Yet he continued to read Russian literature and to drift leftward, and in 1931 he joined the Proletarian Arts Society, a Comintern front. That year the Soviet Communist Party dispatched Tsutomu Yano (also known as Takedo), a prominent Japanese communist who had spent time in Moscow in 1930, to the West Coast of the United States to recruit new members. He picked up Miyagi at a meeting of the Arts Society. Miyagi, displaying a weakness for strong-willed authority figures that would bring him fatally under the sway of Richard Sorge, was talked by Tsutomu into joining the party. The distinguished visitor even filled out

Miyagi's Communist Party card. Tsutomu also, unbeknown to Miyagi, registered him with the Comintern – though not with the Communist Party of the USA – under the codename of Joe, which he would bear for the rest of his future career as a spy.

Miyagi had married a fellow Japanese immigrant, Yamaki Chiyo, in 1927. The couple took lodgings with a poor Japanese couple in Los Angeles, where Miyagi remained even after he split with Chiyo in 1932. His new landlord, Yoshisaburo Kitabayashi, was decidedly not a communist. But his wife Tomo, a tiny, anxious-faced woman, was both a member of the party and of the Proletarian Arts Society.[47] This humble pair would play a fateful role in Miyagi's – and Sorge's – future.

Like Vukelić before him, the sickly, low-born Miyagi was a far from obvious candidate for recruitment into the Fourth Department's Tokyo spy ring. His only apparent qualifications were a cheerful demeanour, a fluency in English and Japanese, and a ready-made cover as an artist. Nonetheless in spring 1932, two party officials came to call on him at the Kitabayashi house. One was Miyagi's original recruiter, Tsutomu Yano. The other was 'an American' – or so Miyagi claimed to the Japanese authorities – who called himself Roy, an old acquaintance from Los Angeles party circles. Roy remains a mysterious figure. It is possible that he was a cousin of Miyagi's father, Yosaburo, a second-generation Japanese immigrant who was arrested in January 1932 at a Communist Party meeting in Long Beach and charged with plotting the overthrow of American institutions.[48] Though the Japanese-American 'Roy' was indeed a US citizen, perhaps Miyagi was trying to throw investigators off the scent of his communist relative by implying that his recruiter was a Caucasian.[49]

The visitors proposed that Miyagi help the cause by travelling to Tokyo for 'a short time' to establish a Comintern group in Japan – the same false flag used with Vukelić in Paris and with Hotsumi Ozaki in Shanghai. Miyagi, pleading the prevalence of tuberculosis in Japan, protested his ill health. But in September 1933, Yano and Roy were back. The moment had come for Miyagi to serve world peace, they said, promising their new agent that his mission would last no more than three months.[50] Miyagi, who had been eking out a precarious existence selling paintings that summer, accepted.

Before he left, Roy gave Miyagi instructions to look out for a certain classified ad in the *Japan Advertiser* and handed him $200 for expenses, plus an extra dollar bill for identification when he reached Japan. His contact would be carrying a bill with the consecutive serial number. Miyagi boarded the *Buenos Aires Maru* at the Californian port of San Pedro. He arrived at Yokohama on 24 October. Soon after he left, Miyagi's landlady, Tomo Kitabayashi, severed her ties with the party and became a Christian, joining the Seventh-Day Adventist Church and the Women's Christian Temperance Union.[51] It would be some years before she would remember her young communist lodger and his mysterious visitors.

Miyagi met Vukelić outside the offices of an advertising agency in Kanda district in early December 1933. They successfully compared dollar bills and doubtless marvelled at the mysteriously efficient logistics of the secret organisation they had just joined. A meeting with the boss was set up.[52]

Sorge rendezvoused with his newest recruit at an art gallery in Ueno. Sorge wore a black tie, Miyagi a blue one. Cautious even with agents recruited and sent by Centre, Sorge confined himself to general chat. Miyagi, too, was nervous. In coded telegrams, Sorge told Centre that he had doubts about the young artist's commitment.[53] But for the moment the last component of Sorge's new team – a native Japanese agent – was now in place. The Tokyo spy ring was almost complete.

8

At Home with the Otts

'He was much more intelligent and charming than was reasonable, and also wicked. He loved what he was doing. Betrayal was his element'[1]

John le Carré on Kim Philby

By Christmas 1933, Richard Sorge's infiltration as a respected member of Tokyo's tight-knit German community was nearly complete. In early December the *Tüglische Rundschau* had published his first essay on Japanese politics, a piece which, according to Sorge, 'received a very good evaluation in Germany'.[2] More importantly it won him the respect of the embassy's staff. Commercial Secretary Josef Knoll was, in Sorge's estimation, 'the number one as far as political knowledge was concerned'. Hearing of Sorge's article, 'Knoll came to trust me not a little.'[3]

By the time the new German ambassador, Herbert von Dirksen, arrived to take up his new posting in mid-December, Sorge was already developing a solid reputation as a *Japan-kenner* – a Japan expert.[4] Dirksen was a Prussian aristocrat of the old school who had just completed a five-year stint at the German embassy in Moscow, one of the Reich's most important diplomatic missions. His appointment to Japan, a far smaller embassy, was something of a mystery, even to Dirksen himself. Germany's war minister General Werner von Blomberg had dropped one hint: Hitler intended 'to establish closer relations with Japan'. Both Germany and Japan had left the League of Nations in 1933. Both were making a bloody transition to fully fledged authoritarian states.

Dirksen – and Sorge – came to the obvious conclusion. Realising 'the necessity of applying some kind of brake to the Russian machine, after the relations with Germany and the Soviet Union became more strained', Hitler intended to build an alliance with Japan in order to effect a military encirclement of Russia, Dirksen wrote in his 1950 memoir. 'I never believed in the possibility of a Russo-Japanese war on Japanese initiative [alone].'[5] In other words the Japanese would, when the time came, have to be pushed into war with the USSR. It would be the German ambassador to Tokyo's job to push them.

Dirksen took over a staff of just one counsellor, four secretaries, two service attachés and two typists. His relations with Sorge were cordial and respectful from the beginning, but never became friendly. In Dirksen's world view, journalists existed on a lower plane of being from diplomats. Nonetheless, Sorge's immodest assessment that he was soon 'regarded as a man of consequence' by the ambassador and his staff was probably not far from the truth.[6] Sorge's position at the embassy was to become the core of one of the most successful penetrations of an enemy institution in the history of espionage. 'The fact that I successfully approached the German embassy in Japan and won absolute trust by people there was the foundation of my spying activity in Japan,' Sorge would later confess. 'I could carry out my spy activity only standing on this foundation. In Moscow the fact that I infiltrated into the centre of the embassy and made use of it for my spying activity was evaluated as extremely amazing, having no equivalent in history.'[7]

Sorge's rapid conquest of the embassy's senior staff was testament to his charisma and intelligence. But Tokyo's German community was also a tiny village. Any new arrival was an event. The arrival of a charmer like Sorge was a sensation. 'Women were fascinated by him, and if the men envied him they tried hard not to show it,' recalled Frieda Weiss, the wife of a German diplomat. 'At any social occasion he attended he attracted a crowd of admirers, men and women. He was the life and soul of any party … he was a social lion.' Weiss recalled how Sorge swung her around in a fiery tango at a party.[8] Araki Mitsutaro, a Japanese society hostess who often visited the embassy, remembered 'first the beauty, then after study the ugliness of his face, but always it was an interesting face'.[9] Paul Mousset, a French journalist who met Sorge in early 1934, was struck by Sorge's 'strange combination of charm and brutality'.[10] Reuters' veteran Japan correspondent Captain Malcolm

Kennedy found Sorge 'quiet, unassuming, intelligent'.[11] In Sorge's own estimation, the embassy staff thought of him as 'an eccentric, first-class journalist' who was 'completely isolated from political parties and factions, being neither a follower of Nazism or Communism'. As on outsider to the embassy, Sorge's brilliance posed no threat. 'I think I gave not a little humanistic charm to ... members of the embassy because I was not ambitious. I did not seek for position; I did not seek benefits.'[12] No benefits, at least, from the point of view of the diplomats whose trust and confidence Sorge was so thoroughly to exploit in the cause of defending the USSR.

Soon after the German community celebrated Christmas Eve at their modest clubhouse, Captain Paul Wenneker reported for duty as the new naval attaché. Sorge recognised a fellow gregarious soul. Wenneker was 'very sociable, charming, and friendly', remembered Araki Mitsutaro.[13] Dirksen described the new naval man as 'a frank and outspoken sailor, a cheerful and reliable comrade'.[14] Sorge and 'Paulchen' Wenneker quickly became 'boon companions'. In the accelerated hierarchy of expatriate life, Sorge was already an old hand and was able to take the young officer under his wing. Wenneker 'was a man of noble, martial character', wrote Sorge. 'But he was quite out of his depth in political matters when he arrived and I was able to be of some help to him there ... Like me Wenneker was a bachelor and we travelled together.'[15] The two new friends travelled to the ancient *onsen*, or hot springs, of Atami, a hundred kilometres south of Tokyo. And together they caroused in Ginza.

Ginza is today a crowded, overwhelming, neon-lit maze of upmarket shops and restaurants. Behind the glass-sided skyscrapers of the main avenues are warrens of small streets full of bars, beer halls and eating establishments. Even in 1934, the area was rumoured to have over two thousand bars. Ginza was where traditional Japanese culture met the West, the place where modern Japan's thrilling synthesis of the two was born. Electric trams shared the streets with rickshaws. Women in kimonos mixed with women in modern dresses, with hems just below the knee. Traditional *samisen* music mingled with jazz and the latest craze to come to Tokyo, tango – played at the Florida Dance Hall and the Silver Slipper. Sorge loved to tango with the 'taxi-dancers' – ladies in elegant gowns who would be paid to dance by the number. He also frequented the area's brothels, though perhaps it was more for the amusement of visitors and for sociological research than for his own carnal purposes. His friend, the leftist writer Friedrich Sieburg, noted that in brothels Sorge was 'obsessed with the fate of all these girls who had been ruthlessly sent to the big cities … he was unbelievably popular in the *milieu*'.[16]

Then there were the German bars and beer halls, which were just coming into fashion among Japan's bourgeoisie. Sorge and Wenneker frequented the Die Fledermaus bar and Lohmeyer's basement restaurant, which was run by an army veteran from the German colony of Tsingtao, home of the Germania Brewery, then (and now, under the brand Tsingtao) the producer of the finest pilsner in Asia.[17] But their favourite was the Das Rheingold bar, run by the genial Helmut 'Papa' Keitel. Papa was also a Tsingtao veteran who had been captured when the colony fell to the Japanese in 1915,[18] married a Japanese woman and set up his bar in Tokyo a year after the great earthquake of 1923. He created the Das Rheingold as a *gemütlich* – cosy – little corner of the Fatherland in Tokyo. He selected pretty young Japanese women to be his waitresses, dressed them in uniforms of Bavarian dirndls and pinafores and gave them German names such as Bertha, Dora and Irma.

Something of the spirit of the Das Rheingold survives in the splendid 1934 Ginza Lion Beer Hall which still stands, now improbably enveloped inside a much larger modern building in Ginza. The cavernous interior is built in bizarre neo-Aztec style, executed in glazed brick, perhaps a tribute to Lloyd Wright's Imperial Hotel, via Albert Speer's angular modernism. The waiters and waitresses are still dressed in Bavarian outfits and struggle under vast plates of sausages and steins of beer. In the 1930s beer halls like the Ginza Lion were becoming fashionable among the salarymen of the Japanese petit bourgeoisie. Sorge himself preferred smaller, more authentic drinking establishments. Perhaps he found cavernous, rowdy spaces like Ginza Lion too redolent of the Nazi Munich he had seen the previous year. A handful of cosier, hole-in-the-wall beer joints still survive under the brick railway arches of Ginza station. Built in 1934, the overground railway runs over the top of a row of tiny bars, filled with the excitable chatter of tipsy Japanese and the explosive laughter of foreigners, wreathed in the savoury smoke of grilling seafood and cigarettes.

Certainly Sorge fell deeply in love with the city. 'He who finds himself on the streets of Tokyo for the first time in those new year days could return home delighted by the wonderfulness of the colours, transformed into delight by the touchingly happy holiday mood of the Japanese and a little frightened by the Asian noise of Ginza the main commercial street of Tokyo,' Sorge would later write in the *Frankfurter Zeitung*.[19] Many later visitors would be impressed by Sorge's deep affection and fascination for Japan.

In December 1933, with the help of Aritomi Mitsukado of the *Jiji Shimpo*, Sorge found a house to rent at 30 Nagasaki Street, in the then quiet residential district of Azabu.* It was a modest, two-storey wooden building, surrounded by similar houses (one of his neighbours was an engineer for Mitsui Mining; the other a clerk at a credit union). One of the three approaches to the Sorge residence led visitors past the Toriizaka police station. There was no back door, and no way to enter or leave unobserved by ever-vigilant neighbours. In short, it was an utterly impractical place for a spy to live. That was the point. Sorge would remain there, hiding in plain sight, for nearly a decade.

'I get the impression of leading [the police] by the tips of their noses,' he reported breezily to Moscow on 7 January 1934.[20] But Sorge could have been under no illusions that the police surveillance was anything other than a constant and deadly threat. He knew that police would search his home whenever he left town ('this was standard procedure for all foreigners', he told Centre), and he knew that his elderly maid, Honmoku, would be regularly questioned by the Tokko – the special higher police – and later by the Kempeitai military police. Indeed Sorge joked to Clausen about collecting matchboxes from various brothels and leaving them for Honmoku to find.[21] But the danger was very real. In March 1934, William Bickerton, a young New Zealander teaching at Ichiko high school, was arrested under the Peace Preservation Law on suspicion – entirely correct as it later emerged – that he had been acting as a liaison between the Comintern and the underground Japanese Communist Party. Despite protests from the British embassy, Bickerton was brutally interrogated and beaten (though he refused to talk) and was eventually released and deported.[22] Unlike in Shanghai, foreignness was no protection from the spy mania.

---

*Today this area, including the site of Sorge's house, is occupied by a hulking shopping mall, office building and multiplex cinema.

The ground floor of Sorge's little wooden house consisted of a living room of eight tatami mats – the traditional rice-straw floor mat, measuring about 1.6 square metres each, that served as the standard measure of living space in Japan – a dining room of four and a half mats, a small kitchen and a bathroom with a Japanese-style squatting toilet. Up a narrow staircase was an eight-mat study that was filled with bookcases, filing cabinets and a sofa, the only Western-style item of furniture. The house also had a private telephone line, a great novelty in the district. The six-mat bedroom was furnished with several traditional Japanese futon mattresses piled on each other to create something more like a European bed.

German visitors found the house tiny, spartan and impossibly untidy. The writer Friedrich Sieburg called the place 'hardly more than a summerhouse',[23] and remembered the two or three rooms he saw as scarcely larger than tables, 'stuffed full of books, papers and all possible kinds of articles of everyday use'.[24] Rudolf Weise, head of the official German news bureau (Deutsches Nachrichtenbüro, or DNB), found that 'the shortcomings' of the two upstairs rooms, 'in furnishings, comfort, and even cleanliness, cannot easily be described'. One or two good bronzes and porcelain pieces were the only evidence that the place was home to a man with some pretensions to good taste.[25]

Sorge's daily routine was to rise at five, bathe in the small Japanese-style wooden tub-bath, then do his callisthenics and chest-expander exercises. His maid Honmoku would arrive to make him a Japanese breakfast, with the German addition of coffee. He would spend the morning at his typewriter and reading the *Japan Advertiser*. After going out for lunch he would return home for an hour's nap, then head out for the embassy, the German Club, and the German News Agency in the offices of Domei, Japan's official news bureau. After 5 p.m. Sorge was usually to be found at the bar of the Imperial Hotel for aperitifs, followed by dinner in town, or parties with the German community.

In early 1934 Prince Albrecht Eberhard Karl Gero von Urach, a member of the royal house of Württemberg and a first cousin to the King of Belgium, arrived in Tokyo as the correspondent of the rabidly pro-Nazi *Völkischer Beobachter*. He carried a letter of introduction to Sorge from Hasso von Etzdorff, the former first secretary in Tokyo who had recently moved back to Berlin.[26] Urach was eight years younger than Sorge, carefully dressed and more reserved than his hell-raising older colleague. Nonetheless they became close. The Great War, of course, bound them. Though Urach had been too young to serve, his father had commanded the student division, ironically known as the Berlin Mayflies, in which Sorge had served in 1915. Urach found Sorge 'a typical Berliner' with his raucous love for drinking and women, but respected his knowledge of Japan. He also found his friend refreshingly forthright in his political beliefs. Sorge never made any attempt to conceal unorthodox views, such as an often-expressed admiration for the Red Army and for Stalin.[27] Again, Sorge was adept at using honesty – or an appearance of honesty – as a species of camouflage. If the man could praise the Bolsheviks to the correspondent of the *Völkischer Beobachter*, what could he possibly have to hide?

Sorge himself understood that his peers saw him as 'a slightly lazy, high-living reporter'.[28] That was, indeed, part of Sorge's true nature. But it was also his cover. Some, in hindsight, saw through the false ingenuousness of Sorge's lovable, louche alcoholic act. It was 'a calculated part of his masquerade', American reporter Joseph Newman of the *New York Herald Tribune* wrote later. 'He created the impression of being a playboy, almost a wastrel, the very antithesis of a keen and dangerous spy.'[29]

In March 1934, Eugen Ott was mercifully released from his Nagoyan exile and joined the embassy staff in Tokyo as senior military attaché, with a promotion to full colonel. Both Ott and Sorge were, for different reasons, delighted by the move. Ott may have been 'rigid and stiff', as Araki remembered him, but like many self-possessed men he seemed to have gained vicarious satisfaction from flamboyance in others. The Otts moved into a European-style villa in the bourgeois Nagai compound in Shibuya in downtown Tokyo. Sorge became a regular visitor, even reluctantly donning evening dress when other guests were present. He would often stay behind to play chess, drink whisky and chat – off the record, naturally – about the politics of Germany and Japan.[30]

Ott quickly developed contacts with pro-German officers in the top ranks of the Japanese military – men like Colonel Oshima Hiroshi and the Japanese military intelligence spy chief Colonel Kenji Doihara – who were to play a central role in transforming Japan into a military dictatorship and ally of Hitler's. At the same time Sorge applied his considerable energies to establishing himself as a serious authority on Japanese culture and politics – in other words, into making himself something more than merely a journalist or even a diligent, run-of-the-mill *rezident*. 'I plunged into an exhaustive study of Japanese affairs,' Sorge explained in his prison confession. 'I did not believe that I should concern myself exclusively with the technical and organisational work of receiving orders and conveying them to my co-workers and forwarding reports to the Moscow authorities. I could not reconcile myself to such a simple concept of my responsibilities as the leader of an intelligence group operating in a foreign land. I had always felt that a man in such a position should cultivate a thorough understanding of all problems related to his activities. The collection of information had an importance of its own, but I was convinced that the ability to appraise it and to evaluate the over-all political picture was of vital importance.'[31]

In early 1934 the first courier sent by Centre from Shanghai – pre-arranged before Sorge's departure – arrived in Tokyo. He (or conceivably she – the courier is not named in the archives) wrote to Sorge care of the German embassy. They met in a room in the Imperial Hotel to establish their bona fides. The next day they met again at the Ieyasu shrine, where among the forest of stone lanterns the courier handed over a package 'chiefly containing money' and the number of a postbox in Shanghai for emergency communications.[32]

Sorge put Centre's dollars to good use – at least as he saw it – embarking on an extensive series of tours around Japan. His companion for trips to Nara, Kyoto and Yamada was the writer Friedrich Sieburg, whom Sorge probably knew from Berlin. The journeys were an insight not only into the ancient culture of Japan but also into the almost maniacal scrutiny under which all foreigners were kept.

'In those two or three journeys to the provinces there were many police, in uniform and plain clothes, who controlled us closely, starting conversations with us almost by force,' Sieburg wrote. 'For the most part they were these eye-catchingly "nondescript" young men who always accepted with pleasure the visiting cards that I had ordered in a Japanese print shop on Sorge's advice. On trains people would constantly begin to talk to us in broken English or German, asking us for our visiting cards and accepting them as though they were valuable documents. They would ask extremely politely if they may be allowed to keep the card. In the station at Yamada we were stopped by a whole group of uniformed policemen who bowed and asked if they could photograph us.'[33]

Sorge also set about amassing a private library, which by the time of his arrest numbered nearly a thousand books on Japanese history, economics, politics, and philosophy. He commissioned several translations of Japanese classics and in his spare time – still dreaming perhaps of a future in academia – worked on a book about the eleventh-century epic *The Tale of Genji*. With the help of various translators – Sorge's knowledge of Japanese never rose beyond the colloquial – he read magazines and government pamphlets in the libraries of the German embassy and the Tokyo East Asia German Society.[34] And he corresponded with at least a dozen *Japan-kenners* around the world. Combined with the confidential information that Ott would share with him and intelligence from his Japanese network, Sorge soon became, without exaggeration, the best-informed foreign observer of Japan in the world.

With the arrival of Wendt, Vukelić and Miyagi, Sorge's network was, in theory, ready to start its covert work. In practice, however, the cadres that Centre had hastily, and apparently randomly, selected for the *rezidentura* were proving useless. By spring, Wendt had assembled his transmitter in the attic of his house in Yokohama and successfully made contact with the powerful Soviet military radios of 'Weisbaden' (Vladivostok). But though the radio man was supposedly under less scrutiny than Sorge was in Tokyo, Wendt clearly lacked his boss's iron nerve. Even when he did pluck up the courage to communicate with Centre, Wendt's transmissions were often incomplete. Wendt 'drank all the time and often neglected to send out the information', wrote Sorge. 'Spying work must be done bravely. He was cowardly.'[35]

Miyagi was also proving anything but a natural-born spy. He had come to Japan under the impression that his help was required to set up a Comintern group of idealistic Japanese socialists, not to act as a secret agent. 'What Sorge asked me was things about Japanese political and military issues,' Miyagi told interrogators. 'He was not trying to organise a Comintern ring' at all.[36] Sorge finally put his cards on the table during their fifth meeting, in January 1934, and told Miyagi bluntly that he needed his help to undertake espionage against his fellow countrymen. The naive, Tolstoy-loving artist had a crisis of nerve, or perhaps of conscience. But Sorge was clearly a persuasive man. He convinced Miyagi, by the latter's account, that he had been chosen as a soldier of the revolution, and that a soldier obeyed orders.

The clinching argument was that Miyagi's secret work would be 'an important mission from the viewpoint of world history and ... the main task was to prevent a Japanese-Russian war'.[37] At the same time Miyagi made Sorge promise that he could return to California as soon as a better qualified man could be found (none ever was). In the meantime, Miyagi agreed to 'participate in the ring, understanding completely that this activity was against the laws of Japan and that I would be executed in wartime for my espionage'.[38]

The first report Miyagi compiled for Sorge was on the mood of the army, gleaned mostly from newspaper reports and street gossip. Sorge was unimpressed. Miyagi had no local contacts of any sort, and though friendly and gregarious, Miyagi did not move in the kind of circles that could be of any use to the spy ring. What Sorge needed to make his Tokyo assignment worthwhile was a Japanese agent of a much higher calibre.

Ozaki Hotsumi had spent the two years since the end of his Shanghai posting working in Osaka at the foreign desk of the *Asahi Shimbun* and living a quiet family life with his wife Eiko and young daughter Yoko, born in November 1929. A sweeping purge of Japanese communists had caught several of his old friends and comrades, but since Ozaki had always been careful never to formally join the party he remained above suspicion.

In May 1934, Sorge decided that the time was ripe to seek out his old Shanghai collaborator. He sent Miyagi as his emissary. Using the alias of Minami Ryuichi, Miyagi tracked down Ozaki at the offices of the *Asahi* and passed on the invitation to meet 'an old foreign friend from Shanghai days'. Ozaki was naturally suspicious, at first assuming that 'Minami' was a police provocateur. It took two further meetings before Ozaki agreed to meet the foreigner that he assumed was Agnes Smedley's American journalist friend, Mr Johnson. It would be two years before Ozaki discovered, by chance, Sorge's real name.[39]

Sorge and Ozaki met on a Sunday afternoon in early May of 1934 on the steps between the Sarusawa-ike Pond and the Kofukuji Five-Storey Pagoda in the deer park of the old Imperial city of Nara. It is one of the few places in the Sorge story that has been preserved absolutely intact. Then, as now, Nara park was a favourite destination for day trippers eager to feed the eerily tame deer and visit the ancient temples. In a tea pavilion, among crowds of Japanese tourists, 'Johnson' explained that he was now posted to Tokyo, and asked Ozaki to help him gather information 'for the Comintern' as he had done in Shanghai. Ozaki, by his own account, readily agreed without qualm. 'I made up my mind to do spy activity with Sorge again. I accepted his request readily, and since then up to the time of my arrest I have been engaged in espionage activity,' Ozaki would later tell his interrogators.[40]

After the war Ozaki was to become a hero for Japanese leftists as a true patriot who put his conscience before blind obedience to his country.[41] In Junji's Kinoshita 1962 play *A Japanese Called Otto*, Ozaki is portrayed as a man moved by high humanist ideals. Principled he may have been, but Ozaki's confession suggests that he was, from the beginning, a willing and conscious spy for Moscow.[42] 'I have thought that … the role of protecting Russia was one of the most important activities,' Ozaki would later tell the police. 'Keeping the Comintern or Russia accurately informed of the various situations inside Japan, which is the most probable attacker of Russia among the world powers, and let her take measures as a means of protecting Russia, was the most important mission for us … I sometimes thought secretly that, as a communist in Japan, it is even something to be proud of that I engaged in such difficult and disadvantageous work.'[43]

At the same time Ozaki was no naive novice. He knew – and immediately warned Sorge – that any covert work in heavily policed Japan would be a very different proposition from operating in freewheeling Shanghai. Sorge, for his part, seems to have underestimated just how valuable Ozaki's position and contacts at the *Asahi* would become. It appears that Sorge at first envisioned Ozaki as a kind of high-functioning Miyagi, a busy go-between operating at the *rezident's* beck and call. Sorge suggested that he quit his job and find work as a private tutor in Tokyo, an idea that Ozaki sensibly rejected – especially since Sorge offered him no salary for his secret work.[44] Instead Ozaki agreed to apply for a transfer to the *Asahi's* Tokyo office. He also wanted to finish a translation of Smedley's *Daughter of Earth*, on which Ozaki had been working ever since he left China in 1932 (the finished book, entitled *A Woman Walks the Earth Alone* and extensively filleted of overtly communist references by Japanese censors, appeared in August 1934 under Ozaki's pen name of Jiro Shirakawa).[45]

In the event, the devil's own luck that would recur so often in Sorge's espionage career struck over the summer. Ogata Taketora, the

Asahi's august editor-in-chief, persuaded the paper's board to sponsor a think tank in Tokyo, to be known as the Toa Mondai Chosa Kai, or 'East Asia Problems Investigation Association'. The idea of the association was to bring together top *Asahi* writers and senior Japanese policymakers to produce learned papers on pressing current events – while in the process offering the paper a privileged insight into the highest councils in the land. Members of the new research centre included economists, political analysts, representatives of the Foreign Ministry, army and navy, delegates from the General Staff, other government ministries, Japan's major financial-industrial groups, various intellectuals, and of course an expert on Soviet affairs.[46] Naturally Ozaki, as the paper's respected expert on China, was asked to join.

By early September the Ozakis were setting up home in Tokyo. In a single stroke, Sorge's main agent would have access to the latest top-level information – albeit unclassified, the association being a public forum – on every strand of Japan's political, economic and military life. And so was born the virtuous circle that would link Ozaki, Sorge and Ott and help propel them all to greatness in their respective fields.

The key to Sorge's success was that he seldom stole secrets – he traded them. Ozaki fed Sorge all the information he gleaned at the Association. Sorge shared it with Ott, making himself indispensable to the rising star of the embassy and boosting Ott's own standing in the eyes of his masters in Berlin. In turn Sorge would feed back what he had seen and heard from Ott – as well as titbits gleaned from British and French journalists by Vukelić – to Ozaki, giving him an unprecedented insight into the workings of German and European power politics.[47] And all the time, the sum total of this gold mine of intelligence would pass to Moscow. Of the three, Ott was of course the only unwitting party. But he was also the only one, in the final reckoning, to escape the hangman's noose.

Prosecutor Mitsusada Yoshikawa, who questioned Ozaki extensively in prison and developed considerable sympathy for his prisoner (before calling for him to be sentenced to death) was convinced that Sorge's information was the key to Ozaki's rise. Ozaki 'wanted to be associated with Sorge because the latter was an important source of information and analytical interpretation'.[48] Ott, for his part, found that Sorge's information helped him quickly to become Dirksen's most valued adviser on political affairs – an unusual position for a military attaché.[49] In autumn 1934, Sorge's luck struck once again when Dirksen developed severe asthma that rendered him a semi-invalid for much of the winter in Tokyo's damp, smoggy climate.[50] By the following year Ott would effectively be running the embassy.

In September, Eugen Ott set out on an official trip to Manchuria. He asked Sorge, his new friend and confidant, to accompany him as an official embassy courier.[51] In 1932 the Japanese had established a puppet state in Manchuria and part of Inner Mongolia they named Manchukuo. In the same year Ott's acquaintance, Colonel Kenji Doihara – chief of Japanese military intelligence and one of the pro-German ultra-nationalist officers who dominated the Japanese Kwangtung Army in Manchuria – had organised the kidnapping of the deposed Emperor of China, Henry Pu Yi. The hapless young Pu Yi was established as the putative emperor of the new state – though Manchukuo remained unrecognised by any nation other than Japan itself. Dirksen, after lobbying from Japan's foreign minister Koki Hirota, recommended to his superior in Berlin that Germany recognise it too as a way of bringing Germany and Japan closer together. State Secretary Bernhard von Bülow was initially sceptical.[52] But it was already clear by the time of Sorge and Ott's official visit that Manchuria would be a crucial bellwether not only of Japan's imperialist intentions but also of the power struggle between the hotheads of the Kwangtung Army and their supporters in the General Staff and the more cautious political establishment in Tokyo.

As honoured guests from a country whose favour Japan was actively courting, Ott and Sorge were entertained lavishly. Ott inspected troops and visited Manchukuo's new capital, Hsinking (modern Changchun). They travelled on the South Manchuria Railway, almost certainly on the brand-new *Asia Express*. Built at the Showa steel works in Japan specially for the Chinese rail gauge, the *Asia Express* reached a top speed of 133 kilometres per hour and was the fastest scheduled train in Asia – as well as one of the fastest trains in the world – at the time.

The technological wonders of the South Manchuria Railway were of more than casual interest to Sorge. Between the Russian handover of the railway to Japanese control in the aftermath of the Russo-Japanese war in 1905 and the annexation of Manchuria in 1931, the Mantetsu company that ran the railway had functioned as a state within a state inside China. It was wildly profitable, providing over a quarter of the Japanese government's tax revenues in the 1920s, thanks to its freight trade of soybeans and oil from the Chinese interior. In 1927 the Mantetsu was carrying fully half the world's supply of soy to Japan and other Asian markets,[53] and by the mid-1930s the railway was transporting over 17 million passengers per year.

The real importance of the Mantetsu, however, was as a vehicle of Japanese colonisation of Manchuria. The company had its own army (infamously, it had been the railway troops of the Kwangtung Army who had organised the provocation that had led to the invasion of Manchuria) as well as its own research bureaus, urban planning departments, police and secret service, and company towns. As Japanese colonists piled into Manchuria with official encouragement – numbering over 800,000 by 1940 – the Mantetsu built up-to-date modern settlements for them all along the length of the railway, with modern sewer systems, public parks, and creative modern architecture far in advance of what could be found in Japan itself. The ideological message was clear. The Japanese had arrived as the civilisers of China – and the rest of Asia too.

The railway was also a vital military asset, as important to the Japanese Army as battleships and coaling stations were to its navy. And here was the rub. Under the terms of the 1905 Treaty of Portsmouth that settled the Russo-Japanese war all lines north of Changchun were still controlled by Russia.[54] At Kuanchengzi station the width between the rails changed from the standard gauge of 4 feet 8½ inches (originally invented by British railway pioneer George Stephenson) to the much wider Russian gauge of 5 feet (a uniquely Russian gauge invented in 1842 by George Washington Whistler, an American railway engineer and father of the artist James McNeill Whistler). In practice – and this practical detail would play a vital role in the escalating tensions between Moscow and Tokyo – that meant that Japanese rolling stock could not physically cross on to the Soviet-controlled part of the track. It also meant that after Japan overran all of Manchuria, a large section of strategically vital railway running deep into Manchukuo remained, bizarrely, under Moscow's control. By the time Sorge visited in 1934 the Japanese government was making increasingly emphatic overtures to the Soviets to buy the Manchukuo section of the railway – with the clear implied threat that in the event of a refusal they would simply take it.

On their return to Tokyo, Sorge and Ott both penned lengthy reports on the political and military situation in Manchuria. Ott was so impressed by Sorge's account of the mission that he asked permission to forward it to General Georg Thomas, chief of the Economics Department of the General Staff headquarters in Berlin. It was the beginning of a long-term association between Thomas and Sorge that would result in the commissioning of many more reports from Sorge – with the result that until late 1941 the Wehrmacht's main source on Asia's economics was a ranking Soviet spy.[55]

The most immediate benefit of the Manchurian expedition was to cement the trust and friendship between Sorge and Ott, and confirm Sorge as a trusted and authoritative source on all things Japanese. Ott's only reservation about his charming, well-informed friend was Sorge's drinking, which worried Ott considerably. 'I had him watched for months,' Ott would later recall, 'because I feared that while drunk he might talk about things from our conversations.'[56]

This delicate juncture in Sorge's relationship with his most valuable source was not, perhaps, the wisest moment to seduce Ott's wife. Yet that was precisely what Sorge did, soon after his return from Manchuria.

Helma Ott was six-foot tall, haughty and imperious, with grey hair and a grave manner. Her Japanese friends nicknamed her *matsu no ki*, 'the pine tree'. She had a reputation for rudeness with the wives of Ott's subordinates, and she looked down, not only literally, upon Japanese women.[57] Helma was a year older than Sorge when they embarked on their affair in the autumn of 1934. But perhaps the most remarkable thing about Helma was that she had once been a communist, and had indeed been a member of the party.[58] Her first husband, Ernst May, was a visionary architect who had studied in England under Raymond Unwin, the prophet of the garden city movement.[59] He was also an enthusiastic socialist. May and Helma moved in left-wing circles in May's native Frankfurt until their divorce in 1918. It is possible that Sorge may even have met Helma during the revolutionary fervour of 1919. Certainly they must have had many common Red friends and acquaintances from Frankfurt.

Regrettably for Helma's new role as good Nazi wife to the upstanding Colonel Ott, May went on to become something of a socialist celebrity. As architect and planner for the city of Frankfurt he created the revolutionary large-scale housing development programme known as Neues Frankfurt. Many of his prefabricated constructivist buildings – such as the bow-fronted Siedlung Römerstadt and the Zickzackhausen, or zigzag houses – survive today. In 1930, with Neues Frankfurt complete, May left Germany for the USSR where his team of progressive architects – known as May's Brigade – set to planning entire socialist utopian cities including the Urals mining city of Magnitogorsk.[60]

In any case, Helma's communist past continued to be, even in Tokyo, a source of mild embarrassment. Perhaps she and Sorge found common ground in Tokyo as fellow left-wingers in an increasingly Nazi world. More likely, Helma was in a loveless marriage and found the hell-raising, handsome new arrival too much of a temptation. Sorge's prodigious libido certainly seems to have got the better of his judgement.

In the event, Ott did not object to his wife's dalliance. The only sign he gave of knowing of his wife's affair with his new best friend was to nickname Sorge '*der unwilderstehliche*' – the irresistible one. What private pain was masked by this jocularity we cannot know. Helma seems to have had oddly maternal feelings for Sorge. She attempted to make his bohemian den on Nagasaki Street more *gemütlich* – as well as more private – by having curtains made. In any case, the affair was brief. Sorge remembered it with his usual lack of sentimentality. Some years later, after the Shanghai radio man Max Clausen had joined Sorge in Tokyo, Clausen's wife Anna suggested that Helma Ott was 'beautiful'. 'Oh, don't talk to me of that woman,' answered Sorge. 'But what do you want me to do? We need her.'[61] And when Sorge's last Japanese mistress found snapshots of a grey-haired Western woman whose eyes were 'full of happiness and shone beautifully', she was convinced that the woman in the photo loved whoever had taken it. When she quizzed Sorge on this subject, he identified the woman as his old lover Helma Ott. 'But there is nothing between us now. She is just a friend. Mrs Ott is kind and good.'[62]

Eugen Ott's continued faith in his wild friend was confirmed in the most public way when Sorge's Nazi Party card, number 2,751,466, finally arrived at the Tokyo chapter of the National Socialist Workers' Party. Sorge was officially enrolled in the local party organisation on 1 October 1934 – making him possibly the only person in history to have been a simultaneous member of both the German Nazi Party and the Soviet Communist Party. He became a regular at party meetings, and when the chairman left later in the year Sorge's fellow Nazis urged him to take the position. Sorge consulted Dirksen and Ott, who supported the idea. 'You should become head of the branch,' Ott told Sorge. 'Then the Nazis will have another intellectual leader.'[63] Sorge apparently heard no irony in the remark. But Ott's approval of his candidacy was a clear endorsement of the esteem in which he was held both in the community and by Ott himself.

In the event, Sorge declined the honour – sensibly, since by no means all members of the German community in Tokyo were Nazis and many, including several German Jews and Lutheran Christian missionaries, were openly opposed. Nonetheless, Sorge made a point of sporting a Nazi lapel badge while at the embassy. He also gave occasional lectures after party meetings, including one memorable evening when he spoke to the assembled Nazis, presumably with remarkable authority, on the Comintern and its techniques of spreading revolution.

In January 1935 a new Soviet agent arrived in Tokyo on a solo mission. Her name was Aino Kuusinen, the estranged first wife of Otto Wille Kuusinen, the Finnish-born secretary of the Comintern's Executive Committee. She and Sorge had first met in 1924, when he was working in the Comintern's secretariat. After her separation from her husband, Aino was recruited by the Fourth Department and assigned to secret work in the United States. In the 'free air' of America, Aino's doubts about communism grew – or so she claimed after retiring to Italy in 1965.[64] She seems to have kept her wavering faith to herself, for Berzin assigned her to Tokyo with the unusually cushy assignment of infiltrating Japanese high society while posing as a writer. Centre provided her with a Swedish passport in the name of 'Edith Hansson' and plenty of funds. But unlike Sorge, Kuusinen was not required to recruit agents or establish her own communications with Centre. Instead, she was to receive cash and send her messages via Sorge, an arrangement which obviously irritated him. As in Shanghai with the Noulens, Centre was ready to compromise Sorge's security in order to solve the Comintern's – in this case marital – problems. The two also got off to a bad start when Aino objected to Sorge taking her out to a 'German ale house of the lowest kind', presumably the Das Rheingold, for their first meeting.[65]

Despite the irritation of having to deal with Aino Kuusinen, Sorge must have been pleased with his achievements. After just a year and a half in Tokyo, he had built the foundations of a formidable espionage machine. His recruitment of a Japanese source as well-connected as Ozaki, his friendship with the increasingly influential Eugen Ott, the position he had carved out in the Nazi Party, the Tokyo press corps and the German community – this was already penetration on a level that few Soviet agents had ever achieved. However, Wendt remained a problem. There was still no effective communication with Moscow other than by microfilm, laboriously couriered by hand via Shanghai by the otherwise fairly useless Vukelić. But beyond the Fourth Department's poor choice of radio man, Sorge's own planning had been meticulous. Unlike the chaotic arrangements he had inherited in Shanghai, in Tokyo Sorge was able to operate freely without any compromising entanglements with local communists, uncontrollable left-wing foreign celebrities, and most importantly bumbling Comintern cadres.

There was only one structural flaw in Sorge's system: the freelance recruiting efforts of his enthusiastic Japanese acolytes, Miyagi and Ozaki. It would ultimately prove fatal to everyone in the group. Soon after his arrival in Japan, Miyagi had run into Akiyama Koji, an old acquaintance from California whom he had met through his communist landlady Mrs Kitabayashi. Forty-five years old and unemployed, Akiyama was looking for work, so Miyagi engaged him to translate materials he had gathered into English for Sorge for 100 yen a month, freeing up Miyagi for his field work.[66] It was a risk, as Akiyama was neither a fully fledged communist nor even a fellow-traveller. Sorge, for one, was nervous, particularly since the military reports that Miyagi was giving Akiyama to translate were certainly suspicious if not outright compromising. 'Lately it seemed that Miyagi was often meeting with a former friend from America,' Sorge wrote in his prison memoir. 'He talked about him several times, and whenever I expressed my anxiety about his association he declared emphatically that the man was trustworthy.'[67]

Ozaki had also engaged in some recruiting of his own. In early 1935 he decided to write to his old Shanghai informant – and Smedley protégé – journalist Teikichi Kawai, asking him to come home in order to 'study the situation in Japan'. Kawai readily agreed, doubtless remembering how impressed he had been by Sorge and Smedley during their earlier association in China. Kawai arrived in Tokyo in March and took a room with another old friend from Shanghai, Fujita Isamu, a virulent ultra-nationalist. Fujita was a risky room-mate but also a useful one, as he was deeply involved in the intrigues of the Japanese Army's power structure and knowledgeable about its constantly shifting factions.[68] Ozaki enrolled Kawai in his own second-tier, exclusively Japanese, subset of the Sorge spy ring.

'Until the spring of 1935 the execution of our duties was completely out of the question,' Sorge wrote. 'The time was spent in getting to grips with the especially difficult Japanese situation.'[69] Nonetheless, by March 1935, and well ahead of the two-year schedule that Berzin had set him for setting up a Tokyo *rezidentura*, Sorge was ready to report in person to Centre – and to see his wife Katya once again. More conveniently still, Ozaki had announced that he would be spending the spring and summer on an extended fact-finding mission in China with a team from the East Asia Problems Investigation Association. They arranged to rendezvous in September, on their mutual return to Tokyo.[70] Sorge also hoped to be in Moscow to catch up with old friends who would be attending the Seventh International Congress of the Communist International in July.

After an exchange of messages with Centre preparing the logistics of his journey, Sorge told Ott that he was ready for a holiday 'in America'. In May 1935 he boarded a steamer from Yokohama bound for San Francisco, the first stage of his long journey back to Moscow.

9

Moscow 1935

'He had been transformed into a boisterous, hard-drinking man'[1]
Hede Massing

Sorge was met in New York by a Fourth Department agent who supplied him with an Austrian passport with which he would travel to Russia. It bore the real owner's 'long and outlandish' name, but the alias would protect Sorge's genuine German passport from showing Soviet entry stamps. Sorge visited a tailor to order a new American suit, visual evidence for his Japanese friends of his time in the States.[2] He was unused to the tradecraft of travelling under an assumed name. At the steamship office he had to consult his new Austrian passport to remind himself of his new identity. Once on board the ship an American customs official discovered that Sorge had omitted to pay US exit tax. To avoid being taken off the liner he paid the man a bribe of $50 – something unthinkable in Japan. ('Things are very flexible in the United States,' Sorge noted.[3]) He was naturally keen to avoid a thorough inspection by US law enforcement, as his suitcase was full of secret microfilmed material. As he cockily told the Japanese after his arrest, this was a violation of standing instructions that expressly forbade any agent to 'make a long journey carrying articles to be delivered through many countries'.[4] Once more Sorge's luck carried him through.

Sorge found Moscow much changed. Photographs of the city from 1935 show Soviet-made Moskvich cars and brand-new, twenty-seat GAZ buses jockeying horse-drawn carts for road space on the newly named Gorky Street, formerly Tverskaya.[5] A grand 'General Plan for Moscow' was transforming the city into a new socialist metropolis. The first line of the Moscow Metro had just opened. New constructivist buildings by radical architects such as Le Corbusier and Konstantin Melnikov (though none by Helma Ott's former husband, Ernst May, who had left Moscow in 1933 after his plans had been rejected) were replacing the pre-revolutionary wooden and baroque merchant palaces. The boxy new Hotel Moskva rose over Manezh Square, its facade asymmetrical because Stalin had signed two different sets of alternative plans and no one had dared question which one the *khozain* actually wanted. And to symbolise the victory of the future over the past, new electrically lit Soviet stars were that summer being installed on the tops of the Kremlin's towers.

Sorge's first call was, naturally, to Katya. Her friend Vera Izbitskaya, remembered the couple coming to find her at the Intourist travel agency offices on the second floor of the Metropol Hotel on the day of Sorge's arrival. 'Shining with happiness,' Katya cajoled her friend into coming to celebrate her husband's return. Vera protested that she needed to stay until the end of the working day but Sorge refused to be thwarted. 'No, girls, we must mark my arrival,' he told them.[6] Vera found Sorge 'charming and humorous', though the women 'didn't know what was true and what was made up' about his banter. But Sorge was serious about one thing. Speaking only to Katya, but within earshot of Izbitskaya, he promised that 'now I will not go anywhere, my Katyushka. We will not part again. They promise me work in Moscow in the Institute of Marxism and Leninism. I love my work ... and now we will go to the South. I have been dreaming of going to the Black Sea.'[7] Perhaps, at the moment he said it, Sorge even believed his own promise.

The couple were able to enjoy at least a little of the settled married life about which Sorge always claimed to dream. Katya took a holiday from her factory job to spend more time with her husband. Visiting friends would only call by for a moment, knowing that the couple wanted to be alone. Katya's tiny room felt like a kind of home. A whole bookcase of Sorge's German books stood by one wall, as well as the old cross-country skis that he would never use again.[8]

It was, in many ways, a happy time to be in Moscow. Food rationing that had been in place since the civil war had just ended. A brand-new metro station – Kominternovskaya, now Aleksandrovsky Sad – had opened a few metres from Katya's communal apartment on Nizhny

Kislovsky Lane. The papers were full of the news of the production exploits of hero miners in Donbass and record-breaking long-distance flights. The first Moscow International Film Festival was held that summer, with Sergei Eisenstein as chairman of the jury. The avant-garde Chinese opera director Mei Lanfang was visiting with his troupe. Perhaps Sorge, with his interest in the Orient, and Katya with her passion for theatre, went to see it.

Despite her obvious happiness at seeing Sorge, Katya's life was also shot through with regret. Her neighbours at Nizhny Kislovsky, Boris and Sonya Glovatsky, had left for a summer tour of Siberia with a theatre company to perform plays to builders, miners and foresters. Katya, her dreams of a theatrical career abandoned, did not accompany them. She told her friends at work that her husband 'worked in defence' and that she received the status and perks of being the wife of a Red Army officer. Her sister Marfa never met Sorge but felt 'that we knew him well … Katya said he was a scholar-specialist on the East. Katya always called him a brilliant revolutionary. We knew he was doing hard and dangerous work.' But Katya confided to her friend Vera: 'I don't know if I am married or not. We count our meetings in days and the time were are apart in years.'[9]

Moscow's political climate was changing as fast as the city itself. The previous December a lone assassin had shot Sergei Kirov, Stalin's last rival for leadership of the party, in his office at the Smolny Institute in Leningrad. Though Stalin had acted as pallbearer and wept at Kirov's funeral, the murder was his work. Finally the undisputed master of the party, Stalin set about purging his enemies among the old Bolsheviks. Sorge's old mentor, Comintern founder Grigory Zinoviev, had been expelled from the party (for a second time) and arrested in December 1934. In January 1935 Zinoviev was tried with his old comrade Lev Kamenev, forced to admit 'moral complicity' in Kirov's assassination and was sentenced to ten years in prison.

Most importantly for Sorge, he found the Fourth Department in disarray and his old boss and recruiter Jan Berzin gone in the wake of a serious espionage disaster. In February 1935, Danish police had ambushed a meeting of senior Soviet military intelligence officers in a Copenhagen apartment. Four top European *rezidenty* were arrested, along with ten local agents. The debacle was the worst mass arrest of illegals in the history of Soviet intelligence. Blame was laid, Sorge may not have been entirely surprised to hear, at the feet of Alexander Ulanovsky, his old chief in Shanghai.

Just as in China, Ulanovsky had disregarded Centre's instructions not to have anything to do with local activists and recruited five of the ten arrested local agents from the ranks of the Danish Communist Party. One turned out to be a police informer. Worse, at least two of the Fourth Department officers who had just arrived from Germany had no reason to be at the meeting other than just 'to catch up with old friends', according to a report into the disaster prepared for the People's Commissar for Defence, Artur Artuzov. Another of Ulanovsky's mistakes was to recruit the American chancer and assassin George Mink, a former taxi driver from Philadelphia who had made a career as a communist trade union organiser in Maine. Mink had made himself useful to the OMS by murdering at least one potential traitor to the Party in Hamburg. But with his multiple links to the underworld, as well as the thoroughly infiltrated local branches of the Profintern, Comintern and Danish Communist Party, Mink was a five-bell liability.[10] With a lack of judgement that characterised his various disastrous personnel choices in China, Ulanovsky nonetheless recruited Mink as his deputy. Both Mink and another American comrade were scooped up at the fateful spies' get-together in Copenhagen.[11] All were jailed for up to five years. Worse, the identity of British comrades who had assisted in the establishment of the Danish Fourth Department station the previous year were also revealed.[12]

The mass arrests were a major blow to Berzin's fledgling apparat. Copenhagen had become Soviet military intelligence's major European espionage hub after the Nazis' rise to power had rendered Berlin too risky an environment. The underground West European Bureau of the Comintern had also been evacuated to Copenhagen.[13] All those networks now lay exposed and unusable. Artuzov's ruthless deputy, and soon to be successor, General Kliment Voroshilov, wrote scathingly on the Fourth Department's report into the disaster, 'from this unclear and naive account it is obvious that our foreign intelligence is still lame in all four of its legs'.[14] Berzin offered his resignation and was demoted to deputy commander of the Far Eastern Army.

So it was General Semyon Uritsky, Berzin's former deputy, who greeted Sorge on his triumphant return to Moscow. Uritsky was a former pharmacist and keen amateur novelist from Odessa who had made a career organising the Red partisan movement against the Whites in south Ukraine during the civil war. Like Berzin before him he had proved himself a ruthless commander in the field, leading a punitive expedition against anti-Soviet partisans in the Caucasian enclaves of Chechnya and Ingushetia in 1919–30.[15] Promoted to *komkor* (corps commander, or lieutenant general), Uritsky had headed a secret Soviet mission to Germany in 1932 where he negotiated the final phase of the covert military training of German pilots and tank commanders on Soviet territory.[16] It is possible that while in Berlin Uritsky also came across Eugen Ott, who at the time was still actively involved in the undercover training programme as a liaison officer to Sondergruppe R.

Uritsky received Sorge with unfeigned enthusiasm. Sorge had the impression that his new chief had thoroughly vetted his background and the reliability of the information he had sent, and been impressed. First and foremost, Sorge had proved that 'spy activity was possible' in Japan. They discussed in detail 'the bright prospects I foresaw there'.[17] Both men seem to have learned from the debacle of the Noulens affair that a *rezident* must be allowed to make his own operational decisions, free of Centre's micro-managing tendencies. Sorge asked for 'absolute freedom to contract any relations I deemed necessary with the German embassy' and also, crucially, for formal permission to share information with the Germans in order to build his bona fides with Ott. He also requested that the newly registered agent Ozaki be recognised as 'a direct member of our group' – presumably to avoid the danger of some Fourth Department functionary attempting to reassign Ozaki to other work elsewhere in Asia.[18]

Uritsky agreed to all Sorge's conditions – at least by Sorge's own account – promising that he would have 'freedom of activity to select problems to work on as the situation would develop and change'.[19] The chief also outlined a detailed list of seven questions that were of crucial importance to the security of the USSR. What was Japan's policy toward the Soviet Union, with particular attention to whether or not Japan planned to attack? Were there any signs of reorganisation and strengthening of such Japanese Army and air units that might be directed against Russia? Were Germany and Japan planning to form an alliance? Was Japan planning any further expansion in China? Was Japan likely to strike any deals with Britain and America to encircle the USSR?

Was the influence of the Japanese Army on national policies growing? What was the status of Japan's breakneck industrialisation? In short, Sorge's task was to keep Moscow informed of whether Japan intended to invade the USSR – either alone or in alliance with Germany – and how well equipped is was to do so.

The last outstanding question was how to get the *rezidentura's* communications on a professional footing. Before he left for Moscow, Sorge had briefed the hapless Wendt on the dangers that faced him if he remained in Japan. Exactly why Sorge did not simply tell him that he was about to be fired for incompetence is not clear. Perhaps he wanted to help Wendt save face. In any case, the sobering talk had the desired effect and the inept Wendt resigned from the job on his own initiative. By the time Sorge began searching for a new radio man, Wendt was already safely back in Moscow with his wife, ready to brief his replacement.[20] Men in Moscow with the operational experience necessary to work in Tokyo's hazardous environment formed a shortlist of just two: Sorge's old China comrades, Sepp Weingarten and Max Clausen.[21]

There was one problem. Clausen was, in Sorge's view, by far the better radio operator, both in terms of his technical skill and his ability to work under constant danger. But in the two years since he had last worked with Sorge in Shanghai and Canton, Clausen's relations with the Fourth Department had deteriorated almost to breaking point. The difficulty was Clausen's wife, Anna. Anna Wallenius's late husband had seen his factories expropriated by the Bolsheviks and the couple had been forced to flee to Shanghai with nothing except what they could carry. Max had never told Anna about his secret life because of her hatred of communism. Not surprisingly, Berzin judged Anna a liability – and indeed for a spell had refused to allow Max to marry her. When, in autumn 1933, Clausen was recalled to Moscow from his last post as radio man in Harbin, the Fourth Department tried to insist that he left Anna behind in China. They even offered to provide him with a dummy wife – a Soviet agent – with whom to travel back to Moscow, possibly because his Chinese visa mentioned that another had also been issued to Clausen's spouse.[22]

Clausen balked and refused to leave China without Anna.[23] With bad grace Berzin agreed – evidence that specialists of Clausen's calibre and experience were hard to replace. But when the Clausens did finally step off the Trans-Siberian express in Moscow in October 1933 they were treated with suspicion. On their first night all their luggage, as well as their passports, disappeared.[24] Anna – who soon discovered that her husband was in fact an officer of the Red Army, not least because he took to wearing his uniform during their strolls around town – quickly soured to the delights of the capital of socialism.[25]

Things got worse. After six-weeks' leave in a sanatorium on the Black Sea, Clausen was summoned to Fourth Department headquarters in January 1934 and dressed down for supposedly 'unsatisfactory' work in China. He was to be consigned to a spell of 'reform through labour' at a collective farm deep in the Russian provinces. Exactly why the Fourth Department would go to the trouble of bringing its star radio man and his wife back to Moscow only to send them into humiliating exile is not clear. In any case, the Clausens were soon on a train to Engels – formerly Pokrov – the capital of the Volga German Autonomous Soviet Socialist Republic. This curious community was peopled by the descendants of Saxon German settlers who had been brought to Russia in the 1780s by Catherine the Great. In 1934 it was home to the ZiU bus factory and boasted two municipal newspapers printed in the archaic dialect of Volga German.

From the railway station at Engels the Clausens were driven 120 kilometres eastwards across the featureless Volga steppes to Krasny Kut, a small settlement on the Yeruslan river. To the east, across the vast seas of grassland, lay Kazakhstan, to the south Stalingrad. They must have felt they had reached the end of the earth. Max was assigned to work at Krasny Kut's motor tractor station, one of a newly founded system of bases spread across Russia that lent out brand-new Soviet-made tractors to local collective farms.[26] He set up a system of radio-telephones to link the farms spread out over the vast landscape, something of a demotion from his former activities setting up international clandestine transmitters. Clausen also set up mobile radio clubs that would broadcast Radio Moscow and other improving programmes to audiences of wondering peasants. Anna found a part-time job as a teacher.[27]

The couple soon adapted themselves to their harsh new life, showing a toughness and stoicism that were among Clausen's best qualifications for life as a spy. By February 1935 he was so settled that he chose to ignore a telegram from the Fourth Department ordering him back to Moscow. He had no idea that the call had ultimately come from his old boss Sorge. Whatever the message from Moscow was about, Max clearly did not want to find out. A month later, Berzin followed up with another more peremptory summons, which Clausen again proudly refused to answer. In March the regional party chief personally drove from Engels to Krasny Kut bearing a third telegram, this time signed by the deputy People's Commissar for Defence, General Voroshilov himself.[28] Handing Clausen the message, the party man said simply: 'So – Max must go back to Moscow.'[29] Leaving Anna behind, Max set off for the two-day journey to Centre.

Clausen found Berzin, not a man used to being defied, in an unfriendly mood. (Unbeknown to Clausen, Berzin was dealing with the fallout of the Copenhagen debacle and was on the verge of resigning.) The general demanded why Clausen had twice ignored orders. 'I rejected them because my position was stable and life was getting better in the Volga Republic,' Clausen bravely told his boss – or so he claimed to his Japanese interrogators. 'As a result I did not want to return to Moscow.'[30] The meeting was 'the crossroads of whether I would lead my life as an honest worker or whether I would be sent abroad as an international spy', Clausen wrote in his post-war memoir. In fact, as a serving officer under military discipline, he formally had no choice. Berzin ordered him back to the radio school in the suburbs of Moscow, where he found his old comrade Weingarten studying the structure and capacity of American transmitters and – surely a clue to the Fourth Department's plans – Japanese short-wave receivers.

A month later, to Clausen's surprise, his old boss Sorge appeared. True to Shanghai form, he chose to interview the two radio men at a bar near the radio school. By the end of their meeting it was clear that it would be Clausen whom Sorge wanted as his Tokyo radio man.[31] Clausen, who had always liked and respected Sorge, agreed. It was to be Clausen's greatest, and final, mission.

Sorge and Katya left for a short holiday, as he had promised, at the Black Sea resort of Gagra. According to her sister, Marfa, Sorge told Katya that he forgot which language he should be speaking when he woke up in a hotel in strange town. 'He remembered, of course, but [Katya] decided that his nerves were giving out,' wrote her sister. All the same, Katya told Marfa that on the whole she found her husband a 'calm, quiet, well-balanced person'.[32]

During the summer Sorge also saw old comrades. One was Ignace Reiss, born Nathan Markovic Poreckij, one of the founders of the

Fourth Department and one of the great Soviet illegals, and his wife Elizabeth.[33] Reiss had worked with Sorge in Moscow in 1933, and it is more than possible that they also knew each other in Berlin in the late 1920s. Sorge also caught up with his old Comintern patron Otto Kuusinen and Grigory Smoliansky, the former first secretary of the party's central committee. Neither Comintern leader could have been optimistic about the future. Stalin, always suspicious of the Comintern, was now in unrivalled control of the party. At the same time the Comintern itself was veering into what would soon be called 'rightist deviation' – the heretical willingness to make pacts with non-Soviet controlled leftist parties in the face of the rising fascist threat. Grigory Zinoviev had already been purged, while the old Comintern boss Nikolai Bukharin had been sidelined from politics and was at that time editing the Party newspaper *Izvestia*. Foreigners, even loyal communists, were being treated with undisguised suspicion.

By mid-July the Hotel Lux was filling up with delegates from around the world, arriving in Moscow for the Seventh Comintern Congress. The Fourth Department ordered Sorge to stay away. His new mission in Japan was too important for him to expose himself, even to loyal party members, just for the sake – in the words of the report on the Copenhagen debacle – of 'catching up with old friends'. Even his old recruiter to the OMS, Manuilsky, agreed, also vetoing Sorge's request to attend the conference. So tight was the security around Sorge's precious new cover in Japan that he had even been removed from all but the most secret membership rolls of the Communist Party of the Soviet Union.

Uritsky may also have been protecting Sorge by keeping him away from the failing Comintern. At the congress, in defiance of Stalin's line, Bulgarian party leader Georgy Dimitrov and his Italian counterpart Palmiro Togliatti insisted on advocating a new policy of forming 'popular fronts' with fellow leftists – as opposed to only 'united fronts' with Soviet-approved workers' parties. They were backed in this act of political suicide by Manuilsky. The scheme, heretical to Stalinists, was overwhelmingly approved by the delegates. The idea of uniting socialist forces was in fact an eminently sensible one. It would soon yield results in Europe, leading to the election in France of leftist prime minister Léon Blum in 1936 and the victory of the leftist Popular Front in Spain. But to Stalin any movement not under his direct control was an anathema. By backing popular fronts, the Comintern had, in effect, signed its own death warrant. Stalin was already plotting the destruction of its leadership. The Seventh Congress was to be the Comintern's last.

In August 1935, just as the congress was drawing to a close, Sorge took the risk of meeting with the Finnish communist Niilo Virtanen, an old friend from the IKKI secretariat. The account of this meeting – albeit at second hand, through Otto Kuusinen's estranged wife, Aino – suggests that Sorge was far from enthusiastic about returning to Japan, and had developed serious doubts about his relationship with the Soviet Union. The two men met at the Bolshaya Moskovskaya Hotel and drank heavily. Virtanen confided his anguish at the destruction of the Comintern and his disillusionment with Stalin. Sorge, in turn, admitted that he was tired of working as a spy. Virtanen later told Aino that Sorge had complained of wanting to leave the Soviet secret service but was unable to do so. He sensed that he was in danger in the Soviet Union, but could not flee to Germany. The Soviet hagiographic tradition has Sorge as a steely, determined and ruthless professional, the indefatigable spider spinning a web of deception. But in truth Sorge was as much trapped in the web he had made as any of the agents he charmed and seduced. As he prepared to leave for Tokyo, Sorge realised that he simply had no choice but to continue his mission, despite his personal misgivings.[34]

When Sorge broke the news of his imminent departure to Katya she called her friend Vera to comfort her. 'Come,' Katya told her friend tearfully. 'Richard is leaving and I am staying behind.'[35] Had Sorge perhaps promised Katya that she could join him in Japan, as Vukelić and Wendt's wives had? If so, it had been an impossible proposition. Centre would never have allowed its star agent a Soviet wife *en poste*. As a concession Uritsky promised Sorge that he would be away for no more than two years. They also agreed that regular couriers would carry Sorge's personal mail to and from Katya so that they could stay in closer touch. Uritsky also confirmed that Sorge and his team would be solely responsible to the Fourth Department, 'and did not have any duty to receive any instructions from any other place ... even if Stalin himself ordered me'.[36]

In late August, Sorge had to leave for Japan. According to Katya's sister Marfa, Sorge asked her to sew a large package of money into the lining of his coat before he left. ' "What a lot of money they entrust you with," Katya said. "They entrust me with more than money," Richard replied, not without pride.'[37]

We know from their later letters that Sorge's parting from Katya was painful. 'It has been a year since I left you early in the morning,' he wrote to his wife in August 1936. 'I am closer and closer to you and more than ever. I want to come back to you. But in our life it is not personal wishes that are in charge – they must regretfully take second place.'[38] Sorge was not hypocrite enough to mention duty, communism or protecting the Motherland, despite the fact that both he and Katya knew that their correspondence would be read by the Fourth Department through whose secret post it was sent. He had privately told Virtanen that he felt trapped; he told Katya that he dreamed of settling in Moscow and living the life of a scholar. Most probably, Sorge believed that this departure would be his last and that he would return soon. Two more years and he would be able to hand over the *rezidentura* to another man. His communist and internationalist duty discharged after nearly twenty years of service to the party, Sorge could reasonably look forward to an honourable retirement. More important, he perhaps hoped that two more years would be enough time for him to excise the demons in his nature – his thirst for danger, the call of the booze, and beer halls and whorehouses – and the narcotic thrill he seems to have drawn from his endless betrayals of all those around him.

Sorge spent a few days in Berlin visiting his mother and sister. In Amsterdam he destroyed – or possibly handed back – his Austrian passport and boarded a ship to America under his own name.[39] Stopping at the New York tailor's to pick up his new suit, he forgot that he had left it under his assumed name. The tailor seemed unfazed by the discrepancy. 'People in the United States do not think it strange if the same man uses two different names,' Sorge noted dryly in his memoir.[40]

Sorge called Hede Massing, his old friend from Berlin days who was now working under cover in New York. 'But how did you find me?' she exclaimed when she heard the familiar voice. Sorge just laughed. They met at the Café Brevoort on East 8th and 5th in Manhattan. Massing found her comrade much changed. 'He had been transformed into a boisterous, hard-drinking man,' she wrote later. 'Little of the charm of the romantic idealistic scholar was left though he was still startlingly good looking. His cold blue eyes slightly slanted and heavy browed had retained their quality of looking amused for no reason at all. His hair was still thick and brown, but his cheeks and the heavy sensuous mouth were sagging.'[41] They arranged to meet in New York again before his departure, but Sorge never showed up for the rendezvous. It would be the last time they ever saw each other.

Hanako and Clausen

'A gay, dissolute adventurer with a brilliant mind and unassailable conceit'[1]

Hans-Otto Meissner on Sorge

While Sorge was away in Russia, Ozaki and Miyagi had been busy cementing their own spy ring. Ozaki invited Kawai to a conspiratorial dinner at the Sakai restaurant near Tokyo's Ueno Pond, where he introduced the journalist to Miyagi as 'an artist from France'.[2] After an evening of heavy drinking the three repaired to a *machiai* – a species of shady bar – where they summoned young geishas to entertain them. Miyagi asked for a round, chubby one.[3] The next day the three met again, their comradely conspiracy sealed by the previous night's revels. Kawai was inducted into the methods of Miyagi's growing team of informants, agreeing that as Japanese they had no need to conceal their meetings as they were forced to when seeing Sorge. Kawai was to show up at Miyagi's studio whenever he had anything to report, and Miyagi would take notes on tiny pieces of paper that he would hide among his brushes and paints.[4]

Miyagi also busied himself with fulfilling Sorge's order to provide 'information on the Japanese Army based on documents and pamphlets'.[5] It turned out that a remarkable amount of apparently sensitive intelligence was – as every foreign correspondent knows – available in the public realm, if one only knew where to look. At a specialist bookshop in Kanda, Miyagi bought magazines and military and technical pamphlets filled with articles 'by Japanese military officers on the introduction of Soviet weapons, anatomy of Red forces and the new weapons of France, Germany and England'. Miyagi gave the important bits to Akiyama to translate into English for the boss.[6]

Ozaki also unearthed an old acquaintance, Shinotsuka Torao, who owned a small factory in the industrial Tokyo suburb of Kansai that produced military equipment. Pretending that he needed technical information for his studies at the Association, Ozaki asked Shinotsuka for help – introducing Miyagi as a student of military affairs who was 'helping him with his work'.[7] Happy to do his patriotic duty, the unwitting new informant turned out to be a fund of knowledge. Over dinners in Ginza, Shinotsuka told Miyagi all about Japan's newest aircraft, the Kawasaki 88 and the Mitsubishi 92, as well as the exact numbers, armament and capabilities of the army's bomber fleet and details of the navy's complement of 'reconnaissance planes, scout planes, attack planes, fighters and torpedo planes'. At a later meeting the garrulous factory owner shared details of the layout and locations of the army's flying units and the navy's bases at Yokosuka, Kasumigaura, Sasebo, and Omura. He also chatted about the navy's new aircraft carriers *Akagi* and *Kaga* – which six years later would wreak devastation at Pearl Harbor.[8]

With such a valuable source to mine, Miyagi had to stay in Tokyo and postpone his plans for field trips around Japan to gather military information. He tried to persuade Kawai to go in his place, disguised as a travelling book salesman, but Kawai did not initially share his friend's work ethic nor his devotion to the cause. 'Kawai's communist conviction was low and his private life was not good either,' Miyagi would tell his interrogators. 'Therefore, from the viewpoint of spying activities, he could not be trusted.'[9] He had no idea how much pain Kawai would soon endure at the hands of police torturers in order to keep his own and Sorge's secrets safe.

Sorge returned to Tokyo in early September 1935. Parading in his new American suit, he seemed his old, boisterous, bachelor self. To his German cronies he praised American women, joking that 'the girls over there are fully grown!' He had no way to communicate with Moscow Centre – or with Katya – until Clausen's expected arrival later in the year.

On the evening of 4 October, Sorge celebrated his fortieth birthday at the Das Rheingold on Chome 5 in West Ginza. He sat with the

'From the schoolroom to the slaughterhouse' – Richard Sorge, aged 20, after being wounded, 1916.

Baku days – the oil engineer Wilhelm Sorge and his Russian wife Nina with their children. (*Richard in white*)

The Sorge's house in the once-affluent Baku suburb of Sabunchi today.

Sorge and his cousin, Erich Correns.

Osip Pyatnitsky, the Comintern commissar who recruited Sorge in Frankfurt in 1924.

Sorge's official Comintern identity photograph, Moscow, 1924.

General Jan Karlovich Berzin, the founder of Red Army Intelligence who headhunted Sorge from the disintegrating Comintern.

Sorge's signature in the Comintern files in Moscow, 1924.

Konstantin Basov, the brilliant Berlin spymaster who launched Sorge for his Fourth Department career.

Katya Maximova (*top*) and her two sisters around the time she met Sorge.

Fourth Department officer Boris Gudz.

The only surviving photograph of Katya and Sorge together.

The Shanghai Bund, 1930.

Alexander Ulanovsky, Sorge's charming but indiscreet boss in Shanghai.

Swindler, spy and former secret policeman Evgeny Kozhevnikov, aka Captain Pik.

Humanitarian, journalist and spy Agnes Smedley, in Chinese uniform. Sorge unchivalrously called his lover 'a mannish woman'.

Ursula Kuczynski, alias Ruth Werner.

Hede Massing.

Hotsumi Ozaki, the idealistic
Japanese journalist who worked
with Sorge in Shanghai and became
his most valuable agent in Japan.

The Tokyo Spy Ring (*top left to right, bottom left to right*): Yotoku Miyagi, the consumptive painter who became the spy ring's most indefatigable leg-man; Branko Vukelić, the failed Croatian journalist recruited in Paris as the ring's photographer, with his Japanese wife Yoshiko Yamasaki; Max Clausen, Sorge's trusty radio man in Shanghai who followed him to Tokyo; Max's wife Anna Clausen.

Ambassador Major General Eugen Ott, whose unshakeable trust in his friend Sorge enabled a great espionage career.

Helma Ott, wife of Eugen and lover of Sorge.

The German Embassy in Tokyo.

Eugen and Helma visit the palace, Tokyo, 1938.

proprietor, 'Papa' Keitel, who had recently redecorated to reflect the mood of the times: a large Nazi swastika flag hung behind the bar; framed photographs of Adolf Hitler decorated the booths where homesick Germans and curious Japanese patrons scoffed beer and sausages.[10] Sorge's waitress that night, dressed in a uniform of Bavarian dirndl skirt and bodice, was Hanako Miyake.[11] She was pretty and slender, with a round face marked by two beauty spots on her nose and eye. Papa had given her the German name of 'Agnes'. At five feet five inches Hanako was tall for a Japanese woman, and self-conscious about her height. The first thing she noticed was Sorge's broad shoulders and unkempt hair. The handsome stranger looked 'German to his last bone', Hanako recalled when interviewed in 1965.[12] Sorge ordered champagne. Keitel turned to the waitress to relay the order. 'Agnes,' he announced, 'today this man turned forty. It is his birthday.' Sorge nodded, smiling broadly, and said, '*So des, so des.*' ('It is so, it is so.'). Hanako asked another waitress: 'Who is that foreigner talking to Papa? Is this his first visit here?' Her colleague 'Berta' replied that 'he used to come here quite frequently, but he has not come recently. He is a very nice person … He does not speak Japanese, but he is very generous.'[13]

Hanako carried the champagne to Sorge's booth, then took a small folding chair from one of the nearby tables and joined the two men. They popped the cork and drank to Sorge's health. Hanako would later recall her first meeting with Sorge in great detail:

'Are you Agnes?' Sorge asked.

'Yes, I am,' she answered.

'I am Sorge,' he replied, shaking her hand. His voice sounded to her Japanese ears somewhat hoarse and unmusical, Hanako told the interviewer, but his tone was kind and his 'whole demeanour proclaimed a man of good breeding'.[14]

'How old are you, Agnes?' Sorge asked in English.

'I am twenty-three years old,' Hanako replied in her few words of German (she was actually twenty-five, but Papa had instructed his girls to subtract a few years from their age).[15] Sorge smiled at her accent and began chatting up the pretty waitress, not realising that Hanako understood only two phrases in German: 'I am very happy today', and 'Agnes, what would you like to have? I want to buy you a present.'

'Please give me a record,' she said.

'Let us go buy you one tomorrow.'

Hanako loved music. So did Sorge. He produced his notebook and wrote the time of their date, the next day at Sorge's favourite record shop. At the end of the evening he left a memorably large tip, which Hanako shared with 'Berta'.[16] Anxious that Sorge made a habit of picking up waitresses, Hanako quizzed Berta on whether 'that foreigner has anyone he likes especially in this bar? ... Does he have a favourite?'

'Dora used to serve him occasionally when he came here,' 'Berta' replied. 'But since he does not call for anyone specifically, I don't think he has a favourite.'[17]

Hanako found Sorge already at the music shop when she arrived, listening to records. He told her she could choose anything she liked, so she found three records of arias sung by one of her favourite tenors, Beniamino Gigli. Sorge added some of his own favourite piano and violin sonatas. 'I am very fond of Mozart,' he told her. 'Please accept these.'[18]

Sorge suggested going for dinner, which 'Agnes' accepted. They went to Lohmeyer's, the German restaurant Sorge often frequented with Wenneker and Ott. Hanako was shy – all the more so because a Japanese woman walking with a Westerner drew curious and disapproving stares. They also, between Hanako's halting English and German and Sorge's basic Japanese, had almost no common language. Nonetheless, when Sorge suggested another date she agreed. After dinner, with characteristic disregard for bourgeois niceties, he told her he had to go to the office of Domei, the Japanese press agency, and therefore could not walk her home.

They began seeing each other regularly, though for months Sorge forbore to make any sexual advances on the bashful young woman. For Hanako it would be a fateful and life-changing relationship. For Sorge, less so. For their first dates Sorge called her 'Agnes'. When Hanako eventually told him her real name, Sorge mistakenly thought that Miyake was her given name, so took to calling her 'Miyako' and continued to do so even after she had corrected him. She did not object, saying she found Hanako – which means 'little flower' – 'a child's name'.[19]

Clausen had set off for Japan, via Shanghai, in September. Though he 'felt a big pride' at being appointed radio operator to such a crucial station, he must have had mixed feelings about leaving Russia.[20] The

Fourth Department had forbidden him from taking Anna with him, effectively keeping her hostage against his good behaviour. Even more insensitively, Uritsky blithely suggested that he divorce his present wife and 'take a German woman ... If you are willing, I can introduce you to one'.[21] Clausen flatly refused, and instead arranged to meet Anna in Shanghai in November, where they would be officially married far from the irritating scrutiny of Uritsky.

The Fourth Department furnished Clausen with two genuine passports, one Austrian and one Canadian, doctored with Clausen's photograph. They also gave him $1,800 in American dollars. One thing he did not take were any radio parts, since Clausen was planning to improvise a radio using the bits and pieces assembled by Wendt and left for collection in Yokohama. Like Sorge, he travelled via New York, where he was contacted by a Soviet agent named Jones who offered to give him more money. Rashly, Clausen declined. After being fined $300 by US customs in San Francisco on 14 November – it is not clear why – he found that he now no longer had the money he needed to bring Anna from Shanghai to Tokyo and set up home with her in Japan.[22] In the event Clausen need not have worried. When the *Tatsuta Maru* liner docked in Shanghai, Anna was nowhere to be seen. It would not be until the spring of 1936 that the Soviet authorities grudgingly – and at Sorge's insistence – finally issued her an exit visa. Clausen proceeded alone to Japan.

Because Sorge had no way to communicate with Centre before the arrival of his radio operator, they had arranged that the chief would wait for Clausen every Tuesday evening at the Blue Ribbon Bar off Sukiyabashi.[23] Clausen arrived in late November with some days to spare before his rendezvous. He decided to pass the time by going to a party at the German Club, where he had been invited by a fellow German passenger. There, Clausen was surprised to bump into his past and future boss dressed as a Berlin sausage-seller, draped in strings of cardboard bratwursts and in an exuberant mood. The two men ignored each other until they were formally introduced by the club's director, a public meeting that happily removed the necessity of concealing their previous acquaintance.

Clausen took rooms in the Bunka Apartments and set to work building his improvised transmitter. Though separated from his 'Anni', Clausen's 'technical ability and enthusiasm for his work knew no bounds', Sorge wrote.[24] The radio apparatus he cobbled together may have resembled a Heath Robinson device, but its effectiveness was formidable. For the receiver Clausen cannibalised an ordinary Japanese-made radio, discarding the case and speaker in favour of headphones and adding three American-made vacuum tubes he found in a radio parts shop to modify it for short-wave reception. The transmitter was a Bakelite panel attached to a wooden box, the tubes and coils readily detachable. The tuning coils were fashioned from copper gasoline tubing intended for automobiles, which he purchased at a hardware store in Kyōbashi-ku. The entire apparatus was made to fit inside a suitcase.[25] When the Japanese police finally captured Clausen's transmitter, an official radio specialist called it 'one of the strangest conglomerations of various stray parts I have ever seen – a terrific assortment of materials that included one or two beer bottles and other miscellaneous items'.[26]

While Clausen was assembling the radio that would become so essential to the spy ring's operations, a chain of events that could have sent the entire Sorge group to jail was set in train by the arrest of a lowly Comintern informant in Manchuria. Back in 1933, before he ever worked for Sorge, Kawai had been sent on an intelligence-gathering mission in northern China and Manchuria by Ozaki and Smedley. During this trip Kawai recruited one Tatsuoki Soejima as an assistant. Two years later, in the autumn of 1935, Soejima was picked up by Manchukuo police in Hsinking on suspicion of passing military secrets to the Comintern. During his brutal interrogation the terrified Soejima mentioned his old acquaintance with Kawai. A formal request to bring Kawai in for questioning duly made its way from the Japanese consulate in Hsinking to the Tokyo police.[27]

At dawn on 21 January 1936, eight policemen charged into Kawai's apartment in Suginami-ku and dragged him out of bed. After a couple of days in Suginami police station he was transported to Manchuria in uncomfortable stages, arriving two weeks later in a Hsinking prison in Manchukuo to answer to thirty-seven charges of espionage.[28] Kawai was beaten by two policemen armed with an iron bar as his interrogator screamed questions. Even in his agony Kawai realised that his questioners suspected nothing of his recent spying activities for Sorge in Tokyo. He denied all knowledge of Comintern activities in China. To confuse his captors he claimed to be a *Shina ronin* – a member of one of the secret right-wing patriotic societies who had a sinister reputation and enjoyed semi-official protection from the Kwangtung Army. After an hour of torture, Kawai passed out. But he had said nothing about Sorge. Of all the members of the ring who were eventually interrogated, Kawai was the only one who never talked.

Kawai's arrest and subsequent disappearance into the Manchurian prison system was obviously an existential threat to Sorge – but for the time being one with an unknowable outcome. While he waited for news of whether Kawai had betrayed them, Sorge set about the challenging problem of finding a safe place from which Clausen could transmit. Any short-wave receiver was capable of detecting Clausen's signal and establishing its approximate direction. Pinpointing the source was more complicated, requiring at least three receivers to lock on to the transmission and triangulate the origin. In order to make the police's job harder the sender, therefore, should be in a densely inhabited section of town. The signal would have to be sent from a wooden, rather than a steel-framed, building. The transmission would also have to come from a house at least two storeys high because the magnetic attraction of the earth would swallow a signal sent from ground level.[29] Sorge and Clausen briefly considered using Sorge's own house as a base station, but quickly dismissed the idea because of the likelihood of unexpected visits from the boss's German drinking buddies from the embassy and the press, and also the dangerous proximity of Toriizaka police station.

Sorge decided to ask Gunther Stein, a fellow journalist, for permission to use his apartment on Motomachi-Cho in Azabu-Ku for the radio transmissions. It was a calculated risk. Stein was a German writer of leftist sympathies who had known Sorge 'for a long time', as Sorge later confessed to the Japanese. Stein had been a correspondent in Moscow for the *Berliner Tageblatt*, but as a half-Jewish socialist was fired when Hitler came to power. He wisely decamped to London and joined the staff of the London *News Chronicle*, which sent him to Tokyo in the spring of 1935. Sorge and Stein ran into each other at a Foreign Ministry press conference – 'an extremely happy event' for both men, according at least to Sorge. The *rezident* confided to his old acquaintance that he was 'engaged in something more than news reporting'. Later he told Stein that he was 'working for the Moscow authorities'. Sorge reported to Centre that Stein was 'a useful man' whom he was 'manoeuvring … gradually toward participation in our work'.[30] He asked for permission to recruit Stein as a full member of the ring – a request that Centre, without giving its reasons, denied.

Sorge, never one to take no for an answer, began using Stein as a collaborator and part-time helper – albeit a reluctant one – regardless. Stein's reticence was hardly surprising given the inordinate risks he was being asked to take. Sorge's request to set up a transmitter in Stein's house 'visibly disturbed him', but nonetheless he agreed. 'Stein and I discussed radio and he drew a map to show me where he lived,' Clausen later confessed. 'I visited him several days later at his home … examined the house to see whether it was suitable for the installation of radio equipment, and decided, with his consent, to use two of his upstairs rooms'.[31]

Clausen began testing his equipment in February 1936. Because he could not, for obvious reasons, use an outdoor antenna, the radio man strung two tin-plated, seven-metre long copper wires across Stein's ceiling. And though the transmitter was portable, the electrical transformer it required was not. Clausen therefore constructed a permanent transformer in Stein's attic – and would create a new one in every location he would ever use to transmit. Aside from the bulk of the transformer, Clausen's set-up was miraculously discreet. He could unpack it in ten minutes and dismantle it in five.[32]

Within a week of his first experiments, Clausen made his first contact with 'Wiesbaden', the familiar Soviet military transmitter at Vladivostok with which he had communicated from Shanghai.[33] Since his device had no instrument for measuring wavelength, Clausen improvised with a wavelength of 37–39 metres for transmitting and 45–48 metres for receiving. His guess proved to be spot on.

Clausen's timing was fortuitous, because Sorge had momentous news to report. On 26 February 1936 an ultra-nationalist faction in the Japanese Army attempted yet another murderous coup d'état. Officers of the First Division, under orders to ship out to Manchuria, rallied some 1,400 soldiers to assassinate top members of the government. Their hit list included the prime minister, Admiral Keisuke Okada, and the Minister of Finance, as well as the Imperial Grand Chamberlain, the Lord Keeper of the Imperial Seals and other moderates who had the emperor's ear.[34] Makoto Saito, the Keeper of the Imperial Seals, had just returned from dinner and a movie at the American embassy when the killers shot him and wounded his wife as she tried to shield him from the volley of shots. The prime minister escaped by hiding in a toilet. The murderers shot his brother-in-law by mistake. His family pretended that the killers had succeeded in their mission and Okada walked in disguise behind the hearse at his relative's funeral. Count Nobuaki Makino, an intimate of the emperor, also survived an ambush at a country inn by diving down a hillside with his granddaughter and playing dead after they were wounded by rifle fire.

The rebels, despite their failure to kill their key targets, issued a chilling proclamation. 'Now is the time to bring about an expansion of the power and prestige of Japan,' they declared. 'In recent years many persons have made their chief purpose in life the amassing of wealth regardless of the general welfare and prosperity of the people, with the result that the majesty of the Empire has been impaired … The Elder Statesmen, the financial magnates, the government officials, and the political parties are responsible.' Claiming that it was 'our duty to take the proper steps to safeguard our fatherland by killing those responsible', the rebel officers declared that they had done their 'duty as subjects of His Majesty the Emperor'.[35]

Was this the long-feared turning point when Japan's militarists finally seized power? The German embassy was taking no chances. Food and furniture were carried to the cellar in case the fighting spread, and the confidential files carted down to the boiler room ready for incineration. Eugen Ott had to smuggle Ambassador Dirksen through narrow alleys to the embassy to avoid roadblocks of loyal troops who were guarding the nearby War Ministry.[36]

When Sorge arrived at the embassy the following day he found Ott bewildered by the coup attempt and unable to understand the failure of the government and the army's top brass to control it.[37] The rebels raised the standard of revolt (in fact a white tablecloth from the Peers' Club, purchased for 100 yen) over the occupied prime minister's residence.[38]

However the coup swiftly unravelled. In the provinces, suspect officers were quickly arrested before they could muster troops. The mutineers' positions in Tokyo were surrounded by loyalist artillery. After four days the rising fizzled out in a typically Japanese face-saving way, with the surrender of the rebels under offer of Imperial pardon. A decorous two-hour pause followed the formal surrender during which the mutineers were expected to commit ritual suicide.[39] Only two did. Fifteen of the ringleaders would eventually be executed – on charges of 'using the army without Imperial sanction' – but the War Ministry's announcement of the end of the revolt contained no promise of an investigation nor any condemnation of the mutineers.[40]

Under a veneer of continuity, everything had changed. The coup attempt – euphemistically known as 'the February 26th incident' – showed that it was the army, not the government, that now held the balance of power in the Japanese Empire.[41] In the days that followed the collapse of the putsch, Sorge struggled to make sense of what had happened for his masters in Moscow – and assess the impact of the new order on the security of the Soviet Union.

Miyagi, the artist and joker, began to show his skill at gleaning top-level intelligence from the gossip of soldiers. He told Sorge that he believed the revolt was doomed from its inception, as the Young Officers had only small arms to oppose the loyalists' tanks, artillery and aeroplanes. Ozaki, who had recently returned to his research centre after his sojourn in Manchuria, was able to consult with some of the empire's senior decision-makers to form a uniquely well-informed picture of what had happened.

Ozaki submitted a long dissertation to Sorge with his findings. He wrote that the rebellion had been spearheaded by officers from rural backgrounds who had a deep loathing for capitalism, inspired by the 'revolutionary ideology' of ultra-nationalist writer and propagandist Kazuki Kita.[42] More practically, Ozaki predicted that it was only a matter of time before the right-wing officers took control of the army. Indeed, by 18 May 1936, after the resignation of the cabinet in the wake of the rebellion, the army further demanded that any ministers of war and the navy in any future government must be active-duty officers. Since these ministers were, by law, able to choose their own successors, the military had effectively freed itself from civilian government control. The only question worth answering in Japanese politics now became: what faction was in control of the army? The radical young Action Group, who advocated immediate war with the Soviet Union, or the more cautious Control Group?[43] Miyagi, for his part, believed that the Control Group would hold power for a while yet – and choose to expand in China rather than immediately attack the USSR.[44]

In addition to Ozaki and Miyagi's well-informed insights, Ott also showed Sorge a copy of the Japanese Imperial General Staff's own confidential report into the February 26th incident. Using a special miniature camera, Sorge photographed the report in Ott's office – the first, but by no means the last, time he would photograph the most secret documents of the Germans and Japanese for the Kremlin's perusal. Ott also showed Sorge 'very detailed reports on to what extent Japan had military force for an anti-Russian war' that showed that Japan's eight or nine divisions in Manchuria, or even the entire Japanese Army of about sixteen divisions, were insufficient to take on the the USSR – for the time being at least.[45]

The report that Sorge wrote for the German embassy was hailed as a triumph of informed analysis by Dirksen, Ott, and Wenneker. 'In this way,' wrote Sorge, 'I accomplished the same effect of killing two birds with one stone, in that I gained trust from the Germans by studying and writing ... And at the same time I spied valuable materials.'[46] A copy was sent to General Thomas in Berlin, who officially requested more such excellent work. Thomas's patronage gave Sorge an iron-clad excuse to peruse the embassy's files for information that he then shared with Ozaki – and of course Moscow. To cap it all, Sorge also penned a long article on 'The Army's Revolt in Tokyo' that appeared in the May issue of Haushofer's *Zeitschrift für Geopolitik*, as well other pieces for the *Frankfurter Zeitung* that cemented his status as an authoritative contributor to Germany's most respected newspaper.[47]

All the elements that would make Sorge's spy ring the greatest such espionage network of the age – Ozaki's contacts among the Japanese elite, Sorge's access to the secret Japanese military documents the army shared with Ott, Miyagi's assiduous groundwork – were in place. More impressively still, every piece of information that passed back and forth served to buoy the reputations of Ott, Sorge and Ozaki in the eyes of their respective superiors. Information was power, not just to governments but to all the principals of the spy ring, both witting and unwitting.

Ott's trust and admiration for Sorge in the aftermath of 26 February had grown so deep that it was to Sorge, rather than any other member of the embassy staff, that Ott turned to when he picked up a startling piece of gossip during a visit to the Japanese General Staff. Bursting into the office that Dirsken had allocated to Sorge in the embassy, Ott excitedly confided to his friend that he had just got wind of secret talks in Berlin between Major General Oshima Hiroshi – the pro-Nazi military attaché at the Japanese embassy in Berlin – and Germany's foreign minister, Joachim von Ribbentrop. The negotiations were being carried out behind Dirksen's back and, Ott reported, brokered by Germany's military intelligence chief, Admiral Wilhelm Canaris. Incredibly, Ott asked Sorge to help him compose a coded telegram to Berlin to ask what was going on, asking his friend to 'swear that you will not tell this to anyone else'.[48]

It was a promise that Sorge, to put it mildly, did not keep.

The news of the secret Japanese–German talks was the first truly sensational espionage scoop of Sorge's career. 'I reported the development of these negotiations constantly to Moscow through wireless,' he later confessed. 'Since at that time nobody in the world knew about such negotiations except a limited number of related persons, the report to Moscow must have been highly sensational to them.'[49]

Berlin's replies to Ott's enquiring telegrams about the Ribbentrop–Oshima talks were suspiciously non-committal. But Ott's further enquiries among his friends in the Japanese Imperial General Staff discovered that a political and military alliance was being mooted between Germany and Japan, unbeknownst to the foreign ministries of either country. Obviously alarmed by the consequences of such an entente for the Soviet Union's security, Sorge took it upon himself to convince Dirksen and Ott that the pact would be both undesirable and dangerous.[50] 'Germany would be smart to tie in with Russia and so be able to cope with Britain and France,' Sorge argued, adding that in the wake of the 26 February revolt the Japanese military was unstable and 'could not be trusted'. For good measure Sorge also cast the talks as 'an adventurous attempt by ... Oshima and Ribbentrop to obtain their own advancement'.[51]

Sorge's word may not have been decisive. Nonetheless, the ambassador was in strong agreement with Sorge in being 'dead against the pact with Japan', as Dirksen recalled in his memoir. Dirksen sailed for Germany via Vancouver on the *Empress of Canada* on 9 April 1936 to check on the rumours with his superiors in Berlin and attempt to reverse the mooted alliance before it was too late.[52] The ambassador, along with the German Foreign Ministry and the General Staff, found Hitler's pro-Japanese stance foolish and preferred to strengthen Germany's ties with Chiang Kai-shek instead.[53]

When Ribbentrop sent a confidential agent, Dr Friedrich Wilhelm Hack, to Japan to confirm the details of a possible alliance, Sorge quickly sought him out in order to convince him of the folly of such a pact. Hack, officially an employee of the Heinkel Aircraft Company, was an old Japan hand. After being interned along with Papa Keitel and the rest of the German garrison of Tsingtao after its capture by the Japanese in 1915, Hack had returned to Japan often and was instrumental in persuading the Japanese Army and Navy to buy German armaments from 1921 onwards.[54] Assured by Ott that Sorge was entirely trustworthy, Hack confided to Sorge that Soviet agents had been posted outside the Berlin homes of Oshima, Ribbentrop, and Canaris, and had 'even taken pictures during the secret negotiations for the Anti-Comintern Pact'. Hack had been chosen as a go-between, he told Sorge, so that 'the negotiations could continue without further Russian detection'.[55] Hack could not have made a more unwise choice of confidant.

It is not clear exactly when Sorge received the news that he was about to become a father. But we do know that he wrote Katya a letter, photographed on microfilm, on 9 April 1936 expressing his excitement. 'If it's a girl I would like her to have your name ... today I will arrange a second parcel of things for the baby.' By this point the pregnancy must have been at least eight months advanced. 'This is sad and, perhaps, cruel, as is our separation on the whole,' he wrote. 'But I know that you exist, that there is a person whom I love very much and about whom I can think, whether my affairs go well or badly. And soon there will be something that will belong to both of us ... Of course, I am very worried about everything you are enduring, and if everything will be all right. Please take care to see that I receive the tidings at once, without delay.' Sorge hoped that Katya's family were not angry because he had left her alone. 'Later,' he promised, 'I will try to rectify all this with my love and tenderness for you.'[56]

Despite his melancholy – or perhaps because of it – Sorge decided to celebrate the news of Katya's pregnancy by redoubling his efforts to seduce Hanako Miyake. After taking Hanako to another one of their now-regular romantic dinners at Lohmeyer's, accompanied by the gift of more phonograph records, Sorge suggested going back to his place. He claimed that he had 'something to show' her. Hanako agreed. They stopped off at German bakery for a box of chocolates and caught a taxi to the little house on Nagasaki Street. Hanako recalled being startled by the eccentric mixture of the Japanese and Western decor. The place was piled with books and papers and the walls were covered in maps. The *tokonoma* in the study – a niche traditionally used to display decorative objects – held not only the usual flower arrangement and scroll but also Sorge's portable phonograph, a clock and a camera.[57]

Sorge brewed coffee over an alcohol burner while Hanako ate chocolate on the couch. German classics played on the record player. To amuse his nervous guest Sorge seized a samurai sword and began twirling it above his head in a parody of a traditional sword dancer, then he pushed her abruptly back on the couch and began trying to kiss her. '*Dame-o, dame-o!* – It is wrong, it is wrong!' Hanako shrieked, offended, and bursting into tears. She told Sorge that she wanted to go home, so he walked her to the main road and put her in a taxi, giving her money for the fare. 'His face looked very sad,' Hanako remembered. Though shaken, she agreed to meet him again.

Sorge's approach a few nights later was slightly more refined. This time there was no sword dancing. He invited Hanako once more to his house and persuaded her to try a Turkish cigarette. He wooed her with talk of his passion for ancient Japanese literature – especially his favourite, *The Tale of Genji*, a story of courtly love and the art of seduction. 'What an extraordinary conversation!' Hanako remembered of their first night together as lovers.

Sorge would be the love of Hanako's life. The reverse, sadly for her, was not the case. Around the time he embarked on his affair with Hanako it transpired that another young woman, a waitress named Keiko (from the Die Fledermaus rather than the Das Rheingold) had fallen in love with Sorge. It is not clear whether they were already lovers, but when she saw her beloved show up at the bar with a beautiful European woman in tow – possibly Helma Ott's friend, Anita Mohr – Keiko despaired and resolved to kill herself. She left a farewell note and a gift of flowers on Sorge's doorstep and took a steamer for Oshima, where she planned to throw herself into a volcano. The Die Fledermaus' German proprietor got wind of her plan and called the police, who tracked the lovesick girl down and brought her back home. She eventually recovered from her heartbreak, and even brought herself to sit with Sorge when he visited, spitting into his dice cup for luck.[58]

Sometime in late spring, Katya sent news that she had lost the baby – possibly at an advanced stage of her pregnancy, though with an unpredictable delay of several months in their microfilmed correspondence it is hard to know more precise timings. 'Everything turned out quite differently than I had hoped,' Sorge wrote in a bleak letter that focussed more on his own despair than Katya's feelings. 'I am tormented by the thought that I am getting old. I am seized by the mood to come home quickly, but for the time being that is all dreams ... it's hard here, really hard.'[59]

'What do I do? It is hard to say,' he wrote to Katya in a letter that was probably delivered by Sorge himself to a courier in Shanghai in the summer of 1936. 'It is hard to bear the heat here. It is as though you are sitting in a greenhouse covered in sweat. I live in a little house built in local style, inside mostly sliding doors and on the floor woven mats. The house is quite new and quite cosy. One old lady makes everything I need, boils me some lunch if I am at home,' he told her. 'I have acquired another bunch of books – you I know would be happy to search around in them and I hope that you will one day be able to. Sometimes I worry about you not because something will happen to you but because you are alone and very far away. I always ask myself ... would you not be happier without me? Don't forget that I would not blame you.' He tried to explain, as gently as possible, that he would not be coming back soon. 'I am *en poste* and know that this must be for some time. I don't know who can take over from me in our important work. Be healthy my dear. Write more often.'[60]

In public, despite his private anguish, Sorge kept up his facade of cheerful cynicism. At an embassy reception in September 1936 the newly arrived Third Secretary Dr Hans-Otto Meissner found Sorge in apparently buoyant mood. "So you are Meissner. I heard you had just arrived," Sorge said, tipping a glass in a half-mocking, half-gracious salute. "Welcome to our Oriental paradise!" Sorge had not bothered to introduce himself, assuming that the young diplomat already knew who he was. Meissner judged Sorge 'a gay, dissolute adventurer with a brilliant mind and an unassailable conceit'.[61] (Another new member of the rapidly expanding staff, Press Secretary Count Ladislaus von Mirbach-Geldern, sniffily dismissed Sorge as 'the most uncultured fellow in the world'.[62]) But Meissner noted that Sorge was 'accepted by everyone, everywhere', and clearly enjoyed the confidence of his superiors. Indeed, Ott hinted to Meissner that Sorge was some kind of German special agent. The young diplomat found it 'hard to resist'

Sorge's 'obvious high zest for living and careless disregard for pomp and ceremony'.[63]

At least Max Clausen was able to enjoy a happy family life. Once Clausen had established radio contact to their satisfaction, the Fourth Department decided to allow Anna to join her common-law husband in Tokyo. Over the winter she had been living alone in Moscow, under Centre's close eye, and thoroughly disliked it. 'There is no life, no freedom, and no peace' under communism, she bluntly concluded.[64] But early one morning in March 1936 a German woman who had been closely monitoring Anna unexpectedly handed her a train ticket to Vladivostok and told her to be ready for departure by ten o'clock on the same day. Anna was shunted off to China with an accompaniment of a string of Fourth Department blunders. The contact who was meant to give her money and a false passport in Vladivostok was late, so she missed her boat to China and had to wait a month. When she finally reached Shanghai, the post office could not find Clausen's letter with his contact details.

Eventually Clausen tracked Anna down through the poste restante service of the Thomas Cook office. He had travelled to Shanghai with twenty to thirty rolls of microfilm that he kept in his pocket at all times, ready to fling them into the sea at the first sign of trouble.[65] Finally, he and Anna had been able to have their marriage legally sanctioned by the German consul general, which entitled her to a German passport in her own name. By late summer they were installed in Tokyo as man and wife in Clausen's new house in Azabu-ku.[66]

'Are you busy with the secret work as usual?' Anna asked her husband shortly after they had settled in. 'Of course,' Clausen replied. 'But just a little bit.' Clausen assured his wife that he was going into commerce. What he did not tell her was that the seed capital of $20,000 was Fourth Bureau money sent at Sorge's request in order to set Clausen up with a cover business. At first Clausen experimented with importing forestry equipment, then powerful Zündapp motorcycles (one of which he sold to the speed-loving Sorge, which would soon have fateful consequences). But the project which eventually prospered was the manufacture and sale of blueprint copying machines. In early 1937 the Fourth Department's latest covert commercial venture was duly registered as 'M. Clausen, Shokai'.

Meanwhile Ozaki was busy penetrating ever deeper into the heart of the Japanese establishment. In August he sailed with a top-level Japanese delegation to California for the sixth annual conference of the Institute of Pacific Relations. Founded in 1925 by American philanthropists, the institute was a regional discussion forum in the spirit of the League of Nations that attracted some of the most senior figures in Japanese and American diplomacy. The theme for the 1936 meeting, naturally enough for the turbulent times, was Japan–China relations. Ozaki had been invited as a leading China expert.

On board the liner *Taiyo Maru* were two old acquaintances. One was Prince Kinkazu Saionji, the Oxford-educated adopted grandson of the liberal constitutionalist Prince Kimmochi Saionji, one of Japan's most distinguished elder statesmen.[67] The younger Saionji would later become a passionate socialist. But in 1936 he was a rising statesman who enjoyed the patronage of his grandfather's friends, Prince Fumimaro Konoe, the future prime minister, and Yosuke Matsuoka, soon to become foreign minister. Ozaki knew Saionji slightly through the East Asia Problems Investigation Association. On board the ship they shared a state room and became firm friends.[68]

Ozaki's other friend was a school and university mate, Tomohiko Ushiba, who was now a secretary of the Japanese council of the Institute of Pacific Relations. The conference itself, held in a lodge in Yosemite National Park, turned out to be 'very aristocratic and also pedantic, and did not fit a heretic like me', Ozaki remarked. Ozaki observed at first hand how 'fastened to nationalistic consciousness' and 'narrow-minded' the Japanese were; he also noted that the 'British and Americans did not try to cover their arrogance as the rulers of the world'.[69] The main 'crop' of the conference, as Ozaki put it bluntly, was 'to promote my personal friendship with Japanese delegates'.[70] After the trip Saionji would become a daily visitor to Ozaki's offices and they would regularly dine at each other's homes. 'Saionji trusted me well, treated me as a bosom friend, and disclosed secret matters to me without any caution. Thus, as his political position rose, I was able to obtain important information from him,' confessed Ozaki.[71]

Ozaki penned a widely read report on the conference entitled 'Recent Developments in Sino-Japanese Relations'. It was an apologia for Japan's imperialistic adventures in China, emphasising Japan's status as a great power and calling for China to recognise Manchukuo. The report was also statement of Ozaki's outward political orthodoxy. Its spirit was not entirely cynical, however; nor was it that far from Moscow's own party line. The USSR had no desire to see a resurgent Nationalist China on its borders. And while Japan was busy cannibalising its neighbour it would have no time to attack the Soviet Union. By cheering on Japanese expansion southwards into China, Ozaki (and later, Sorge) were distracting Tokyo's militarists from the temptation to strike northwards into the USSR.

In September 1936, just as Ozaki was returning from California, Aino Kuusinen reappeared in Tokyo. She had been urgently recalled to Moscow the previous November – doubtless to the relief of Sorge, who saw this Comintern princess with no obvious job or usefulness as a security risk for his hard-working spy ring. On arrival in Moscow, Aino had made an appointment to see General Uritsky only to be told that her recall had been a mistake, and that she should return to Tokyo forthwith. She refused. Aino could afford such caprices, at least as long as her ex-husband still ruled the Comintern. Instead of returning she set to writing a book entitled *Smiling Japan*, a vapid account of the country's history and culture, penned with the sole purpose of ingratiating herself with her new friends in Tokyo.

Amid the general confusion she found at the Fourth Department, Aino heard some disturbing criticism of Sorge's new *rezidentura*. Uritsky warned Aino to stay away from Sorge and expressed irritation that he had requested so much money to set Clausen up in business. 'Those rascals – all they do is drink and spend money,' Uritsky had told Aino – which she reported to Sorge when she eventually deigned to return to Japan. 'They won't get one kopek.'[72]

Sorge mentioned nothing of Centre's odd – and frankly inexplicable – ingratitude in his confessions or prison memoir. But he could only have been deeply hurt. In Tokyo and Berlin, Ott and General Thomas appreciated him as an exceptionally perceptive observer of Japanese affairs. However Moscow, which had learned the deepest secrets of the unfolding alliance between Germany and Japan and had an ear, via Ozaki, to the topmost echelons of Japanese politics, scorned him. Worse, Aino brought news of various old Comintern comrades who had been imprisoned in a gathering purge of foreign cadres, including her own brother.

At least Aino – known to the Fourth Department as Agent 'Ingrid' – was well launched on her quixotic mission to penetrate Japanese high society. The Foreign Ministry arranged for *Smiling Japan* to be translated into Japanese (from the original Swedish) and the Swedish ambassador took her to a garden party at the Imperial Palace, where she met Emperor Hirohito. Aino also struck up a cordial relationship with Prince Chichibu, the emperor's brother, and found him surprisingly liberal in his views.

Aino's report from Moscow was not the only ominous news to reach Sorge that monsoon season, his third in Tokyo. In Nuremberg in September 1936, Hitler treated a rally of the Party Congress of the Workers' Front to what Dirksen described as a 'terrific diatribe against Bolshevism', an ominous sign of his implacable hatred for Soviet Russia.[73]

Worse was to come. On 25 November 1936, Japan and Germany officially announced the culmination of the talks that Sorge had caught early wind of back in March – an official Anti-Comintern Pact.[74] Superficially the five-year pact was relatively innocuous, committing the signatories to exchange information on Comintern activities and to 'take drastic steps within the bounds of existing law, in dealing with persons who, at home or abroad, directly or indirectly, are serving with the Communist International or foster its destructive activity'.[75]

The sting was in the pact's secret annexes, which Dirksen (now back from Berlin) sent to Ott, who shared them with Sorge. In the event of an 'unprovoked attack or unprovoked threat of attack' by the Soviet Union, each party would act 'to preserve their common interests'. It was not a full military alliance, and Dirksen in his official report to Berlin – which Sorge photographed – believed that the Japanese government was too divided ever to take decisive action against the Soviet Union. Nonetheless, any kind of deal between the USSR's most powerful and volatile enemies to the west and east was the sum of all Moscow's fears.

Sorge's information rang around the Kremlin and down the chains of command – even coming back to Tokyo, where the Soviet ambassador to Japan, Konstantin Yurenev, told his US counterpart Ambassador Grew that 'his Government possessed definite evidence that a secret military pact existed'.[76] The effort to avoid a two-front war with Germany and Japan became the basic motive of every Russian diplomatic action from the last months of 1936 almost until the end of the Second World War.

Sorge had good reason to feel pleased with his work. 'I hope that soon you will have the opportunity to rejoice for me and even to be proud and convinced that "yours" is quite a useful fellow,'[77] he wrote to Katya. But if Sorge thought that his outstanding work in Tokyo was being gratefully received in Moscow, he was quite wrong. In late November he summoned Aino to come and see him urgently. She found him at home, alone and dead drunk with a nearly empty bottle of whisky. 'We have all been ordered back to Moscow, including me,' he informed Aino. 'Immediately, via Vladivostok.' Sorge had already made his decision to refuse Uritsky's order. 'Pass a message to our chiefs about the excellent contacts we have made. I will not return before next April at the earliest.'

Aino, despite her forebodings of why Centre should have suddenly recalled all its agents, had no such excuse and agreed to return. She tried to persuade Sorge to do the same, to avoid the wrath of the Fourth Department. Again he refused. 'My judgement', he said, 'is better than yours.'[78]

Bloodbath in Moscow

'In the atheists' paradise, their souls, like Sorge's, may survive in peace'[1]

John le Carré

Sorge was right: his decision to defy Centre probably saved his life. Aino returned, and within a year found herself in the Gulag, along with thousands of other loyal Comintern comrades. Stalin had finally set in motion the machinery of terror that he had spent years putting in place. By the end of 1938 the Soviet secret police (by 1937 known as the NKVD, or People's Commissariat for Internal Affairs) painstakingly recorded the arrest of 1,548,366 citizens – many of them party members – on charges of counter-revolutionary activity and sabotage. Of those, 681,692 were shot.[2] Stalin's Great Purge would decimate the party and consume almost the entire Fourth Department apparat. Of the Comintern's 492 staff, 133 were imprisoned or executed. Three of five Soviet marshals, 90 per cent of all Red Army generals, 80 per cent of Red Army colonels and 30,000 officers of lesser rank were arrested.[3]

Was it the good judgement that Sorge blithely ascribed to himself that saved his skin – or was it intuition, or even his usual fiendish good luck? By the time he and Aino spoke in Tokyo in November 1936, there were clear signs that a major bloodbath was under way – the purge that Virtanen had warned Sorge about during their drunken dinner at the National Hotel in Moscow the previous year. In August 1936, Grigory Zinoviev and Lev Kamenev, two of the most prominent former party leaders to have opposed Stalin's rise, were publicly tried alongside sixteen other old Bolsheviks. After confessing to plotting to murder Sergei Kirov and Stalin himself, all the defendants were immediately executed.[4] By 11 October, when the Politburo voted to replace NKVD commissar Genrikh Yagoda with Stalin's loyal lackey Nikolai Yezhov, the Purge was ready to move down the social scale to the rank-and-file of the party.

Yezhov had made his name by personally orchestrating the show trial of Kamenev and Zinoviev – 'working all the time, not taking any leave, and, it seems, not even getting ill', as his then-boss Yagoda recalled. With these scalps in the bag, the ambitious Yezhov turned his attention to 'restructuring of the work of the NKVD itself' where he divined 'in the leadership moods of complacency, calmness, and bragging … they now only dream about decorations'.[5] Once Yezhov was finally rewarded for his zeal with the NKVD's top job he set to his great work of cleansing the party, the army, and the foreign intelligence apparat of spies and traitors.

Yezhov came to power with a detailed plan in place to eliminate 'agents of foreign intelligence services, disguised as political emigres and members of sister parties' who had allegedly penetrated the Russian Communist Party. Yezhov's report 'On Measures to Protect the USSR Against the Penetration of Spy, Terrorist, and Sabotage Elements' was accepted by the Central Committee in February 1936. He appointed a commission headed by the new head of the Comintern's OMS, Mikhail Moskvin, to draw up detailed lists of suspect foreigners associated with the Comintern, International Red Aid, or the Red Trade Union International. Moskvin was not who he seemed. In reality he was named Mikhail Trilisser, and his true job was chief of the Foreign Department of the NKVD. He had been installed in the Comintern under his new alias in August 1935 specifically to root out traitors.

Trilisser found plenty. By 23 August he presented the NKVD with a list of 3,000 comrades who were 'under suspicion of being saboteurs, spies, agents provocateur, etc.'. Several hundred German communists who had fled from Nazi Germany or been actively invited – as Sorge had been – to work in Moscow were liquidated. More than a thousand more were handed over to the Nazi authorities in Germany.[6] The leaders of the Indian, Korean, Mexican, Iranian, Mongolian and Turkish communist parties were executed – including Agnes Smedley's former lover, Virendranath Chattopadhyaya.[7]

Sorge's old Comintern comrade Leopold Trepper recalled terrifying nights waiting for arrest. 'In the house where the party activists of all the countries were living no one slept until 3 o'clock in the morning ... At exactly 3 o'clock the car headlights began to appear ... we stayed near the window and waited [to find out] where the car would stop.'[8]

The Red Army, to Stalin and Yezhov's paranoid minds, had been thoroughly contaminated by its decade-long secret cooperation pact with Germany. Between 1924 and 1933 many senior Red Army officers had had close contact with their German counterparts – including with Eugen Ott in his former role as liaison to the Sondergruppe R. Hundreds had participated in military exchanges. Many had even been admitted as senior students into the German Military Academy in Berlin, where the German and Soviet officers had jointly developed sophisticated operational thinking about how to storm the defences of their common enemy, Poland. Indeed the very concept of blitzkrieg, or lightning war, had been hatched during secret German Army manoeuvres on the plains of Belorussia, with Soviet advice.[9]

Almost every Soviet officer who had ever visited Germany or worked with the Reichswehr was murdered in the purges. Among them was the Red Army's most senior officer, Marshal Mikhail Tukhachevsky, who was arrested in May 1937 and charged with creating a 'right-wing Trotskyist' military conspiracy and espionage for Nazi Germany. The Germans were all too happy to participate in the destruction of their former colleagues. The NKVD, tasked with concocting information on a plot by Tukhachevsky and the other Soviet generals against Stalin, contacted Reinhard Heydrich, the chief of German intelligence (Sicherheitsdienst, or SD), with a request for more information.[10] Heydrich, seeing an excellent opportunity to dupe Stalin into executing his best generals, forged documents implicating Tukhachevsky and other Red Army commanders that he passed back to the Soviets via the Czech leader Edvard Beneš. In his quest to destroy all his potential enemies and rivals in the Soviet General Staff, Stalin was ready to enlist the help of the Nazis – who were only too happy to help him destroy the best of the USSR's officer corps.

Stalin was similarly convinced that Soviet intelligence was thoroughly riddled with 'wreckers, saboteurs, Trotskyist-fascist spies and murderers who infiltrated all our echelons of power'. On a personal visit to the headquarters of the Fourth Department in May 1937, Stalin claimed that 'the whole Directorate has fallen into German hands'.[11]

Richard Sorge, whether he knew it or not, was now in every possible kind of danger. He was a German in the Soviet secret service. He had been a Comintern member and was close to many top leaders who were now under arrest or under deep suspicion. He was a Red Army officer, many of whose superiors were tainted with ties to Germany. He was an intelligence agent who had spent many unsupervised years overseas.

Clearly, Sorge sensed danger when the general recall of all Fourth Department agents all over the world was ordered by Yezhov in November 1936. But it is also likely that when Sorge promised that he would return to Moscow by April 1937, he probably meant it. His only personal contact with Centre was through other Fourth Department agents, like Aino Kuusinen. In Tokyo he avoided contact with any Russians, especially with Soviet diplomats – who were in any case unaware of his true identity. News of the purges would have come obliquely, through the dispatches of Western correspondents such as the *New York Times*'s Walter Duranty (who famously wrote in his Pulitzer Prize-winning coverage of the Great Famine of 1931–32 that 'you can't make an omelette without breaking eggs'). Centre's radiograms contained only the driest summaries of personnel changes at Fourth Department HQ, and gave no sense of the rising panic as the department was decimated by the NKVD.

In a sense, Sorge was protected by his ignorance and isolation. Other agents in Europe who had a closer understanding of the death trap into which they were heading ran for their lives. 'Suddenly, revolutionists with a lifetime of devoted activity would pop out, like rabbits from a burrow, with the [NKVD] close on their heels,' recalled American communist spy Whittaker Chambers in his 1952 memoir. Veteran agent Alexander Barmine fled from the Soviet legation in Athens, Fyodor Raskolnikoff from the Soviet legation in Sofia, Walter Krivitsky from Amsterdam, Ignace Reiss from his station in Switzerland. Reiss – aka Ignace Poretsky, Sorge's old acquaintance from Moscow – sent a defiant letter of resignation personally to Stalin. 'Murderer of the Kremlin cellars! I herewith return my decorations and resume my freedom of action,' Reiss wrote before going underground.[12]

Almost all the defectors were hunted down and killed by NKVD assassination squads, some of them after years on the run. Yezhov would spend over 300,000 French francs on such *mokriye dela*, or 'wet operations', the NKVD slang for murder.[13] Only Barmine succeeded in outrunning the NKVD hunters, escaping to the United States and enrolling in the US Office of Strategic Services, forerunner of the CIA.[14]

The spies who obeyed Uritsky's recall were equally doomed. Theodore Maly, the former priest who recruited Kim Philby and the rest of the Cambridge Five spies as idealistic young students in the early 1930s, was among the star agents who returned and were shot. Sorge's own survival came down to the fact that he had neither returned to Moscow nor run. But just as Sorge was unaware of just how close he had come to danger, so he also could not know that his refusal to travel to Moscow in 1937 had stained his reputation with the Fourth Department for ever.

Colonel Boris Ignatyevich Gudz was on the Japan desk of the Fourth Department as the Purge broke over the department. 'We were busy with concrete cases concerning the security of our country, but in the next door building [the NKVD] was busy fabricating cases,' Gudz told Russian television in 1999. 'We called them *lipochi* ['little nonsenses'], but they presented these nonsenses to their bosses to show their successes ... Many of my chiefs protested, including my own superior, the head of counter-intelligence Olsky. But he was quickly fired and sent to work in the State Restaurant Directorate. They were all later shot.'[15]

Gudz, an ethnic German born in Ufa in 1902, had spent 1934–36 as a spy in Tokyo working in the NKVD's own *rezidentura* under official cover as Third Secretary of the Soviet embassy. Though they lived in the same city Gudz had no idea of Sorge's existence, in part because of the institutional rivalry (that continues today) between Russia's civilian and military intelligence services, but mostly because the Fourth Department kept Sorge's identity a closely guarded secret. On his return to Moscow in the summer of 1936, Gudz found his bosses more preoccupied with the hunt for traitors than with his reports from Tokyo. 'I was met coolly. The years of repression had begun, and search was on for enemies of the people,' Gudz recalled. 'My boss didn't even want to hear my report on my residency and sent me on holiday.'[16]

It was only when Gudz was transferred to the Fourth Department's Second (Far Eastern) Department in 1937 that he began to read Sorge's telegrams. 'Immediately on seeing his file and his reports I understood the enormous value of this spy,' Gudz said. 'Everything about him was of the highest class. He was a wonderful, gregarious journalist, an experienced political analyst and – very important for a spy – an excellent actor. And this despite the fact that he had never undergone any specialist training as an intelligence officer. Sorge had access to unique information. It was our job to supply Sorge with information and instructions based on thorough, detailed investigation of his operations ... But Sorge mostly acted on his own initiative, often taking huge risks.'[17]

But despite Sorge's obviously excellent work, there was a problem. Sorge was, in Gudz's words, a *'nevozvrashenets'* – literally, a 'non-returned person' – and therefore inherently unreliable. 'Sorge was a great spy,' Gudz recalled. But after 1937 Agent Ramsay would never again be fully trusted.

'It wasn't just him that Stalin distrusted. Once I entered Uritsky's study when he was reading a report on preparations for war in Berlin. [Uritsky] repeated several times – "How can I go in and tell [Stalin] this when he believes in nothing?"'[18]

Gudz would play his own odious role in the Great Terror. In late 1936 he wrote a secret denunciation of his sister Galina's husband, the journalist and short-story writer Varlam Shalamov, for supposed anti-Soviet attitudes.[19] Shalamov had already been imprisoned once for protesting against Stalin in 1929 – and had in fact met his future wife, also a political prisoner, in the Vishera camp in the North Urals. On the night of 12 January 1937 the NKVD came for Shalamov at the communal apartment they shared with Gudz at Chisty Lane 8 in central Moscow. His harrowing memoir of his years in prison camps, *Kolyma Tales*, published in the West in 1966, became a classic of Gulag literature. But the denunciation did not save Gudz or his family. In May 1937, Gudz's other sister Alexandra was arrested (she would die in 1945, in a bitter irony, in a Gulag on the Kolyma Peninsula, close to her imprisoned brother-in-law). Gudz himself was immediately fired from the Fourth Department and eventually found work as a bus driver. He was lucky. A colleague from his tour in Tokyo was arrested and confessed to working as a Japanese spy, naming Gudz as an accomplice. 'Every night I awaited arrest,' Gudz remembered. But the Purge had its own incomprehensible logic. Nobody came for him and he continued to live at Chisty Lane, in the apartment directly below this author's, until his death in 2006 at the age of 104.

Back in Tokyo, Sorge decided to take his mind off work – and the alarming news from Moscow – by taking Hanako on a short holiday.

He bought her a new suitcase for the occasion. They went to the Atami hot spring resort eighty kilometres south-west of Tokyo, a Western-style hotel 'famous for steaks and geishas'.[20] They took a train that wound up a steep and wooden valley, through Hakone and up towards Mount Fuji. It was December, and natural hot springs steamed in the cold. 'Sorge took a very long bath,' Hanako recalled. 'We had dinner in the room, drank hot sake, and went to bed. He was very passionate, but gentle, not like a wild animal bearing its teeth. That wasn't Sorge's way.'[21]

The following day it was raining. Sorge spent most of the day typing on his portable typewriter, while Hanako 'looked out at the rain tap-tapping on the window pane'.[22] After a while she got bored and began to compose a poem. Sorge joined her in bed. 'Miyago, do you want to study?' he asked in Japanese, using the name that had begun as a mistake and become a pet name. 'Sorge will help you study.' She replied that she wanted to study opera and that she dreamed of becoming a professional singer. 'Sorge knows a German music teacher ... I will take you to him immediately. Does that make you happy?' True to his word, on their return to the city Sorge arranged piano lessons for Hanako with his friend, Dr August Junker of the Musashino Music College. 'What a fine character he had,' Hanako told an interviewer in the 1980s. 'When Sorge made a promise, he always kept it!'[23]

Katya, of course, had a different experience of Sorge's promise-keeping. He continued to assure his wife that he would soon return, and at this stage he almost certainly believed it. 'I hope sincerely that this will be our last year apart and we will meet the next one together and forget about our long parting,' he wrote to Katya on 1 January 1937. 'Here it is twenty degrees – and where you are it's probably twenty degrees of frost. But I would prefer to live in the cold with you.'[24] He confirmed that he had just received letters from Katya (and from her friend Vera) from August and October – a five-month time lag that would account for the delay in discovering Katya's pregnancy, and its sad end.

Early in 1937 Katya moved out of her basement on Nizhny Kislovsky lane into a large room on the fourth floor of an apartment building on the Sofiiskaya Embankment,[25] next to the British embassy and directly opposite the Kremlin. The view from the window 'is so big you couldn't walk around it in a year', Katya wrote in delight. She assured Sorge that she had taken his entire bookshelf of German books with her. 'Often I try to imagine it,' Sorge wrote of the apartment that was intended to be their future marital home. 'But I cannot.'[26]

Katya concentrated some of the affection that she could not lavish on her absent husband on a new female work colleague, Marfa Ivanovna Lezhnina-Sokolova. She had come from a village near Vyatka and was assigned to Katya's brigade at the factory. The young woman was so unused to life in the big city that she even thanked the speak-the-time machine in the metro.[27] Katya took the new arrival under her wing and began giving her lessons in reading and writing. Soon Marfa moved into a corner of Katya's apartment.

Katya told her that the young woman's company 'made her happier and younger'. They would go to the cinema on Pyatnitskaya Street together, and when summer came go swimming on Sundays at the river beach at Serebryanny Bor to the west of the city. When Marfa admired a stuffed tiger toy that Sorge had given Katya she immediately made a gift of it. Marfa remembered that they would read books together in the mornings and become so absorbed that they would be late for work, running for the tram stop across the bridge and sometimes taking a taxi. In the car Katya would give her young protégée biscuits and sandwiches to make up for her missed breakfast. Katya Maximova 'made me a person', Marfa said in a 1965 interview. 'She helped me to learn my profession and gave me a passion for books for life. She gave me all her soul.'[28]

Sorge had promised Uritsky that he would come to Moscow by April 1937. But by that time details of the gathering pace of the Purge had reached even distant Tokyo. He would have to further delay his return, Sorge wrote to Katya in spring 1937, due to the 'unhealthy atmosphere in Moscow'.[29] A second show trial in January 1937 had another Comintern founder, Karl Radek, as its sacrificial victim, along with seventeen others. Ominously, in his public confession on the defendants' stand Radek had spoken of a secret 'third rightist-Trotskyite organisation' of enormous size that was devoted to organising a 'Fronde [armed uprising] against the Party'.[30] The hunt for the adherents of this mysterious secret conspiracy would be Yezhov's carte blanche for expanding the Purge still further.

Meanwhile Aino Kuusinen was discovering just how serious a mistake she had made in obeying Uritsky's summons. She found the director in the same irascible mood that she had left him in the previous year. The general again railed against Sorge's 'inadequate' work and his free spending of the Fourth Department's money. Most of all, he was furious at having been defied. Uritsky tried several times to get Aino to write letters to Sorge persuading him to return, claiming that Sorge had disobeyed orders and that Stalin himself had personally ordered him back to the USSR. Aino, logically enough, responded that if Sorge did not listen to Stalin it would be unlikely that he would heed her.

The bullying ceased only in July 1937, when Uritsky was fired. He was replaced by his former boss Jan Berzin, just back from directing Soviet efforts to help the Republican side in the Spanish Civil War. In a month Berzin himself was gone, to be replaced by another chief who lasted only a fortnight. By the end of the year both Uritsky and Berzin would be arrested, tried for spying for the Germans and Japanese, and eventually shot. In all, Soviet military intelligence had six different heads between 1937 and 1939, five of whom would be executed.[31] Aino was herself arrested in early 1938 and spent fifteen years in the Gulag and internal exile.

Unbeknown to Sorge, Uritsky's ongoing irritation at the Tokyo *rezidentura*'s expense claims and the *rezident*'s failure to return to Moscow when summoned had unleashed the full paranoia of the Purge against Agent Ramsay and all his works. The Japanese department of the Fourth Department split into two factions: those who trusted Sorge, and those who did not. General Alexander Nikonov, the Fourth Department chief who reigned for a single fortnight in August 1937, commissioned a report into the possibility of liquidating the Ramsay group altogether.

In the event Nikonov's successor, General Semyon Gendin, para-chuted in from the NKVD to take over the wreckage of the Fourth Department, found enough of value in Sorge's reports to argue that he should stay *en poste*. But Gendin, while saving the Tokyo operation, also fatally labelled Sorge and his team 'politically inadequate' and 'probably penetrated by the enemy and working under his control'.[32] The Tokyo reports that Gendin forwarded to Stalin from September 1937 until his own arrest on 22 October 1938 were prefaced by deep scepticism. 'To: Central Committee, Comrade Stalin, Top Secret', reads one of Gendin's memoranda. 'I present the report of our source close to German circles in Tokyo. This source does not enjoy our full trust, however some of his material deserves attention.' It was a stain on Sorge's reputation that would have profound implications for the future.[33]

Plenty of once-idealistic foreign communists like Sorge lost their faith as a result of the bloodbath of 1937. 'Millions were massacred, including those communists who made the Russian revolution,' wrote the Soviet spy Whittaker Chambers who, like Sorge, had defied orders to return to Moscow. Chambers rejected communism in April 1938 in disgust at Stalin's crimes. He listed the reasons for his profound disillusionment as: the deliberate mass murder of peasants in Ukraine and Kuban during collectivisation; the deliberate betrayal of the German working class by the communists, who refused on Moscow's orders to cooperate with the Social Democrats to resist the rise of the Nazis; and the betrayal of the Spanish Republican government by the USSR, whose agents were more focussed on massacring their political enemies than helping them win their struggle against fascism. He might have added the ugly fact – of which Sorge was certainly aware – that Stalin's hatred of moderate socialists was so intense that he had ordered the German Communist Party to vote with the Nazis in the Reichstag to defeat the Social Democrats. 'The gigantic ulcer of corruption and deceit had burst,' Chambers wrote. 'Stalin had consolidated his power by massacring thousands of the best men and minds in the Communist Party on invented charges.'[34]

Did Sorge suffer a similar crisis of faith? It is likely that he did. Sorge had already confessed his disillusionment to Niilo Virtanen in 1935. But, trapped in Tokyo, he had no one in whom he could confide his doubts. The Japanese members of the spy ring looked to Sorge as a boss, a pillar of calm, self-assured resolution. Clausen, who was probably the closest Sorge had to a true confidant in Tokyo, also needed his leadership and encouragement. Hanako did not even know he was a communist in the first place. And his confessions and prison memoir were no place to admit to doubts, as Sorge was hoping until the very end that the Soviet Union would save him.

There are clear signs that Sorge began to go off the rails as a result of the strain. He had always drunk heavily. But as 1937 progressed his bottle-mates Wenneker and Prince Urach noticed a marked increase in his already epic consumption. On his debauched progresses through the bars and dance halls of Ginza, Sorge passed through 'exultation, tearful misery, aggressiveness, paranoia and megalomania, delirium, stupor and the grey solitude of the hangover that can only be relieved by more alcohol', Urach remembered.[35] When Weise of the German News Agency asked Sorge to stand in for him during a vacation, he returned to discover that Sorge had been drunk most of the time he was in charge.[36]

Meanwhile Ozaki and Miyagi continued diligently with their work, apparently oblivious to the dramas unfolding in Moscow and in their boss's own heart and mind. The ever-helpful engineering firm owner Shinotsuka handed Ozaki a list of all the major arms manufacturers in and around Tokyo as well as a copy of the army's latest pamphlet on *Principles of National Defence*. Miyagi was busy recruiting more helpers, mostly from among the ranks of known communist sympathisers. One was Kuzumi Fusako, the ex-wife of a Christian minister who had spent five years in jail for her communist beliefs after a wholesale round-up in 1929. Miyagi enlisted Kuzumi for her extensive contacts in leftist circles. Another helper signed up by Miyagi was his personal doctor, Tokutarō Yasuda. Dr Yasuda had a fashionable medical practice with many prominent patients – and as a celebrated anthropologist and historian was also well connected in Tokyo's intellectual circles. Miyagi suggested that the doctor could help 'disrupt the plans to destroy the USSR, to prevent a Japanese-Soviet war'. Yasuda readily agreed to pass on any high-level gossip he heard in his consulting rooms.[37]

Miyagi's web expanded quickly through the less-than-secure network of Mrs Kuzumi's leftist prison friends. Yamana Masazano was an uneducated thirty-four-year-old romantic, recently released from jail where he had been imprisoned for his communist ties. Miyagi signed him up and sent him north to Hokkaido to count army camps and troop movements near the Japanese–Soviet border in southern Sakhalin island (known as Karafuto to the Japanese). Former university professor Ugenda Taguchi had also done prison time for his leftism, and agreed to help Miyagi on economic information from Hokkaido and Manchuria. Another helper was Takashi Hashimoto, also a leftist recently returned from Manchuria, who helpfully told Miyagi that the Japanese military was secretly sending troops disguised as construction workers northward to Karafuto to build army camps.

For good measure, Miyagi also recruited rightists by hinting – as the still-imprisoned Kawai had done after his arrest – that he was linked to shadowy ultra-nationalist secret societies. In this way Miyagi roped in two right-wing journalists, Masahiko Sano and Hachiro Kikuchi, as informants with whom he also socialised for cover. But the most important of Miyagi's new contacts was was Yabe Shu, a secret leftist who worked as confidential secretary to General Ugaki Kazushige, a former Minister of Defence who briefly served as prime minister in early 1937.[38]

Less than two years after arriving in Tokyo, Miyagi, the dishevelled artist with the winning smile and disarmingly frank manner, had proved himself a recruiter and agent-runner of exceptional talent – if not always with perfect judgement. By the middle of 1937 Miyagi controlled a network of friends, paid agents, collaborators and unwitting dupes that stretched from his native Okinawa in the south to Hokkaido in the north. Unlike the overpowering Sorge, whose booze-fuelled charm steamrollered people into either loving or hating him, Miyagi managed to fit quietly into any company, from high-society hostesses whom he met on the Ginza art gallery circuit to semi-educated fishermen from Hokkaido. He could hang out at low bars and engage strangers in easy conversation. Indeed Miyagi complained to his boss about the amount of time he had to spend drinking with casual acquaintances – not a part of the job that bothered Sorge himself.[39] Sorge described Miyagi as 'a very simple, good-natured man' who looked 'very naive and kind'.[40]

Miyagi's *naïveté* may have been the secret to his charm. But it was also extraordinarily dangerous to associate with former communists, let alone recruit so profligately from their ranks. There is no evidence that Sorge ever objected to Miyagi's working with known communists – but Gudz, in Moscow, certainly did. By his own account, Gudz considered that sending Miyagi to work with Sorge was General Berzin's 'major mistake ... How could one work with communists? They were everywhere under surveillance abroad,' Gudz told Russian television in 1999. 'It was Berzin's idea to take a Japanese artist from a normal environment in the United States and send him to liaise with Sorge. But Sorge did not realise that he must not associate so often and so openly with a communist.'[41] But again there is no evidence that Gudz, or anyone else in the Fourth Department, warned Sorge and Miyagi to fish for informers in less risky waters.

While Miyagi was busy gathering agents for his ring, a new crisis in China would bring Ozaki even closer to the top councils of power in Japan. On 12 December 1936, Generalissimo Chiang Kai-shek, head of the Kuomintang Party and leader of Nationalist China, was arrested by his ally and subordinate Marshal Zhang Xueliang. 'Young Marshal' Xueliang – the former warlord of Manchuria and now commander of China's North Eastern Army – was frustrated by Chiang's refusal to fight the Japanese. Instead of resisting the Japanese expansion into Manchuria and Inner Mongolia, Chiang Kai-shek had continued to spend men and resources fighting the Chinese communists, on the principle that the Japanese were 'a disease of the skin, the communists a disease of the heart'. Xueliang, who had attempted to resist the Japanese, had been ordered to retreat.[42]

Now it was time for Xueliang's revenge. He kept Chiang Kai-shek and his staff prisoner for two weeks at the regional military command headquarters at Xi'an. By 25 December, the generalissimo had been persuaded to change his mind and sign a truce with the communists, allowing a united front against the Japanese. The reversal of Chiang Kai-shek's policy of appeasement of the Japanese invaders set the stage for full-scale war between China and Japan.[43]

The Soviet Union's role in the Xi'an incident was deeply controversial (and would later serve as a major bone of contention between the ultimately victorious Chinese communists and Moscow). Essentially, as Japan and Germany rearmed and became more aggressive, Stalin sought to improve relations with all nations who were also potentially threatened by their rise. Top of the list of potential Soviet allies, by this logic, were the United States and Nationalist China. In 1933 Moscow normalised its relations with Washington, and in the same year Stalin's foreign affairs commissar Maxim Litvinov encouraged America to sponsor a treaty of non-aggression between the US, the USSR, Japan and China.

Stalin was also acutely aware – in part thanks to the efforts of Sorge and the Shanghai *rezidentura* – that Nazi Germany was making strong overtures to Chiang Kai-shek in the form of vast sales of military hardware and military advisers. A pro-Nazi China would leave the Japanese a free hand to attack the USSR. Therefore, from the mid-1930s Stalin had supported a united front with Chiang Kai-shek against the Japanese.

An open alliance with the Chinese nationalists would have left the USSR's ideological allies, the Chinese communists, out in the cold. Stalin solved the problem in characteristic fashion by playing a double game. The USSR promised Communist Party leader Mao Zedong weapons and encouraged him to set up his own Soviet state in Shaanxi province that might also be a buffer against Japanese aggression. But at the same time Stalin was also making overtures to Chiang Kai-shek, attempting to nudge him towards war against Japan – but without involving the USSR. Simultaneously, the Comintern was working on persuading Marshal Xueliang to drop his own hostility towards Mao, sending a senior Moscow-trained Chinese comrade[44] to negotiate with the marshal and encourage him to make a move against the arch-appeaser of the Japanese, Chiang Kai-shek.

The Xi'an incident was in many ways a triumph of Stalin's diplomacy. Indeed Chiang Kai-shek's advisers at the time clearly blamed the Comintern for Xueliang's mutiny and the generalissimo's temporary imprisonment.[45] Stalin had successfully forced China's nationalists and communists to bury their differences and unite against their common enemy – Japan. In order to concentrate on fighting the Japanese, though, Chiang Kai-shek needed an assurance from his Soviet friends that Mao's communists would not stab them in the back – a trade that Stalin was more than happy to offer on Mao's behalf. The USSR quickly abandoned its two-track policy and abruptly ordered Mao to abandon his dream of a separate communist state and work with the nationalists. Mao's fury over this betrayal was witnessed by American journalist Edgar Snow, who spent much time with 'the Chairman' during this period.[46] But for Stalin, Mao's ambitions and even the triumph of communism in the Far East were secondary to the importance of uniting China against the Japanese.

In Tokyo, Ozaki penned another influential article on the incident, 'The Significance of Chang Hsueh-liang's [Xueliang's] Coup d'Etat', correctly predicting a truce between the communists and Nationalists against the Japanese. His editor was so impressed that he recommended Ozaki for membership of a rising new think tank – the Showa Kenkyu Kai (Showa Research Association) – that would soon become a kind of shadow cabinet for a would-be premier, Prince Fumimaro Konoe.[47] Konoe was an impeccably educated aristocrat who enjoyed the respect of both civilian moderates and the military – thanks in large part to his refusal to condemn the army's unsanctioned adventures in Manchuria. The British ambassador to Japan, Sir Robert Craigie, found him exasperatingly hard to pin down on any topic – a slipperiness that would be Konoe's strongest political asset. Craigie called him 'the dilettante Konoe, who, surrounded by the young men of his "brains trust", delighted to toy with dangerous political experiments' such as appeasing Japan's radical nationalists.[48] Ozaki's companions in the brains trust were such luminaries as the editor-in-chief of the Domei News Agency, Japan's leading labour lawyers, political philosophers and economists.

In June 1937, Prince Konoe became prime minister. From his ringside seat at the Showa Association, Ozaki was able to report to Sorge that Konoe's appointment was 'the last trump card of the upper class in Japan' who hoped that their man would check the 'political pressure of the army'. But Ozaki was under no illusions. The military welcomed Konoe as a useful puppet who would allow them to 'bring about the aggressive national policy they had always wanted'.[49]

Ozaki was right. In July 1937, Japanese forces clashed with Chinese troops near Beijing at the Marco Polo Bridge. The pretext was tiny. After some unannounced night-time manoeuvres by the Japanese Army, one soldier – Private Kikujiro Shimura – failed to return to his post. His commanders demanded permission to enter the town of Wanping to search for the missing man. When the local Chinese commander refused, the Japanese began shelling.

In Tokyo, Konoe felt he had little choice but to dispatch three divisions of troops to defend Japanese honour. Japan coveted no Chinese territory, he told the diet (parliament) on 27 July, only 'cooperation and mutual assistance – a contribution from China to Far Eastern culture and prosperity'. Konoe also admonished the military to be sure not to escalate the conflict. He was roundly ignored. By mid-August Japan's Imperial General Staff – now without any civilian oversight – launched a general assault that would by December 1937 bring them to the gates of the Chinese Nationalist capital of Nanking.[50] Though none of the principals yet realised it, the skirmish at the Marco Polo Bridge would mark the beginning of the Second World War in Asia.

12

Lyushkov

'The mechanism at work seems to have been much the same for both [Kim Philby and Richard Sorge]: beginning by finding that alcohol is instant friendship, and a bar the ideal place to elicit information – and discovering, as many a drunkard has, that booze offers a respite from nagging fear – the two spies went on to court attention by their conduct, thinking no one would guess that ostentation is a kind of camouflage'[1]

Murray Sayle

At two o'clock in the morning of Saturday, 14 May 1938, Papa Keitel closed up the Das Rheingold bar and turned Sorge and his friend Prince Urach out into the Ginza night. Urach was staying at the Imperial Hotel. He was drunk enough to accept Sorge's terrifying offer of a lift home. Soviet spy and German prince mounted Sorge's powerful black motorcycle and zoomed across town. The Imperial's bar was already closed, but Sorge knew an Austrian businessman who had invited him to help himself to the private bar in his room, whether he was in or not. Urach resisted his friend's pleas to join him and went to bed, leaving Sorge to raid the Austrian's room on his own. Alone, Sorge polished off a bottle of whisky, then returned to Urach's room to attempt to persuade him to come home to Nagasaki Street for yet more drinking. Again, Urach wisely declined.

Sorge always drove at terrific speed, even when sober – as a thrilled Smedley and a petrified Clausen testified. The motorcycle he drove was one of the heaviest and most powerful models available, a 1934 Zündapp flat-twin K500 that he had bought from Clausen two years before. The 498cc monster weighed 180 kilos and had a top speed of 120 kilometres per hour. Sorge, now drunk and alone, accelerated his roaring machine toward Toranomon and turned left down a narrow dirt road that skirted the US embassy. Just past the embassy grounds he lost control and ran the motorcycle full tilt into a stone wall.[2] A policeman on duty at the gate heard the crash and hurried to help. 'Here, here!' Sorge called out. Through a shattered jaw he managed to ask the policeman to telephone Urach at the Imperial.[3]

Urach was soon on the scene. The first thing Sorge asked him was to 'tell Clausen to come at once!'.[4] Doubtless Urach found it strange that Sorge would call on an apparent acquaintance rather than his girlfriend or someone from the German embassy, but he complied. By the time Clausen – and wife Anna – arrived at St Luke's American hospital they found Sorge barely conscious. His left arm had been sprained, and one of the handlebars had smashed into his teeth and jaw, fracturing his skull. Sorge whispered to Clausen to send out all the doctors and nurses, and once they were alone he managed one final sentence before passing out: 'Empty my pockets!'

In Sorge's bloodstained jacket Clausen found documents that could have cost them both their lives. There were several intelligence reports, written en clair in English ready for encoding, plus a large quantity of American dollars. Grabbing the compromising material, and Sorge's house keys, Clausen rushed to Nagasaki Street and frantically cleared Sorge's study of all suspicious-looking papers, including his chief's diary. Minutes after Clausen left, Weise of the DNB news agency arrived – probably after a call from Urach – to put Sorge's effects under seal in case the Japanese police were tempted to search the place and discover classified embassy information. Clausen spent the rest of the night terrified that the police would come knocking on the door of his house – which contained an antenna built into the wall and all his radio equipment – demanding to know why Sorge had summoned him to the hospital so urgently.[5]

Sorge's behaviour had been insanely irresponsible. The documents he carried in his pocket while driving drunk around Tokyo in the small hours of the morning would have cost him not only his own espionage career and his neck but also triggered a major manhunt that would have snared all his known associates – including his star agent Ozaki. More, the exposure of a communist espionage ring operating from inside the

German embassy and so close to the centre of the Japanese government would certainly have strengthened the hand of the militarists in the army who were lobbying to attack the USSR. Sorge's alcoholism and his addiction to danger had nearly destroyed the security of the Soviet Union that he claimed to be dedicated to preserving.

The risk was especially reckless given that Sorge had risen to a position of unprecedented trust in the German embassy. In the wake of the Marco Polo Bridge incident, Ambassador Dirksen had formed a 'study group' composed of Ott, Sorge and deputy military attaché Major Erwin Scholl to analyse the escalating war in China. Their focus was on gathering information on Japan's armed forces and their deployments. Sorge's official inclusion into the embassy's innermost circle – one that handled the most urgent and sensitive secrets – took his relationship with the German state to a new level. Ott could share all the private information he liked over breakfast or drinks with his personal friend, the journalist Sorge. But including Sorge in formal, classified meetings made him something very close to an official member of Germany's intelligence establishment.

Obviously Ott trusted Sorge and relied on the unusually well-sourced political information on Japan he provided. But to persuade Dirksen to approve Sorge's participation in the study group Ott would have had to cite more than personal trust. It seems that Dirksen accepted that Sorge was already some kind of German special agent (which had also been Third Secretary Meissner's assumption). The confidential reports Sorge was now regularly writing for General Thomas in Berlin would have given him such status.

Soon Sorge would be pulled even more deeply into the official orbit of German intelligence. Evidence of the high esteem in which Berlin held him emerged in 2015, when an employee at the Tamura Shoten antique book dealers in Tokyo's Jinbocho district discovered a personal letter from the newly appointed Nazi foreign minister, Joachim von Ribbentrop, to Sorge. The letter, dated May 1938, congratulated Sorge on his forty-second birthday (somewhat belatedly) and praised his 'outstanding contribution' to the work of the embassy in Tokyo. The letter came with a signed photograph of Ribbentrop. While there has never been any question that Sorge remained a devoted Soviet agent, the fact remains that from 1937 the Germans considered him almost as valuable an intelligence officer as the Russians did.

The German embassy study group received regular reports from naval attaché Captain Wenneker and air force attaché Lieutenant Colonel Nehmiz on everything they discovered from their Japanese counterparts. As a result, Sorge had access to detailed material on Japanese mobilisation plans, equipment and facilities, allocation of troops in Manchuria and China, battle techniques in China, logistics, aircraft, mechanisation, officer training, army casualties and the wartime economy of the nation. 'In addition, when a particularly important battle was fought in China, a detailed investigation and study were made of it and a report was sent to Germany' – and, by Sorge, to Moscow.[6]

The injuries Sorge sustained after his motorcycle accident left his already ravaged face looking, as he wrote to Katya, 'like a battered robber-knight'. As during his wartime hospitalisation in Königsberg, Sorge charmed the female staff at the American hospital. During a minor earthquake during a visit by Meissner, three nurses rushed to protect Sorge from falling plaster.[7] An infection set in that caused most of his teeth to fall out, and his new false ones fitted uncomfortably. The doctors at St Luke's also attempted some plastic surgery. But Sorge's face had become 'somewhat like a mask, demoniacal', remarked his friend Sieburg.[8] The accident also left psychological scars. Sorge 'has been subject to nervous disorders, the after-effects of a skull fracture in a motorcycle accident', Ott would report in 1941.[9]

The Otts generously took Sorge in after he was discharged from hospital. Helma Ott, the doubly rejected wife and mistress, nursed him at the ambassador's residence. She also seems to have attempted to rekindle her romance with Sorge, while her husband was away in Berlin having an audience with the Führer himself. 'Lavishing unwanted intimacy – she is good at that!' Sorge ungraciously told Hanako.[10] Sorge, the difficult patient, was laying incapacitated in the Otts' guest bed when the greatest challenge yet of his espionage career materialised from a wholly unexpected direction.

At around 5.30 on the morning of 13 June 1938, a two-man Manchukuo police patrol made out a suspicious figure lurking in the dawn fog along the frontier zone that divided the USSR from Manchuria near the Changlingtzu Heights, about 120 kilometres south-west of Vladivostok. The man wore a civilian mackintosh and tweed cap and was armed with two pistols. When the Japanese policemen challenged him the intruder threw down his weapons, put his hands up and began to speak rapidly in Russian. The man was 'stout, black haired, [and] black-eyed with a Charlie Chaplin moustache and a strongly Jewish cast of countenance'.[11] He seemed only too happy to be taken into custody at the Japanese border patrol headquarters, where he was jovial and talkative. Under his mac the man wore the full uniform and medals of a Soviet general officer, with boots and red-seamed cavalry breeches. But the defector was not a soldier. His identity card – signed by secret police chief Nikolai Yezhov himself – identified him as Genrikh Samuilovich Lyushkov, Commissar of State Security 3rd Class,* NKVD chief for the entire Soviet Far Eastern region.[12]

Among Lyushkov's personal effects were a Longines watch, Russian cigarettes, a pair of sunglasses; 4,153 yen in small bills issued by the banks of Japan, Korea and Manchukuo; 160 Soviet rubles; the Order of Lenin and two Orders of the Red Banner; and a photograph of his wife Ina. More importantly, he carried an empty typewriter case filled with a trove of classified military documents, including details of Soviet armed forces units, air bases, border posts, and military factories all over the Far East. Under the tightest possible security, the high-profile defector was spirited to the Manchukuo Security Bureau in Hsinking, then to Seoul and finally, after some wrangling between the Kwangtung Army and the Imperial General Staff, to Tokyo.[13]

Sorge heard of the defection of a senior NKVD general from the German embassy officials who visited his bedside in the ambassador's residence. The news must have chilled Sorge's blood. With the NKVD crawling all over the Fourth Department in Moscow, questioning its top leaders and probing its files, could Lyushkov have known about the Red Army's top spy network in Tokyo? Flight was not an option in his battered state. Sorge had no choice but to lie and wait, questioning his colleagues to glean any details he could.

Lyushkov was the most senior NKVD officer ever to flee Stalin's Russia. Until the moment of his defection, his career as a secret police-man had been meteoric. Born in Odessa in 1900 into the family of a Jewish tailor, Lyushkov had made a bloody name for himself fighting for the Bolshevik underground in Crimea during the civil war. He was promoted to brigade political commissar at the age of twenty. He

*The equivalent of a major general.

joined Dzerzhinsky's fledgling secret police in 1920, and worked for a while undercover in Germany. By 1934 Lyushkov was deputy head of the Secret Political Department of the NKVD in Leningrad, where he personally led the investigation into the assassination of Sergei Kirov – the senior Bolshevik those murder at the Smolny Institute in Leningrad had served as the pretext for Stalin to launch his terror. He confirmed to his Japanese interrogators that the charges implicating Kamenev, Zinoviev and dozens of others in the Kirov murder were fabricated – largely by Lyushkov himself.[14]

Yezhov had personally selected Lyushkov as one of his most trusted hatchet men. Another NKVD officer recounted a visit Lyushkov made to a colleague at the NKVD headquarters in Rostov-on-Don in 1937.[15] 'Armed with all the arrogance of his Moscow authority, [Lyushkov] marched into my friend's office, accused him of inefficiency and slackness and shouted, "Get marching, you son-of-a-bitch, and do something or I'll have you arrested!"' After berating the entire staff, Lyushkov pointed out a handful of 'traitors' who were immediately arrested and later shot.[16]

Lyushkov told his Japanese hosts that he had been experiencing doubts about the Soviet Union's 'deviations' from 'true Leninism' during his investigations into the Kirov murder. But the real reason for Lyushkov's flight in 1938 was clearly that he had caught wind that he would soon himself be consumed by the Great Purge. This was highly ironic, because Lyushkov had, by his own account, been personally sent by Stalin to Vladivostok with the express intention of directing a purge against the top party and military cadres of the Far Eastern Military District. He had personally orchestrated the execution of over five thousand supposed enemies of the people before realising that he would soon be next.

One of the most fascinating passages in Lyushkov's confessions to the Japanese is his account of a one-on-one interview with Stalin in the Kremlin in spring 1938 that gives a penetrating insight into the dictator's state of mind in that pre-war period. According to Lyushkov, Stalin accepted that war with Japan was inevitable and that the Far East would undoubtedly become a theatre of war. Lyushkov's mission was to purge the Far Eastern Army of all spies and pro-Japanese elements, particularly those linked to the recently executed Marshal Tukhachevsky. Stalin believed that a subversive group led by Far Eastern

NKVD commander Terenty Deribas and his deputies was planning to provoke a collision with Japan and, in agreement with Tokyo, to turn the troops against Stalin. 'The [Russian] Far East is not Soviet,' Stalin told Lyushkov. 'There, the Japanese rule.'[17]

Stalin also ordered Lyushkov to keep supreme commander in the Far East, Marshal Vasiliy Blyukher[18] – a civil war hero and one of the generals who had helped Stalin frame his colleague Marshal Tukhachevsky – under close observation. No objective evidence of the kind of pro-Japanese sympathy described by Stalin, let alone any plot, has ever surfaced. Rather, the picture of Stalin that emerges from Lyushkov's testimony is of a ruler with little grasp of the realities of international politics – but with a mob-boss-like predilection for eliminating underlings whom he despised or feared. When the Japanese asked Lyushkov whether he ever had any pangs of conscience over his assignment, he replied that 'emotion or human feelings were impossible in dealings with Stalin. The dictator possessed an abnormal suspicion.'[19]

On arrival in Vladivostok in early 1938, Lyushkov had quickly got to work, ordering dozens of arrests and assembling a 200-strong staff of 'field-tested experts' to concoct a complex web of conspiracy from the arrested men's confessions, extracted under torture. He also ordered the mass deportation of 165,000 ethnic Koreans and 8,000 Chinese from border areas on the pretext that they harboured pro-Japanese sympathies. He arrested 11,000 Chinese on the same grounds, as well as 4,200 officers and political workers as 'anti-Soviet elements' – including dozens of generals, admirals and senior commanders.

But the one scalp that Lyushkov was not able to provide was that of Marshal Blyukher. Nicknamed 'the emperor of Siberia', Blyukher proved too able, too well-connected in Moscow and too wary to be ensnared in Lyushkov's nets. Both men were manoeuvring for their lives, and Lyushkov lost. In May 1938, Lyushkov received a telegram requiring him to return to Moscow for a 'new assignment' – a euphemism, as he knew better than most, for liquidation. He began making preparations for his flight by sending his wife and daughter to the capital, with instructions to flee to Poland as soon as they could. The signal that Lyushkov's family were safely out of the USSR would be a telegram to Papa in Vladivostok conveying 'affectionate regards'.[20] With his family en route to Moscow, Lyushkov arranged for an urgent tour of inspection of a thinly policed border region, donned his civilian disguise and left his escort and driver behind saying that he was proceeding on foot to liaise with a confidential Japanese agent. As a rainstorm raged about him, Lyushkov walked out into the Manchurian night, clutching his typewriter case full of stolen secrets.

Lyushkov would later claim that by absconding with his trove of secret papers he was acting only against Stalin personally and not against his Motherland. The defector wanted to 'rescue his beloved homeland from the hands of a frenzied Stalin, to release 180 million people from bloody fear and falsified politics', according to an August 1938 article in Tokyo's *Nichi Nichi Shimbun* newspaper, based on an interview with the interpreter assigned to live with Lyushkov. 'He wanted to bring happiness to the populace.'[21]

This, like all of Lyushkov's attempts at self-justification, was nonsense. The secrets in his typewriter case and in his head were the general's life-insurance policy. From the moment he met his first Japanese interrogator until the Japanese finally murdered him in 1945, Lyushkov sang like a canary to save his own skin.

The Kremlin was as appalled by Lyushkov's defection as the Japanese and Germans were delighted. In Berlin, military intelligence chief Admiral Canaris judged the information so vital that he sent a personal agent to debrief the Soviet general in Tokyo. The bedridden Sorge, effectively imprisoned in the home of the German ambassador, was in no position to instruct Clausen to cable the Fourth Department and ask whether Lyushkov constituted a deadly danger. Nor could Clausen do it on his own, as Sorge was the only member of the ring who knew the secret Soviet cipher codes needed to communicate with Wiesbaden.

The best Sorge could do for the time being was to play down the importance of Lyushkov's revelations about the USSR's alleged weakness to his German visitors. 'Lyushkov is not a big figure, and an unreliable person,' Sorge stressed to Ott and Scholl. 'It is very dangerous to judge the internal condition of Russia by trusting such a person's words. When the Nazis took over the government of Germany many Germans escaped abroad and by reading their books many people got the impression that the Nazis would be collapsing any day. But it wasn't so, and Lyushkov's case is exactly the same.'[22]

By 20 June 1938, Lyushkov had been installed in the heavily guarded but luxurious Kaikosha military compound in Kudan, just outside

Tokyo. He was treated like an honoured guest (the Japanese interrogators noted dryly that although Lyushkov was a general, he had terrible table manners – and though he was Russian he did not like to drink, though he became jolly when he did imbibe). Ten days later the Japanese authorities made the defection public. Japanese newspapers printed special editions on the sensations that Lyushkov revealed – primarily his bitter criticism of Stalin and the bloodthirsty Purge; the supposed growing discontent inside the USSR and the failure of communism; and the danger of foreign war fomented as a distraction by Stalin. Soviet newspapers, by contrast, remained grimly silent.

Soon afterwards Lyushkov appeared in person at a carefully orchestrated press conference at the Sanno Hotel.[23] He wore a newly tailored polar-weave summer suit and smoked Cherry brand cigarettes in a long ivory holder. To his previous revelations he added that Stalin was testing out Russian ordnance in China and had sent many Soviet officers to help the Kuomintang in order to provide Soviet commanders with battlefield training for the coming war with Japan.

More importantly for the Japanese – and for Sorge and his Centre – were the military secrets that Lyushkov had revealed. The Japanese and international press reported that the Soviet Far Eastern Army, combined with the Trans-Baikal Military District and Lyushkov's own NKVD forces, numbered some twenty-five rifle divisions, or 400,000 troops, as well as 2,000 military aircraft, and ninety large and small submarines based at Vladivostok and Nakhodka. Nationwide, according to Lyushkov, the Red Army numbered over a hundred divisions, or some two million men.

These numbers came as a serious shock to the Japanese – and to the Germans, who had seriously underestimated the speed of the Soviet military build-up. Hitler may have found some comfort in Lyushkov's claim, made in an exclusive interview with Ivar Lissner of the the Nazi paper *Der Angriff*, that revolution was 'inevitable' inside the USSR and the people had lost confidence in Stalin. Lyushkov added, with more accuracy, that the Soviet military had also been seriously weakened by the purges. 'The endless arrests of commanders and political agents of the Red Army have brought discredit upon the remaining officers in the eyes of the men ... a feeling of mistrust pervades all and is poisoning the minds of the people.' Lyushkov also predicted that 'if the Japanese Army struck, the Red Army would collapse in one morning'.[24] The defector's words would soon lead directly to war.

Sorge's challenge, following insistent orders from Centre in July and August 1938, was to find out in exact detail what operational details Lyushkov was telling the Japanese Army – and the names of allegedly rebellious Soviet officers that Lyushkov had identified. The task was beyond Sorge's Japanese network. Though brilliantly connected inside the civilian government, Ozaki only had oblique access to the inner workings of the Imperial Army's intelligence wing. Miyagi was able to report only that Lyushkov was being 'treated well'. This was certainly true. To distract Lyushkov from his worry about his family, his handlers took him clothes shopping at the upmarket Matsuya department store, treated him to meals at the Tenkin restaurant in Ginza and even accompanied him – with a generous budget of 300 yen – to a brothel in Maruko Shinchi, where the honoured guest unfortunately contracted gonorrhoea.[25]

Sorge's breakthrough came with the appearance of Admiral Canaris's personal envoy, a military intelligence colonel and a Russia specialist who arrived in Tokyo in October and spent several weeks personally debriefing Lyushkov. Sorge met the colonel several times at the embassy (though could not later recall his name), and got few details out of him. He did not need to. Major Scholl showed Sorge the envoy's full report, running to several hundred pages, as soon as it was complete. Sorge, now back on his feet, secretly photographed about half the document – omitting Lyushkov's tirades about Stalin and his analysis of the political situation in Moscow – and sent it by courier to Moscow.

The information that Lyushkov had given was highly detailed and specific – from the deployment sites, organisation, and equipment of each Red Army division in the East to lists of names of pro-Japanese elements in the army. Sorge was able to inform Moscow that Lyushkov had revealed the Soviet military codes, which were immediately changed. The defector had also told the Japanese that Moscow was aware of a secret bacteriological warfare institute which the Japanese had established near Harbin. Most crucially of all – from Sorge's own point of view – he was able to confirm that Lyushkov knew nothing of the Sorge ring operating in Tokyo. The NKVD man had told the Japanese that the centres of Russian espionage activity in Manchukuo and Japan were, respectively, the Soviet consulate general in Harbin and the Soviet embassy in Tokyo.

Lyushkov also revealed specific details of the Soviet military weaknesses about which he had spoken in general terms to the press. The Russians' 1,000 air observation and signal points were in wretched condition, causing delays of up to three hours between the alert and the actual take-off of planes, Lyushkov told the Japanese. Soviet planes were shoddily manufactured and the pilots badly trained, and sometimes up to half the aircraft of the Soviet Air Force were out of action at any given moment. Many Red Army artillery units had been supplied with the wrong calibre of ammunition; supply chains were dysfunctional; gasoline was in desperately short supply; officers and men were demoralised by non-existent housing and lousy food. It was a similar story in the Soviet Navy – not enough transports, poorly equipped repair facilities, malfunctioning submarines. The Russian railways were in chaos because of disintegrating track beds, bad coal, a lack of locomotives – and because so many experienced administrators had been arrested. All forces suffered from a desperate shortage of men, in large part because Yezhov had sent nearly 470,000 political prisoners from all over the USSR to hastily built Gulags in the Far East which also needed to be supplied and guarded.

Finally, the anti-Soviet feeling that Lyushkov had so ruthlessly persecuted during his days as Yezhov's executioner was not entirely fabricated. Thousands of peasant soldiers had seen their families dispossessed and starved in the recent collectivisation and purge of wealthier peasantry. Many officers feared becoming victims – especially commanders of Polish, German, 'Lettish' (Latvian) and similar minority backgrounds. In short, Lyushkov told his captors that the Soviet forces in the Far East were not ready for active operations because they lacked senior command personnel (thanks in large part to Lyushkov's own purge), had insufficient training and logistical structure and relied on unserviceable artillery and aviation. Most fatefully of all, Lyushkov claimed that the top command of the Soviet Far East – including Blyukher himself – believed that with Japan so heavily involved in China, the time had come to stop the constant purges and weaken Stalin by launching a pre-emptive attack on Japan.

The picture Lyushkov painted was a dangerously tempting one for the Japanese – a mixture of temporary Soviet weakness combined with the apparent certainly of a military build-up, or even an imminent Soviet attack, in the future. Everything that the defecting general had told the Japanese pointed to the wisdom of an immediate strike against the Soviet Far East while it was in a weakened state.

The Japanese had, therefore, every incentive to start a war against the USSR. But the Soviet military archives in Moscow reveal that it was in fact the Russians, not the Japanese, who actually provoked the first military clash between the Red Army and the Japanese in Manchuria.[26] On 6 July 1938 the Kwangtung Army decoded a message sent by the Russian commander in the Posyet region to his headquarters in Khabarovsk recommending that some strategic heights in an ill-demarcated section of the Soviet–Manchurian border be occupied and fortified. Several thousand Soviet troops moved up to the Changkufeng Heights and began digging trenches and installing barbed wire entanglements.[27] The Japanese military attaché in Moscow demanded a Soviet withdrawal. When the Russians refused, some 1,500 Japanese troops launched a night sortie to retake the heights, killing forty-five Soviet soldiers and knocking out several tanks. The second Russo-Japanese war in half a century was under way.

The People's Commissar for Defence, Kliment Voroshilov, ordered the Soviet First Coastal Army and the Pacific Fleet to combat readiness. Marshal Blyukher had initially been reluctant to get into a fight with the Japanese but a bracing phone call from Stalin soon brought him to heel. 'Comrade Blyukher, tell us honestly,' Stalin shouted down the phone on 1 August. 'Do you have the wish to fight the Japanese properly?'[28] Blyukher duly took personal command of a massive counter-attack.[29] The Soviets fired more shells in a day than the small Japanese force was able to fire in a week, though Blyukher lost at least two thousand men in the attack.[30] It was soon clear that without a massive redeployment of troops from the Chinese front the Japanese could not hold the heights – even with the ever-obliging Lyushkov personally advising the Japanese high command during the campaign. On 11 August the Japanese, losing the nerve to escalate the incident into a full-scale war, abandoned the Changkufeng Heights to the victorious Soviets.[31]

The Changkufeng incident taught both sides important lessons – all of them, as it turned out, mistaken. The Russians falsely concluded that the Japanese lacked the will and skill to take on Soviet troops in Manchuria. And the Japanese concluded that the Russians were pathologically aggressive and bent on destruction of Japan's fledgling Asian empire. More, Tokyo's military strategists came to believe that only a pre-emptive attack, in massive force and at a time and place of Japan's choosing, was necessary to curb Soviet expansion.[32]

Sorge's information would be vital in helping the Red Army plug the strategic gaps that Lyushkov had revealed (and that the Japanese would be attempting to exploit). But first Stalin did what he knew best – purge the traitors in the Far Eastern high command that Lyushkov had identified. Blyukher's head rolled first. Despite his effectiveness at Changkufeng, the old civil war hero was summoned to Moscow in September 1938, berated by Stalin for ineffective leadership, dismissed from his post, arrested and severely tortured.*[33] He refused to confess, and died as a result of injuries sustained during interrogation in the Lubyanka in November 1938.[34]

Lyushkov's defection also helped bring down his old boss, NKVD chief Nikolai Yezhov. On 23 November 1938, Yezhov wrote to Stalin asking to be relieved of his duties – an attempt to pre-empt arrest and execution, which was the fate he had meted out to his own predecessor. Yezhov had failed to cope, he admitted, with the job of operating a 'huge and responsible commissariat' and, among his mistakes, had recommended personnel for promotion who proved to be spies. Yezhov's attempt to save his skin, predictably enough, failed. He was arrested, confessed to a range of anti-Soviet activities (which he later claimed were extracted under torture) and eventually followed his hundreds of thousands of victims in the NKVD's execution pits.

*Just before his recall, Blyukher honourably warned his senior staff of the danger. One of his aides-de-camp was Air Force Major Yakov Lvovich Bibikov, whose wife was heavily pregnant at the time. Blyukher ordered the whole family to take the seven-day train journey to Moscow immediately, ignoring Bibikov's protests that labour was imminent. Bibikov's wife gave birth on the train. But when the slightly enlarged family party arrived in Moscow they were spared the arrests that wiped out many of Blyukher's staff. Bibikov rose to the rank of lieutenant general and oversaw the Soviet Union's ballistic rocketry programme after the Second World War. Bibikov was brother of the author's grandfather, Boris Lvovich Bibikov, a party official executed in the Purge of 1937 in Kiev.

13

Nomonhan

'If it were not for loneliness, all would be well with me'[1]
                                        Richard Sorge, letter to Katya

In Moscow the madness of the Purge seemed to have burned itself out –
at least enough for Sorge to feel sufficiently safe to apply for permission
to return home. In February 1938 he wrote to Katya apologising for
not being able to visit the previous autumn and promising to be in
Moscow by summer. In April, Sorge sent a formal request to his latest
boss, General Semyon Gendin, to bring his Japanese mission to an end.
Katya's sister Marina – 'Musya' – remembered that Katya even sent away
her room-mate Marfa before the May Day 1938 celebrations, convinced
that Richard would arrive in time for the holiday.[2] But Gendin refused
Sorge's petition. Agent Ramsay would never come home again.

Sorge had become a victim of his own extraordinary success. In the
febrile atmosphere of the purges, Gendin had voiced public misgivings
about Agent Ramsay's political reliability as a 'non-returner'. But at the
same time Gendin had resisted his predecessor's call to dissolve Sorge's
Tokyo *rezidentura*. It is likely that the director realised that many of
the fantastical charges that had sent so many of his colleagues to their
deaths were, as Gudz put it, '*lipochki*' – little fictions. Gendin was forced
to pay lip service to the pervasive atmosphere of suspicion in order
to survive – but as a professional intelligence operative he recognised
the extraordinary quality of Agent Ramsay's access. And so the Fourth
Department's paradoxical attitude to Sorge as simultaneously a vital
source and a potential traitor was born. If Sorge was, in fact, still loyal,

his rise in the German embassy was fast making him the most highly placed Soviet agent in the world. No new officer sent by Moscow could ever hope to replicate his extraordinary access. In short, Sorge had become irreplaceable. And if he could be relied on, Sorge's information was of the utmost importance to the security of the Soviet Union. That 'if' would become a question of life and death, not only for Sorge but for Russia itself.

In February 1938, Ambassador Dirksen resigned his post, plagued by asthma that had been exacerbated by Tokyo's damp. Ott was offered the job in his place. Even before telling his wife, Ott consulted his friend Sorge on whether to accept. Sorge strongly advised him not to. The probable reasons why Sorge should not wish his closest friend and best source to become Germany's senior diplomat in Japan are significant. It is possible that Sorge was concerned Ott would become more careful with his new role and stop sharing secret military documents with Sorge. Much more likely, however, is that Sorge feared – rightly – that Ott's promotion would reduce his own chances of ever being allowed to return to the Soviet Union. For once Ott disregarded his friend's advice. On the bright spring morning of 28 April 1938, Ott, in full court dress and wearing the Order of the Sacred Treasure, 2nd class, that he had previously received, drove in an open carriage past the famous *sakura* cherry trees in full blossom in the Imperial Palace gardens to present his credentials to Emperor Hirohito.

Rather than losing his access, Sorge became an even more trusted confidant of the new ambassador. And as the representative of Japan's closest foreign ally, as well as by his own diligence, Ott would soon become the best-connected and best-informed member of the diplomatic corps in Tokyo. 'Of all his foreign colleagues, only Ott had real access to Japanese politics and the holders of power,' US Ambassador Joseph Grew confided to Jan Sieburg. 'And that was due more to Ott's human qualities than to German policies.'[3]

In April, Sorge sailed for Hong Kong on a courier-run for the German embassy – and also, of course, for Moscow Centre. Ambassador Ott entrusted him with confidential official German dispatches and issued him with a diplomatic pass to ease his passage. On his way back, Sorge also stopped off at Manila to deliver further papers – almost certainly including the latest diplomatic code books – to the German embassy in the Philippines. The courier activities of the spy ring were not only being financed by the Third Reich but were conducted under German diplomatic protection.

Sorge put a brave face on Gendin's refusal to allow him to come home. 'Dear Comrade: Do not worry about us,' he wrote to the director in October 1938, just days before Gendin's arrest on charges of espionage that were becoming the traditional end to all Fourth Department chiefs' careers. 'Although we are exhausted and tense we remain disciplined, obedient and resolute, prepared to carry out the tasks of our great cause. Our warmest greetings to you and your friends. Be so good as to pass on the enclosed letter to my wife and add my regards. Please look after her from time to time.'[4]

To Katya he wrote, 'do not forget me ... I am sad enough without that'. He complained about the Tokyo monsoon heat – 'so difficult to bear, above all when the work demands a perpetual tension' – and feared that his wife might become tired of 'this eternal waiting'. He hoped that there was still 'a little chance of realising our old dream of five years of living together'.[5]

Sorge made another attempt to come home in early 1939. His old friends and bottle-mates, the military and naval attachés Major Scholl and Captain Wenneker, had been rotated out of Tokyo, meaning that his access to the day-to-day military intelligence they once provided so freely was no longer as good as it was. Sorge also claimed to Moscow – quite falsely – that Ott no longer had much time for him now that he was ambassador. Perhaps it was time for a new Fourth Department man to come in and make new contacts? Sorge suggested. 'Please pass on my best wishes to Katya,' he concluded his cable. 'It is unbearable for her to have to wait so long for my homecoming.'[6]

But by this time Sorge almost certainly knew that his request would once again be refused. Japan's military had signalled its continued aggressive intentions in China by overrunning the Nationalist capital of Nanking, massacring upwards of 250,000 civilians. In Europe, Hitler had annexed Austria, the Sudetenland area of Czechoslovakia and, shortly after, the rest of the country too. A major European war was coming, and the Kremlin's urgent priorities were twofold: to ensure that Hitler attacked anyone but the Soviet Union, and to prevent Germany and Japan concluding an alliance that would threaten Russia from both east and west. Sorge had made himself indispensable to the USSR's national security. He knew that he would be trapped in Tokyo until the end of the war.

Over the summer of 1938 the reach of Sorge's spy ring reached its apogee. Ozaki was formally appointed a *shokutaku*, or 'unofficial assistant', to the office of Prime Minister Prince Konoe. Ozaki and the other members of Konoe's bright young brains trust now had the ear of Japan's rulers – at least in affairs that the civilian government of Japan still ran. Ozaki gave up his job at the *Asahi* and moved into a basement office inside the prime minister's official residence, where he had access to all government papers that crossed the desks of his colleagues in the cabinet office. Konoe's confidential secretaries, Ushiba and Kishi, began convening an unofficial kitchen cabinet of ministers, experts and advisers over the traditional Japanese breakfast of miso soup – earning the council the nickname of Asameshi kai, or Breakfast Group.[7] Barring a seat at the inner councils of the Imperial General Staff, Ozaki was as close to the heart of the decision-making of the Japanese state as a spy could get.[8]

When the hostilities broke out at Changkufeng Heights, for instance, Ozaki was able to consult the cabinet's information department, dispatches from the Governor General of Korea and the official reports of the army. The incident was not a deliberate provocation by the Japanese high command, Ozaki reported to Sorge, and the government and General Staff in Tokyo had no intention of escalating the conflict. Sorge's information was tactically important to the Soviet commanders at Changkufeng, who were able to pile on the military pressure knowing that they did not risk kicking off a full-scale war. But there was one ominous note for the future in Ozaki's scoop. Soon after fighting had broken out with the Soviets in Manchuria, 'contact between the cabinet and military was cut completely'.[9] In other words the Japanese General Staff was becoming a state within a state, so far beyond civilian control that it was not even bothering to report to its nominal masters in the cabinet.

Ozaki was also becoming something of a celebrity pundit on China. In 1937 he wrote two well-received books: *China Facing the Storm: The Foreign Relations, Politics and Economics of China at a Turning Point* and *China Seen from the Point of View of International Relations*, as well as fourteen major articles. He also found time to translate another Agnes Smedley book, *Macao: Pearl of the East*, once more using his pen name Jiro Shirakawa.[10] Most importantly, Ozaki was one of the authors – alongside Breakfast Group colleagues Royama Masamichi and Miki Kiyoshi – of a bold economic plan for the development of the whole of Asia, led of course by Japan. The Greater East Asia Co-Prosperity Sphere[11] sketched out 'a "new order" ... on the basis of an anti-capitalist, anti-imperialist liberation of the colonised peoples in Asia and the creation of a pan-Asiatic culture'.[12] Conceived by Ozaki and his associates along socialist lines the Co-Prosperity Sphere would, ironically enough, soon be co-opted by ultra-nationalists and became the blueprint and ideological fig leaf for the Japanese conquest of all of Southeast Asia.

Ozaki's fame as a China expert led directly to another appointment – one that put him at the heart of the Kwangtung Army's logistical operations. On 1 June 1939 he was hired by the Investigation Department of the South Manchuria Railroad, or Mantetsu. The railway had been the economic powerhouse of Manchuria since its construction by the Russians in 1898–1903. The Kwangtung Army had indeed originally been formed as an adjunct to the all-powerful railway administration. And since the Japanese takeover of Manchuria in 1931, the railway had also become the central military artery of Japan's expansion. From his office on the fourth floor of the Mantetsu Building in Tokyo's Toranomon district, Ozaki had an unrivalled insight into Japan's war effort in China. The railway's innocuous-sounding Investigation Department included a Chinese Resistance Capacity Measurement Council that reported on Chinese troop movements, an International Situation Research Council that gathered intelligence on Chinese politics, and a Current Materials Section which monitored the Chinese economy.[13] 'I was able to obtain a large amount of information and materials on politics, economy, foreign policy, etc.,' Ozaki would later confess to his Japanese interrogators. 'Moreover, I was able to find out some part of the movement of the Kwangtung Army and, furthermore, the movement of the Japanese military.'[14] In short, there was no better vantage point than Ozaki's from which to watch for a Japanese offensive against the USSR.

Miyagi's enthusiastic, if reckless, recruitment efforts also turned up an unlikely gem. The Fourth Department had demanded that Sorge find some serving Japanese officers to work for the ring – a 'very difficult problem', as Sorge remarked when Clausen handed him this message.[15] The army was the ideological home of ultra-nationalism and rampant anti-communism. Moreover, the military had recently set up their own political police force, the Kempeitai, which was fast emerging as

Japan's most ruthless counter-espionage outfit. Any attempts to recruit collaborators from among the officer corps was therefore risky in the extreme.

Miyagi cracked the problem by enlisting not an officer but a reserve corporal who quickly proved his worth as one of the ring's best informants. Koshiro Yoshinobu – also known by his nickname of Kodai – was an old acquaintance of Miyagi's via a fellow Okinawan and socialist who had studied with Kodai at Meiji University. Kodai had flirted with communism as a student but was drafted into the Japanese Army in 1936, spending two years on active duty in Manchuria and Korea. By the time Miyagi looked him up in March 1939, Kodai was back home in Tokyo, a corporal with the army reserves, working in a paper shop.[16] 'If a war should break out between Russia and Japan it would mean a great sacrifice not only on the part of the farmers and labourers of both countries but also on the part of the whole Japanese people,' Miyagi told Kodai at their first meeting. 'To avoid such a tragedy … I am sending various data on the situation in Japan to the Comintern.'[17] Revealing himself as a communist agent was a risky strategy – but it paid off when Kodai agreed to obtain military information from his friends. The idealistic corporal also refused payment.

Sorge was sufficiently intrigued by this new recruit to meet with him in person at least twice in Tokyo restaurants. He even telegraphed a biography of Kodai to Moscow, who approved the recruitment and allocated him the codename of Miki.[18] Miyagi urged Agent Miki to rejoin the army's active list and get a job in the War Ministry's mobilisation bureau. Soon Kodai would become a key source on the organisation and equipment of the Japanese Army – and provide detailed information on the shipment of tanks, planes and troops.

Anna Clausen had also taken her place on the team – albeit reluctantly. After her months of exile in the Volga steppes and in Moscow under the unfriendly eye of Fourth Department minders, Anna was not greatly enamoured of the Centre and its diktats. Nonetheless, as her husband, Sorge and Vukelić were increasingly busy with their spying work and could not spare the time to act as couriers themselves, Centre suggested that Anna become the ring's mule to smuggle urgent microfilmed material out of Japan. When Clausen broke the news to his wife, Anna resisted bitterly. Shanghai had fallen to the Japanese after a three-month battle in 1937, so Centre suggested Anna make a courier-run to the

British colony of Hong Kong instead. But Anna spoke no English and felt much safer in the familiar surroundings of Shanghai. And then there was the important issue of shopping. 'I don't like Hong Kong because I have no friends and there is nothing to buy there,' Anna told her husband.[19]

Anna was eventually persuaded to set sail on the first of her eighteen courier-runs to Shanghai in November 1938. She carried $3,000 in cash in her luggage (a favour to a business partner of Clausen's who needed the money wired to Switzerland, which was easier to do from Shanghai than Tokyo), and a small package of personal gifts from Sorge to Katya. In a rolled piece of cloth concealed under her breasts, Anna carried between twenty and thirty tiny cans of microfilm containing the secrets of Lyushkov's interrogation. She landed in Shanghai, the contents of her brassiere unmolested, around 10 December. She waited for her rendezvous at the cafe of the Palace Hotel in the lobby of the Cathay Hotel. Centre's instructions were for her to carry a yellow handbag and wear white gloves – an idiotic plan that only a man could have thought up, in Anna's view, since nobody wore white gloves in mid-winter.[20]

Nonetheless she complied, and in due course a Fourth Department courier made contact to accept the microfilm and hand over a package containing some $6,000 in mixed Chinese and American money, ostensibly for the *rezidentura*'s needs. In fact Anna immediately rewarded herself by spending $700 on a fur coat, sent $500 to a private account in Hamburg belonging to her husband and deposited another $1,000 in her personal account at the Hong Kong and Shanghai Bank.[21] After making some more purchases for her husband's business, the money was almost gone – perfectly fair, in the Clausens' view, because Sorge had been freely dipping into the profits of Max's business in order to fund the ring's expenses for years. Anna had been drawn into acting as a Soviet secret courier by her own avowedly capitalist interests. Most of the Fourth Department cash had gone into the Clausen family's pockets, raising the inevitable question of who had the right to the profits of the business set up with Moscow's money – Clausen, or Centre? The question was further complicated by the fact that in early 1939 Sorge delegated the accounting duties of the ring to Clausen, meaning that he had to pay his own salary and expenses as well as also those of Branko and Edith Vukelić. Since the only source of funds from Moscow was irregular courier-runs to Dutch and American banks in

Hong Kong and Shanghai, the actual cash flow for the whole operation was increasingly coming from Clausen Shokai, Inc. In essence, Max Clausen was personally bankrolling the Soviet Union's most successful – and expensive – spy ring. As the dangers grew over the coming years, so Anna would increasingly question whether not only the risks but the costs to herself and her beloved Max would be worth it.[22]

Sorge generally took a loftily cavalier, officer-class attitude to the ring's finances. Of much greater concern to him was the growing possibility of a German–Japanese military alliance of far greater scope than the existing, vaguely worded Anti-Comintern Pact. Berlin's interest in such an alliance was obvious – the possibility of a Soviet attack on Germany would be greatly reduced if Japan were committed to retaliate against Russia's eastern flank.

Tokyo's interests were not so clear. The Japanese Army had its eye on conquering not only large swathes of China but also the Soviet Far East. Its most vigorous officers – including the members of the ultra-nationalist Cherry Society, the prime force behind the Manchurian incident and led by War Minister Seishiro Itagaki – applauded Hitler's expansionism and sympathised with his glorification of the nation, his anti-communism and his contempt for an old world order dominated by the victors of the First World War. Hitler had just humiliated the British prime minister, Neville Chamberlain, by arrogantly ignoring the assurances they had signed at Munich the previous October in the wake of Germany's occupation of the Sudetenland and annexing the whole of Czechoslovakia on 15 March 1939. The Japanese Army's Action Group yearned to do the same in Asia.

Japan's Imperial Navy had similar expansionist ambitions, but different targets. Japan's admirals dreamed of dominating the islands' maritime neighbours, from the Philippines to Malaya and beyond to the oil-rich Dutch East Indies – modern-day Indonesia. Their two main obstacles were the British Royal Navy, operating a force far more powerful than Japan's from the apparently impregnable base of Singapore, and the US Pacific Fleet out of Pearl Harbor, Hawaii. Japan's influential navy minister, Admiral Mitsumasa Yonai, was adamantly opposed to any alliance that would commit Japan to follow Hitler on to the war path against Britain, France, the Netherlands and the Soviet Union – all while the draining and apparently endless war in China continued. Yonai argued that Japan was heavily dependent on the Dutch, British and Americans for raw materials, meaning that an all-out war would quickly suffocate the Japanese economy. The Japanese Navy preferred to conduct their expansion, if possible, with US and British acquiescence.[23]

This fundamental clash between the army and navy's differing visions of empire would dominate Japan's foreign policy for years – and would only be finally decided on 7 December 1941 with the navy's dramatic surprise attack on Pearl Harbor. Yet over the German alliance, the battle-lines between Japan's army and navy were less clear-cut. Even the navy recognised that Germany was Japan's closest ally in the world, while the USSR was its most likely antagonist. In Tokyo the newly appointed Ambassador Ott did his best to persuade Japan's civilian government and the navy to sign a closer alliance with Berlin – even though his friend Sorge argued forcefully that Japan would never agree to become Hitler's puppet in Asia with no advantage to itself.

Over months of negotiations, led in Berlin by General Oshima – the former military attaché who had masterminded the Anti-Comintern Pact, now promoted to Japanese ambassador to Germany – the Japanese Army's position appeared to have gained the upper hand. The final document, signed on 22 May 1939, was grandiosely dubbed 'the Pact of Steel', and committed Germany, Italy and Japan to retaliate against any country which attacked them. Public celebrations were held in Berlin and Tokyo, with crossed Nazi and Japanese flags hung across the streets. At Papa Keitel's Das Rheingold, a special party was held in honour of the new pact, the bar decorated with swastika flags and the rising sun of Nippon.

In reality, however, Hitler was unsatisfied. After all Japan's prevarications, he did not believe that the Japanese would make truly reliable allies against the Russians. As Hitler would tell his generals later in the year, 'the Emperor [Hirohito] is the companion piece of the latter Czars. Weak, cowardly, irresolute, he may fall before a revolution. My association with Japan was never popular ... Let us think of ourselves as masters and consider these people at best as lacquered half-monkeys, who need to feel the lash.'[24] Hitler's displeasure with the Pact of Steel had set the stage for another alliance, altogether surprising and conducted in complete secrecy, with Stalin himself.

*

There was another reason for Hitler's disinclination to rely on Tokyo as an effective bulwark against Russia. Japanese troops were once again fighting the Soviets around a barren stretch of the Soviet–Mongolian border – and losing. The 'Nomonhan incident', known in Russia as the Battle of Khankin Gol, was a bizarre little conflict that was to have profound consequences for the eventual outcome of the Second World War.

It began on 11 May 1939, when a detachment of cavalry from the pro-Soviet Mongolian People's Republic numbering between thirty and ninety horsemen entered an area claimed by Japan. They were driven back by a force of Kwangtung Army cavalry. Two days later the Mongolians returned in greater numbers. But this time they were backed by Soviet troops, sent under the terms of a 1936 mutual assistance pact between the Moscow and Ulaanbataar which stipulated that Russian troops could defend their neighbour from aggression – effectively extending the USSR's defensive border to the southern and eastern edge of Mongolia. The joint Mongolian–Soviet force routed the reconnaissance regiment of the Kwangtung Army's 23rd Infantry Division sent to repel them, killing 102 men of the Japanese-led force.

From this small beginning, the incident quickly escalated as both the Soviets and the Japanese poured troops and aircraft into the desolate region. By June 1939 the Kwangtung Army had deployed some 30,000 men, while the Soviet Far Eastern Command mobilised its most able young commander, Komkor (Lieutenant-General) Georgy Zhukov, with a force of motorised infantry. The two sides faced off over a mosquito-infested area of quicksands and ravines that surrounded the Khankin-Gol river.

What makes the story of Nomonhan especially curious is that after the previous year's humiliation at Changkufeng, the Japanese imperial high command strongly opposed fighting another war against the USSR. In the first weeks of the incident Tokyo was in the final stages of the delicate negotiations of its Pact of Steel with the Nazis. And it was clear to the Japanese General Staff in Tokyo that the Kwangtung Army lacked the resources to fight the far more powerful Soviet Army. A year had passed since Lyushkov's defection, and the Soviet operational and political weaknesses that the defecting general had gleefully revealed had almost certainly been patched up. From the outset of the conflict the generals in Tokyo knew that a war against the Soviets while most of the Japanese Army were heavily engaged in China could only end in a humiliating defeat.

The Nomonhan incident was, in effect, a freelance war begun 'single-handedly' (in the words of a subordinate) by the local Japanese commander, Lieutenant General Michitaro Komatsubara. At the outset Komatsubara greatly exaggerated the numbers of Mongol cavalry who had originally crossed the border (he claimed a force of 700), and he personally ordered forces mobilised from Hailar 'in order to liquidate these enemy forces with all our might' without the approval of the Kwangtung Army headquarters, let alone the imperial high command.[25] Even more bizarrely, Komatsubara's 23rd Division was not trained as an offensive force. The unit had recently been formed for purposes of border defence and military reconnaissance. Both Komatsubara and his chief of staff, Colonel Ouchi Tsutomu, had spent most of their careers as Japanese intelligence officers. In other words, in combat terms Komatsubara's division was the Kwangtung Army's weakest link.

The high command in Tokyo, presented with a war they did not want and could not win, faced the impossible task of trying to keep the conflict as localised as possible while avoiding a catastrophic defeat. The result was a series of bizarre manoeuvres where Japanese successes were deliberately not pushed home for fear of escalating the conflict. On 27 June, for instance, the Japanese Army Air Force's 2nd Air Brigade struck the Soviet air base at Tamsak-Bulak in Mongolia, scoring a significant victory. But Tokyo promptly ordered the JAAF not to conduct any more air strikes against Soviet airbases.[26]

In Tokyo, Sorge tried to make sense of Japan's convoluted war aims. Colonel Gerhard Matzky, the new German military attaché who had replaced Scholl, told him that his contacts in the Japanese General Staff were being evasive – but he had the impression that the Japanese would go as far as they dared without bringing the whole weight of the Soviet Union down on the Kwangtung Army.[27] Ozaki brought the reassuring news from the Breakfast Group that the Japanese government was 'adopting a policy of solving the problem locally and not expanding it. It does not have any intention of daring an overall war with Russia. Also the general public does not want to have a war with Russia.'[28] Miyagi also brought news from his informants, Corporal Koshiro and the aircraft-parts manufacturer Shinotsuka, that while aircraft and tanks were being dispatched to Nomonhan there were no plans for a larger mobilisation of troops from the Japanese home islands.

The Soviets had no such qualms about escalation – thanks to Sorge's information about the Japanese high command's fears over widening the war. Zhukov mobilised the Soviet Union's best tanks and planes for an all-out offensive at Nomonhan. His force included twenty-one crack pilots, every one a Hero of the Soviet Union, who soon gave the Russians air supremacy. Zhukov also assembled a fleet of 2,600 trucks to supply his troops from the nearest railhead at Chita, 748 kilometres away. Branko Vukelić, who visited the front line at Nomonhan as one of a group of foreign journalists taken on a tour by the Japanese Army, reported to Sorge that the Russian Army was performing much better than was being reported in the Japanese newspapers, that the Russians had more heavy guns than the Japanese, and that he saw 'very many trucks moving behind' the Soviet lines.[29]

A Japanese breakthrough around the Bain-Tsagan mountain from 3–5 July was fought to a standstill when Zhukov organised a lightning-fast counterstrike of 450 tanks and armoured cars. Komatsubara ordered another offensive in August, despite knowing that his division was not ready for a major assault. The result was a massacre. By the time Zhukov pressed home his victory at the end of August, nearly 12,000 of the Kwangtung Army's 23rd Division's 15,000 men had been killed or wounded, a casualty rate of 80 per cent. Komatsubara's decision to launch the premature offensive was 'the worst in history', according to his subordinate Major Ogi Hiroshi.[30]

Was Komatsubara simply incompetent – or had the whole Nomonhan incident in fact been orchestrated by Soviet intelligence? There is intriguing – though not conclusive – evidence that Komatsubara could have been a Soviet agent. He had spent much of his early career in Russia, beginning with a year in St Petersburg learning Russian in 1909, returning in 1919 to Moscow as assistant military attaché, and again from 1927–30 as chief military attaché to the Japanese embassy.[31] Komatsubara was much given to 'drinking, debauchery, and profiteering', according to the Soviet counter-intelligence official who was shadowing him in Moscow when interviewed by Soviet historians in 1983.[32] According to this source, the OGPU secret police launched a honeytrap operation to compromise Komatsubara, sending a beautiful female agent to seduce the attaché during a trip to Estonia in 1927.[33] Back in Moscow,

Komatsubara and another colleague from the embassy got so drunk with this mistress that he lost the keys to the safe in his room – or, more likely, they were stolen by the OGPU's wily female operative. Komatsubara was 'ready to agree to anything' in order to prevent his misbehaviour from being reported to Tokyo.[34]

The story is plausible, not least because several Japanese diplomats fell victim to similar OGPU honeytrap operations during the same period. Komatsubara's fellow attaché, Captain Kisaburo Koyanagi of the Japanese Navy, was seduced by the attractive Russian language teacher assigned to him by the Soviet diplomatic service agency. On 3 February 1929, according to the Soviet newspaper *Vechernyaya Moskva*, Koyanagi was hosting one of his allegedly regular sex orgies in his apartment at 44 Novinsky Boulevard. The party ended up in a brawl during which Koyanagi supposedly wounded his pretty teacher with a table knife and then chased her down the corridor where he threw a table and dishes at her.[35] Soon after the publication of the article – presumably after Koyanagi's refusal to bow to OGPU blackmail – the unfortunate attaché committed ritual suicide in his office at the embassy by slashing his own stomach.

What is clear is that after 1927 wherever Komatsubara was posted a stream of misinformation to Tokyo – and leaks to Soviet intelligence – followed. Komatsubara was head of the Japanese special mission in Harbin from 1932–34. The Russian Army's central archive in Podolsk has detailed information on Japan, China and Manchukuo coinciding exactly with Komatsubara's posting in Harbin – but very little before or after. In 1933, confidential Japanese telegrams appeared in Moscow exposing Japan's intention to seize the Chinese Eastern Railway from the Soviet Union. And secret material from an unnamed agent includes a chilling presentation given in Harbin in August 1932 by the head of the Russian Department of Tokyo's General Staff Headquarters on the importance of biological warfare as a potential weapon against the USSR. The report was so alarming that it was personally read by Marshal Tukhachevsky and Stalin.

Komatsubara may very well have been put 'on the hook', as Soviet intelligence jargon has it, in Moscow and passed information from Harbin. However, what is lacking in the espionage case against Komatsubara as a Soviet proxy at Nomonhan is any paper trail in the Soviet archives suggesting that he had any controller or direct contact with Soviet intelligence during his time as commander of the 23rd Division in Manchuria. Nor is there any evidence of any Kremlin discussions about provoking a Japanese attack. It is intriguing to speculate that the Nomonhan incident was a brainchild of Stalin's and effected by a senior agent in the Japanese Army. A short victorious war, provoked by Japan and won decisively by the USSR, was precisely what Stalin needed to cauterise Japanese ambitions to invade the Soviet Union. But the case, for the time being, remains unproven.[36]

The now-forgotten war at Nomonhan was to have profound repercussions. The battle won Georgy Zhukov the first (of four) decorations as Hero of the Soviet Union. The Soviets lost some 9,703 killed and missing at Nomonhan – but gained valuable lessons in the concentrated use of airpower against enemy armour.[37] The battle experience of the units which fought the Japanese would be put to good use when Stalin mobilised these Siberian troops in the crucial defence of Moscow in November 1941. And Zhukov himself would use the tactics he had honed at Nomonhan – holding the enemy fixed in the centre, building up an undetected mass force in the immediate rear area, and then launching a pincer attack on the wings to trap the enemy – to surround the German 6th Army at the Battle of Stalingrad.[38]

More important was the effect the engagement had in Tokyo. The humiliation of the Kwangtung Army strengthened the hand of the 'South Strike' Group – led by the navy – who argued for Japan to attack its Asian neighbours and leave the USSR alone. The Japanese reluctance to risk another trouncing at the hands of the Red Army would become a major factor in the outcome of the coming world war.

14

Ribbentrop–Molotov

'There are only three great statesmen in the world: Stalin, myself, and Mussolini'[1]

Adolf Hitler

On 24 August 1939 news came across the wire that took Sorge, the German embassy and the Japanese government by complete surprise: Hitler had concluded a non-aggression pact with his arch-enemy Stalin. The talks between the Nazi foreign minister, Joachim von Ribbentrop, and his newly appointed Soviet counterpart Vyacheslav Molotov had been held in absolutely secrecy. The Nazi–Soviet pact came as a shock even to Ambassador Ott. To Sorge – and for communists around the world – Stalin's decision to do a deal with the devil was a profound and inexplicable betrayal.

It had been clear since spring of that year that a major European war, and probably a world war, was imminent. But exactly who the full cast of combatants would be remained an open question, and would remain so until the end of 1941. When Hitler invaded Czechoslovakia in March 1939, in violation of the Munich Agreement, he stood revealed as an aggressor and a liar. On 31 March, Neville Chamberlain pledged to support Poland in the event of an invasion. Britain and France also began urgent talks with Stalin to secure the USSR's support against Hitler. At the same time the Nationalist Japanese press began clamouring for a full military alliance with Germany against Britain, France and the USSR. Which side would Stalin choose?

The idea that the Soviet Union would choose an alliance with fascism rather than stand alongside the Western democracies seemed inconceivable to devoted communists around the world. Earl Browder, head of the Communist Party of the USA, scoffed just months before the pact that there was 'as much chance of [a Nazi–Soviet] agreement as of Earl Browder being elected president of the Chamber of Commerce'.[2]

And yet the advantages of an alliance for both Hitler and Stalin were clear. Hitler needed to cover his eastern border in order to leave his armies free to conquer Western Europe. Hitler had once hoped that the Pact of Steel with Japan, threatening Russia's own Far Eastern provinces, would be enough to keep Stalin in check. But the Japanese failure at Nomonhan convinced Hitler that more direct measures were needed to keep Russia out of the war – namely, a direct deal with his counterpart in the Kremlin. 'I have decided to go with Stalin,' Hitler told his generals on 22 August. 'On the whole, there are only three great statesmen in the world: Stalin, myself, and Mussolini.'[3]

The Soviet Union had secretly helped the Weimar Republic re-arm and train between 1923 and 1933. Now, reasoned Hitler, Stalin could be persuaded to help once more – this time to provide the raw materials for the German economy that would be cut off in the event of war with Britain by the Royal Navy's command of the seas. Hitler had often decried the 'Jewish-Bolshevik' rulers of the Soviet Union and spoken of an inescapable battle against Pan-Slavism, the victory in which would lead to 'permanent mastery of the world'. But Hitler had also said as early as 1934 that he was ready to 'walk part of the road with the Russians, if that will help us'.[4]

Stalin, for his part, was anxious to direct Nazi aggression away from the USSR at almost any cost – and frankly distrusted the old imperialist powers' promises to help Russia in case of a German attack. Molotov, who negotiated with Hitler in Berlin in August 1939, later explained the pact in terms of simply buying time before an inevitable German invasion. 'We knew the war was coming soon, that we were weaker than Germany, that we would have to retreat,' he told a biographer in 1982. 'We did everything to postpone the war. And we succeeded – for a year and ten months. We wished it could have been longer, of course.'[5]

Molotov was ordered by Stalin to buy not only time but space. 'The question was, retreat to where – to Smolensk or to Moscow, that's what we discussed before the war,' remembered Molotov. 'We knew we would have to retreat, and we needed as much territory as possible.' Over a series of top-secret meetings in Berlin and Moscow in late July and

August, a protocol to the Nazi–Soviet non-aggression pact was agreed, effectively dividing Poland in half between Germany and the Soviet Union and establishing 'spheres of influence' for both powers from the Baltics to Romania. The logic, for Stalin, was clear: to establish a buffer zone around the Soviet Union that would allow defence in depth. In return, over the first year of the pact, the USSR would supply Germany with one million tons of cereals, half a million tons of wheat, 900,000 tons of oil, 100,000 tons of cotton, 500,000 tons of phosphates and considerable amounts of other vital raw materials, along with the transit of one million tons of soybeans from Manchuria.[6]

Molotov would later scoff at the idea that Hitler had lulled Stalin into a false sense of security. 'Such a naive Stalin? No. Stalin saw through it all. Stalin trusted Hitler? He didn't trust all his own people!' Molotov recalled. 'We had to delay Germany's aggression, that's why we tried to deal with them on an economic level – export-import. No one trusted Hitler. Stalin wanted to delay the war for at least another half a year, or longer.'[7]

On 19 August the Soviets abruptly broke off alliance negotiations with British and French officials in Moscow and signed their economic agreement with Germany. Three days later Ribbentrop was invited to the Kremlin where he drank vodka with Molotov and Stalin and signed the political part of the non-aggression pact in front of photographers. The final brake on war had been removed. On 1 September 1939, German troops crossed the Polish border in overwhelming force, unleashing the blitzkrieg they had perfected on the plains of Belarus during the days of German-Soviet cooperation. Britain had signed its defensive pact with Poland six days before: by 3 September Britain therefore found itself at war with Germany.[8]

Stalin did not make any move in Eastern Europe until the final peace had been signed with the Japanese at Nomonhan on 15 September 1939. With the Far East secured, Stalin ordered Soviet troops to invade Poland on the thin pretext of 'protecting' their ethnic Ukrainian and Belorussian brethren from Nazi aggression.[9] Molotov later admitted to German officials that this feeble excuse was necessary because the Kremlin could find no more convincing justification for the Soviet invasion.[10] Within less than a fortnight, German and Russian forces had met in a line that stretched from Königsberg in the north to Uzhgorod on the Hungarian border. In the city of Brest-Litovsk on 22 September

1939, Major General Heinz Guderian of the Wehrmacht and Brigadier General Semyon Krivoshein of the Red Army held a joint victory parade, featuring crossed swastikas and hammers and sickles.[11] Poland had been wiped from the map.

The Ribbentrop–Molotov Pact served Hitler's tactical needs in Europe. But it left his relations with the Japanese in tatters. The Japanese government was furious at having been kept in the dark over Hitler's brazen violation of the Anti-Comintern Pact. More intriguingly, the collapse of confidence in Hitler opened the way for an entirely different alliance for Japan.

Many senior Japanese military officers advocated a rapprochement with Britain, France, and the United States. Most prominent among them was Admiral Kichisaburo Nomura, who was appointed Japan's foreign minister on 25 September. Nomura argued that an alliance with the Pacific's greatest naval powers had much to offer Japan: ready access to the raw materials so vital to its economy, for one, as well as powerful allies who shared an interest in keeping Asia free of both German and Soviet influence. A new government led by General Nobuyuki Abe, a moderate who distrusted the ultra-nationalists, came to power. Abe named emperor's former chief aide-de-camp, General Shunroku Hata, as war minister – another safe pair of hands who distrusted military adventures. Unwittingly, Hitler's deal with Stalin seemed to have stalled, for the moment at least, the progress of militant nationalism in Japan. 'This cabinet will be much weaker than the previous one,' Ozaki reported to Sorge. 'And will be cooperative with the United States and Britain.'[12]

During this brief – and in retrospect bizarrely counterfactual – period it seemed as if the Soviet Union would remain at peace with Germany, and that Japan would sit out the Second World War either in isolation or even possibly as a partner of Britain and America. Some firebrands in the Japanese Army may have admired Hitler's aggressive policies. But Hitler's perfidious pact with Stalin had discredited the pro-German faction. For the most part, Sorge noted, 'pro-British and US groups successfully turned the feeling against Germany, and the German embassy was possessed by anxiety that the Japanese Government might directly join the British and US side'.[13]

The Fourth Department, for its part, did not feel any need to explain or justify the Soviet leadership's abrupt volte-face to its agents. Instead, the tone of the cables coming from Moscow became increasingly peevish and permanently displeased. Between the dismissal of Jan Berzin in August 1937 and the signing of the pact there had been four directors, every one of whom had been (or soon would be) shot. Gendin had been dismissed in October 1938 and was executed four months later. Like his predecessor the latest director, General Ivan Proskurov,[14] valued the Ramsay *rezidentura*'s information – but completely misunderstood the motivations of his star agent in Tokyo. When he had to refuse yet another one of Sorge's requests to return to Moscow in June 1939, Proskurov sent an internal memo to his subordinates in Centre's Japanese department. 'Think carefully about how we could compensate for Ramsay's [Sorge's] recall,' instructed Proskurov. 'Prepare a telegram and letter to Ramsay with excuses for the delay in replacing him and listing the reasons it is necessary for him to remain in Tokyo. Give Ramsay and the other members of his organisation a one-time monetary bonus.'[15] Proskurov, insultingly, assumed that money was all that was needed to maintain Sorge's obedience.

On 1 September, Proskurov wrote to scold Sorge. 'Your activity seems to be getting slack,' the chief snapped. 'Japan must have commenced important movements (military and political) in preparation for war against Russia, but you have not provided us with any appreciable information … You should utilise all the capacities of Joe, Miki and Otto to the fullest extent.'[16]

There was no evidence, either from Ozaki's regular meetings with top policymakers, nor from Miyagi's network in Japan's military industrial complex, nor from the German embassy, that Proskurov's fears of Japanese aggression at that moment were in any way justified. Nonetheless the tone was set for the final, ultimately tragic, period of Sorge's career with the Fourth Department. 'From then on,' recalled Clausen, Sorge 'regularly got telegrams with scoldings and admonitions.'[17] Stalin was convinced he knew the truth about Germany and Japan's intentions. No information that Sorge could provide, however solidly sourced, was capable of swaying the paranoid *khozain* – boss of the Kremlin – from his belief that Germany had been successfully contained but that Japan remained a fatal threat. The truth was precisely the contrary.

Proskurov's criticism was especially unfair in light of the increasing danger in which the Sorge spy ring was working. Even back in 1934 when Sorge first arrived in Tokyo, the atmosphere of suspicion and surveillance was suffocating. But with the escalation of the war in China and the humiliations of Changkufeng and Nomonhan, Japan was overtaken by fully fledged spy mania that quickly evolved into a national psychosis.[18] The government flooded Japan's cities with anti-spy posters, slogans, shop-window displays and even anti-spy matchbooks. In all the propaganda images, the evil spy was invariably depicted as a tall, blond Westerner – a caricature portrait, in fact, of Sorge himself. Local authorities organised anti-spy days and weeks where citizens were harangued to report any suspicious behaviour on the part of their neighbours and passers-by. The Tokko political police and the military's own Kempeitai counter-espionage force routinely questioned any Japanese seen to be talking to a foreigner, and the government even sent agents to Berlin, Rome and San Francisco to monitor Japanese radicals and cut off any Comintern literature that might reach Japan.[19]

The indefatigable Miyagi continued with his recruitment efforts despite the escalating dangers. With anti-Japanese feeling rising in the United States, a steady stream of Japanese expatriates were returning home, among them several of Miyagi's old communist acquaintances. In April 1938 Miyagi travelled to the small town of Kokawa on the island of Honshu for an emotional reunion with the wife of his old landlord from San Francisco, Tomo Kitabayashi. She had found work as a sewing instructress, joined the local Seventh-Day Adventist Church and was saving money for her husband to join her in her native town. With her modest station in life and remote provincial existence it is not clear how Tomo Kitabayashi could be of use to the Sorge spy ring. Nonetheless, Miyagi signed her up as an informant apparently more on the strength of their old friendship than because of any lingering communist sympathies or practical usefulness.

In Tokyo, Sorge, Clausen and Vukelić had done well to establish cast-iron bona fides before the full onslaught of spy mania. Nonetheless, all of them were coming under ever-closer scrutiny. Sorge and Vukelić, as journalists, came under particular suspicion. 'With Japanese nationalism mounting to the point of fanaticism, almost anything in the possession of a foreign correspondent could be construed as evidence of his guilt as a spy,' recalled Joseph Newman of the *New York Herald Tribune*, who often saw Sorge on the seventh floor of the Domei news agency building, where most foreign reporters had offices. 'They suspected German and Italian newsmen much more than Americans. They understood that the

Axis correspondents had been sent to Japan not only to report to their newspapers and agencies but to gather whatever secret information they could for the German embassy.'[20]

By 1939 Sorge was also under regular, though sporadic, police surveillance. The officer assigned to keep tabs on him was twenty-eight-year-old Harutsugu Saito, a proud and intelligent young German-speaker from the five-man-strong department of the Tokko's Foreign Section that was charged with monitoring the 700 Germans in Tokyo.[21]

Sorge was an easy man to follow. His small Datsun, which he had switched to driving after his motorcycle crash, was as distinctive as the tall German himself. Saito was well aware how well connected with the German ambassador his subject was and took extreme pains not to be observed as he trailed Sorge around town. He made regular attempts to question Sorge's new housekeeper, Fukuda Tori, who had taken over from the elderly Honmoku, but was firmly rebutted. 'I won't answer your questions or those of the Kempeitai,' Fukuda snapped. 'My master is a fine man. Leave him alone!'[22] Eventually Fukuda relented to the extent of allowing the personable young officer to accompany her to the temple to pray to her favourite deity, Oinari-san, the fox god revered by many Japanese peasants. As the old lady lit incense sticks in the small shrine she may have offered a prayer to that most appropriate of deities for the safety of her employer.

Over a period of two years Saito got to know Sorge's routes to and from work, his favoured drinking haunts and restaurants. But Sorge's predictability and high profile were of course just the public face of a (usually) meticulous tradecraft. Saito and his four Tokko colleagues had 140 Germans each to keep tabs on, which meant that his surveillance of Sorge was necessarily patchy. He never succeeded in trailing the careful Sorge to his monthly rendezvous with Miyagi, and less frequently Ozaki, in Tokyo teahouses, restaurants and occasionally in the city's numerous 'love hotels'. The Tokko never linked the fictitious 'Mr Otake' who made the restaurant bookings with the government adviser Ozaki. Neither Ozaki nor Miyagi's name ever appeared in the Tokko's surveillance files in connection with Sorge.[23]

Another pair of eyes observed Sorge on a daily basis from the vantage point of the Toriizaka police station, 300 metres from his home. In the wake of Sorge's motorcycle accident Aoyama Shigeru, a young police officer from Toriizaka was assigned to watch over Sorge's house during his convalescence. With his usual talent for befriending those who could be most dangerous to him, Sorge charmed the young policeman. But from the beginning Aoyama 'had the impression that something fishy was going on' in the modest wooden house on Nagasaki Street. Sorge and Clausen spoke frequently on the telephone and Clausen visited Sorge's house even when he was out – but when they happened to meet in the Das Rheingold or other German hostelries they never drank together. 'They acted almost like strangers, only nodding to one another,' Hanako recalled.[24] Saito also sensed something strange in Sorge and Clausen's relationship.

Aoyama, too, attempted to question the housekeeper Fukuda. She told him nothing – except to say that her employer often burned documents after typing them.[25] Soon afterwards a 'gentle-looking' young man visited Hanako and questioned her politely but persistently on her relationship with Sorge. Delicately insisting that he would ask nothing of Hanako that he would not ask of his own sister, the agent requested that she steal Sorge's papers. 'I could not steal without telling him!'[26] Hanako protested. When Hanako told Sorge of the visit he appeared unconcerned. 'Would you like to have my papers?' he offered with a laugh. Hanako declined – though she admitted that the visit had made her nervous. If the police ever came back, she was to refer them directly to him, Sorge told her.

Clausen's constitution was not so steely. His duties as radio man involved him taking his life in his hands every few days to transport his radio gear around town to his various transmission stations. The close calls began to mount up, taking a toll on his nerves. In early 1939 Clausen was in a taxi clutching his black leather suitcase when the driver mistakenly raised his turning signal. A vigilant traffic officer flagged them down and peered curiously at the foreigner in the back with his mysterious luggage. But instead of questioning Clausen the policeman summoned the driver to the nearest police box, where he interrogated him, leaving Clausen sweating in the back of the cab for a 'very painful' thirty minutes. When the driver returned and they resumed their journey Clausen felt, he later told his Japanese captors, 'as though I had just emerged from a tiger's lair'.[27]

What neither Sorge nor Clausen knew was that from 1938 onwards, their every coded signal was being intercepted and transcribed by the Japanese Ministry of Telecommunications. Thanks to their own radio monitoring, and after a tip-off from the military government in Korea, the Japanese authorities knew that a powerful illegal transmitter was regularly operating from various sites in the Tokyo area. An all-points bulletin was sent out to all municipal police stations, including Toriizaka, to try to spot the source of the signals. But the Japanese were never able to successfully triangulate Clausen's radio. And happily for Sorge, the Russian military code he used proved unbreakable – though the messages were faithfully monitored and transcribed by the Japanese into an ever-thickening file of unintelligible strings of number groups.[28]

Sorge's spy group had come to resemble a numerous and unruly family, united less by common loyalty to the communist cause than by the fatal secret they all shared. And it was to Sorge, as the charismatic and apparently unwavering head of the family, that all its members turned for money, advice and moral support.

Clausen's complaints were primarily financial, and connected with the extraordinary stress of his job. Branko Vukelić's were personal. Vukelić had always been a kind of general dogsbody to the spy ring, gathering small titbits of information from his journalistic contacts and performing the relatively menial task of developing Sorge's microfilms for dispatch to Moscow. His wife Edith was wife to a dogsbody. She received no salary from Moscow, and supplemented the family's meagre income with her callisthenics lessons. Their little son Paul helped keep the family together – 'Voukelitch bought his son an electric train and played with it himself,' recalled a friend.[29] But Vukelić's marriage was in trouble within a year of his arrival in Tokyo. On 14 April 1935 he went alone to a Sunday afternoon performance of a Japanese Noh play at the Nogakudo theatre in Tokyo's Suidabashi. Sitting next to him was a charming young Japanese woman, chaperoned by her father. Vukelić approached her in the lobby afterwards and introduced himself. Yoshiko Yamasaki turned out to be a daughter of a good family, a graduate of the Tsuda English College in Tokyo who spoke good English. In an interview in 1976 she recalled her excitement and nervousness at being approached by a foreigner. Vukelić was immediately smitten. The next day he sent her the first of ninety-one love letters that would eventually lead to their marriage.[30]

In 1965 one of Vukelić's Japanese interrogators claimed that Moscow Centre had ordered Vukelić to divorce Edith and marry a Japanese woman in order to integrate himself into the local population more closely.[31] There is no trace of such an instruction in the Soviet archives. The story seems unlikely – not least because Sorge, knowing from personal experience that relations between a Japanese woman and a Westerner were strongly frowned upon by traditional Japanese families, would almost certainly have opposed such a hare-brained scheme. But what is clear is that as Vukelić and Yoshiko's affair continued, his scorned and increasingly erratic wife Edith presented Sorge with a growing security risk.

Hanako told Sorge that it was 'common knowledge' that Vukelić made love to his Japanese mistress downstairs while his wife wept upstairs. (Hanako took a generally dim view of Vukelić – 'he had no manners to speak of', and rudely stretched out on the couch whenever he came to visit Sorge.[32]) Sorge and Clausen also knew that, since her husband had started his affair with Yoshiko, Edith had begun to see other men.[33] Though all the members of the group were, at least nominally, ardent communists, Sorge hit on a thoroughly capitalist solution to the Edith problem: he paid her off. Edith moved into her own house in March 1939, and in exchange for setting up one of Clausen's radio stations in the new location, she began to receive a modest salary of 400 yen a month from Centre's funds, plus 100 more for expenses. 'She was like a prostitute in a way, because she was permitting me the use of her house for radio work,' was Clausen's unpleasant characterisation of Edith's new role. Edith's 'generous' allowance was justified, Clausen told his interrogators, because she and the radio man engaged in the 'illicit relations' of espionage.[34]

In December 1939 the Vukelićs' divorce was finalised and Branko prepared to marry Yoshiko. Edith's world began to fall apart, an early victim of the brutal human toll that the spy ring wrought on its members. Clausen, when he visited for his transmissions, found her house filthy. 'After I worked in her home I did not feel like eating anything at all,' he would haughtily confide to his interrogators. Nonetheless Clausen felt a degree of sympathy for Edith's predicament. 'Men simply used her body and soon went away from her. Thus she deteriorated gradually through her sexual life. But like most other women she is a woman. Although she was not bright she had sense enough to be able to use other people for herself … If she had had a stronger man than Vukelićh she might have been different. She cannot be said to be bad in everything.

Simply her living conditions made her what she is.'[35] Clausen might have added, with more truthfulness, that it was the Fourth Department that ultimately had ruined her life.

Edith had been neutralised, her mouth sealed with money and her complicity in her husband's espionage. Yoshiko was another question. Clausen had warned Sorge that Vukelić would not be able to keep quiet to his girlfriend about his communist faith and his participation in a clandestine spy ring. It is clear from their subsequent interrogations that Clausen was right. Vukelić had indeed told Yoshiko everything just before their marriage on 26 January 1940. Wisely, Vukelić did not let on to Sorge that Yoshiko knew his secret.

The outbreak of war in Europe had one profound, practical effect on the day-to-day workings of Sorge's group. Courier-runs for post and cash to Shanghai and Hong Kong ceased to be practicable as German nationals were not welcome in the International Settlement or in the British Crown Colony. Clausen, as an enemy national, was no longer a valued customer at the few British and American banks in Tokyo. As the courier-runs dried up in 1939, Clausen found himself personally bankrolling the ring in its entirety. He protested, to Moscow, that his cash flow was not enough to cover the 3,000 yen a month that Sorge demanded. This was not true, as Clausen himself later admitted: he could easily afford to contribute more, as his blueprint business had prospered considerably on the back of a vast increase in Japanese military spending on engineering commissions of every kind. By the end of 1939 Clausen had opened his own factory that turned an annual net profit of 14,000 yen.[36] He opened a branch in Mukden to do work for the Japanese Army and had contracts with the Mitsui, Hitachi and Nakajima machine-building factories, as well as with the Ministry of the Navy. Clausen drove a Mercedes and his wife wore mink. But, as Clausen told his interrogators, he was unhappy about the prospect of his hard-won profits going to subsidise the work of the Soviet government. More, he was fed up with Sorge always treating him 'like a sort of servant, since he had no one else to help him'.[37]

Unfortunately for all concerned, the solution that Centre approved in November 1939 – to arrange handovers of cash and microfilm to diplomats from the Soviet embassy in Tokyo – was fraught with yet more risk. Hitherto the members of the Sorge spy ring had worked completely independently of the embassy for the sound operational reason that all

Soviet diplomats were kept under constant close surveillance. It was with some unease, therefore, that Anna Clausen received an invitation from her husband to accompany him to the Teikoku Gekijo, Tokyo's Imperial Theatre.

'I'm supposed to meet a friend,' Clausen claimed. Anna immediately guessed the truth – that this was the first clandestine meeting with a Soviet courier on Japanese soil. On 27 January 1940, Clausen and Anna found themselves sitting in a darkened theatre box next to a European of nondescript appearance. It was only two years later, when shown photographs by the Japanese police, that Clausen identified the courier as the Soviet consul, Helge Leonidovich Vutokevich. Fifteen minutes into the performance, the man slipped about 5,000 yen wrapped in a white cloth from his left hand into Clausen's right, which Clausen exchanged for a packet containing thirty-eight rolls of microfilm.[38]

In addition to running a fast-growing business by day, Clausen spent his evenings encoding and decoding lengthy documents in Centre's fiendishly complex number cipher. At least once a week he would pack up his transmitter for the nerve-wracking car journey to one of his radio stations, where he would often work from three to six in the morning, straining to pick up the crackle of apparently random numbers as they streamed over the airwaves from Vladivostok.[39] By 1940 Clausen had become very fat. His evenings, when not busy with encryption, were spent drinking with Sorge or other members of the German community. The only exercise he took was walking from a taxi to the bar at the Das Rheingold, and lifting heavy steins of beer. He was by nature a cheerful and stoical man, happily married, and increasingly prosperous. But by April 1940 he had begun seeing a German physician, Dr Wirtz, and was undergoing periodic hospital check-ups for shortness of breath and chest pains – an infirmity which he blamed on the fumes he inhaled in the factory rather than on his extraordinarily stressful lifestyle. When on 18 April Clausen made another courier contact – this time at the Tokyo Takarazuka theatre, with the Soviet embassy's second secretary, Viktor Sergeyevich Zaitsev, to collect $2,000 and 2,500 yen – he asked the courier that in future Sorge take over this risky task.[40] It is telling that Clausen chose to make this request through his unknown Soviet contact rather than face his hard-driving boss.

In late May 1940, to nobody's surprise except perhaps his own, Clausen suffered a serious heart attack. He survived, but Dr Wirtz ordered him to bed for three months of complete rest with an urgent recommendation to hand over his business affairs to his Japanese manager. Sorge, implacable, was having none of it. He ordered Clausen to continue transmitting, from his sickbed if necessary. The radio man dutifully obeyed, organising a slanting bed-table where he could encode and decode messages and at night instructing Anna how to assemble the radio, which she plugged into the antennas built into the siding of their house. When the set-up was ready the apparatus was balanced on two chairs by Clausen's bed so he could transmit without getting up. As he tapped through the night, Anna kept watch on the street from a second-storey window. This was not exactly the convalescent regime that his doctor had ordered.[41] Nonetheless, from Sorge's point of view the problem had been solved. 'Clausen has had a heart attack,' Sorge reported with callous brevity to Moscow on 12 July. 'He operates the wireless lying in bed.'[42]

The arrangement was not only risky to Clausen's health but to the security of the whole operation. On several occasions Clausen's Japanese employees and Dr Wirtz breezed into the room while the table was scattered with secret documents. 'Don't write when you are sick,' was the doctor's only comment after glancing at the sheets of numbers. For several days Clausen lay in fear that Wirtz would become suspicious and make a report to the police or to the German embassy, but the incident passed without consequences – at least not in the sense that Clausen was arrested. But the years of constant fear, the pain of the coronary, and Sorge's pitiless ingratitude was beginning to gnaw at the radio man's hitherto unshakeable loyalty.

'It is very difficult to explain Sorge's personality,' Clausen later told the Japanese, his words tinged with unmistakable resentment. Sorge 'has never shown his true self. But he is a true communist ... He is a man who can destroy even his best friend for the sake of communism. But judging from what I have observed, if he were in a different position he would be a miserably small-minded person ... [He] did not need to have much courage in working in the embassy. On the other hand ... he collected all information from his spy ring members and he himself tried to stay away from danger,' Clausen confided. 'When I myself was seriously ill and was being told by the doctor not to work, Sorge requested me to work the same as though I were well. Therefore he may be said to be inconsiderate of other people ... [He] does not give money even when necessary but at the same time he spent money as though he were throwing it away. Thus his character cannot be said to be ideal. [He] always treated me as a kind of a servant ... But he always treated women well. However, he did not like my wife.'[43]

Ironically, both Sorge and Clausen, for all their shared communist ideals, had in a sense reverted to the class types of Wilhemine Germany. Sorge was the high-handed, luxury-loving bourgeois ordering his subordinate about with no regard for his well-being, Clausen the dogged and hardworking mechanic, grumblingly submitting to his fate. Certainly, Sorge seemed to make no special effort to be nice to his long-suffering and long-serving associate. Sorge never 'showed a smiling expression toward Clausen', Hanako said. 'Sorge did not feel any necessity to be amiable to him.'[44]

The news of Germany's economic upswing under Hitler had, as Clausen admitted under interrogation, brought him 'to have a very favourable attitude toward Hitler's way of doing things'. The Nazi–Soviet pact doubtless further blurred the lines between Clausen's conflicting loyalties to ideology and Fatherland. As he lay in his sickbed, Clausen's commitment to spying, and to the man he had followed to Tokyo, was steadily draining away.[45]

15

Attack Singapore!

'Nobody could ever disturb his inner loneliness; that was what gave him his independence and probably explains how he was able to influence the people around him'[1]

Christiane Sorge, *Memoir*

In the spring of 1940, as the Wehrmacht stormed to victory over the Netherlands, Belgium and France, it seemed that the future world might indeed belong to the Third Reich. The tide of war had trapped Sorge in Tokyo. His only hope for a speedy return to Moscow was for Hitler's victory over Western Europe to be swift and total, and that it would leave the Soviet Union unharmed. 'The Germans here say that the war will soon be over and I must know what will become of me,' Sorge wrote to Centre. 'May I count on being able to return home at the end of the war? ... It is time to settle down, put an end to this nomad existence ... We remain, with health somewhat undermined it is true, always your true comrades and co-workers.'[2]

But a return home remained a vain hope while Japan pondered whether to enter the world war. Sorge's mysteriously intimate knowledge of Japanese politics made him a man much in demand not only by his querulous spymasters in Moscow but also, and especially by, the Germans. Ambassador Ott had been trying to persuade Sorge to join the embassy staff for much of 1939. His proposal was followed up by an official offer from the Reich Foreign Ministry of 'a high position to administer activities related to information and newspapers in the embassy'.[3] Effectively, the ministry wished to headhunt Sorge's excellent brain and have him all to themselves.

The offer put Sorge in a tricky position. He already had informal access to the embassy's secret files and telegrams through his close friendship with Ott. As an embassy official that access would be freer, and formalised. But Sorge also needed plenty of spare time to conduct the arduous business of meeting with his agents, writing and encoding reports – not to mention the relative freedom to travel and meet contacts that his journalistic cover allowed him. More important, an official job at the embassy would entail a full security check – including a scan of the police records at all his former addresses in Berlin, Hamburg, Solingen and Frankfurt. 'If I had accepted the position I would have had to present my identification,' Sorge told his interrogators. 'What I am could have been discovered after checking my past career.'[4]

Sorge refused the job offer. Ott became angry, but eventually offered a compromise. Sorge would have a desk at the embassy and fulfil some official duties, such as turning out a daily news summary for the embassy staff. But he would not become an employee of the Reich. At the same time, crucially, Sorge would 'continuously maintain the role of a private collaborator to ambassador Ott'.[5] The two old friends signed a formal contract confirming Sorge's strange, semi-official status, at the heart of the embassy but not one of its staff.

Sorge, in his new capacity as Ambassador Ott's private adviser, began showing up to the embassy at six in the morning. At that early hour he had the place virtually to himself and was able to read the overnight telegrams from Berlin, scan the news wires, and rummage through colleagues' desks. At the beginning of his espionage career Sorge had snapped photos of important documents during snatched moments when left alone in Ott's or Scholl's office. Now he had an office of his own where he could lock the door and photograph all the documents he needed in privacy. Moreover, since his job included selecting 'important items of information and arranging them so that higher members of the embassy could look at them immediately', he had official access to every report that came into the embassy with the exception of 'eyes-only' telegrams addressed personally to Ott.[6] This security precaution proved no obstacle, however, because at seven on most mornings Sorge and Ott would breakfast together. A table would be set for them on the lawn, or in the plant-filled winter garden in case of rain, and a house boy would bring fresh rolls from the German bakery. Sorge would summarise the night's news, while Ott would share his confidential correspondence from Berlin.[7] The data and information he obtained at the embassy 'were not obtained by means of plot, conspiracy, or violence', Sorge told his captors. 'I was shown them by Scholl and Ott, who asked for my cooperation.'[8]

After his convivial early-morning chat with the ambassador, Sorge would return to his embassy office and compile the *Deutscher Dienst*, the embassy's daily news-sheet distributed to staff and German expatriates. By ten in the morning his duties to the Reich were discharged, and Sorge would get into his Datsun and drive home to hammer on his typewriter. After lunch and his customary nap he would then head off to check the wires at the Domei news agency and spend the evening on the town.

Sorge also continued to contribute almost weekly to the *Frankfurter Zeitung*. As with the embassy, he insisted on remaining a freelancer rather than a staffer in order to be able to control his own time. Over his six years in Japan the editors in Frankfurt commissioned a total of 163 articles from Sorge, and remembered him as 'a most serious and thoughtful person, gifted with both an understanding of a newspaperman's job and political insight'.[9]

Today Sorge's articles make for rather dense and often platitudinous reading. But he was considered by contemporaries to be one of Germany's foremost commentators on Japanese affairs.[10] Sorge, for his part, was proud of the prestige that his association with the *Frankfurter Zeitung* gave him and boasted in his prison memoir that the newspaper 'represented the highest standards of German journalism'.[11] He also sent occasional – and even more turgid – longer articles to Haushofer's *Zeitschrift für Geopolitik*, which kept Sorge's name in the eye of senior Nazi Party circles.

From Moscow's point of view, Japan remained an urgent threat. From mid-1939 onwards Tokyo began negotiations to set up another Manchukuo-style puppet state in the occupied parts of China. Such an arrangement could have brought an official partition between Japanese-controlled China and the areas still held by the Kuomintang and communists – and in its wake possibly peace. That would be the most disastrous outcome for the Soviets, who counted on continued hostilities in China to keep the Japanese Army pinned down. A handwritten copy of the proposed secret treaty between Japan and its chosen puppet, a discontented Kuomintang official named Wang Ching-wei, found its way into the hands of Prince Saionji, and through him to Ozaki, Sorge, and Moscow.[12] The Fourth Department passed copies of the document to its communist allies in China and agents in the Kuomintang with urgent instructions to scupper any peace deal with Japan's proposed puppet state. Thus Sorge played his part in keeping the flames of conflict alive in China, the better to protect the USSR.

The Fourth Department also remained intensely interested in Japan's rearmament, which was fast making the Imperial Japanese Army a match for the Soviet forces in the Far East. 'Investigate the production capacity of the Japanese Army and Navy arsenals and civilian factories about cannon, tanks, airplanes, automobiles and machine guns,' the Fourth Department ordered Sorge on 19 February 1940.[13] The cable ended with the kind of snippy criticism that was becoming commonplace from Centre. An army manual, obtained by Corporal Koshiro and sent to Moscow by courier, was not confidential and did not need to be obtained by clandestine means, griped Centre. In fact the second part of the manual was indeed secret, but the Fourth Department simply was not paying attention. 'If you think it can be [bought] why don't you use your legal agency and let them buy it?' Sorge snapped back.[14]

This tiny spat revealed a growing gulf between Sorge's team in Tokyo and their distant masters in Moscow. The purges had claimed five successive heads of the Fourth Department and dozens of senior personnel. Over 'the past two years … organs of the NKVD have arrested more than two hundred persons, replacing the entire leadership, including chiefs of departments', Fourth Department chief Proskurov reported in May 1940 to a commission of the Defence Commissariat and the Central Committee on the effects of the purges. 'During the period when I was in command in the central [military intelligence] apparatus and its subordinate units, 365 persons were dismissed for political and various other reasons. Three hundred and twenty-six new persons were hired, the majority of whom were without intelligence training.' The loss was evidently painful to Proskurov, both professionally and personally. 'I reported on the *rezidenty* I had met – that is, those who were still there [not purged],' recalled one agent sent to Europe to report on the state of Centre's intelligence gathering apparatus in mid-1939. 'I noticed that as I spoke Ivan Iosifovich [Proskurov] squeezed his cheekbones, the muscles in his face twitching,' as he realised how many good men had gone. It may be that Proskurov's refusal to allow Sorge to return in 1939 was intended to save him from a second wave of purges instigated by his own deputy (and eventual successor) Ivan Golikov.[15]

By 1940 very few officers remained at 19 Bolshoi Znamensky Lane who had known Sorge personally. Sorge and his *rezidentura* had become abstract figures to most of the consumers of their intelligence. General Gendin had followed his predecessors to the NKVD execution grounds the previous year. But Gendin's suspicions that Sorge's network had been 'penetrated by the enemy' and was 'working under his control' remained, hovering over the relationship between Centre and Sorge like a noxious smell.

Worse, in the wake of the signing of the Nazi–Soviet non-aggression pact, Stalin and the Defence Commissariat became even more critical of Soviet military intelligence than ever. Lieutenant Colonel Maria Poliakova, one of the few of Proskurov's subordinates who had managed to survive the purges, recalled the director returning from a visit to the General Staff in a fury of frustration. 'What do they take us for – fools? How could this be disinformation?' Proskurov exclaimed. In May 1940, at a meeting with the deputy Commissar for Defence, Proskurov declared: 'No matter how painful it is, I must say that no other army has such disorderliness and a low level of discipline as ours.'[16]

The operational consequence of this atmosphere of distrust from the top was Centre's constant, nagging insistence on seeing primary documents rather than word-of-mouth information, however highly placed the source. Sorge's reputation may have been tainted – but Proskurov nonetheless recognised solid raw intelligence when it saw it and wanted more.

'It is very essential to have details about aircraft manufacturing plants,' a typical message from 2 May 1940 read. 'Also it is necessary to estimate the actual 1939 production totals in cannon manufacturing arsenals and factories. What measures are they taking to expand cannon production?'[17] Another, of 25 May, scolded that 'information must be obtained in advance. To report after-the-fact information is not good enough.'[18] Sorge dutifully borrowed the reports of the German air attaché to the Mitsubishi aircraft factory in Nagoya, the Aichi-Tokei Company, and Nakajima Aircraft.[19] General Thomas, head of the military's Economics Department in Berlin, unwittingly helped Sorge's task by commissioning a report from Sorge on the 'The problems of

Japanese wartime industry', for which military attaché Maztky helpfully furnished extensive information, including 'specific studies on aircraft, automobiles, tanks, aluminium, artificial petroleum, iron and steel among Japanese wartime industries'.[20]

Sorge's team were excellent at obtaining statistics on propeller production or new engine modifications. But the *rezident*'s particular talents were wasted on such details. Sorge's true value as a spy was an observer of the epochal diplomatic game that was unfolding between Germany and Japan, featuring Ott as a major player. By 14 June 1940, Germany's blitzkrieg on Europe was more or less complete when Hitler entered a defeated Paris and had himself photographed in front of the Eiffel Tower. The British had evacuated their battered Expeditionary Force from the beaches of Dunkirk and abandoned their positions in Norway, the last outpost of resistance on the Continent. Mussolini had finally joined the war on Germany's side and prepared to crush British armies in Egypt and Malta. Sorge, in his cups and ranting to fellow correspondents, called the Nazis 'grave-robbers'.[21] But Stalin was also doing some robbing of his own. On 15 June 1940 he sent the Red Army into independent Lithuania, Latvia, and Estonia and installed pro-Soviet puppet governments in the territories to the east of the demarcation line that had been agreed with the Nazis.

Only one part of Hitler's plan did not work: Britain did not collapse under the onslaught of bombing that the Luftwaffe unleashed on its cities in May 1940. Unlike his appeasing predecessor Neville Chamberlain, Britain's new prime minister Winston Churchill vowed uncompromising resistance to what he referred to in his stirring radio addresses as the '*Narzis*'. Hitler ordered a vast invasion force massed on the coasts of France and Belgium ready to invade Britain. Known as Operation Seelöwe (Sealion), it was Hitler's biggest military mobilisation yet. But no amphibious invasion of Britain could succeed as long as the Royal Air Force still challenged the Luftwaffe's air supremacy, or as long as the Royal Navy outgunned the Kriegsmarine in the English Channel.

It was knocking out the Royal Navy, more than bringing the British Isles themselves under the German Reich, that was Hitler's major preoccupation. As long as the British could blockade the Atlantic, North Sea and Mediterranean, Hitler's vision of a greater German Reich could never prosper. Germany's major military and diplomatic manoeuvres of the early part of the Second World War were driven by the need to destroy Britain's naval power – specifically, to destroy the naval base of Malta, to break Britain's control of the Suez Canal, and to take Singapore, the key to British naval supremacy in the Pacific and Indian oceans. As Sorge himself put it, reporting a conversation with Ott in the summer of 1940: 'The Germans believed that a Japanese attack on Singapore would reduce British naval forces in the Mediterranean and Atlantic and so make it possible for Germany to invade England itself.'[22]

From June of 1940, therefore, it became an urgent priority for Ribbentrop to persuade Japan to enter the war on Germany's side against Britain and take Singapore. But Ott faced a major problem in executing his chief's demand. On the one hand, there had always been deep admiration for Hitler among Japanese militarist circles – an admiration that grew stronger after the success of Hitler's blitzkrieg tactics. The Wehrmacht had shown that a new kind of mechanised lightning war could cut deep into the territory of even the most entrenched and technologically advanced enemy. The fall of the Netherlands and France left Indochina and the Dutch East Indies – a key source of oil and rubber – vulnerable.

On the other hand, Tokyo had so far been officially neutral in the unfolding world war, largely because Japan chose to remain in aggrieved isolation in the wake of the Ribbentrop-Molotov Pact. Admiral Yonai, the dominant figure in the government, was a strong opponent of a full alliance with Germany and instead argued – rightly, as it ultimately turned out – that Japan would be crushed if it attempted to go to war against both Britain and the United States. Tensions ran so high between the army's Control Group and Action Group that one militarist faction even hatched yet another plot to murder Yonai and all the anti-German members of the government.[23]

The assassination plot was uncovered and thwarted. However, Yonai's objection to military adventures was being fast eroded by the tempting prizes piling up in the Asia-Pacific region. Japan demanded, and received, a commitment from defeated France that it cease traffic in munitions from French Indochina to the Chinese nationalists. Japan also, with Germany's blessing, signed a generous new deal for oil and rubber from the East Indies with the government of the Nazi-controlled Netherlands. The era of European domination in Asia appeared to be over.

In July 1940 the war minister Shunroku Hata demanded a reorganisation of the Japanese state along Nazi lines, as well as a full alliance with Germany. When Yonai refused Hata resigned, precipitating a constitutional crisis that brought Prince Konoe to power for a second time. Konoe may have spoken regularly of curbing the army's power, but in reality he was a witting stooge of the militarists. Konoe's new war minister was General Hideki Tojo, a militant nationalist and ideologue of Japanese imperialism popularly known as 'Razor Brain'. Tojo's presence in the cabinet was visible proof that Konoe was not his own master. Konoe also named Yosuke Matsuoka, a garrulous and ambitious politician with close ties to the Kwangtung Army, as foreign minister.

The Action Group of the Imperial Army had effectively mounted a soft coup against their opponents. The Konoe government was now under their control. Immediately upon formation of the second Konoe cabinet, the Breakfast Group – including Ozaki – re-formed, meeting at the official residence of the chief secretary, Kenji Tomita. Ozaki also maintained his position in the Investigation Department of the South Manchuria Railway, the nerve centre of military intelligence for China.

With the moderates now out of the way, negotiations could begin in earnest for a full-blown Japanese–German military alliance. Japan's aims were clear, even from Miyagi's ground-level point of view. 'Japanese diplomacy hopes to strengthen the German-Italian alliance, exclude or boycott United States and British power from the Orient, resolve the war in China and establish a self-sufficient East Asia and new order in East Asia,' Miyagi reported.[24] On 23 August, Ribbentrop sent Heinrich Stahmer as his personal envoy to Japan to negotiate a new alliance.[25] The South Manchuria Railway was in charge of all logistics of his visit to Tokyo, so Ozaki – and therefore Sorge and Centre – were aware of Stahmer's itinerary almost as soon as Ribbentrop himself.[26]

By mid-September, Stahmer and Matsuoka had concluded negotiations for a tripartite alliance between Nazi Germany, Fascist Italy and Japan – or as Mussolini more snappily dubbed it, the Axis.[27] In essence, the Axis entailed a global carve-up of spheres of influence in a future, Nazi-dominated world. Japan agreed to 'recognise and respect the leadership of Germany and Italy in the establishment of a new order in Europe', while Japan was accorded similar 'leadership ... in the establishment of a new order in Greater East Asia'. Japan's sphere would encompass Manchuria and China, French Indochina and the Pacific Islands, Thailand, British Malaya and Borneo, the Dutch East Indies, Burma, Australia and New Zealand. British India was, in a curious nod to the spirit of the Ribbentrop–Molotov Pact, to be considered as within the sphere of the Soviet Union.

Importantly, the Japanese would be allowed to choose whether and when they wished to join the war against Britain. Also, crucially, Germany shared Japan's keenness to keep America out of the war – and hoped that the prospect of fighting in both the Atlantic and Pacific would encourage Washington to stick to its current policy of isolation. To that end, Matsuoka appointed Admiral Kichisaburo Nomura, a high-profile advocate of US–Japanese friendship with many allies in Washington, including President Roosevelt himself, as Japan's new ambassador to the United States.

Keeping Soviet Russia out of an alliance with Britain and America was also vital. Article V of the Tripartite Pact specifically affirmed that 'the above agreement affects in no way the political status existing at present between each of the three Contracting Powers and Soviet Russia'. And Stahmer strongly hinted during his visit to Tokyo that better relations between Japan and the Soviet Union would help keep America neutral.[28]

The Japanese did not wait for the formal signing in Berlin on 27 September ('in the 19th year of the Fascist era [1941]', according to the document's grand preamble[29]) to enact their side of the grand carve-up. A Japanese expeditionary force sailed from Taiwan to French Indochina on 19 September, overrunning Tonkin province after a few brief skirmishes. This was excellent news for Sorge. Every step Japan took south was a step away from the Soviet Union – and presumably towards the end of the war, and his return home.

'I have just turned 45 and have been on this job for eleven years ... the conditions here would undermine the strongest constitution,' Sorge reminded Centre in October 1940. 'I beg you not to forget that I have been living here without a break, and unlike other "respectable foreigners" have not taken a holiday every three or four years. That may look suspicious.' He also claimed that 'Max is unfortunately so seriously ill that a return to his former work capacity cannot be counted on ... I am learning his job now and will take his work on myself.'[30]

This was untrue. Max was in fact back at work and being driven harder than ever. Despite his heart attack and three months in bed, Clausen managed to transmit about sixty times during 1940 – ten more than the previous year – encrypting and sending a gruelling 29,179 words, a record for the Tokyo *rezidentura*. But if Sorge's lie was meant to hasten the recall that he and Clausen wished for so badly, the response from Centre was so tactless that it might have been calculated to extinguish the last vestiges of loyalty that Clausen may have retained for the cause, and for his bosses in Moscow.

Yet another new director had taken over. Proskurov had proved too outspoken in his views on the possibility of Hitler reneging on the Ribbentrop–Molotov Pact. In June 1940 he fell victim to yet another purge of the top ranks of the Red Army, and was arrested and later shot. Proskurov's successor was his one-time deputy General Filip Golikov, a man whose prime concern was remaining alive by feeding Stalin only information that conformed with the dictator's prejudices. Keeping his demanding Japanese *rezidentura* happy came low on Golikov's list of priorities.

'Dear Ramsay, having carefully studied your materials for 1940 I believe that they do not answer to the tasks set before you ... the majority of your materials are not secret and not timely ... I demand that you activate your work and supply me with operative information,' Golikov cabled in February 1941. 'I believe it is necessary to curtail the expenses of your firm to 2,000 yen a month. Pay your sources only for valuable information and carefully. Use the income of the firm of Fritz [Clausen] for additional financing of our work.'[31]

Sorge protested vigorously. 'When we received your orders to curtail our expenses we took that as a kind of punishment,' Sorge cabled on 26 March 1941. 'If you insist on curtailing our budget then you must be ready for the destruction of this small apparat which we have created. If you do not find it possible to agree with these suggestions then I will have to ask you to call me home. Having been here for seven years and becoming physically weakened I believe that this is the only way out of these difficulties.'[32] But Centre was adamant. It was time to see a return on its investment in Tokyo's blueprint-producing industry.

This was not welcome news to Clausen, who had worked for years at building Centre's seed money into a highly profitable business.[33] Indeed, by the beginning of 1941 Clausen, by his own account, had become more interested in his capitalist cover operation than in his supposed main job as an intelligence officer.

'As I became disinterested in spying work and as my belief in communism became shaky, I came to devote myself seriously to this business,' Clausen said in prison. 'I put all of my money into this business and worked as hard as I could.' Once, Clausen had considered himself '100 percent communist' who 'thought that the work of secret spying was sacred and important work'. Years of stress, bullying and callous treatment by Centre and especially by Sorge had made him 'sick and tired of spy work'. Max had undergone, albeit somewhat belatedly, the ideological transformation that thousands of German communists of his class and generation had experienced. He told his interrogators that he had originally become a communist 'because all of the people could not find employment'. But now that Hitler had succeeded in eradicating unemployment, Clausen felt a swelling pride in his homeland. 'For the first time I felt that I am a German,' he said. 'I have been wandering between my old communist ideology on the one hand and the newborn Germany and the patriotic Japanese people.'[34]

In his years in Tokyo, Clausen came to feel that the Japanese seemed quite content without the dictatorship of the proletariat. 'This country does not need communism,' he decided. As for his masters in the Kremlin, Clausen felt that Stalin had sacrificed the communist dream in the interests of rebuilding the Russian Empire. He concluded, therefore, that his 'spying work was nonsense'. The order from Moscow instructing him to fund the ring personally proved the final straw for Clausen, who finally resolved to 'stay out of involvement with Moscow'.[35] Evidently scared of Sorge's wrath, Clausen prevaricated about informing his chief that he 'could not accept such instructions' until January 1941. But in the meantime he took his own small revenge on Sorge, on Centre, and on his own former servile self. From November 1940, Clausen began destroying parts of Sorge's reports without bothering to transmit them to Centre.

In his prison testimony, Clausen was trying to prove to his captors that he was no longer a communist fanatic, and had not been for some time. Sorge, on the other hand, hoped that the Soviet Union would step in and save him, as they had the Noulens in their Chinese captivity, so confessed to no weakening in his loyalty to communism. Nor could Sorge make any such an admission to Hanako, nor the wavering Clausen or the doggedly loyal Ozaki; much less to the Otts or through his letters to Katya, which were all read by Centre. In those climactic years of his Tokyo career, Sorge was utterly alone with his doubts, and his secrets. Perhaps the stress of keeping these emotions bottled up helps explain why Sorge so readily confessed to the Japanese, and in such detail and at such length. But he lied and concealed from his interrogators too. Our single insight into Sorge's inner mind is his crie de coeur to Niilo Virtanen in Moscow in 1935, when he confessed to feeling desperate and disillusioned – and his often-repeated pleas to Moscow be allowed to return home.

After the start of the war Sorge became closer than ever to the Otts, not just professionally but personally. Sorge spent much of the summer and autumn of 1940 at the Otts' summer residence at Akiya, thirty kilometres south of Tokyo. He and Eugen would spend days walking around the countryside, Sorge snapping photographs of peasant life (on one occasion Ott saved Sorge from arrest by spy-crazy police by producing his diplomatic pass). Sorge was also frequently ill – despite his enthusiasm for chest-expanding and physical fitness, he was not a healthy man – and Helma Ott reprised her role as nursemaid and mother, bringing him nourishing soups at home.[36] But the real pain – of separation from Katya, and of being trapped in his secret life – remained, private and implacable.

In early autumn 1940 Colonel Matzky headed back to Berlin – via Vladivostok and the Trans-Siberian railway through friendly Russia – carrying Sorge's latest essay for General Thomas among his papers. As the colonel drove through central Moscow en route from the Kazan station to the Belorussian station he would have passed close to the Fourth Department headquarters, where the report's contents had been filed some weeks before. Matzky's replacement was Colonel Alfred Kretschmer who, like his predecessors, had been briefed by army top brass that Sorge was a man who could be trusted.

Hitler's planned invasion date for Britain had been set for 15 September 1940. A crew of film-makers from Berlin was sent to the Belgian port of Antwerp to film tanks and troops pretending to land in Britain from barges and storming dunes under a volley of blanks. Since the actual landings were due to happen under cover of night, propaganda minister Joseph Goebbels wished the people of the Reich to have a newsreel-ready version of the invasion.[37] But the RAF's unexpected resilience, and the superiority of the Royal Navy, made the planned operation a near-suicidal prospect. On 17 September 1940, Hitler held a meeting with Reichsmarschall Hermann Göring and Field Marshal Gerd von Rundstedt during which the Führer became convinced the operation was not viable as long as control of the skies was still lacking. Grand Admiral Karl Dönitz admitted that 'we possessed neither control of the air or the sea, nor were we in any position to gain it'.[38] Later that day, Hitler ordered the postponement of the operation and ordered the dispersal of the invasion fleet in order to avert further damage by British air and naval attacks.[39]

Officially, in order to maintain pressure on Britain, Operation Sealion was merely postponed until the following spring.[40] In private, Hitler was already moving towards the most fateful decision of his life. At noon on 29 July 1940, after a routine situation report from his senior commanders, Hitler asked his chief of operational staff, Generaloberst Alfred Jodl, to stay behind. The Führer was worried: the Russians might ignore the non-aggression pact and attack while Germany's forces were tied up in the West. Hitler was concerned that there were too many Russian troops on the other side of the German–Russian border: 'In the East we have nothing.' If the Soviets seized Romania they would cut the Reich off from the only source of petroleum in mainland Europe, the oilfields of Ploesti, strangling Hitler's war effort. 'Then the war would be lost for us,' Hitler told Jodl.* Hitler then asked Jodl whether there was any chance of redeploying the Sealion forces to the East and, if necessary, attacking and defeating the Soviet Union in the autumn of 1940. Jodl replied that such an offensive would take four months at least to prepare.[41]

On Hitler's orders, a secret group in the German high command began working on plans to invade the Soviet Union under the codename 'Operation Otto'.[42] The Führer received the preliminary military plans for an attack on the USSR on 5 December 1940. Two weeks later Hitler issued his top-secret Directive No 21 instructing the Wehrmacht to be ready for an imminent attack along the Reich's 1,600-kilometre

---

*Hitler was right – Romania was Hitler's only source of oil and the destruction of Ploesti would have stopped the German war machine at any time of the war. Hitler's much touted synthetic oil represented only a very small part of Germany's consumption. It remains one of the great mysteries of the Second World War why the Allies did so little to attack it, other than a single major USAF raid in August 1943.

long Eastern front with the USSR. The operation was renamed after
the medieval Holy Roman Emperor who had led the Third Crusade,
Frederick Barbarossa. The launch date of Hitler's invasion of the Soviet
Union was set for 15 May 1941.

Despite the enormous movement of men and materiel that it entailed,
Operation Barbarossa remained a closely kept secret. In Japan, the first
inklings of a major shift of German policy came in the form of urgent
instructions to the new military attaché Kretschmer to redouble efforts
to persuade the Japanese to join the war by attacking Singapore. Ott,
too, was mobilised by a personal cable from Ribbentrop.

The ambassador, ever practical, knew the respect in which German
military planning was held by the Japanese. He therefore formed a
working group at the embassy to come up with a detailed military plan
to take Singapore, based on the information they possessed about Japan's
military and economic capabilities. The group – composed of Ott's three
senior service attachés, plus the chief of the Economic Section, Alois
Tichy – even constructed a special sand table representing the geography
of the southern tip of the Malay Peninsula. By the end of January, Ott,
Kretschmer and naval attaché Wenneker (Sorge's old bottle-mate, back
in Tokyo for a second tour of duty with the rank of rear admiral and a
pretty young bride) came to a crucial conclusion. 'It would be possible
to conquer Singapore if Japan would attack from the direction of the
Malay Peninsula,' Sorge reported to Moscow. Furthermore, the attack
should be 'sudden' and supported by Germany, who would 'assist Japan
indirectly by taking the offensive in the Atlantic during the period and
by thus drawing British forces there'.[43]

The Germans' simple realisation that Singapore was impregnable from
the sea but almost undefended from the land was a brilliant piece of
creative tactical thinking. However, despite the cleverness of the plan,
Ott's campaign to persuade the Japanese to attack Singapore ran into a
snag almost from the outset – a complication of the Germans' own making
and the fruit of a fateful naval engagement in the South China Sea.

At around 7 a.m. on 11 November 1940, the British Blue Funnel cargo
liner SS *Automedon* was spotted by a German surface raider about 340
kilometres miles north-west of Sumatra. The *Automedon* was carrying
crated aircraft, motor cars, spare parts, liquor, cigarettes, and food and was
bound for Penang, Singapore, Hong Kong and Shanghai. Her German

pursuer was the *Atlantis*, a heavily armed converted freighter. Within an hour the faster *Atlantis* had closed to within gunnery range. She ran up her Kreigsmarine ensign and uncovered her guns. *Automedon* did not have enough time to finish sending a distress signal before German shellfire destroyed her bridge, killing all the senior British officers at a stroke.

The boarding party from the *Atlantis* took the surviving crew members prisoner. Among the cargo they discovered fifteen bags of top-secret mail intended for the British Far East Command in Singapore. Among the haul of documents were the new Royal Navy fleet codes valid from 1 January 1941, the newest fleet orders and gunnery instructions, $6 million in new Malayan dollars – as well as some sixty sealed packages containing mail from Britain's Secret Intelligence Service to their stations in Singapore, Hong Kong, Shanghai, and Tokyo, including summaries of the latest intelligence reports of Japanese military and political activities.

The most significant find, however, was a small green bag discovered in the chart room below the wreckage of the bridge. The bag, marked 'Safe Hand – British Master Only' was weighted with lead and equipped with holes to allow it to sink if it had to be thrown overboard. It contained documents prepared by the British War Cabinet's Planning Division and addressed to Air Chief Marshal Robert Brooke-Popham, British commander-in-chief in the Far East.[44] The report was a summary of the Cabinet's military strategy in the Far East. It was an explosive document, frankly admitting that Britain did not have the ships or men to go to war against Japan. The papers also made it quite clear that no reinforcements could be spared from the European theatre of war, and that Hong Kong, Malaya, the Dutch East Indies and even Singapore itself were all indefensible in the face of a Japanese attack. In effect, the document confirmed that Britain could not send a fleet to defend Singapore and that in the eyes of Downing Street, the fortress had already been abandoned.*,[45]

---

*Even as Churchill was privately giving up on Singapore, he was nonetheless also attempting to persuade President Franklin Roosevelt to station units of the US Pacific Fleet there. Churchill sent Roosevelt a report called 'Notes on the Action at Taranto', a study on how a 11–12 November 1940 Royal Navy surprise attack had, for the first time, used torpedo bombers to destroy a significant part of the Italian Regia Marina fleet at anchor. Churchill had hoped that the Taranto operation would warn the Americans that the same thing could be done to their own fleet at Pearl Harbor. But Roosevelt did not send any ships to Singapore, nor did he prepare for the kind of surprise aerial torpedo attack that Churchill had so cannily predicted.

The *Atlantis*'s captain, Bernhard Rogge, recognised the significance of the captured dispatches and sent them to Wenneker in Tokyo, who immediately composed a message to Berlin on his Enigma encoding machine.[46] Wenneker's telegram was immediately shown to Hitler who scrawled in the margin: 'This is of the utmost importance.' On 12 December the Führer authorised a copy to be given to the Japanese. Wenneker hurried to show the document to Admiral Nobutake Kondo, deputy Chief of the General Staff.

Wenneker believed that the report, showing as it did British weakness in the Pacific, would strengthen his argument for an attack on Singapore. Instead the Japanese reached a very different conclusion – one that did not suit Germany's interests at all. The commanders of the Japanese Imperial Navy took the British War Cabinet report as an assurance that Britain would not – and could not – interfere with their Asian expansion. Even more significantly, navy commander Marshal Admiral Isoroku Yamamoto concluded that their only remaining serious enemy in the Pacific was the Americans.

From the beginning of Japan's naval rearmament in 1922, Japanese Navy planners had had to contend with the likelihood of a two-power threat in the Pacific. Thanks to the revelations in the *Automedon* papers, it became evident that the Japanese naval staff could concentrate with single-minded equanimity on the US Pacific Fleet.[47] In January 1941 Yamamoto ordered his staff to plan a surprise attack that would destroy American naval power at a single stroke.[48] The plan, developed in absolute secrecy even from the civilian government and the army, centred on a strike by naval aircraft on Pearl Harbor.[49]

Neither Sorge nor Ozaki, nor even Prime Minister Konoe himself, had any inkling of Yamamoto's Pearl Harbor plan. However, evidence of Germany's preparations for war against the Soviet Union continued to accumulate. An economic mission from Berlin arrived in Tokyo. It was headed by Helmut Wohltat, a Finance Ministry official who specialised in the Reich's strategic oil supplies and its task was to negotiate a grand economic bargain between Germany and Japan.[50] From economic attaché Tichy, Sorge learned that Japanese wanted parts for machines, tanks, submarines, and anti-aircraft guns, assistance in mass production of war materiel, and patent releases on such items as artificial petroleum and aeroplanes.[51] Wohltat asked, in return, for 60,000 tons of rubber a year, soybeans, whale oil, various minerals, and a guarantee of German rights in China.

Why would Germany be seeking to find alternative sources of the raw materials it was currently receiving from the Soviet Union? Why the sudden urgency to cripple the Royal Navy? Piece by piece, an observer as intelligent and well informed as Sorge must have been fitting together the truth about Hitler's plan to attack Russia within weeks of Directive No 21. 'Germany at that time was already determined to have a war against Russia,' Sorge would explain to his captors. 'And since she could not give any time to Britain, she was eager for the Japanese to join the war against Britain.'[52]

Later Sorge would claim that he never doubted that Hitler would eventually attack Stalin. 'Even though Germany had come to terms with Russia, anti-Soviet feeling in the Nazi Party ran high,' Sorge told the Japanese. He became convinced that 'despite the existence of the [non-aggression] Pact, sooner or later a break with the Soviet Union would inevitably occur'.[53] Hanako, in her memoir, confirmed that 'by the end of 1940 Sorge had the conviction that someday Germany and Russia would fight. Sorge was deeply troubled by this prospect. It gave him many anxious moments.' Sorge certainly despised Hitler. Hanako recalled him explaining to her, in his babyish Japanese, that Hitler was 'not a very big man' whereas Stalin was 'a great man'. But, in Hanako's judgement, her lover 'had a deep inner conflict. He spied for the Russians, but he both liked and respected the Germans and he did not want to see Germany and Russia fight.'[54]

Even as Barbarossa was still in its earliest stages, Sorge picked up more snippets of information from visiting German officers. The first inkling was Berlin's growing preoccupation with keeping Romanian oil out of Soviet hands. Another was speculation by visiting German officers about the battle-readiness of the Soviet Army. On 28 December, Sorge reported to Moscow that a new reserve army of forty divisions had been created in the Leipzig area of eastern Germany.[55] He also warned that several new arrivals from Berlin had mentioned a force of eighty German divisions deployed on the Soviet border with Romania.[56] The purpose of the new army, in Sorge's understanding, was to protect the oilfields of Ploesti, the Reich's single source of petroleum in Europe. If the USSR 'begins to develop activities against German interests, as happened in the

Baltic, the Germans could occupy territory on a line from Kharkov through Moscow to Leningrad,' Sorge explained. 'The Germans know that the USSR would not risk this, as the Soviet leadership is aware, particularly after the Finnish campaign, that it will take twenty years for the Red Army to become a modern army like that of Germany.'[57]

Like Clausen, Sorge still felt himself to be German, even after all his years among foreigners. And Centre was doing little to encourage Sorge's loyalties for his adopted Motherland. With its constant carping and demands for confirmation, Centre was making it abundantly clear that it frankly distrusted his information. Nonetheless, whatever qualms he may have felt about the coming war between the Motherland and Fatherland, Sorge's first loyalty remained to his network and to the Soviet Union. The year of the snake – 1941 – promised to bring terrible danger for Russia, and for Katya.

16

The Butcher of Warsaw

'So utterly bestial and corrupt as to be practically inhuman'[1]

SS-Brigadeführer Walter Schellenberg
on Gestapo colonel Joseph Meisinger

It is not precisely clear just how Nazi intelligence first got wind of the fact that their contributor, informant and trusted source on all things Japanese, Dr Richard Sorge, might, in fact, be a communist. What we do know is that by the end of 1940, SS-Brigadeführer Walter Schellenberg, head of foreign intelligence at the Reich Main Security Office (or RSHA), was fully aware that Sorge had deep, long-standing connections with the German Communist Party.

The first tremors of doubt about Sorge's bona fides had begun to circulate in Berlin in the middle of 1940, when the Foreign Department of the Nazi Party received expressions of concern about Sorge's 'political past'. Such a denunciation could only have come from members of Sorge's Tokyo Nazi Party group – probably triggered by Sorge's increasingly frequent and outspoken diatribes against Hitler in the bars and restaurants of Ginza. Rather than raising the matter with the embassy, where Sorge's personal connections with Ott would doubtless have quashed any investigation, the complaint went direct to Berlin, where party headquarters referred the matter to one of Sorge's official employers, Wilhelm von Ritgen, the head of the German News Agency (or DNB). Von Ritgen, who had been the grateful recipient of detailed news reports and personal letters from Sorge for some years, in turn took the allegations to Schellenberg at the RHSA.

Schellenberg had the makings of a most dangerous enemy for Sorge. He had joined the SS, Hitler's elite stormtroopers, in 1933 immediately after graduating from law school. A fanatical Nazi, Schellenberg subscribed to the Führer-Prinzip – the idea that Hitler's directives were beyond the framework of the legal system and should be carried out unquestioningly, regardless of legal niceties. In 1935 he was handpicked by RHSA chief Reinhard Heydrich for counter-intelligence work. Schellenberg's SS personnel file described him as 'open, irreproachable, and reliable … firm, tough, possesses energy [and] very sharp-thinking'. His national socialist worldview was judged 'thoroughly fortified'. Heydrich entrusted him with the less official aspects of the SS's empire-building. One of Schellenberg's tasks was to amass a real-estate portfolio from confiscated properties – including a handsome villa on Berlin's Wannsee where the SS's leaders would soon gather to plan the Final Solution to the Jewish problem.

The allegations against Sorge presented Schellenberg with a tricky problem. By 1940 Sorge's judgement on all things Japanese was trusted by a swathe of the Reich's top brass – not only Ambassador Ott, but also General Thomas of the Wehrmacht's Economic Department and by the DNB, which had by this time become an arm of the Reich's intelligence network. Von Ritgen told Schellenberg that Sorge had never given him any reason to doubt his integrity. Indeed, his recent report on Japan's war economy had been circulated to some of the most senior officials in Berlin. Sorge was, in von Ritgen's estimation, 'indispensable'.

And yet when Schellenberg called up Sorge's files from 'three or four' security agencies – the Gestapo, the SD Internal Security Department, and the RHSA's own archive – it was immediately clear that in the 1920s the man had deep, extensive and unmistakably suspicious contacts with a swathe of known Comintern agents. While no definitive proof could be found that Sorge was an active member of the German Communist Party or Comintern, 'one could not help coming to the conclusion that he was at least a sympathiser', Schellenberg wrote in his post-war memoirs. 'But he had close ties with people in influential circles and had always been protected against rumours of this sort.'[2] The mystery remains as to why these compromising files were not discovered back in 1934, when Sorge applied for his Nazi Party membership, well before his 'influential' contacts from Tokyo had any reason to cover for him.

A less subtle and more brutal man than Schellenberg would have immediately moved to shut Sorge out of the embassy, or denounced him to the Japanese authorities as a communist. Instead, Schellenberg decided to continue to use Sorge's undoubted talents, while all the time watching for him to make a slip. According to Schellenberg, von Ritgen insisted that 'even if we assume that Sorge had connections with the Russian Secret Service, we must, after safeguarding our own interests, find ways of profiting from his profound knowledge'. In the end, Schellenberg 'agreed that I should protect Sorge from attacks by the [Nazi] Party, but only on condition that he included in his reports intelligence material on the Soviet Union, China and Japan ... When I reported this to Heydrich he agreed, with the proviso that we immediately establish surveillance on Sorge. Heydrich was skeptical about the whole thing and warned that Sorge may be furnishing us with disinformation.'[3]

Schellenberg claimed, in effect, that he had agreed with no less a figure than the Reich's security chief that Sorge be treated as a potential Soviet agent nearly a year before his eventual arrest by the Japanese. But this does not fit the facts. If Schellenberg was truly convinced that Sorge was a Soviet spy, leaving him with an office in the embassy, security clearance and the confidence of Ott, Thomas and the DNB would have been a grave security risk. More likely is that the information Schellenberg had dug up cast some suspicion on Sorge, but nothing more concrete. Indeed some parts of the 'evidence' against Sorge – for instance Schellenberg's belief that Sorge was 'in touch with extreme right wing elements in Germany between 1923 and 1928' – were simply untrue. Sorge had lived in Moscow for most of that period, a fact which Schellenberg was apparently not aware of. Schellenberg wrote his memoir *The Labyrinth* while he was on trial for war crimes at Nuremberg in 1949 (it became an international bestseller).[4] The author's aim was to cast himself in the role of German patriot and, more importantly, an all-knowing spymaster. Sorge's future arrest was to prove a shock and deep embarrassment to Schellenberg and the RHSA – such a shock, in fact, that for weeks afterwards the Germans continued to protest that Sorge was innocent. Schellenberg's claim to have rumbled Sorge so early has a distinct ring of hindsight.[5]

What is clearly true is that the suspicions of the Nazi security apparatus had certainly been aroused. But Schellenberg faced an operational problem in fulfilling Heydrich's order to put watchful eyes on Sorge. Reich security had nobody at the German embassy in Tokyo with sufficient experience in counter-intelligence to trap an agent of Sorge's calibre. Until, that is, the file of Colonel Joseph Albert Meisinger landed on Schellenberg's desk in March 1941.

Meisinger had been a Freikorps comrade of Reinhard Heydrich's in the early 1920s, when the future Nazi security supremo had been a minor Bavarian police official. Both men would find their true calling in the Nazi secret police. From 1933 Meisinger carved a niche for himself in the Reich's secret state police, or Gestapo, as an expert on questions of homosexuality, illegal sexual relations between Jews and Aryans, and abortion (which had been made illegal under Nazi law). Meisinger sent thousands of 'social deviants' to the newly established concentration camps, and played a leading role in purging the ranks of the Foreign Ministry of suspected homosexuals.[6] In September 1939 he was appointed deputy commander of Einsatzgruppe IV in newly occupied Poland, a death squad charged with murdering opponents of the Nazi regime. On 1 January 1940, promoted to *Standartenführer* or colonel, Meisinger was made commander of the state police in the Warsaw District. There, he unleashed a brutal campaign of wholesale slaughter against Poles and Jews.[7] Among his more notorious actions were the mass shooting of 1,700 people in a forest near Palmiry, the execution of fifty-five randomly selected Warsaw Jews as a reprisal for the murder of a Polish policeman, and the execution of 107 Poles as a reprisal for the murder of two Germans.[8]

For these and other, less public, acts of sadism and brutality Meisinger quickly earned himself the soubriquet the 'Butcher of Warsaw'.*[9] By March 1940 his superiors were so appalled by his behaviour that even the Gestapo wanted Meisinger arrested and tried for war crimes. Such actions would become standard operating procedure for Einsatzgruppen operating in Russia after the launch of Operation Barbarossa the following year. But for 1940, they were shocking. Even Schellenberg, no stranger to violence, found that the 'huge file' he had collected on Meisinger 'proved him to be so utterly bestial and corrupt as to be practically inhuman'.[10]

---

*There seems to have been some competition for this nickname: SS-Gruppenführer Heinz Reinefarth was also dubbed the Butcher of Warsaw.

Fortunately for the Butcher, his old *Kampfkamerad*, Heydrich, intervened to prevent Meisinger's impending court martial and possible execution. 'Meisinger knew too much,' according to Schellenberg – apparently a reference to his old comradeship with Heydrich.[11] A face-saving compromise was arranged. With Heydrich and Schellenberg's blessing, Meisinger was to be sent to Tokyo as a police attaché to the embassy. The Gestapo colonel was swiftly packed, like a dangerous bacillus, into a Kriegsmarine submarine and sent east. Schellenberg had found just the right man to investigate the mysterious Dr Sorge.

Meisinger certainly made a powerful impression on his arrival in Japan in early April 1941. One German lady in Tokyo remembered him as 'such a terrifying presence my knees gave way when I went into his office'.[12] A rumour went around the embassy staff in Tokyo that Meisinger ate raw steak with his fingers. His official post was as the Reich security liaison officer to the Japanese Secret Intelligence Service. But word quickly spread that his real role was to seek out enemies of the Third Reich within the German community.

Sorge's response to the arrival of Meisinger, a deadly threat to his spy career and his life, was simple. At the earliest opportunity, he invited this terrifying man to go drinking with him in Ginza. Over beers at the Imperial Hotel, Lohmeyer's, Das Rheingold, Die Fledermaus, Ginza Lion and his usual repertoire of other bars, Sorge worked his old magic – just as he had with Ott, Wenneker, Scholl, Matzky and the rest. Like Sorge, Meisinger had been an infantry private in the First World War, in the 230th Minenwerfer Company of the Bavarian Pioneer Battalion. Like Sorge, he had been wounded, won an Iron Cross, and been promoted to a non-commissioned officer. Sorge's status as a war hero, his rough charisma, his abundant knowledge of both Tokyo's nightspots and its high politics, won the colonel over. By May, according to a German diplomatic colleague, Meisinger 'felt honoured that Sorge valiantly helped him devour his stock of whisky on many an occasion, even though he made great fun of the fat Meisinger while doing so'.[13] Within weeks of his sub-marine arrival in Tokyo, Sorge had converted the Butcher of Warsaw into his newest bottle-mate.

As Sorge was defusing the Meisinger threat, he was also attempting to decipher the diplomatic conundrum of whether Japan was actually going to heed Ribbentrop's increasingly insistent pleas that Tokyo join in Germany's war. Ambassador Ott and his sand-table had, so far, failed to persuade Konoe and the Imperial General Staff of the wisdom of attacking Singapore – not, primarily, because they feared beleaguered Britain but mostly because they were wary of making an enemy of America. 'Germany was somewhat disappointed by the Japanese attitude after the conclusion of the three-country alliance, for Germany expected that Japan would by this alliance take a more aggressive attitude toward the United States and Britain,' Sorge reported to Moscow. 'But all that Japan tried to do was to bring Indochina into the Greater East Asia Co-Prosperity Sphere ... Thus this diplomatic game ended with a complete Japanese victory.'[14]

Ribbentrop attempted to break the deadlock by inviting Foreign Minister Matsuoka to Berlin for an official visit in March 1941. The visit was intended as part of a convoluted web of diplomacy that Hitler was weaving to disguise his preparations for Barbarossa. Hitler was already resolved to invade Russia. But nonetheless, in late 1940 and early 1941, Berlin floated several diplomatic démarches designed to disguise Germany's true intentions until the invasion force was ready. One was a proposed deal with Stalin to carve up the Balkans between the USSR and Germany – a false-flag operation that allowed Hitler to pass off his build-up of troops on the Eastern front as an invasion force intended for Yugoslavia and Romania. The other deal was the (in retrospect) bizarre suggestion that the Soviet Union actually join the Axis.

The deal – which Molotov discussed with Hitler and Ribbentrop in Berlin in February 1941 – would entail the Soviet Union signing up to the Tripartite Pact formula of recognising the 'leadership' of Germany, Italy, and Japan in, respectively, Europe and East Asia. The existing Axis powers would, in turn, agree to respect Soviet territory. All would pledge to give no assistance to the other's enemies. A secret protocol assigned areas of influence beyond Europe's borders. The Persian Gulf and India would be within the Soviet sphere, Japan got the Pacific, Germany central Africa, and Italy northern Africa.[15] Though after the war Molotov would try to pass these negotiations off as Stalin playing for time before the inevitable German invasion, in truth, for several months in early 1941, Stalin seems to have believed that his sworn enemy in Berlin was still more interested in dominating Europe and Africa than invading the Soviet Union.

Matsuoka's role in this scheme, from the German point of view, was as a useful dupe. Berlin had told the Japanese nothing about

Barbarossa. They had also kept quiet about Stalin's demands of chunks of the proposed Japanese sphere of influence – notably in Mongolia and India – as the price of his agreement to join the Axis powers. Hitler needed Japan to attack Singapore, but not other areas of the Pacific rim that might bring America into the war, such as the Philippines, a former US protectorate. And, most immediately, he needed Matsuoka to rubber-stamp his double-dealing with Stalin until such time as Barbarossa was ready.

Sorge believed himself to be supremely well informed about Matsuoka's European visit thanks to Ozaki's friend Prince Saionji, who was to be one of the envoy's travelling entourage. Saionji, at the outset, believed that the foreign minister had no special mission other than to make the personal acquaintance of Hitler, Ribbentrop, Mussolini and Stalin. There would be 'no world-shaking results' from Matsuoka's visit, Ozaki confidently reported.[16]

Both Saionji and Ozaki were quite wrong. Matsuoka made his way via Trans-Siberian express to Moscow, where he held brief and cordial talks with Stalin and Molotov where the idea was floated of a non-aggression pact with Japan along the lines that Hitler had signed two years previously. On arrival in Berlin, Matsuoka was feted with all the pomp the Reich could muster, driven down the Unter den Linden avenue in an open car under the fluttering flags of the Axis powers and accorded a long audience with the Führer in the newly completed Reich Chancellery. The interview consisted mostly of a lengthy harangue by Hitler about the treacherousness of Britain, which revealed nothing of Germany's real game plan to attack the Soviet Union. But under his effusive admiration for Hitler, Matsuoka offered only the vaguest of assurances of Japan's intention to eventually take Singapore. After a brief visit to Mussolini in Rome, Matsuoka boarded his train back to Moscow where Stalin waited to seal the Russo-Japanese non-aggression pact.

Matsuoka spent a week in Moscow. By Molotov's post-war account, the Japanese was subjected to the full force of Stalin's wiles, fuelled by copious amounts of vodka and champagne – true to Stalin's well-known tactic of getting both friends and enemies paralytically drunk during talks. Japan's true interest lay in ensuring that there would be no war on its northern flank, Stalin argued, freeing the emperor's forces to conquer Asia. The clear subtext was that Japan had nothing to gain from joining Germany in any possible attack on the USSR. 'Japan was deeply resentful toward Germany and gained no benefit from their alliance [with Berlin],' recalled Molotov in a 1979 interview. 'Our talks ... had great significance,' Matsuoka told the American ambassador to Russia, Laurence Steinhardt, on 8 April that both Hitler and Ribbentrop had urged him to 'make friends' with the Soviet Union.[17]

Stalin's charm offensive paid off four days into Matsuoka's visit with the signing of a neutrality pact between Moscow and Tokyo. Stalin made a great show of their newly forged comradely relations. 'At the end of Matsuoka's visit Stalin made a gesture that caught the whole world's attention,' recalled Molotov. 'He personally went to the station to see off the Japanese minister. No one had ever expected this; Stalin never met or saw off anyone. The Japanese and the Germans were stunned. The train was delayed for an hour. Stalin and I made Matsuoka drink a lot, and we almost carried him onto the train. Seeing him off was worth it because Japan refused to wage war on us.' Before he left, reeling from Soviet hospitality, Molotov and Matsuoka sang a chorus of the Russian folk song 'The Reeds Were Rustling'. 'Why, he could barely stand up in the station,' remembered Molotov. 'Matsuoka paid for his visit to us.'[18]

Much as it might have pleased Stalin to believe that Matsuoka was a victim of his wiles, in truth the Japanese–Soviet non-aggression pact rested on nothing but the foreign minister's word. And Matsuoka, on his return to Tokyo, was quick to reassure Ott on 6 May that the pact 'did not nullify the Tripartite Alliance'. He also claimed, with a two-facedness that was the hallmark of Matsuoka's career, that Japan would not, in fact, remain neutral in the event of a war between Germany and the USSR.[19]

Nonetheless, it was a setback for German diplomacy. Ott told Sorge 'clearly that he never expected it and that such a Japan–Russia Neutrality Treaty was far from a happy thing for Germany'.[20] Ott, Sorge, and indeed the rest of the Japanese cabinet had been taken by surprise by Matsuoka's move. But news of the unexpected pact was greeted with general approval in Tokyo. Konoe personally met his foreign minister at Tokyo station and accompanied Matsuoka to the Imperial Palace for toasts. The Imperial General Staff also signalled its support – though the powerful pro-Axis faction led by General Araki's group in the army 'was not happy and took an opposing stand', Miyagi informed Sorge.[21]

Despite the new pact, the volatile factional politics of the Japanese military meant that in reality a change of heart towards Stalin remained only one power-shift away. 'Personally I did not think that the treaty made the Russo-Japanese relationship safe,'[22] Sorge would later tell his interrogators.

Moscow, too, continued to keep a wary eye on any Japanese preparations to attack northwards into the USSR. Centre tasked the Ramsay group with drawing up a detailed order of battle of the Japanese military, an enormous undertaking that Ozaki and Miyagi completed by early May. The result was an impressive chart – drawn, naturally, by Miyagi, the artist of the spy ring – that showed the strength, equipment and location of Japan's fifty-division-strong army with extraordinary accuracy. In the early stages of the Pacific War in 1942, the Americans would discover to their surprise that it was their Soviet allies who had by far the most reliable information on their Japanese opponents – thanks to the work of Sorge and his colleagues.[23]

'If we could predict a Japanese attack on Russia two months in advance, that attack could be avoided through diplomatic negotiations,' Sorge later explained to the Japanese. 'If we could tell one month in advance, Russia could move major military forces to the border and could make complete defence preparations. If we could warn two weeks in advance, Russia could at least make defensive preparations at the front line. And if we could advise a week in advance, that should help minimize the sacrifice.'[24] Precisely the same logic applied to the more immediate threat of Operation Barbarossa. If Stalin could be warned in time – or rather if he could be induced to believe the reports of Sorge and others of German invasion plans – then the Soviet Union could be spared a bloodbath, or even complete destruction.

Throughout the spring of 1941 the regular military couriers arriving from Berlin via the Trans-Siberian railway brought yet more snippets of gossip about German preparations for war. These officers were more than glorified postmen. They were all military specialists who under the terms of the Axis agreement came to brief their Japanese counterparts on their respective areas of expertise – mechanised warfare, naval gunnery, bombing patterns and the like – and were briefed by the Japanese in return. Most of these couriers carried letters of introduction to Sorge from his old friends now back in Berlin – including Colonel Matzky, Ambassador Dirksen and even Karl Haushofer. The visitors were all taken on Sorge's inimitable tour of Ginza's nightspots, and in their cups gossiped about plans for war against Russia – as well as what they had learned about the latest Japanese military hardware.

In late April 1941, Sorge learned from Colonel Kretschmer, the embassy's new senior military attaché, that he had received instructions from Berlin to warn the Japanese War Ministry that Germany would be taking 'defensive measures' to counter supposed Soviet troop concentrations on the eastern frontier of the Reich. 'These instructions were very detailed and included a map of Soviet military dispositions,' Sorge recalled in prison. 'Although it was uncertain whether or not the situation would lead to actual hostilities, Germany had completed her preparations on a very large scale ... I understood [from Kretschmer] that the decision on peace or war depended solely on Hitler's will, and was quite irrespective of the Russian attitude.'[25]

This tale of German defence against Soviet aggression was not entirely bluff. The truth was that Stalin did indeed have a plan in place for invading German-occupied Poland and the Reich itself, if the need arose, known as Operation *Groza*, the Russian for thunderstorm. In today's Russia the very existence of this plan remains deeply controversial, as it contradicts the official historiography of an innocent Stalin double-crossed by Hitler. But the document can be found in a so-called *osobaya papka*, or special file, in the Russian Defence Ministry archive.[26] The original plan, dated 18 September 1940, three months before the birth of the Germans' own Operation Barbarossa, was signed by Marshal Semyon Timoshenko and the Chief of the General Staff, Marshal Kirill Meretskov. A slightly later version of the plan, updated after Marshal Georgy Zhukov took over after Meretskov's removal and subsequent arrest for espionage in February 1941, detailed a Soviet offensive across Poland to Berlin and beyond. The plan of Operation Groza listed the military forces available to Stalin as 300 divisions, including 8 million soldiers, 27,500 tanks and 32,628 aeroplanes. On paper, at least, that gave the USSR numerical superiority over the Wehrmacht – which was also at that moment partly tied down in occupied Europe and north Africa.

It is possible that it was Meretskov himself who betrayed Groza to the Germans.[27] It seems that Berlin knew of its existence as early as March 1941, when Walter Schellenberg and the Soviet ambassador to Germany, Vladimir Dekanozov, discussed Groza over drinks in Berlin. Dekanozov asked Schellenberg directly about '"a plan called Operation Barbarossa which means a German assault against us". The RHSA chief remained quiet for a while before replying: "This is correct, this plan exists and it was elaborated with great thoroughness. We communicated this plan through secret channels to the Americans and the British, to make them believe that we are preparing to attack you. If they believe it, we have a good chance to succeed with our Operation Sealion. But we also know about your "Operation Grom".'*[28] Indeed the existence of Plan Groza – and the Soviet General Staff's planning for an invasion of Germany, not a defence of the Motherland – has been cited as one of the reasons for the USSR's unpreparedness for invasion in June 1941. Units along the frontier had been equipped with maps of German territory, but not of the Russian rear.[29]

In Tokyo, neither the Germans nor Sorge knew anything of the Kremlin's contingency plan to invade Germany. They were more concerned with the mounting probability of Hitler's attack in the opposite direction. By early May, both Ott and Wenneker had become convinced that war with the Soviet Union was inevitable. 'I chatted to the Ambassador and the Naval attaché about German-Soviet relations,' Sorge cabled Moscow on 2 May. 'Ott informed me that Hitler is full of determination to destroy the USSR and seize the European part of the USSR as a grain and raw materials base in order to control all of Europe ... German generals estimate the Red Army's fighting capacity is so low that they believe the Red Army will be destroyed in the course of a few weeks ... A decision about war against the USSR will be taken by Hitler alone, either already in May, or after the war with Britain. Ott, who is personally against such a war, has already advised Prince Urach to return to Berlin in May.'[30]

Days later the courier Colonel Oskar Ritter von Niedermayer arrived in Tokyo with even more detailed information. Niedermayer told Sorge – in a bar, naturally – that he had been sent to Tokyo specifically 'to investigate to what extent Japan would be able to participate' in the forthcoming war against Russia.[31] Niedermayer knew the USSR well, having spent nearly a decade living there in the 1920s, during the period when German units were secretly training on Russian soil under the secret deal supervised by Ott himself. The 'opening of a German-Russian war was already a determined fact', Niedermayer confided to

*Schellenberg either mis-spoke or misremembered; *grom* in Russian means 'thunder' and *groza* 'thunderstorm'.

Sorge. 'Hitler believed that it was high time to fight the Soviet Union.'[32] Sorge reported to Centre that Germany had a threefold objective:

(1) to occupy the European grain area of the Ukraine;
(2) to obtain at least a million or two million captives to supplement the German scarcity of labour and use them for agriculture and industry;
(3) to eliminate completely the danger existing at the eastern border of Germany. Hitler thought that probably he could not find another chance if he should pass this one up.[33]

The evidence, from Sorge's point of view, was crystal clear. Massive preparations were under way to attack Russia. The only outstanding question was exactly when and where the blow would fall. But there was a problem. Centre, in the person of Director Golikov, resolutely refused to believe not only Sorge but also the mounting pile of agent reports from around the world that screamed urgent warnings of the coming offensive.

Golikov was a civil war hero who had made a career as an infantry officer before joining the Political Directorate of the Red Army in 1937 under the command of Lev Mekhlis. Mekhlis was the main architect of the purge of the army. Golikov was one of his most grimly efficient lieutenants, conducting brutal interrogations of hundreds of officers prior to dispatching them to the NKVD for execution. One of the up-and-coming young commanders Golikov accused of 'friendships with former enemies of the people and hostility toward political workers' was the rising star Georgy Zhukov, who had escaped from 'Beria's basements' (a reference to Lavrenty Beria, NKVD chief from August 1938) only thanks to the support of his comrades and superiors in the Belorussian Military District. Golikov had come within a whisker of murdering the Soviet Union's most brilliant general, a fact that Zhukov never forgot.

When Golikov was appointed director of the Fourth Department in July 1940 he must have been acutely aware that his five predecessors had all ended up shot. But Golikov was well trained in the kind of dissimulation and buck-passing that prospered in those post-Purge years. 'He never gave straightforward orders or directions but always left it up to his subordinates,' recalled one of his officers. 'If he was not satisfied, he would say, "I never gave you orders like that" or "You did not understand me."' Golikov 'always wore a strange smile whether he approved or disapproved' of work done by his staff.[34] The clear lesson of his predecessors' grim fates was that the best way to stay alive as head of Soviet military intelligence was to tell Stalin precisely what he wanted to hear. As a result, Golikov consistently distorted the information he received about the increasing likelihood of a German attack to conform to Stalin's scepticism. The result was a fatally self-reinforcing circle of delusion between dictator and intelligence chief.

On 20 March 1941, Golikov submitted a report to Stalin and the party's Central Committee entitled 'Opinions on the Possibility of Combat Action by the German Army against the USSR'. It was probably the most misleading document ever produced by Soviet intelligence – and would have disastrous consequences for Stalin's decision-making in the remaining months before Barbarossa.

'The majority of agent reports concerning the possibility of war with the USSR in the spring of 1941 come from Anglo-American sources, the goal of which at present is without a doubt to worsen relations between the USSR and Germany,' the report began. 'Recently, English, American, and other sources speak of the preparations for an alleged German invasion of the Soviet Union.'[35] In the copy of the report intended personally for Stalin, Golikov underlined passages that would appeal to the dictator's conviction that Churchill and Roosevelt wished either to provoke a conflict between Germany and the USSR or to make common cause with Hitler to destroy the 'first socialist state'.

The meat of Golikov's report was a catalogue of sixteen paragraphs containing a variety of hearsay remarks and rumours from foreign military attachés, journalists, and the foreign press – all appearing to confirm that Hitler would only contemplate attacking the USSR after defeating Britain. 'If the Germans don't have success in England, they will be compelled to carry out their old plans for the seizure of Ukraine and the Caucasus,' the American minister in Bucharest was quoted as saying.[36]

The bitterest irony was that Golikov was in fact extremely well informed about Germany's real plans, thanks to the NKGB's – as the NKVD was renamed in February 1941 – brilliant Berlin station chief Aleksandr Korotkov. In defiance of standing orders not to have any contact with networks associated with known traitors, Korotkov deliberately sought out the agents recruited by his predecessor, Boris Gordon, one of the dozens of top *rezidenty* who were executed in the fatal 1937 recall that Sorge had escaped. One of Gordon's most promising contacts had been Arvid Harnack, a communist-sympathising official in the Reich's Ministry of Economics. In September 1940, Korotkov re-established contact with Harnack, who was reactivated as an agent and given the codename Korsikanets – 'the Corsican'. Korsikanets in turn recruited another colleague, Harro Schulze-Boysen – codename Starshina, or 'warrant officer' – a major in German Air Ministry intelligence. As early as October 1940, Korsikanets reported to Moscow that 'Germany would go to war with the USSR in 1941', the initial phase of the operation being the occupation of Romania. A source in the German high command told Korsikanets that 'the war would begin in six months'.[37] Korotkov's warning was ignored.

The Korsikanets network quickly grew as Harnack inveigled other informants, some under false pretences, into giving information. Grek, 'the Greek', was a member of the technical department of the Wehrmacht; Turok, 'the Turk', was principal bookkeeper of the industrial chemical giant I. G. Farben; Italianets, 'the Italian,' was a German naval intelligence officer; Shved, 'the Swede', was a Luftwaffe major who worked as a liaison officer between the Air Ministry and the Foreign Ministry; Albanets, 'the Albanian', was a Russian émigré industrialist and former tsarist officer with good contacts in the German military. Korotkov was also in direct contact with an old friend of Korsikanets, codenamed Starik, 'the old man',* who was able to report on the opposition to Hitler and assisted in communications among the group.[38]

By the early spring of 1941, Korotkov, through this mid-level but extensive network, had access to a broad variety of detailed information on Barbarossa. In early January 1941, Starshina reported that 'an order had been given to begin large-scale photographic reconnaissance flights over the Soviet border area.' At the same time Hermann Göring ordered the Russian Section of his Air Ministry – concerned with logistics of operations over the USSR – 'directly subordinated to the active air staff responsible for operational planning'. On 9 January, Korsikanets

---

*Not to be confused with Starik, the nickname of the executed director Jan Berzin, nor the identical NKVD codename assigned to the exiled Leon Trotsky, who had been assassinated in Mexico in 1940.

reported that 'the Military-Economic Department of the Reich Statistical Administration was ordered by the German high command to prepare a map of Soviet industrial areas'. By mid-March 1941, Starshina warned that 'the photographic reconnaissance flights were under way at full speed … Göring is the "driving force" in planning for a war against the USSR.'[39]

On 20 March 1941 – the day that Golikov filed his report claiming that Hitler would wait for a successful invasion of Britain before attacking the USSR – Korsikanets confirmed that 'only one active division was left in Belgium, thus confirming the postponement of military action against the British Isles. Preparation for an attack against the USSR has become obvious. This is evident from the disposition of German forces concentrated along the Soviet border. The rail line from Lvov to Odessa is of special interest because it has European-gauge tracks.'[40]

Like Sorge in Tokyo, Korotkov was growing increasingly desperate that his snowballing trove of information seemed to be falling on deaf ears. Breaking protocol, on 20 March, Korotkov wrote direct to his boss, NKGB chief Lavrenty Beria, to plead for the credibility of Korsikanets and his network. On the same day, the US Secretary of State, Sumner Welles, notified the Soviet ambassador to Washington[41] that the United States had 'authentic information' that 'it is the intention of Germany to attack the Soviet Union'.[42] But both Beria and Golikov resolutely clung to – and reinforced – Stalin's delusion that no invasion was imminent.

Other sources, too, were sounding the alarm. On 7 February 1941, Agent Teffi, a NKGB spy in the Greek embassy in Moscow, warned that 'there are growing rumours of a German attack on the Soviet Union'. Two weeks later the NKGB's resident in Switzerland, Alexandr Rado (codename Dora), reported that 'the German offensive will begin at the end of May'.[43] Both reports could, possibly, be dismissed as hearsay. But Rudolf von Scheliha, First Secretary in the German embassy in Warsaw, was an altogether more serious source. He had been recruited as a Soviet spy by Rudolf Herrnstadt, a former Moscow correspondent of the German newspaper *Berliner Tageblatt*, in Warsaw in 1933.[44] After the German conquest of Poland, Scheliha – given the codename Ariets, 'the Aryan' – was reassigned to the German Foreign Ministry in Berlin, giving him an ideal vantage point from which to spy on Germany's diplomacy.[45] On 28 February, Ariets urgently contacted Herrnstadt's mistress (and fellow spy) Ilse

Stöbe, codename Alta, saying he had information of the highest urgency for Moscow. Ariets was not exaggerating. The documents he had seen at the Foreign Ministry included a detailed operational plan of the coming German attack. Three army groups under Marshals Leeb, Bock and Rundstedt would be directed at Leningrad, Moscow, and Kiev, Ariets reported. 'The beginning of the attack is provisionally set for May 20th.'[46]

Ariets's warning did find its way into Golikov's 20 March report to Stalin – albeit in highly distorted form. The intelligence chief claimed that 'after the victory over England, Germany proposes to deliver blows from two flanks against the USSR: an envelopment from the North (they have in mind Finland) and from the Balkan Peninsula'.[47] Golikov's version bore no resemblance to Barbarossa as Ariets had described it – which turned out to be exactly how the Wehrmacht executed it. Golikov also, fatally, remained convinced that the USSR would be safe from German invasion until after Hitler's conquest of Britain.

Ten days later, Starshina described in detail the operational plan prepared by Göring's aviation staff for the attack on the Soviet Union. 'The air force will concentrate its attack on railroad junctions in the central and western parts of the USSR, the power stations in the Donetsk basin, and aviation industry plants in the Moscow area. Air bases near Cracow in Poland are to be the main departure points for aircraft attacking the USSR. The Germans consider ground support for its air forces to be a weak point in Soviet Defence and hope by intensive bombardment of airfields quickly to disorganise their operations.'[48] It would turn out to be a precise description of the first days of Barbarossa. Golikov made sure that Stalin never saw it.

'A good spy can decide the outcome of a battle or the course of crucial negotiations – but of course only if he is believed,' Boris Gudz told an interviewer in 1999. 'It is a very difficult psychological state when you are not believed, when you have obtained secret information that turned out to be right.'

By the end of March 1941 almost every Soviet intelligence officer stationed in and around the Axis nations, including Richard Sorge, was in exactly that difficult Cassandra-like predicament – knowing they were right, but not being believed.

17

Barbarossa Takes Shape

'Now they don't kill us with their swords – but in their hearts they hate us just as much. They smile and behave politely, but don't be fooled'[1]

Richard Sorge on the Japanese

Sorge composed a long cable to Centre with Niedermayer's latest information – but Clausen did not send it. Instead, he composed his own brief summary, leaving out key information and deliberately blurring details. 'I thought it was a very important subject,' Clausen told the Japanese after his arrest, 'but since I had a favourable attitude already at that time toward Hitler's policies, I did not send out this information.'[2] The actual cables received in Moscow confirm this. By the time Clausen actually went on air on 21 May, he sent only eight messages totalling 797 word groups, about a third of the original message. By his own confession, of the roughly 17,472 word groups that Sorge gave him to send in 1941, the radio man transmitted only 1,465 – a stark contrast to his record-breaking output the previous year.

'German officials arriving here from Berlin inform us that war between Germany and the USSR may begin at the end of May,' was Clausen's bare precis of his chief's vital report. 'Germany has nine Army corps consisting of 150 divisions.'[3] Fatally for the credibility of the message, the second paragraph of Clausen's cable apparently contradicted the first. 'They also say that for this year the danger might pass.'[4] It was hardly a ringing intelligence slam-dunk. Golikov wrote on the telegram: 'query Ramsay whether he means Corps or Armies'.

Sorge, with his military experience, had of course meant armies (and finally clarified on 13 June to that effect). Clausen had confused this vital order-of-battle information, further undermining his chief and the seriousness of his warning.[5]

Unbeknown to his boss, Clausen had been systematically sabotaging the ring's work all year. 'I already had doubts about communism at that time and so I sent just a little out of the [information] to Moscow,' admitted Clausen. 'Most of the manuscripts given to me by Sorge were torn up.'[6] Clausen coded and transmitted only what he dared not suppress, dispatching just enough to keep the Fourth Department from suspecting his treachery.[7] Sorge waited impatiently for some indication that Moscow had taken heed of his warning. But there was no news on the wires of diplomatic overtures or Soviet troop movements. For two weeks, Centre did not even acknowledge his telegram. Sorge could not know that much of the delay was attributable to sabotage by his own radio man.

Erich Kordt, Ribbentrop's latest envoy to the Japanese, met Sorge during these tense days. Kordt was expecting to meet the 'the intelligent German journalist who supposedly was more knowledgeable about Japan's complicated political conditions than anyone else' that he had heard so much about in Berlin. He was also, doubtless, hoping to have a good time on the town with a man he had been told was 'decidedly bohemian, very receptive to feminine charms and more than willing to partake of a good drink'. Instead, when he was introduced to Sorge after midnight at the bar of the Imperial Hotel, Kordt found him drunk, 'bizarre', and 'in a belligerent mood'.[8]

The two men, naturally, talked politics. Sorge declared flatly that the Japanese were 'pirates' but that they would never oblige the Germans by striking Singapore. Furthermore, he taunted the visitor from Berlin, there would soon be a deal between the Japanese and Washington. This was a reference to Konoe's recent instructions to Japan's new ambassador in Washington, Admiral Nomura, to try to defuse the escalating tensions with the US – a key snippet of information gleaned by Ozaki over his breakfast miso soup. The US had indeed recently demanded that the Japanese withdraw from the Axis as their price of recognition of Japanese conquests in Manchuria and Tokyo's economic demands in Asia. It was a tempting deal for Konoe – if he could persuade the army in Manchuria to make peace with the Chinese after so much blood and sacrifice.

One more week would tell whether or not Nomura would reach agreement with the Americans, Sorge bragged. Kordt, taken aback, replied that he could not imagine that Tokyo would deal with Washington behind Hitler's back. 'Yes, that's beyond you,' retorted Sorge rudely. 'But in two weeks I can get you all the details.' The Japanese authorities had declared another 'National Spy Prevention Week', Sorge explained, which meant that every city block had to report to the police any neighbour who had contact with foreigners.[9] By next week all this should have blown over, and his 'friends' would be able to visit him once more and inform him of the latest news on the talks. It is a measure of Sorge's desperate mood that he had no qualms about sharing such sensitive information with a senior German diplomat, and a stranger to boot – as well as casually mentioning that his top-level Japanese sources had reason to fear discovery during Spy Week. At three in the morning, having drunk the best part of a bottle of brandy, Sorge departed into the Tokyo night. Kordt had found the famous Sorge 'a real braggart'.[10]

'A funny sort of telegram', as Sorge described it, finally came across the ether from Moscow in the last week of May. Its blunt message was that 'we doubt the veracity of your information'. Sorge was, by coincidence, with Clausen when this infuriating cable came in. It drove him to wild anger, by Clausen's account. 'Now, I've had enough of this!' Sorge shouted, springing to his feet and pacing the room, clutching his head. 'Why don't they believe me? Those wretches, how can they ignore our message!' Somewhat disingenuously, Clausen claimed that 'this was the only time when both of us were beside ourselves'.[11] What Sorge could not have known was that his earlier cable reporting Niedermayer's intelligence, garbled by Clausen and further truncated in Golikov's summary, had actually found its way onto Stalin's desk. Stalin scrawled on the report that the information came from 'a shit who has set himself up with some small factories and brothels in Japan'. The *khozain* of the Kremlin had apparently confused Sorge with Clausen.[12]

In a last-ditch attempt to get his warnings believed in Moscow, Sorge resorted to the extraordinary tactic of leaking his information to the Western press. He summoned Vukelić and ordered him to approach four US papers with Scholl and other couriers' information about Barbarossa – though shorn of the names of the sources. Vukelić could not run the story on his own agency's wire, Havas, as it was now

controlled by the Vichy puppet government of France. But Vukelić did
have some luck with Newman of the *New York Herald Tribune*. On
31 May 1941 the *Tribune* ran a story headlined 'Tokyo expects Hitler
to move against Russia'. The piece was buried deep inside the paper.
A Manhattan news desk had given a little more credence to Stalin's
man in Tokyo than Stalin himself. But not much.

As the disappointments mounted up, Sorge's suave composure began
to show more cracks. He came home reeling drunk more frequently than
ever before. One night in early summer, Sorge lurched into his study
to find Hanako reading. He seized her and made love to her so roughly
that she buried her face in her hands with embarrassment. The abrupt
change from Sorge's usually gentleness and consideration alarmed her
deeply.[13] Some days later Hanako found Sorge on his couch, weeping
with his hand over his forehead. It was the first time she had ever seen
her lover cry, as she related in her 1949 memoir:

'Why do you weep?' she asked.

'I am lonely,' Sorge replied.

'How can this be when you have so many German friends here in
Tokyo?'

'They are not my true friends,' was Sorge's bitter response.[14]

Sorge's daily updates on the state of the secret Japanese–American talks
alarmed Ott, who relied on his exceptionally well-informed friend
for insider news on the Konoe government's covert diplomacy with
Washington. 'We learned a little about these from the American press,
something from our ambassador in Washington, and a good deal from
Richard Sorge,' recalled Third Secretary Meissner.[15] Sorge also shared
the information with Schellenberg in Berlin, further blurring the lines
between Sorge's career as a Soviet spy and his valued role as a German
intelligence source.

'Sorge's intelligence material grew more and more important to
us, for in 1941 we were very keen to know more about Japan's plans
concerning the United States,' wrote Schellenberg.[16] Of particular
concern was the American offer to mediate between Japan and the exiled
Chinese Nationalist government in Chungking. An end to the fighting
in China would have unpredictable consequences for the Soviet Union
and Germany. Moscow worried that it would make an attack on the
USSR more likely. Berlin feared the exact opposite – that a peace deal

with China would encourage Japan to throw its forces southward into its planned Asian empire instead of joining in with their attack on Stalin.

Ott decided to send Sorge to Shanghai to find out more. As before, he was given diplomatic protection as an official Germany embassy courier. Sorge's Shanghai trip presented the perfect opportunity to flee. His duty to warn his masters in Moscow of the impending catastrophe of Barbarossa had been discharged, and they had not heeded him. There seemed little point in continuing his long and lonely mission – though he mentioned nothing of this crisis of confidence to his Japanese interrogators.

Why did Sorge not take this opportunity to disappear into the chaos of war-torn China? He certainly considered the possibility, strongly hinting to Hanako that he might not return. But he also cared, in his brusque way, for what would happen to Hanako if he left her. He attempted to find a new future for her, using the grimly practical logic of a man used to ordering the lives and loves of his subordinates. He suggested that Hanako get married.

'Who should I marry?' she had asked, taken aback, according to an interview she gave in 1965.

'Don't you have a friend?'

'I have no friend,' she replied, hurt. 'Always and only you.'

'I may not be in Japan much longer. Your heart will ache if you keep thinking about me. If you marry a wise Japanese man, you will make a fine wife. A wife has no worries. Yes, I think you should marry.'

'If I must, let it be one of your friends,' she answered.

'I don't know many Japanese men. Let me see.' Sorge reflected for a moment, pacing his study. 'I have a friend who is an adviser to the Manchurian Railroad.' Sorge assured Hanako that Hotsumi Ozaki was a kind, intelligent man who could make her happy.

At his next rendezvous with Ozaki – at Sorge's house, for fear of the current spy mania – he breezily informed his star agent that he had a splendid wife for him. It is revealing of Sorge's obsession with work, and his indifference to his colleagues as people, that despite having worked together for twelve years Sorge never bothered to ask if Ozaki already had a wife. Ozaki, for his part, evidently never considered Sorge enough of a personal friend to talk about his family affairs. It is also telling that it never seems to have crossed Sorge's mind that Ozaki or Hanako might object to his brilliant plan.

'I have found out that Ozaki-san is already married,' Sorge informed Hanako. 'Too bad! I don't know of anyone else.' He looked down at his desk, scratched his head, then turned back to his work.[17]

Prince Urach, the former correspondent on the *Volkischer Beobachter* who was now briefly back in Tokyo on a new assignment, told a more distasteful story. Speaking to *Der Spiegel* in 1951, Urach claimed that Sorge tried to 'sell' Hanako to him, saying that their affair was over.[18] Hanako's version of events is rather different. She claimed that Urach told Sorge that he wanted to take her to Germany with him, but Sorge refused, saying that 'it would be difficult for me to live' without her.[19] Given that during his earlier Tokyo career Urach had annoyed Sorge by 'pawing' Hanako, it is perhaps more likely that the German aristocrat continued to hold a torch for his friend's pretty mistress. In any case Sorge's bizarre attempts to pass Hanako on to his top agent, then to his friend the Nazi newspaper correspondent, had both failed. If Sorge absconded during his trip to China, Hanako would be left alone with the stigma of having been the mistress of a foreigner and a spy.

Sorge's disintegrating mental state did not go unnoticed at the embassy. Ott had become seriously worried about Sorge's heavy drinking and – as much conscious of his position as concerned for his friend's well-being – confided to Urach that he feared a scandal. News had reached the ambassador of at least two incidents in which a drunken Sorge had crashed his Datsun into telegraph poles, and of screaming rows and even a fist fight between Sorge and local Nazis.

'Something needs to be done about Sorge,' Ott told Urach, by the latter's account. 'The man is drinking harder than ever and he seems like a nervous wreck ... It goes without saying that one's first concern is for the good name of the embassy.' Ott 'had some evil premonition that something unpleasant might happen' and asked Urach to try to persuade their mutual friend to return to Germany in early June, which the ambassador had privately warned Urach would be the last possible safe date to cross the USSR before the outbreak of hostilities. Ott proposed to use his influence to secure Sorge 'a good press position in Berlin'. Knowing his man, Ott even donated a quantity of whisky to help Urach's campaign of persuasion.[20]

Urach, knowing Sorge's vocal anti-Nazi attitudes, had little hope that he would succeed in tempting his friend home to the Reich. 'At home he would be just another journalist, while here he was *Sorge*, who knew what was going on,' recalled Urach. 'What would he want in "Germany, the great concentration camp"?' Ott was deeply disappointed when Urach reported his failure. But when Urach suggested that Ott try himself, as Sorge's 'day-in, day-out friend', to persuade him, Ott refused. He would also not countenance simply ordering Sorge back to Berlin. 'That won't do,' said Ott. 'I'm his friend!'[21] Had Ott been less pusillanimous about dealing with Sorge's spiralling personal crisis and actually insisted that he return to Germany – a command that even Moscow Centre could not possibly have argued with – he might have saved his friend's life.

On Thursday 15 May, Sorge called in on Helma Ott at the ambassador's residence after his usual breakfast meeting with her husband. As he passed through the hallway a tall, blonde German woman emerged from the drawing room. She was evidently a house guest of the Otts. There was a moment of awkward silence before Helma appeared and introduced them. 'Ah, you don't know one another. Sorge – Mrs Harich-Schneider.'

Margareta – or Eta, as she preferred to be called – Harich-Schneider had just arrived in Tokyo, leaving her two daughters behind with relatives in Germany. She was a celebrated harpsichordist, whose concerts were often reviewed in the arts pages of the *Frankfurter Zeitung*. 'Not a completely unknown name,' said Sorge, bowing with exaggerated formality before exchanging a few words and hurtling away.

In an interview in 1982, Eta recalled that she had been immediately intrigued by Sorge's craggy, striking face and deep blue, vigilant eyes. Sorge had something demoniacal about him, she thought.

'Who is that interesting man?' she asked her hostess.

'A journalist – *Frankfurter Zeitung*,' Helma answered. She had evidently noticed the spark that passed between Eta and Sorge, because she snippily added: he 'doesn't have any interest in women'.[22]

So began the final, and most dramatic, love affair of Sorge's Tokyo career.

Sometime before 20 May 1941,[23] Sorge boarded the daily 06.30 Japan Air Transport flight from Tokyo's Haneda airport to Shanghai, via Osaka and Fukuoka. Shanghai was a place of happy memories for Sorge. It was the place where he had fallen in love with Asia, and built his first espionage ring. The local German community in Shanghai feted Sorge, the famous newspaper correspondent. A dinner was held in his honour by the German News Agency bureau chief. A young diplomat named Erwin Wickert entertained Sorge to tea at his home, and recalled that the visitor flirted outrageously with his young wife.[24] Armed with letters of introduction from Ott, Sorge made the rounds of senior Japanese officials in Shanghai, including the Japanese consul general and military and naval attachés, as well as meeting various old Chinese contacts.

'About ninety per cent of [the Japanese] were categorically opposed to peace mediation, and said that if Konoe and Matsuoka pushed it through they would be met with fierce resistance,' Sorge later told his captors. 'I got the impression that the Japan-US negotiations [over a peace settlement in China] were doomed to fail.'[25] Sorge reported his findings back to Ott using a top-secret military cipher book that the ambassador had given him – a clear sign that Ott himself was unaware of the suspicions of Schellenberg and of Meisinger's mission to investigate Sorge's reliability.

As it happened, Meisinger was himself also in Shanghai, though there is no evidence that hunter and hunted crossed paths there. Meisinger's official mission was to meet the Gestapo officials in China, who were subordinate to his Tokyo bureau. But the colonel also had another, more esoteric, interest.

Ignatius Timotheus Trebitsch-Lincoln, born Abraham Schwarz, was a Hungarian-Jewish petty thief, actor and sometime Anglican missionary who had briefly worked as a curate in Kent before being elected a member of the British parliament for Darlington in County Durham in 1910. After the outbreak of the First World War he volunteered his services to the German military attache in London – and after being rebuffed, fled to New York where he published a sensational book entitled *Revelations of an International Spy*. Extradited to Britain and convicted of espionage (or rather, attempted espionage), he served time in Parkhurst prison. After a spell in Germany after the war – where he served as the chief press censor for the short-lived Kapp regime in Berlin and met Adolf Hitler – Lincoln moved to China and converted to Buddhism.

By 1941 he had established his own monastery in Shanghai, where all initiates were required to hand over their possessions to 'Abbot Chao Kung' – as Lincoln was now styling himself. He also earned money writing anti-British propaganda for the occupying Japanese authorities.

Lincoln had come to the Gestapo's attention thanks to an eccentric plan that he wished to present to the Reich. He proposed to travel to Tibet (then still an independent state) and persuade the Lhasa government to ally itself to Berlin, thereby turning the mountain kingdom into a base of operations against British India.

Meisinger evidently did not enquire too deeply into how a Hungarian adventurer and multiply convicted fraudster planned to persuade a Buddhist theocracy to join the unfolding world war on the side of the Nazis. He cabled the RHSA in Berlin triumphantly to announce his recruitment of Lincoln. Unfortunately for Meisinger's scheme, the German consul general in Shanghai got wind of this insane plan and cabled Berlin to warn that 'Abbot' Lincoln was a notorious fraud, with no significant connections to the Buddhist community in China and even fewer in Tibet. Ribbentrop sent a stinging rebuke to Meisinger, reminding him that 'the self-evident assumption for his posting to the Tokyo embassy was that he concern himself exclusively with police questions'.[26]

While Meisinger was busying himself with his mountebank monk, Sorge returned to Tokyo. It is not clear why he finally decided not to remain in China, as he mentioned nothing of his plans to his Japanese interrogators and we have only Hanako's account of his deep personal crisis and dreams of flight. One reason may have been practical. The Japanese occupation police in Shanghai required locally issued travel documents for all foreigners which Sorge could only have obtained through the German consulate general. To reach communist-held areas he would have had to cross at last two front lines. The Soviet embassy might have helped – but to do so they would also have had to seek authorisation from Moscow Centre, which would hardly condone the flight of such a crucial agent at this juncture. And then of course there was the unresolved question of Hanako. In short, Sorge was once again trapped.

There was one further reason for his return, linked to the great question of Barbarossa. Sorge's old friend and bottle-mate Erwin Scholl was on his way from Berlin to Tokyo, surely bearing important news about Germany's plans. Scholl, freshly promoted to lieutenant colonel, was en route to Bangkok to take up a new assignment as military attaché after two years at the Foreign Department of the General Staff in Berlin. If Sorge could catch Scholl during his layover in Japan, perhaps his old friend would be able to provide operational information that would finally change Moscow Centre's mind.

Sorge's plane touched down in Tokyo, according to the Japan Air Transport timetable for 1941, at 4.30 p.m. It was probably 27 May. Certainly, Sorge dined with the Otts that evening at the ambassador's residence. The mood was gloomy. As the party sat down to dinner around 8 p.m. Wenneker arrived with the news that the battlecruiser *Bismarck*, the largest ship in the German fleet,* had just been sunk by the Royal Navy's plane-launched torpedoes and naval gunfire in the North Atlantic. The sinking was significant not just for Germany's plans to defeat Britain but also for the Japanese, who could hardly have been encouraged to attack Singapore after this resounding sign of Britain's continuing naval prowess.

Eta Harich-Schneider was also at the dinner. Sorge, in his usual manner, lectured and flirted in equal measure. He learned that since her arrival Eta had seen almost nothing of Tokyo except the embassy compound. Sorge proposed taking her on an excursion the following day, which she eagerly accepted. Helma Ott and her friend Anita Mohr – both former mistresses of Sorge's – were less enthusiastic. 'Are you sure you want to put your life in Sorge's hands?' asked Mohr over a ladies' lunch at the embassy the next day. The sexual currents of the tiny community had become deeply intertwined. Eugen Ott was hopelessly in love with Mohr, Helma had confided to Eta, who had become an unwilling confidante to her older, frustrated hostess. Sorge's cavalier bedding of not only Ott's wife but also his 'love object' was scandalous enough. But to Helma, still possessive of her former lover, Sorge's evident plan to also seduce their pretty new house guest was taking things too far.

Speeding through the crowded streets of Tokyo, even in Sorge's little Datsun, felt like a liberation. 'It's heavenly to be out of the compound and actually get close to people,' Eta told her dashing new friend. 'You feel so remote from the real world when you are being driven around in the Ambassador's car.'27

Sorge was all too willing to chime in with his own gripes about the Otts, the couple he had been forced to befriend for his own secret

---

*Almost named the Adolf Hitler, but changed to the Bismarck when the Führer presciently worried about the symbolic consequences if the ship were sunk.

reasons but whom he had come to heartily detest. The Otts had shown Eta nothing of Tokyo 'because they know nothing about the place themselves. What an unimaginative bunch!' Eta countered that the Otts had been nothing but charming towards her. 'Charming?' reposted Sorge. 'Charming, unimaginative, unprincipled people.'[28] Despite his irritation with the Otts – compounded no doubt by the ambassador's clumsy attempt to have him removed to Berlin – Sorge was nonetheless in one of his buoyant moods. Driving an attractive blonde through the streets of his adopted city had made him playful. As they ascended the steep steps at Agato Park he put a steadying arm around Eta's shoulders and made fun of his own limp. 'The Kaiser took two centimetres from my leg and gave me an Iron Cross in exchange,'[29] he joked.

They counted the steps in chorus as they ascended to the top, with its sweeping view of a low-rise, smoke-veiled city which was soon to be obliterated by Allied bombing. Eta thought it 'ugly ... a mess. Uglier than Naples, even.'[30] They drank green tea at the teahouse and drove on, across the city, to the Aoyama cemetery in the port district of Minato. By the end of May, the cherry trees that still line the main avenue would have lost their blossom, but the cemetery, with its European-style grave monuments in ponderous Victorian style, remained an island of quiet in the busy city. Sorge walked with Eta to the section of the graveyard where the Europeans were buried, segregated from the Japanese in death as they had been in life. For Sorge, it was not a romantic place.

'The first Europeans butchered by the Japs are buried here,' Sorge explained, with typical hyperbole (the first Europeans killed by the Japanese were in fact Jesuit priests buried in unmarked graves in Nagasaki in the seventeenth century). 'Now they don't kill us with their swords – but in their hearts they hate us just as much. They smile and behave politely but don't be fooled ... They wear a mask of courtesy, but even that is wearing thin. When I first came to Japan eight years ago, they were much more tolerant of foreigners. But now – the malevolence towards whites! We Germans are meant to be on the same side, but the fact is that most Japanese make no distinction.' Sorge, oblivious to the horrific picture that he was painting for the new arrival, told Eta that a German woman had recently been slapped by a stranger on a train, 'not because she was German but because she was white'.[31]

Sorge had always liked and respected the Chinese. But the Japanese, he had come to believe, were worse than the Nazis. 'They are breast-fed on chauvinism and conditioned to think of themselves as a divine race,' he told Eta. 'From which it follows that Japan has a holy duty to rule Asia – and the rest of the world as well if we let them get their hands on it. In place of the Nazis' ideology, the Japanese rulers have "the way of the Gods" to bolster their ineffable superiority ... Not even the Nazis have this kind of holy authority for their master-race super-state.'[32]

Eta offered some confidences in return – about her successful musical career in Berlin, and her unhappy marriage. She claimed that her recent divorce was the reason for her self-imposed exile in Tokyo. She did not trust Sorge sufficiently to vouchsafe the real reason for her leaving Germany, which was the disapproval of the Nazi Party when Eta tried to prevent a Jewish student from being expelled from the conservatoire two years previously. But Eta did share with her intriguing companion her frustration and fear at the atmosphere of distrust, intrigue and family quarrels at the German embassy.

It was growing dark. Sorge suggested dinner. It was indecently late by the time Eta finally returned to the residency, where she was greeted coldly by her hosts. Clearly both Helma Ott and her husband felt jealous – for different reasons – of her friendship with the irresistible Dr Sorge.

Sorge finally met his old friend Scholl at the Imperial Hotel, most probably on Saturday, 31 May. The previous day Ott had already communicated the gist of Scholl's message from Berlin, which Sorge summarised to Centre in a brief, urgent cable.

'Berlin informed Ott that the German attack [on Russia] will commence in the latter part of June,' Sorge wrote in a message dated 30 May and promptly – for a change – transmitted by Clausen. 'Ott 95% certain that war will commence ... Because of the existence of a powerful Red Army, Germany has no possibility to widen the sphere of war in Africa and has to maintain a large army in eastern Europe. In order to eliminate all the dangers from the USSR side, Germany has to drive off the Red Army as soon as possible. This is what Ott said.'[33]

Scholl and Sorge met in the lobby of the lumbering neo-Aztec ziggurat of the Imperial Hotel. By Sorge's account, they spoke 'in a corner of the lobby'. In contemporary photographs one can see that the hotel's wide lobby opens onto a large terrace decorated with potted palm trees, with a view of a Japanese garden composed of ponds, bamboo and stone lanterns. It was probably here that Scholl recounted, in detail, what was at that moment the greatest secret in the world. Scholl confided that he had 'orally transmitted to Ambassador Ott special, highly secret instructions concerning the coming German-Russian war'. So secret was the message that Ott had told Sorge only the barest outline during their conversation the previous day. 'Ott hid as much as possible the secret instructions he received from Scholl,' Sorge later told the Japanese. 'And he did not even give any warning to those Germans who were going home via the Siberian Railroad.'[34]

Scholl himself had no such inhibitions. He bluntly informed Sorge that Operation Barbarossa would begin in the middle of June; and though the start date might be postponed for a few days all the preparations were already in place. The Wehrmacht had massed some 170–180 divisions along the Soviet border, all of them mechanised or with tanks. The German attack was to be made simultaneously along the entire front, with the main strike forces heading for Moscow, Leningrad, and Kiev. The German General Staff confidently expected the Red Army to collapse quickly under this overwhelming blitzkrieg, and anticipated that the war would be over in two months. By the winter, Hitler planned to take the Trans-Siberian railway and establish contact with Japanese forces in Manchuria.[35]

Despite the urgency of the information, Sorge had to go through with his promise to take Scholl for a night on the town, just like in the old days. They dined at the Imperial, probably at the fashionable New Grill. Sorge was particularly fond of the Beef Steak *à la Chaliapine*, a dish created at the hotel and named, for obscure reasons, in honour of a great early twentieth-century Russian opera singer.[36] They then headed into the fleshpots of Ginza.

By the end of the evening Sorge was reeling, not only with drink but with the detail and importance of the news he had to impart. In the morning he composed a long message to Moscow, the single most important cable of his intelligence career. He summoned Clausen and handed it to the radio man for urgent transmission, an order that Clausen could find no excuse to refuse.

This time Sorge made sure to spell out that his source was Scholl – 'who left Berlin on May 3rd' – rather than unnamed couriers at unspecified times, as per his previous cable. 'The beginning of the German-Russian war is expected around June 15th,' Sorge wrote in his telegram of 1 June

1941. 'In my conversation with Scholl I established that the German advance against the Red Army is founded on a major tactical mistake by the USSR. From the German point of view, the Soviet disposition of forces against German positions does not have any significant depth, which is a grave error. It will help them smash the Red Army in the first major battle. Scholl informed me that the strongest strike will be undertaken by the left flank of the German Army.'[37] He went on to describe in detail Scholl's descriptions of the plan of attack. Surely now, with such concrete and well-sourced information, Golikov would finally take heed and signal the alarm that would allow the Soviet Union to prepare for the coming storm.

18

'They Did Not Believe Us'

'You can send your "source" ... to his fucking mother'
Stalin, on being warned of Operation Barbarossa

His latest and most important-ever dispatch completed, an exhausted Sorge telephoned the Otts to excuse himself from attending a Whitsun weekend party at their summer house in Akiya. Eta was also in no mood for the wholesome pleasures of a German family gathering, but felt obliged to go. She spent much of the weekend walking alone on the wide, sandy beaches and in the pine woods above the house. She also thought of Sorge. Her first impression of him, she told an interviewer in 1982, was of an arrogant and rather boorish man with low-brow cultural tastes. He was an atheist, a drinker, a glutton and a nihilist for whom nothing was sacred. Eta's Catholic beliefs and middle-class prejudices made her 'a pious petty bourgeois', as Sorge had bluntly told her. She found his habitual mocking tone and incessant sarcasm grating.

But after their day together in Tokyo, Eta had begun to believe that under the outward act, Sorge was a fundamentally decent and humanistic man. She was particularly impressed by his fearless contempt for their fellow Germans in Tokyo – including the Otts – whom she also found hypocritical, smug and stilted. Among this community of time-servers, careerists and *Geldmenschen* (men interested only in money), Sorge stood out 'like a true aristocrat, pure and uncorrupted, natural and spontaneous'.[1] She would not be the first woman, but was the last, to fall for the romanticism of the robber-baron persona Sorge had adopted ever since his schooldays.

Helma Ott was keen to show off Eta, her celebrity house guest. She hosted a lavish reception and concert at the embassy on 10 June, to which the entire Tokyo diplomatic corps and many Japanese notables were invited. Eta played Bach's 'Concerto for Harpsichord and Two Flutes', conducting from her harpsichord as an amateur orchestra drawn from the German community struggled through the piece. After the recital the guests went through to a lavish buffet, both a miracle and an act of calculated German arrogance in a city struggling with shortages of everything from fresh meat to kimono silk. As Soviet ambassador Konstantin Smetanin, in full dress uniform, congratulated Eta on her performance, Sorge cut in. 'You need a brandy,' he said, holding out a drink for her. Famously Helma Ott was the only hostess in the city able to force Sorge into evening dress. For Eta's concert he wore a white dinner jacket and black bow tie.[2]

'Let's get away from here,' Sorge whispered, taking Eta by the arm. It was the night of Tokyo's annual flower festival; he proposed they escape there at once. 'You have to relax sometimes, you know.'[3] Eta knew the Otts would disapprove of the star of the gala disappearing from the reception, but accepted anyway. She slipped upstairs to change out of her ball gown. As she left she caught a wintry glance from Helma. Eta ran across the wide, gravelled drive to Sorge's car and they speeded away, laughing. They drove as far as the crowds would permit, then parked the Datsun and walked arm-in-arm through narrow streets lined with paper lanterns. The physical intimacy with a striking young woman was nothing new to Sorge, but Eta evidently triggered deeper feelings in him.

'I am a lonely fellow,' Sorge confessed – a theme which he had hitherto shared only, as far as we know, with Hanako and Katya. 'I have no friends, no one.' He told her that the 'political situation' was depressing him. 'But your music tonight – that really lifted me up.'[4]

They moved through the throng towards the sound of a booming temple bell, and threw coins in a large chest to take their turn swinging the heavy wooden clapper. Eta noticed Sorge's lips moving in an unspoken prayer. 'Come on,' Sorge said. 'Everyone comes here to pray they'll get rich. Now it's your turn.' He presented her to some of the monks he knew from earlier visits, bowing deeply and introducing his blonde companion as 'a famous musician from Germany who has come to Japan to give concerts'.[5]

They walked down streets lined with stalls selling potted plants and flowers. Sorge was particularly interested in the stands selling miniature bonsai trees. 'They fascinate me, these dwarf trees. They are like a metaphor for the Japanese themselves, rigidly trained to suppress their own nature and turned into artificial, disciplined creatures. Look, I'm going to buy you a wicked little pine.'[6] They continued, cradling Eta's midget tree. Dropping her guard, she told Sorge of how she missed her daughters, of her hopes to travel on to South America, of how the Nazis had hounded her out of Germany.

'The whole German *volk* is diseased,' she told Sorge, happy to finally find a fellow countryman to whom she could speak frankly. She also confessed that her hosts, the Otts, had no idea of her real reason for fleeing Germany. She had claimed to the ambassador that she was in Tokyo at the invitation of the Musashino Music Academy. Ott had graciously invited her to stay on the unspoken assumption that she would play for her supper by entertaining his guests. Eta had also told Ott that she would be heading back to Germany on 11 July, which was a lie. 'Quite frankly, I am in a mess,' she confided.

Sorge listened to her gravely and told her – without elaborating on how he knew – that return via the Trans-Siberian railway would soon be impossible, Eta recalled in her memoir: 'There is no way you can go back to Germany, even if you wanted to,' he told her. 'You will have to stay here. By July we will be in the middle of a war with Russia.'

'But I feel such an impostor.'

'There are other kinds of impostors here, believe me. Imposture can sometimes be a merit.'[7]

Sorge told Eta firmly not to divulge anything of her true history to the Otts. He warned her that Ott was a frightened man who thought someone was watching him all the time. 'He will be finished as Ambassador if he puts a foot wrong. He will not help you.' Sorge admitted that once, Ott was 'alright. He was against the Nazis. When he heard he was being appointed ambassador he asked me whether he should accept. I warned him ... you'll lose your integrity ... And that's what's happened. Whatever principles he started out with have gone out of the window long ago. Now he is trying to drag Japan into the war, into Germany's war, to improve Hitler's chances against Britain. It's not like he likes Nazis or wants to rule the world. No! He is only doing it for the money. For filthy, despicable money, and to advance his career.'[8]

Sorge was in no mood for an early night. He took Eta to a party at the home of Kurt Ludde-Neurath, a secretary in the embassy's political department. They drank red wine and ate sandwiches, then they all repaired to Sorge's more modest digs at Nagasaki Street. It was the first time Eta had visited the little house. Considerably more booze was consumed – with Sorge swilling whisky – before the party broke up in the early hours. The rowdy group piled into Neurath's car to accompany Eta back to the Otts' residence. As they passed the Soviet embassy, Ludde-Neurath turned to his passenger, who had been loudly proclaiming his admiration for Stalin and extolling the Soviet Union as the best partner Germany could ever have. 'Well, Sorge?' quipped Ludde-Neurath mischievously. 'Shall I drive in so we can see your friends?'

When they pulled up outside the German embassy, Sorge drunkenly staggered out of the car and began shouting up at the Otts' darkened bedroom windows. 'Frau Ambassador!' he called. 'Frau Ambassador!' A sleepy houseboy came to open the door and a mortified Eta hurried inside.

The following morning Eta apologised for Sorge's rudeness: 'He was completely drunk.' Helma offered some tart advice. 'There is something you must know about Sorge. No love affair with Sorge lasts very long. It always ends in tears.'[9] She did not reveal that she was speaking from personal experience.

Sorge waited for a response from Centre to his bombshell telegram of 1 June. He could not know that Stalin had personally scrawled across the message: 'Suspicious. To be listed with telegrams intended as provocations.'[10] When Golikov finally responded, his answer was out-of-date, irrelevant and, as usual, carping. Had Ramsay meant corps or armies in his 20 May cable, asked Centre? 'I repeat,' Sorge replied in desperation on 13 June, 'nine armies with the strength of 150 divisions will most likely begin an offensive by the end of June.'[11]

Ott and Colonel Kretschmer were, so far, the only members of the embassy staff to have been officially advised of the date of the invasion. But the matter was by now an open secret. Across the road from the embassy, the Japanese Imperial General Staff were studying their own intelligence reports from Berlin and Moscow of the imminence of war with Russia.

Hanako Miyake, Sorge's longstanding Japanese mistress.

Rear-Admiral Paul 'Paulchen' Wenneker, one of Sorge's most devoted bottle-mates and informants.

Prince Albrecht von Urach, Tokyo correspondent of the rabidly anti-semitic *Völkischer Beobachter*, also joined Sorge on his late night drinking binges in Ginza.

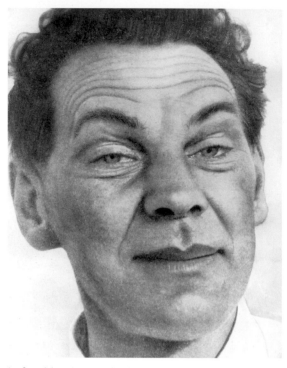

'A face like a ravaged robber baron' – Sorge after drunkenly crashing his motorcycle.

Sorge in Japanese clothes at home on Nagasaki street.

(*left to right*) Sorge at the German Embassy dacha, and on one of his regular tours across Japan.

Eta Harich-Schneider, the celebrated harpsichordist who was Sorge's last lover.

Anita Mohr, the glamorous blonde who was best friend to Helma Ott, Eugen Ott's love object – and Sorge's mistress.

Aino Kuusinen, the Comintern princess sent to summon Sorge back to Moscow in 1937.

Prince Fumimaro Konoe, three times prime minister of Japan, who brought Ozaki into his inner circle of advisers.

General Hideki Tojo, who masterminded Japan's invasion of China as well as the attack on Pearl Harbor.

The Manchurian Railway, or Mantetsu, also controlled its own intelligence agency and the army.

Gestapo Colonel Joseph Meisinger, the 'Butcher of Warsaw' sent to investigate Sorge.

SS-Brigadeführer and spymaster Walter Schellenberg, who suspected Sorge of being a Soviet agent.

Joseph Stalin looks on as Soviet and German Foreign Ministers Vyacheslav Molotov and Joachim von Ribbentrop sign the non-aggression pact that secretly divided Eastern Europe between Berlin and Moscow.

Stalin greets Japanese Foreign Minister Yosuke Matsuoka in Moscow in 1939. By the time of his departure Matsuoka was so drunk that he and Stalin sang folk songs together on the platform.

General Filip Golikov, whose six predecessors as heads of the Fourth Department had all been executed. Golikov suppressed Sorge's urgent reports of an imminent German invasion.

Sorge's police photograph after his arrest.

Immortality (*clockwise from top left*): A Soviet four-kopeck stamp produced after Sorge's official rehabilitation in 1961; Sorge's grave in Tokyo, the original humble gravestone paid for by his mistress swamped by the hulking Soviet monument featuring his posthumous Hero of the Soviet Union star; the monument to Sorge in his native Baku.

On Sunday 15 June, Sorge took Eta to another party. The stifling atmosphere of disapproval at the Otts' was becoming unbearable. 'We are both adults, and here I am creeping through the back gate to meet you in secret as if I were their little daughter,' she said. Sorge advised her to get a place of her own and learn Japanese 'fluently enough so you can bribe the police who handle foreigners'.[12] Eta had other news: Helma had asked her to vacate her quarters in the residency and move into a smaller guest room so that Colonel Meisinger could set up the new Gestapo office in her first-floor suite.

Sorge invited Eta back to his house for 'one more whisky'. In exalted mood, he danced around his little study, carried away with a vision of himself as a slayer of the German Satan. 'If anyone destroys Hitler it will be me!' he shouted, to Eta's puzzled amusement. That night, not without some calculation from Sorge, he and Eta became lovers.[13]

Five days later Eugen Ott finally told Sorge what he had already heard from Scholl – that the invasion was planned for the following week. Sorge sent a final warning to Centre, citing Ott as his source. 'War between Germany and the USSR is inevitable,' Sorge cabled on 20 June. 'German military superiority will allow the destruction of the Soviet Army as effectively as was accomplished at the beginning [of the war] because the strategic defensive positions of the USSR are still as weak as the Polish ones were.' He also reported that Agent Invest (Ozaki) 'has told me that the Japanese General Staff is already discussing the question of the positions that will be taken in the event of war'.[14]

Why did Stalin refuse to heed the warnings that were flowing in from across the world? After the war, Molotov explained away Stalin's scepticism as a form of caution. 'We are blamed because we ignored our intelligence,' Molotov told journalist Felix Chuev in 1969.[15] 'Yes, they warned us. But if we had heeded them, given Hitler the slightest excuse, he would have attacked us earlier.' As we have seen, Molotov always insisted that Stalin knew that war was coming. The *khozain*'s only priority, according to his foreign minister, was to postpone conflict for as long as possible so that the USSR could build up its army sufficiently to resist a German attack. 'Stalin reckoned before the war that only in 1943 would we be able to meet the Germans as equals.' Delaying war was the reasoning Molotov cited for signing the pact with Ribbentrop in 1939. It was also, he claimed, the logic behind Stalin's refusal to prepare for an invasion in 1941.

But Molotov's narrative does not tally with the physical evidence – the actual documents that were recorded as crossing Stalin's desk in May and June 1941. Stalin appears to have developed a profound mistrust of intelligence reports, and expressed his contempt in blue or red wax pencil scrawls across a slew of documents. The sight of that inimitable handwriting still has the power to bring out goosebumps as one turns over the page in the stillness of the archives.

Stalin defaced Sorge's report of 20 May with his dismissive insult about 'a shit' who ran 'small factories and brothels'. On 17 June, five days before the start of Barbarossa, Stalin received a report signed by Pavel M. Fitin, chief of NKGB foreign intelligence, asserting that 'all preparations by Germany for an armed attack on the Soviet Union have been completed, and the blow can be expected at any time'. The source was Agent Starshina, the intelligence officer in Germany's Air Ministry. Again Stalin's blue pencil struck, scrawling a note to Fitin's chief, People's Commissar for State Security Vsevolod Merkulov. 'Comrade Merkulov, you can send your "source" from the headquarters of German aviation to his fucking mother. This is not a "source" but a *dezinformator* – a dis-informer.'[16]

This was neither caution nor healthy scepticism – it was the irrational, hysterical suspicion of a leader convinced that he alone knew the truth while all around him were deceiving him. One has to remember that just three years previously, Stalin's secret police had been ordered to destroy the flower of the USSR's foreign intelligence apparat on the grounds that it was thoroughly infiltrated with foreign spies. There's no reason to believe that Stalin knew that these charges were very largely fabricated. He was certainly aware of Sorge's career – in 1940 the *khozain* had instructed his secretary, Alexander Poskrybyshev, to order up Agent Ramsay's personal file for inspection – and would therefore have also been apprised of Centre's wild suspicions of the 1937 era that the Tokyo *rezidentura* was 'under control of the enemy'.[17] The purges had created such a thick cloud of suspicion that Stalin himself had become blinded by it.

Molotov's reminiscences capture some of the flavour of that pervasive, deadly atmosphere of distrust. 'I think we could not have relied on our intelligence,' Molotov recalled. 'You have to listen to them, but you also have to verify their information. Intelligence agents could push you into such a dangerous position that you would never get out of it. Provocateurs everywhere are innumerable. That's why you cannot trust intelligence without constant and scrupulous checking and rechecking.'[18]

'Some naive people, philistines, have written in their reminiscences that the intelligence agents spoke the truth,' asked his obsequious interlocutor Felix Chuev. 'You couldn't trust such reports,' Molotov answered. 'When I was the *Predsovnarkom* [Chairman of the Council of People's Commissars] I spent half the day reading such intelligence reports. The only thing missing was the date of the invasion! And if we had trusted these reports [and gone on a war footing], the war could have started much earlier.'[19]

In fairness to Molotov, many of the early warnings of Barbarossa — including Sorge's — were indeed inconclusive. On 2 May, Sorge fatally hedged his report with the possibility that the German invasion may indeed wait until after victory over Britain. In his 20 May message Sorge admitted that the danger 'may pass for the year'. Even in his cable of 15 June, he admitted that 'the military attaché is not sure of whether there will be war or not'.[20] But by mid-June the sheer volume of reports coming into the Kremlin from all over the world — including Sorge's account of his conversations with Scholl and Ott — were so detailed and specific that it is hard to read Stalin's dogged refusal to heed them as anything but an act of wilful self-deception. Or, possibly, deception.

Stalin could have been misled by his minions — or perhaps by Hitler himself. Why was Stalin so ready to believe that he was being lied to from all quarters except for Golikov's? Marshal Zhukov, in a series of interviews in 1965–66 with the renowned war correspondent and poet Konstantin Simonov, offered an intriguing explanation: that Stalin had indeed been duped by Hitler. Zhukov recalled a meeting with Stalin at the beginning of January 1941 where he expressed concern over the large numbers of Wehrmacht forces in German-occupied Poland (dubbed the 'Government-General' by the Nazis). Stalin replied that he had 'sent Hitler a personal letter, advising him that this was known to us, that it surprised us, and that it created the impression among us that Hitler intended to go to war with us'. Hitler had responded by sending Stalin a personal, confidential letter where he admitted — according to Zhukov — that the Soviets' 'information was correct, that there actually were large troop formations deployed in the Government-General'.[21]

But these troops, Hitler assured Stalin, 'are not directed against the Soviet Union. I intend to observe the [non-aggression] Pact strictly and swear on my honour as a chief of state that my troops are deployed in the Government-General for other purposes. The territories of Western and Central Germany are subject to heavy English bombing and are easily observed from the air by the English. Therefore, I found it necessary to move large contingents of troops to the east, where they can secretly reorganise and rearm.'[22] As far as Zhukov could tell, Stalin believed Hitler's assurances. (This reference to secret personal correspondence between Hitler and Stalin was not published in Simonov's original book and was not revealed until 1987.) The January 1941 letter was evidently not the only duplicitous communication Hitler sent Stalin. Russian historian and war veteran Lev Bezymensky asked Zhukov in a 1966 interview about the Hitler–Stalin letters. 'Sometime in early June [1941] I decided to try again to convince Stalin of the accuracy of the intelligence reports on the approaching danger,' Zhukov answered:

> Until then Stalin had turned aside similar reports by the chief
> of the General Staff … Defence Commissar Timoshenko and
> I brought along staff maps with the locations of enemy troops
> entered on them. I made the report. Stalin listened attentively but
> remained silent. After the report he sent us away without giving
> us his opinion … A few days passed and Stalin called for me …
> He opened a case on his desk and took out several sheets of paper.
> 'Read,' said Stalin … It was a letter from Stalin to Hitler in which
> he briefly outlined his concern over the German deployments,
> about which I had reported a few days earlier … Stalin then said,
> 'Here is the answer.' I am afraid that after so many years I cannot
> exactly reproduce Hitler's words. But this I do remember precisely: I
> read the June 14 issue of *Pravda* and in it, to my amazement,
> I discovered the same words I had read in Hitler's letter to Stalin in
> Stalin's office.[23]

The communiqué that Zhukov read, issued by the official Soviet news agency TASS and reprinted in the party newspaper *Pravda*, opened by denouncing England for spreading rumours that Germany and the USSR were 'close to war'. Zhukov was amazed to see 'Hitler's very arguments printed in this Soviet document.'[24]

Golikov also did his bit to reinforce Stalin's conviction that the German build-up on the Soviet border was British disinformation. During May and June 1941, as intelligence about Barbarossa from a cornucopia of sources mounted up, Golikov only doubled down on his conviction that an invasion of Britain remained Hitler's primary objective, eagerly seizing on all reports that seemed to contradict the evidence of a planned invasion of Russia. In early May, Golikov sent all top Kremlin and military cadres – including Marshals Timoshenko and Zhukov – a report from a source in the German embassy in Bucharest which claimed that 'a German move to the East in the near future is excluded'. The message concluded that rumours that Germany would attack the USSR 'are being spread deliberately with a view to causing uncertainty in Moscow'.[25] The informant was, paradoxically, precisely the kind of German *dezinformator* that Stalin so feared.

On 31 May, Golikov followed up with another special summary which stated that 'the German command has rather quickly restored its main dispositions in the West, continuing concurrently its movement of troops to Norway ... having in view the execution of the main operation against the British Isles'.[26]

Golikov continued to believe – or claimed to believe – as late as 1961, that Sorge had been under hostile control. Both Golikov and Zhukov attended a Moscow screening of French director Yves Ciampi's hagiographic film *Qui êtes-vous, Monsieur Sorge?* The film takes extensive liberties with the truth – but it does accurately depict Sorge's despair at his reports not being heeded in Moscow. After the premiere Zhukov stood up in the theatre and called over to Golikov, 'Why, Filipp Ivanovich, did you hide these reports from me? Why did you not report such information to the chief of the General Staff?' Golikov replied: 'And what should I have reported to you if this Sorge was a double agent, both ours and theirs?'[27]

For Sorge in Tokyo, the reasons for the Kremlin's stubborn refusal to give credence to his warnings of war remained inexplicable. Moscow must have seemed very remote. Centre had become a ghost, a disembodied stream of numbers whispering across the airwaves, heedless of Sorge's voice crying its warnings from the wilderness. No wonder he drank and wept for his loneliness; even the distant gods in the Kremlin, to whom he had devoted his life, had turned a deaf ear to him.

*

As deadly jeopardy massed on the border of the Soviet Union, Sorge faced his own nemesis closer to home. Colonel Meisinger may have become a bottle-mate. But alcohol-fuelled camaraderie in Die Fledermaus did not mean that the threat from the Butcher of Warsaw had disappeared entirely. Meisinger was soon due to move his office and files into the ambassador's guest suite, currently occupied by Eta. So Sorge recruited Eta to help him obtain a copy of the key before she moved out. It was her first mission as the latest, unwitting, cog in the Tokyo spy ring.

On the evening of Friday 20 June, Eta was once again playing for her supper at the residency, performing Bach for an audience of the Otts' guests. Sorge waited in the clammy heat of the garden. After the concert, Eta accepted compliments and bouquets before claiming sudden tiredness and slipping upstairs. Back in her room she peeled off the pink ball gown, put on dark street clothes and slipped her room key into her pocket. But the guests had by now spilled out into the hallway, making it impossible for her to join Sorge without being noticed. Opening her first-floor window, she jumped down, landing in a flowerbed wet with summer rain. Muddy and bruised, she hurried to her lover's car and they sped out of the embassy gates. At Sorge's house, exhilarated by the escapade, she allowed him to clean the mud from her legs and dress her grazes with bandages. 'You see!' Sorge told her. 'This is what happens when you get mixed up with a gypsy like me!'[28]

That night Sorge came close to confessing the truth of his double life to Eta. He talked about the war, about his life as a communist organiser in the Ruhr, about the Russian woman, 'who was not really his wife, but whom he considered such' and to whom he was, Eta thought, still deeply attached. He admitted that he was working 'for the defeat of Hitler', and that his friendship with Ott was solely to obtain information that would help serve that cause. 'I, Richard Sorge, am going to deal with those pigs in Berlin,' he promised.

'That would be nice,' Eta recalled herself replying, unimpressed. She admired his courage, but his drunken bravado was hard to bear.[29]

The following morning, as Eta packed her things in preparation for her move to a smaller room upstairs, Sorge returned the key that he had copied. He would now have free access to the Gestapo's new Far Eastern headquarters whenever he came for dinner at the Otts' – as long as he took care not to step on the creaky floorboard on the lower corridor about which Eta warned him.

Sunday, 22 June dawned clear and warm from the plains of eastern Poland down to the Carpathian Mountains – perfect flying conditions. In Tokyo the day was hot, with light summer showers. Sorge had arranged to meet Eta in the embassy grounds at five. He wore a smart white linen suit; Eta was in a patterned dress and wide straw hat. She was desperate to tell him the latest outrageous news from the residency. The previous evening, after dinner, Eta had discovered Helma Ott rummaging through her possessions and preparing to confiscate the bonsai tree and bowl that Sorge had given her. A scandal had ensued. But Eta found her lover in a bleak mood. 'Let's go and booze at the Imperial,' he said. 'I need a drink.'

Germany was at war with Russia.

At lunchtime in Tokyo news had come across the wire that Nazi propaganda minister Joseph Goebbels had announced the invasion. 'At this moment an advance is taking place that, for its extent, compares with the greatest the world has ever seen. I have decided today to place the fate and future of the Reich and our people in the hands of our soldiers. May God aid us, especially in this fight!'[30] A few hours later – about the time Sorge drove off with his mistress in the direction of the bar, Molotov took to the airwaves to inform the Soviet people that 'without a declaration of war, German forces fell on our country, attacked our frontiers in many places ... The Red Army and the whole nation will wage a victorious Patriotic War for our beloved country, for honour, for liberty ... Our cause is just. The enemy will be beaten. Victory will be ours!'[31]

In the New Grill of the Imperial, Eta ordered red wine. Sorge asked for a double whisky, the first of very many.

Seven time zones to the west, nearly three million Wehrmacht soldiers advanced along a 1,600-kilometre-long front that stretched from the Baltic to the Black Sea. Luftwaffe bombers crossing the borders found the Soviet territories sleeping and utterly unprepared. 'As we flew above the enemy's country, everything below seemed to be asleep,' wrote Leutanant Max-Hellmuth Ostermann of Luftflotte 1's 7/JG 54 squadron. 'No anti-aircraft fire, no movement, and above all no enemy aircraft were present to confront us.'[32] The Germans bombed as far as Kronstadt, on the outskirts of Leningrad, and Sevastopol in the Crimea.[33] From the Kremlin, Stalin ordered a general counter-attack – oblivious to the reality that the initial momentum of the German ground and air attack had completely destroyed the Soviet organisational command and control within the first few hours, paralysing every level of command from the infantry platoon to the Soviet high command in Moscow.[34]

Eta left Sorge at sunset, preferring even the tedious company of the Otts to that of her heavily drunk lover. Sorge had grown morose and aggressive. Around eight in the evening he made his way to the public telephone in the hotel lobby and dialled the ambassador's private line. 'The war is lost!' Sorge shouted to a startled Ott. He then called other friends, including Anita Mohr and other pillars of German expatriate society, with the same dire message. Helma Ott pooled her indignation over Sorge's behaviour with her friends. The man was drunk, but this was really too much.[35] Helma's personal, profoundly vacuous, explanation for the war was that 'we told the Russians that we needed the products of the Ukraine, and if they're not willing to give them to us, we just have to take them for ourselves, that's all'. So simple. Her only son, Podwick, would freeze to death at Stalingrad two years later.

Sometime later that evening, the embassy's radio attaché Erwin Wickert heard Sorge's raised voice as he crossed the lobby of the Imperial on his way to bed. Sorge was at the bar, haranguing half-a-dozen guests at the top of his voice. 'A fucking criminal,' he shouted in English. 'A murderer! Signs a friendship pact with Stalin then stabs him in the back. But Stalin will teach that bastard a lesson.'[36] Wickert attempted to calm the man he knew to be Ambassador Ott's friend, whose behaviour was drawing frosty stares.

'I tell you, he's nothing but a common criminal,' Sorge told the young diplomat. 'Why does nobody kill him? For instance, some army officers?'

Such careless talk was dangerous, Wickert warned. One never knew who might be listening and pass on his words to the Gestapo.

'Meisinger is an arsehole! You're all arseholes!' was Sorge's reply. 'And if you think the Japanese will attack Siberia, you all have another think coming! There, your Ambassador is completely mistaken!'[37]

Sorge then attempted to make his way to the lavatory, but almost collapsed. Wickert concluded that it might not be wise for Sorge to attempt to drive himself home and hurriedly arranged a room at the hotel for him. With the help of a lift boy, Wickert helped the drunk upstairs. Sorge had to rush to the sink to vomit, then fell asleep in his clothes.

*

On the other side of Asia, day two of Operation Barbarossa had already dawned with German troops eighty kilometres inside the Soviet border on most sectors of the brand-new Eastern front. A thousand Soviet aircraft had been destroyed the previous day, mostly on the ground. At an airfield near Minsk, a young aviation engineer and pilot named Isaac Bibikov climbed into one of the surviving Polikarpov-2 fighters and took off westwards to meet the second day's wave of German bombers that poured over the frontier. Bibikov was shot down somewhere over the cornfields and rolling countryside of western Belarus, and his body never found. His niece, the author's mother, would discover Isaac's fate only in 1944.

On Monday 23 June, Sorge was back in his office at the embassy. His mood was angry. He lashed out furiously at a secretary who chattered excitedly about the German victories, and railed at his colleagues that Hitler's mistake would cost him the war.[38] The economic attaché Kordt was taken aback by how deeply the outbreak of war had affected the usually cheerful – or at least flippant – Sorge. Kordt claimed in his memoir that Sorge confided to him that 'he felt particular sympathy for the Russian people, having been born in Russia of a Russian mother' – though the two men were never particular friends and it seems doubtful that Sorge would choose such an inauspicious moment to share his Russian background.[39]

Centre did not bother giving Agent Ramsay the satisfaction of acknowledging that he had been right all along. Instead Golikov sent an abrupt note the day after the invasion began. 'Inform us of all information you have on the position of the Japanese government in connection to the German war against the USSR. Director.'[40]

The previous evening the Soviet ambassador Smetanin had rushed to the residence of Foreign Minister Matsuoka to seek reassurance that Japan would honour the terms of the non-aggression pact he had signed on his jovial, karaoke-filled stopover in Moscow in April. Matsuoka could give no such assurance. As Soviet forces crumpled and Hitler's blitzkrieg stormed eastwards towards Minsk, Kiev, Leningrad and Moscow, the USSR's ability to fight and win a war on one front hung in the balance. What was clear to the Kremlin, even in the first days and weeks of Barbarossa, was that a war on two fronts against both Germany and Japan would be impossible.

The very existence of the Soviet state depended on the Japanese resisting the temptation to invade the Soviet Far East.

19

Plan North or Plan South?

'Please write what Sorge has said and what Sorge has done. Sorge is a big man. He does good things all the time. Do you know what Sorge is? Sorge is a God ... God is always a man ... People need more Gods. Sorge will become a God ... Do you know what Sorge has done? I have arranged that the Japanese government will be defeated soon'[1]

Sorge to Hanako, August 1941

Ozaki, along with the whole Konoe cabinet, had always been sceptical that Hitler had the appetite for the titanic risk involved in an attack of the Soviet Union. 'Ozaki himself had the opinion that it would be a crazy matter for Japan to go to war against Russia,' Sorge wrote in his prison confession.[2] The reality of Barbarossa, therefore, came as a profound shock to him. It also seems to have triggered a sense of personal guilt at not having seen the danger. In this moment of crisis for the motherland of world revolution, Ozaki decided the time had come to be not merely an observer but an actor.

Neither Sorge and Ozaki were modest men. Like many advisers, they both came to believe that they knew better than their masters. They also knew intimately the process of how the presentation of information could shape major political decisions. Both understood that information is power – and both Sorge and Ozaki in their own ways had long dreamed of stepping out of the shadows and onto the political stage. As early as 1939, Ozaki had suggested to Sorge that he might use his 'considerable persuasive power socially as an expert on Chinese problems and contact politically with influential people' to nudge his powerful friends into a more pro-Soviet position.[3] Back then Sorge had vetoed the idea, fearful that overt lobbying would jeopardise his agent's position.

By late June 1941, however, the time for discretion was past. The Konoe group's 'attitude toward Russia was considerably flexible', Ozaki reported, so 'there was some ground to enable my political manoeuvring'.[4] Even better, Sorge's earlier insistence that Ozaki maintain scrupulous neutrality on the subject of Russia had paid off. The prime minister 'evaluated me fairly highly' for even-handedness and even sought out Ozaki's advice. 'This was a chance for [Ozaki] to disclose his opinion about the current crucial problem of whether Japan should join the war against Russia,' Sorge told his interrogators. To Moscow, he wrote 'saying that we had a possibility of carrying out a positive political activity and asking whether we should go ahead and do it'.[5]

Centre, inundated with disastrous news of retreat and with more emergencies to address, 'did not particularly reject' the Tokyo spy ring's scheme for active intervention, 'but answered that we did not need to do so' Sorge later wrote.[6] That was a sufficient green light for Ozaki. He lost no time in forcefully arguing against any Japanese military adventures in the Soviet Union at the Breakfast Group's early morning meetings. The USSR would never threaten Japan, Ozaki told the inner circle of Konoe advisers on 25 June. Siberia had none of the natural resources such as rubber, oil and tin that Japan needed for its war effort. A winter war in Siberia against an enemy skilled at defensive war would be bloody and hard. As fellow Breakfast Group member Shigeharu Matsumoto, editor-in-chief of the Domei news agency, recalled to an interviewer in 1965 that Ozaki forcefully invoked the memory of the Soviets' unexpected efficiency at Nomonhan two years previously. A war against Russia would also be pointless, Ozaki argued, because Japan's natural economic dominion lay to the south, not to the north – as he should know, as one of the early architects of the Greater East Asia Co-Prosperity Sphere. Furthermore, he concluded, a Japanese–Russian conflict would only play into the hands of the United States and Britain, who very likely would strike Japan 'after her oil and iron reserves were depleted. Moreover, if Germany should succeed in defeating the Soviet Union, Siberia might fall into Japan's lap without her raising a finger.'[7] Ozaki, a pacifist and international communist spy, was passionately promoting Japan's imperial destiny in Southeast Asia in defence of the USSR.[8]

The Breakfast Group debate was lively – not least on the subject of the interpretation of where that imperial destiny might lead Japan. Domei chief Matsumoto, for one, saw Operation Barbarossa as a heaven-sent opportunity to seize a slice of Russia while the Germans did the bulk of the fighting on the Western front. Thus Japan could get rid of its historic northern enemy, as well as confirming the Japanese as the master race of Asia by expelling Europeans from north-east Asia forever.

Ozaki later admitted that the passion of his argument was fuelled by indignation at being contradicted by men he saw as inferior to himself: 'my main motive was caused by my feeling of repulsion because my opinion was being opposed strongly by these people'.[9] Happily for Stalin, Ozaki's point of view proved the more persuasive. The cabinet advisers concluded, recalled Matsumoto, that 'it would have been very difficult to defeat Russia' and 'only the Russians can survive in Siberia … It is much too cold there for Japanese.'[10]

True, persuading the Breakfast Group was not the same as persuading Konoe himself. And even Konoe was not Japan's supreme authority in military matters – as had been proved on a regular basis over the last decade as the Kwangtung Army and the War Ministry repeatedly overruled the civilian government's decisions. Nonetheless, Ozaki's voice was important in stoking the prime minister's scepticism towards an invasion of the USSR. It was all the more significant because, as Ozaki had informed Sorge back in May, 'if Konoe has to choose between a war with Britain and the United States or a war with Russia, he would rather choose Russia, because he doesn't like Russia'.[11]

On 19 and 23 June, the top commanders of the Japanese Army and Navy had held two crucial, top-secret conferences to decide their policy towards the USSR. Within days, Miyagi and Ozaki had jointly gathered the gist of their decision, largely from conversations with Ozaki's loose-tongued Oxford-educated friend Prince Saionji, and Shinjiro Tanaka, the head of the political and economic desk of the *Asahi Shimbun* newspaper.

In essence, Ozaki told Sorge on one of his increasingly regular visits to his boss's house, the current Japanese position was one of *jukushishugi* – waiting for the persimmon to ripen and fall into your lap. In other words, the army and navy had decided to wait and see, observing *both* the Tripartite Pact and the Japan–USSR Neutrality Pact until such time as Hitler convincingly beat the Soviets. At that point Japan would step in to prevent the Nazis from claiming Siberia. This fence-sitting exercise was grandly dubbed 'a unified north-and-south integration strategy ... in accordance with the future changes in the international situation', as Sorge reported to Moscow.[12] In the meantime, Japan's military leaders agreed to continue with their plan to expand into Southeast Asia – while preparing for a possible invasion of Russia if, as Ott had confidently expected, the Soviet forces were overrun within three months.

While Ozaki bent the ears of Japan's civilian policymakers and betrayed their secrets, Miyagi was busy gathering small titbits of intelligence and assembling them into an impressively complete collage of Japan's military strategy. Miyagi, running the gauntlet of police checkpoints and intermittent surveillance of Sorge's house on 26 June, brought him new maps of the northern Japanese islands of Hokkaido and Karafuto (Sakhalin) with airbases and military installations marked on them with the help of Miyagi's Hokkaido-based agent, Ugenta Taguchi. Two days later Sorge penned a long report to Centre and handed it to Clausen. The radio man, with his by now usual mixture of cowardice and resentment, transmitted a truncated version to Centre only on 3 July. The crucial message was further garbled when an agent of the Kempeitai showed up at his door halfway through the transmission, forcing Clausen to cut the power, lock the door of the second-floor bedroom containing his radio equipment and make polite conversation with the policeman until he went away.[13]

Clausen's interrupted transmission makes for confusing reading. He reported both Scholl's prediction – actually based, as we know but Centre did not, more on wishful-thinking than fact – that Japan would attack the USSR 'within five weeks'. The next paragraph contained the exactly contradictory news from Ozaki, who reported that 'the Japanese government has decided to honour the non-aggression pact with the USSR ... and send three divisions to Saigon and Indo-China. Even Matsuoka voted for this, although he had previously spoken for an orientation towards the USSR.'[14] But even in its paradoxical and muddled form this telegram was taken seriously in Moscow. Confirmation that the Japanese had not yet made any firm decision on

'Plan North' was some comfort. Golikov ordered it distributed to top members of the General Staff.

More solid intelligence followed. On 2 July, in conditions of the deepest secrecy, the Emperor Hirohito himself summoned a *gozenkaigi* – a 'conference with the August Presence' – with his cabinet to discuss matters of strategy. The emperor wore a naval uniform and sat on a dais between two incense-burning braziers, while his ministers and military chiefs knelt alongside low tables covered in brocade.[15] It was a rare and fateful meeting of the greatest import for Sorge and his masters. In the days following the meeting Ozaki once more pumped Saionji, who had just learned the secrets of the *gozenkaigi* from Commander Fuiji of the Foreign Affairs Section of the Imperial Navy and was happy to share them with his trusted friend.[16] 'I had no secrets from Ozaki,' Saionji would later recall.[17] By 4 July, Ozaki was able to pass Sorge a precise account of Hirohito's secret conference. The emperor had given his blessing to the plan for his armies to attack southwards. But at the same time Siberia and the Soviet Far East were also included in plans for Japan's Co-Prosperity Sphere, a clear sign that Hirohito expected the persimmon to fall soon. Japan certainly wanted its slice of the Soviet Union – it just didn't expect to have to fight for it.

There was another consideration holding Emperor Hirohito and the cabinet back from an immediate attack on Russia. With the overland route via Russia severed by the war, Japan could no longer import the military equipment from Germany which had been flowing as long as the Ribbentrop–Molotov pact had held. Now Japan hoped that perhaps the United States might become an alternative supplier of vital military technology, from radar and electronics to machine tools and engine parts. Saionji told Ozaki that Japan must 'take a compromising attitude toward the United States' – which meant supporting Ambassador Admiral Nomura's continuing attempts to strike the kind of non-aggression pact with Washington as it had agreed with Moscow the previous year.[18]

Even as Admiral Yamamoto's naval strategists worked on their secret plans to destroy the US Pacific Fleet, official Tokyo still held on to the hope that a peace deal with America would give them a free hand to expand in Asia. The possible consequences of an accord between Washington and Tokyo in the summer of 1941 – chief among them the cancellation of Japanese plans to make an attack on Pearl Harbor and consequently

the removal of any reason for the US to enter the Second World War –
remains one of the most tantalising might-have-beens of the conflict.

In a meeting with Ambassador Ott soon after the *gozenkaigi*,
Matsuoka attempted to put a brave face on the setback to German plans.
He told Ott that the emperor was concerned that if Japan attacked the
USSR, Stalin would bomb Japanese cities – to which Ott, not very
reassuringly, countered that according to German intelligence the
Soviet Union had a mere 300 heavy bombers capable of reaching Japan
stationed in the Far East and none of its latest aircraft.[19] According to
the foreign minister's personal secretary Toshikazu Kase, Matsuoka then
disingenuously attempted to persuade Ott that 'Japan's effort to restrain
the United States and Great Britain in the Pacific constituted a no less
vital contribution to the common [Axis] cause than an intervention
in the Soviet-German war'.[20] But in the end Matsuoka, evidently
embarrassed at his own defeat at the Imperial Council, also gave Ott
the quite false impression that 'Plan North' would eventually win out
and that the Japanese attack on Vladivostok was just a matter of time.
'Everything indicates that Japan will enter the war against Russia,'[21] Ott
optimistically reported to Berlin on 3 July.

Sorge knew better. Over the embassy breakfast table, Sorge quizzed Ott
on the progress of his efforts to persuade Japan to join Hitler's attack
on Russia. Ott passed on Matsuoka's assurance that Japan would go to
war within two months. But of the two men it was Sorge who had the
clearer insight into Japan's true intentions.

'Matsuoka told such a story to Ambassador Ott in order to please
him,' recalled Sorge. But he knew from Ozaki that 'the truth might be
different'.[22] On 12 July, Sorge wrote another lengthy cable to Centre – a
message that Clausen did not mangle quite as badly as the previous one.
Sorge reported that Ott had doubted that the Japanese would attack
Vladivostok before the Germans took Sverdlovsk, the capital of the
Urals. Since the Germans were at that moment only at Smolensk – some
2,200 kilometres to the west of Sverdlovsk – this remained a remote
possibility. 'If the Red Army suffers defeat then there is no doubt that
the Japanese will join the war, and if there is no defeat, then they will
maintain neutrality,' Sorge wrote.[23]

The version of this telegram in the military archives bears Stalin's
initials alongside those of Molotov, Beria and army chief Marshal

Voroshilov. A handwritten note on the bottom written by a Fourth Department official says: 'in consideration of the high reliability and accuracy of previous information and the competence of the information sources, this information can be trusted'.[24]

Sorge's reports were, finally, receiving the credence they deserved.[25] Centre even broke the habit of a lifetime and sent explicit thanks to Agent Ramsay. A message acknowledging the 12 July cable began with 'a portion expressing their gratitude for our previous information'.[26] But at the same time, Centre decided to do a thorough check on the reliability of its suddenly vital agent in Tokyo.

In the first days of the war Stalin had relieved Golikov of his post and sent him on a top-secret mission to London and Washington to ask for military aid to the USSR and to drum up support for the opening of a second front in Europe.[27] The new director of the Fourth Department was General Konstantin Kolganov, who ordered the old archives combed and all the old accusations against the Tokyo *rezidentura* re-examined. The result was a scathing document entitled 'On the Sources of Political Distrust of INSON [Sorge]' that Kolganov submitted to the Red Army leadership on 11 August 1941.

'For a prolonged period INSON worked under the former leaders of the Intelligence directorate who turned out to be enemies of the people,' read Kolganov's report. 'From this emerges the conclusion – that if enemies of the people sold themselves to foreign intelligence agencies why could he not sell out INSON also? ... The former chief of the Japanese department Sirotkin turned out to be a Japanese spy. Sirotkin told the organs of the NKVD that he gave INSON up to the Japanese with all his sources ... at the end of 1938.' Kolganov was either unaware or ignored the fact that Sirotkin had withdrawn his charges against Sorge at his trial. But that was only one of many confusions in the damming report. Kolganov confused Clausen with Vukelić: 'In 1935 Inson was sent a radio operator code-named FRITZ, an extremely murky character. It is clear only that he is a Serbian officer who is married to a Russian white émigrée.' And he overlooked Sorge's years of work with the Comintern prior to joining the Fourth Department. 'INSON has no previous history of work for the Party ... how he came into the Party and then into the intelligence directorate is unclear,' wrote Kolganov – without pausing to consider that the reason for this gap in institutional memory was because most of the Fourth Department who had known

Sorge personally had been murdered in the Great Purge. 'The question of INSON is not a new one … The basic question is: why have the Germans or the Japanese not destroyed him, since he has been betrayed to them? There is always one answer – that [they] do not liquidate him in order to send him here for intelligence work. Therefore it is necessary always to compare the information provided by INSON with other sources … and in general thoroughly to analyse it and take a critical attitude to it. INSON is extremely arrogant and has a high opinion of himself that is necessary to bear in mind when directing him.'[28]

In any normal intelligence organisation in normal times, the devastating conclusions of the Kolganov memorandum would have destroyed the reputation of any *rezident*. But these were not normal times. The archives show that despite his reservations, Kolganov continued to circulate Sorge's information to the highest echelons of the Kremlin and the army. The universal pall of suspicion cast by the Purge seems to have devalued the very meaning of the terrible accusations Kolganov bandied about so freely. If Sorge was under the control of the Germans, why did he try so desperately to warn Stalin of Barbarossa? If he was being run by the Japanese, why was so much of the important top-secret information he revealed provably true? It seems that Kolganov did not trouble himself with such questions. By the crazy illogic of the period, as far as Centre was concerned the Tokyo *rezidentura* was both thoroughly compromised and vitally important.

The stakes, for the Soviet Union, could not have been higher. An attack by Japan on the USSR in the summer of 1941 would have spelt the end of Stalin's regime and utterly changed the outcome of the Second World War. Even without the benefit of hindsight, it was clear at the time to both Sorge and Ozaki that the Japanese position in the two months between the beginning of Barbarossa and the onset of winter in the Soviet Far East would be crucial to the outcome of the conflict. As Sorge reported to Centre on 3 July, Ott and the Japanese were all too aware of exactly how powerful the armies and aircraft that Stalin had stationed in the Far East were. These forces would soon be desperately needed to defend Moscow. Indeed, in early July Stalin ordered four divisions from the Far Eastern garrison westward. Could Stalin risk leaving Siberia undefended by transferring even more of those vital troops? The answer to that question depended on what Agent Ramsay could report on Japan's intentions.

Ott suffered a further setback when Matsuoka – the most pro-German member of the government – quit along with the whole cabinet on 16 July. Konoe's dramatic resignation was a protest against the Japanese high command's resistance to his efforts to strike a peace deal with the United States and end the war in China. Konoe's drastic démarche worked. The emperor summoned him back to power immediately, and even gave his valued prime minister permission for a last-ditch attempt to avert war with America by proposing a personal summit with US President Roosevelt. But Matsuoka, Germany's most vocal ally, remained out of power.

As the stakes rose for the Sorge spy ring, so did the risks. The Tokyo authorities stepped up their spy mania another notch by forbidding the use of any language but Japanese in long-distance telephone conversations. Security in the institutions where Ozaki worked grew tighter. When Kawai went to see Ozaki at the offices of the South Manchuria Railway in June, he was made to present his credentials and sign a form. 'They are even watching you inside your own office,' Kawai warned his recruiter, 'so you have to be careful.' Ozaki did not seem unduly troubled at being singled out for special surveillance. 'They are watching me closely because I am one of Matsuoka's boys,' he replied easily.[29]

But by late July, Ozaki was less sanguine. He had grown tense, lost his usual bonhomie, and had become fearful of arrest, Kawai recalled. When he met Kawai by chance on a crowded commuter train in Ginza the two old comrades went for a quick beer (probably in one of the little bars that still exist today, tucked under the railway arches). Ozaki confided that he felt 'like a rat in a bag'.[30] Miyagi, too, was nervous. He believed that he was being shadowed as he criss-crossed Tokyo on errands for the ring and dreamed of retiring to the quiet life of a painter in his ancestral Okinawa. 'It is foolish for people like us to engage in this sort of thing,' Miyagi told Kawai. 'I never intended to do this on a permanent basis. Now I can't seem to get away from it!'[31]

The growing jeopardy did not, however, make Ozaki any more cautious. When Kawai went to call on Ozaki at his house on 27 July he was again followed for part of his route by police agents, who he managed to shake off. Ozaki was not at home; but Kawai was surprised to see his wife pouring tea for an old party comrade, Ritsu Ito. Ito had served two years in jail in the 1930s for his links to the Communist

Youth League, had been rearrested in November 1939 and then, curiously, released in August of 1940 to resume his old job as Ozaki's deputy at the South Manchuria Railway's Investigation Department. Had Ito been released on condition that he became a police informer on the activities of Ozaki, Kawai wondered?[32]

By mid-July it was also becoming alarmingly clear that the Japanese Army was mounting a mass mobilisation. New training camps were being hastily built all over Japan, Miyagi reported, still dutiful to the ring despite his growing fear. Thousands of call-up papers had been issued, including to Miyagi's sometime helper Yoshinobu Odai, who heard rumours at his recruiting centre that his unit was bound for Manchuria. The key question for Sorge was whether the main thrust of this mobilisation would be directed at Siberia, or Southeast Asia.

This was the moment when the careful bookkeeping of the South Manchuria Railway came into its own as a source of intelligence. Every movement of troops, armour and war materials across Japan and China could be traced in precise detail through the Mantetsu's meticulous hour-by-hour timetables, updated nightly by a team of slide-rule-wielding technicians. More, the origin, destination and make-up of each train – the number of passenger carriages, boxcars, cattle wagons or flatcars – gave a complete, if coded, picture of Japan's land-based war effort.

The problem was that even with this insider information Ozaki could still not reach any definitive conclusion. His Mantetsu colleagues estimated that 250,000 troops were being sent north, 350,000 to the south. But, worryingly, the railway had mobilised a team of 3,000 experienced railway workers accompanied by special cranes to lift rolling stock in order to change the wheel gauge. There was only one possible use for such equipment: to transform Japanese wagons for use on the Trans-Siberian railway. New track was also being laid to provide more passing places for locomotives near the Soviet border crossing of Ushumun, evidently the likely focus point of a possible invasion. Ozaki was also disturbed by a meeting of the Showa Research Association where the chief of the Military Affairs Section of the War Ministry frankly stated that 'if Russia should be defeated in her fight with Germany ... Japan should naturally send troops to Siberia. It is ridiculous not to eat the food being set before you.'[33]

Miyagi attempted to help solve the conundrum in the way he knew best: by gathering small, apparently insignificant details. Exuding his usual clownish charm, Miyagi travelled tirelessly around the provinces chatting to soldiers in teahouses and bars. Asking direct questions about their destination would have resulted in Miyagi's immediate arrest as a spy, so he instead gossiped about the quality of the kit that the conscripts were issued. Weren't the new army-issue greatcoats splendidly warm? Thank goodness for those tropical cotton uniforms in this summer heat. And so on. Piecing together the recruits' gripes about their new equipment, Miyagi was able to make informed guesses about where each unit was heading. He found a disturbingly high number were ready to wrap up warm for a winter war in Siberia.

On 28 July, the Japanese troops who had been occupying parts of French Indochina since the previous year moved into the capital, Saigon, and occupied the city without a shot being fired under an agreement with the Vichy puppet government. Indochina offered excellent ports, a rich supply of rice and labour for the Japanese Empire. The first ripe persimmon had indeed fallen quite effortlessly into Japan's lap.

This easy victory would have profound consequences for the course of the war. In response to the invasion of French Indochina, the US swiftly imposed an oil embargo on Japan. In a stroke, Japan was cut off from 80 per cent of her fuel supplies. Washington also froze all Japanese banking assets – followed soon after by Britain, Australia and the Netherlands, which together controlled the entire banking infrastructure of Asia. With no possibility of buying vital oil and steel supplies, Japan would now be forced either to curtail her plans for a pan-Asian empire – or to seize the oilfields of the Dutch East Indies to make up for the loss of Texas and Pennsylvania oil. The US oil embargo, more than any other event in 1941, set Japan on a collision course with its Asian neighbours and with America itself.

Though Berlin had pressured the defeated French not to resist Japan in Indochina, the fall of Saigon was also bad news for German hopes of pushing the Japanese to attack Russia. More Japanese troops and ships were steaming south at the exact moment that Berlin needed them heading in the opposite direction. The German General Staff had also begun to realise that they had grossly underestimated the strength of the Red Army. On 16 July the Germans finally took Smolensk after intense fighting, but failed to prevent most of the Soviet Army escaping eastwards to defend Moscow. Opening a second front against the Soviet Far East was, therefore, becoming an increasingly urgent priority for Berlin if the Russian war was to be won quickly.

Ribbentrop began badgering Ott in a series of urgent cables to hurry up the Japanese assault on the Soviet Far East – an assault that both Scholl and the ambassador had blithely promised was imminent. To help the Japanese in their decision, Kretschmer and his aides again got to work on the basement sand table Wenneker had used to plan an attack on Singapore, this time to plot tactics for amphibious assaults on the Soviet Pacific ports of Vladivostok and Khabarovsk. For Ott, the only unequivocally good piece of news from the Russian front was that advancing Wehrmacht troops had captured Soviet soldiers drafted in from Far Eastern garrisons, revealing that Stalin had already begun denuding his Siberian defences to save Moscow.

Both Sorge and Ott were under enormous pressure from their respective masters – the ambassador to deliver a Japanese offensive against Siberia; the spy to avert it. The strain was beginning to tell. For the first time in their seven-year friendship they argued openly over politics. Sorge insisted, banging the breakfast table, that Germany would be defeated within three years and that Hitler's plan was as doomed as Napoleon's Russian campaign had been. Sorge made a point of pouring cold water over Ott's hopes whenever he could. Whenever he 'obtained various information items from Ozaki and Miyagi', Sorge recalled, he 'distorted them conveniently, propagandised them, and worked so that the German side should not have a hope that Japan would join the war'.[34] At the Domei news agency, Sorge – by now the longest-serving German correspondent in Tokyo – even summoned a meeting of his German press colleagues and harangued them on the folly of Barbarossa. He also raised eyebrows in the Japanese Foreign Ministry by insisting that he had secret information that Soviet air strength was in reality much larger than the Germans had been telling them.

On 2 August, Sorge drove up to the embassy dacha at Karuizawa, leaving the summer heat and pressure-cooker atmosphere of Tokyo behind him, to spend the weekend with Ott, and his old friend Erwin Scholl. Karuizawa, a town in the mountains near Nagano, was a traditional summer resort where the wealthy bourgeoisie of Tokyo escaped the humidity of the capital on the pine-forested slopes and hot springs of Mount Asama. Perhaps the irony of taking a holiday on the slopes of an active volcano was not lost on Sorge. At least he would have felt at home. In recent years Karuizawa had become a favourite vacation spot for Tokyo's German community, and boasted a German bakery that made pumpernickel bread and *apfelstrudel*. That weekend the main cinema was showing the latest film from Berlin, *Verklungene Melodie* ('Faded Melody'), a romantic melodrama starring Brigitte Horney.[35]

The German embassy's summer residence was a pretty two-storey wooden building, set in a lush garden. In the evenings the three old comrades, free of the oppressive claustrophobia of Tokyo, relaxed in the bar of the Mampei Hotel. The hotel, built in 1936 in an odd mixture of Japanese and half-timbered Bavarian styles, still stands today. Pre-war photographs show a cosy, club-like bar furnished with leather armchairs and art deco brass lamps. Remarkably, an archive photograph in the hotel's 2017 brochure shows a pair of Westerners contentedly playing chess in the lounge sometime in the late 1930s. They are – unmistakably – Ott and Sorge.

Over drinks, the three old friends conferred over politics and the news from the Russian front. Ott confided that, despite Berlin's relentlessly upbeat propaganda, German progress was slow and the losses heavy. Barely six weeks into Barbarossa, it was clear that the invasion was not going to plan. Sorge, for his part, seems to have shared his own insider knowledge of Japanese politics.

On their return to Tokyo, Ott was so impressed by Sorge's knowledge of the workings of the Konoe cabinet that he suggested to Colonel Kretschmer, the senior military attaché, that he pick Sorge's brains on Japanese strategy. 'Sorge's connections are really incredible!' remarked Kretschmer, thanking Ott for the tip.[36] Kretschmer cabled the key points of Sorge's analysis – strongly sceptical of Japan's desire for Plan North, naturally – to Berlin on 9 August. For the first time in his career Sorge had the undivided attention of the top spymasters of both Berlin and Moscow.

Around 5 August, Sorge met with Ozaki for the first time in a month. Ozaki reported a rumour that the Japanese Army had scheduled an attack on the Soviet Union for 15 August, but postponed the plan because of German setbacks on the road to Moscow. Three days later Clausen transmitted part of Sorge's message to Centre. 'The Germans are pressing the Japanese to join the war on a daily basis. But the fact that Moscow was not occupied last Sunday, contrary to what the German

Supreme Command promised, has cooled Japanese enthusiasm.'[37] That was the part of the message that got through. The rest, which Clausen failed to send and was later discovered in draft when the police raided his house after his arrest, read: 'Even Green Box [Japanese Army] has the impression that the White-Red [German-Russian] war may develop into a second China Incident because White is repeating the same mistakes as Green in China.'[38]

Both Sorge and Ozaki knew that these August days would be critical for the outcome of the war. Ozaki had told him the Japanese Army calculated that an offensive could not be launched later than the end of August because the Siberian winter would render large-scale operations impossible after mid-November. 'In the coming two to three weeks Japan's decision will be made,' Sorge warned Moscow in a 12 August cable. 'It is possible that the General Staff will take the decision to intervene without prior consultation.'[39]

Both senior members of the ring also realised that Tokyo's policy would be dictated by something more immutable than politics or even the seasons – the vital factor of Japan's strategic supplies of oil. In the wake of the American embargo on imports at the beginning of August, the entire Japanese military had only its existing supplies to fuel the rest of the war effort. If the stocks were low, Plan North would necessarily have to be abandoned and all resources concentrated on capturing the oilfields of the Dutch East Indies.

Ozaki turned to Yoshio Miyanishi, a colleague in the economic department of the South Manchuria Railway, to help him understand how much fuel Japan actually had left. Claiming that he needed the information for a government report on energy supply and that the picture would not be complete without knowing how much oil the army and navy had privately stockpiled, Ozaki persuaded Miyanishi to obtain the latest, top-secret numbers. Within a few days Miyanishi had come back with a detailed answer. A total of 2 million tons of petroleum, including naphtha, heavy oil, crude oil, and lighting oil, was available for civilian purposes. The same quantity had been hoarded by the army, and under nine million tons for the navy. At normal consumption rates, this meant that Japan had less than six months' supplies of fuel in its stockpiles.

'An examination of the oil supply situation revealed that Japan was placed in a position of choosing one out of two solutions: advancing to the south and acquiring oil in the Netherlands Indies, or yielding to the United States and receiving a petroleum supply from her,' Ozaki would explain to his interrogators.[40] The Imperial General Staff's freedom of action was being shrunk every day by the American oil embargo. However much the army may have wanted to take Siberia, Japan simply did not have the petrol to do it.

On 9 August, Sorge returned for a second weekend to Karuizawa, this time with Eta Harich-Schneider and Helma Ott. Eta was by now gripped with 'Richard Sorge fever', as she would later tell an interviewer.[41] Sorge, by Eta's account, had promised her that all his other affairs – including with Helma and her friend Anita Mohr – were firmly in the past. He also told her that 'the little Japanese woman' who had lived with him 'at times' had been sent away in May.[42] This was less than the full truth. In fact, Hanako was spending at least three nights a week in the house at Nagasaki Street and would continue to do so until September. Eta was there most other nights, though she did not notice any sign of female presence in the house.

During their weekend at the embassy dacha, Eta found her lover tense and irritable, but also dreaming of – or perhaps reconciling himself to – the idea of escape. 'Germany is sliding towards total destruction,' Sorge complained. Yet all the local German diplomats could 'worry about is getting a bigger petrol ration'.[43] He also urged Eta to break free of the Otts' hospitality and get a place of her own. 'Make yourself independent from these wretched people,' he urged her. 'I won't be around all that much longer. One of these days you will be on your own here.' Shocked by Sorge's talk of leaving Japan, Eta pressed him to tell her more. 'I may have to leave the country suddenly. I may have no choice. I cannot explain the reason. But if it happens, and some people at the embassy tell you I have run off with another woman, don't believe them!'[44]

One night soon after their return to the city, Eta attempted to soothe Sorge's brooding mood by playing Beethoven's 'Moonlight Sonata' to him by candlelight in the embassy ballroom. After the impromptu concert Sorge slipped away and let himself into Eta's old room – now the embassy Gestapo headquarters – with the key that she had stolen for him. There, as the Otts slept upstairs, he rifled the contents of Meisinger's files. Sorge discovered that his Gestapo codename was 'Post' – and that the Butcher of Warsaw had reported to Berlin that Sorge was entirely politically reliable, noting his regular attendance at

Nazi Party meetings. That probably did more to ease Sorge's anxieties, or at least one of them, than Beethoven could ever do.

The Meisinger threat may have receded, but the Japanese police were taking an ever closer interest in Sorge, Hanako and Clausen. By now all the members of the ring – in common with most foreigners in Tokyo – were receiving regular home visits from the local police. These visits were superficially scrupulously cordial, but no less nerve-wracking for it.

The early August visit by an unknown Kempeitai agent to Clausen's house in the middle of his radio transmission had been an anomaly. His more usual caller was Officer Shigeru Aoyama, Sorge's old acquaintance from the Toriizaka police station.[45] Aoyama usually dropped in at the Clausen house when he was out, questioning the maid on details of her employers' lives. Amid the usual round of domestic gossip, Aoyama picked up one intriguing gem. 'My master gets up in the middle of the night and fiddles around with a machine with shiny knobs,' the Clausens' servant told Aoyama, as he recalled in a 1965 interview. As an amateur radio operator himself, Aoyama recognised the description and had a flash of recollection. About ten days before, an official of the Ministry of Telecommunications had been at the Toriizaka station asking questions about unregistered short-wave transmission in the Azabu area. Arresting a prominent German businessman without very good reason was a formidable step for a young police constable. But Aoyama wondered if he had now possibly stumbled across the rogue radio station.[46]

Aoyama politely questioned Anna Clausen about her husband. Either careless or, more likely, scared, Anna blurted out that if she asked her husband what he was doing after midnight, he 'would get very angry and scold her severely'. She also blamed her husband's friend Richard Sorge – whom Aoyama had never before connected to Clausen. 'Sorge is a bad influence on my husband,' Anna told the courteous policeman. 'He takes my husband, who has a very weak heart, to all sorts of outlandish places at ridiculous hours, such as Kunenuma to go fishing. So please, Mr Aoyama, when you next see Sorge, please scold him for me.'[47] Aoyama concluded that the Clausens 'were a very close and intimate man and wife'. He also decided that even if her husband had any questionable relationship with Sorge or had been sending out illegal messages, Anna knew nothing of it.

The keen young policeman decided to follow up this intriguing lead by paying a visit to Dr Sorge himself sometime in early August 1941. When no one answered his knock, Aoyama assumed that the house was empty. He tried the door and found it unlocked. Overcome by curiosity, he mounted the stairs and entered Sorge's study. He found Sorge sitting at his typewriter, fixing him with a furious glare. Sorge yelled that the policeman was trespassing. Knowing himself in the wrong, Aoyama retreated in a flurry of apologies. Sorge's anger soon evaporated and the men parted with assurances of mutual respect.

The next encounter with the police was less amicable. Sorge's loyal old housekeeper Fukuda Tori had retired and been replaced by another, slightly less elderly woman. The new housekeeper was summoned to Toriizaka station by officers who wanted to know Hanako's address. When she protested that she had not worked for Sorge very long and did not know where Miyake-san lived, the questioners became aggressive. 'You had better let us know the next time Miyake-san comes, or we won't put up with it!' the police told the woman, according to Hanako's later hearsay account. 'I cook my master's meals and get paid for it!' the servant replied defiantly. 'There's no reason why you people should push me around!' More amused than annoyed, the policemen joked: 'This old bitch is fresh!' and smacked her backside. Weeping with rage, she fled to Sorge's kitchen.[48]

A few days later Aoyama was back, again asking for Hanako. Sorge was out, but Hanako was at home and Aoyama brought her in to the station.[49] In a narrow upstairs room, she was questioned by the local chief of police, a severe-looking elderly man in plain clothes. The interrogation began with routine queries on Hanako's name, age, address and education, which the chief took down in pencil on a long form. Then the tone changed abruptly. 'I don't see why an educated woman like you … lives with a foreigner,' said the officer sharply. 'Aren't there enough men in Japan?'

Longing for escape, Hanako tried to claim that she had been separated from Sorge for a long time. 'There is nothing between us now.'[50]

'If you have nothing to do with him, why do you go there all the time?' the chief retorted.

Hanako ventured that he must be mistaking her for someone else.

'Stop lying!' her interrogator shouted. 'You're the only Japanese woman who visits Sorge. I know exactly when you get there and when you leave. From the window here I can see you lying in bed with your backside bare!' The policeman told Hanako that she should separate from Sorge immediately. 'You know that a Japanese woman who lives with a foreigner is not considered a Japanese national,' he said. 'We will get severance pay from him. We will take care of the details.'

The suggestion that she lived with Sorge only for money stung Hanako into defiance. 'What will you do about it if I refuse?' she asked, but her anger quickly dissolved into tears of anger and humiliation and she turned to the window to hide them.

'What do you see in these hairy *ketto* [barbarians]?' said the chief, continuing his tirade. 'We cannot compete with these hairy foreigners. They are so sweet and nice to our women.'[51]

'May I leave now if you have no more questions?' Hanako responded coldly. The police had no reason to detain her. But they told Hanako to return when next she visited Sorge to sign a written transcript of their interview to be used as the basis for a report on her to the Ministry of Home Affairs. Hanako departed without answering.

When Hanako told Sorge about the incident the following day, he was furious. 'If Japan takes you away from me, I will have Germany take all German girls away from their Japanese men,' he ranted, becoming ridiculous in his impotent rage. 'I can do it! I'll send a telegram to Germany!' Calming down a little, he took his lover's hand. 'I am strong,' Sorge assured Hanako, she recalled twenty years later. 'You needn't worry.'[52]

Sorge may have been powerless against the collective might of the Japanese police force, but against a single officer, his physical strength and the aura of untouchability that still surrounded him as a well-connected foreigner still made him a formidable opponent. A few days after Hanako's first interrogation Aoyama made the mistake of knocking at Sorge's door once more. Hearing a familiar voice talking to his maid, Sorge strode out of the dining room to confront the policeman. Aoyama asked for Miyake-san. 'What do you want with Miyake-san?' demanded Sorge. 'Anything concerning her I'll answer.'

'You don't understand,' the officer retorted, and attempted to push past Sorge. Aoyama began to tell the maid that she should send Hanako to the police station when she next appeared when Sorge knocked him to the ground with a short uppercut.[53]

Sorge had made many impulsive mistakes in his espionage career, all involving fellow foreigners. Seducing the wife of his most important intelligence source, crashing his motorcycle while carrying a pocketful of compromising documents, drunkenly praising Stalin to a roomful of Nazis. But an assault on a Japanese police officer was a different level of error. Sorge, realising that he could be in handcuffs within minutes, quickly attempted to apologise as he helped the stunned young policeman to his feet. 'I am very sorry about this,' said Sorge. 'I did not think. I was so worried about Miyake-san.' He instructed the maid to bring a pair of his best shoes, which he presented to Aoyama with a bow. The young man accepted both apology and shoes and made his exit.

'I didn't think Mr. Sorge would get so angry,' he told the maid as he left. 'He is touchy! It will be awkward for me to try to reach her [Hanako] here.'[54]

Once again, Sorge's fiendish luck had held (though, unbeknown to him, it was at this point that it had finally run out). Aoyama told his colleagues about the assault, but they did not show up in force to arrest him. But it was also becoming clear to Sorge that his relationship with Hanako must end, for her own safety. Back in Moscow he had lectured the besotted Hede Massing on 'how lonely and ascetic the life of an apparatchik must be, with no attachments, no strings, no sentimentalities'.[55] The time was approaching for Sorge to perform painful triage on his own personal life.

Hanako's second interrogation sealed the break. Aoyama had spotted Hanako in the street on her way to Sorge's house, and called from an upper window of the police station. This time both Aoyama and his boss were more courteous, though the former complained – fortunately in a jocular tone – about the power of Sorge's punch. The senior policeman showed Hanako a thick file of Japanese women who had broken off their relationships with foreigners – all, he claimed, in exchange for substantial compensation. But their former aggressiveness had disappeared. Perhaps Sorge's gallant violence in defence of his mistress, and Hanako's loyalty, had struck a chord of respect in the policemen. In any case, they made Hanako sign a transcript of their earlier interview with a thumbprint, and sent her on her way.

The situation clearly could not go on. Agitated and pacing up and down his study, Sorge hit on a plan. Urging Hanako to send her mother and niece to their native village for their own safety, he told Hanako to ready herself to flee to Shanghai. 'I have lots of money in the bank at Shanghai,' Sorge told her – the only hint that this dedicated servant of the revolution may have been preparing his own private golden parachute in a Chinese bank, as the Clausens had done. He proposed that Hanako travel alone, and that he would join her later. 'My work here will be finished soon,' he said, by Hanako's own account. 'Then I will join you in Shanghai and we will live together there.'[56]

It took Clausen to identify a serious flaw in his boss's plan. The three of them had gathered in Lohmeyer's restaurant to plot Hanako's exfiltration from Japan. Most of the conversation was conducted in German between the two men and Hanako could not follow. But it was clear that Max had pointed out that it would be impossible for Hanako to travel without a passport. And in the circumstances it would be extremely unlikely for the police to issue her one. The mood of the dinner turned bleak.

'I feel very depressed,' Sorge told Hanako in Japanese. 'Tonight I am not going to work. Tonight I am going to get drunk,' he announced. 'You drink, too,'[57] he ordered his companions.

Back home together, Sorge played some of the popular German classics he loved, Beethoven and Mozart. Drunk and sorry for himself, he contemplated the future. 'I don't know what to do … When Sorge is gone, you will think, "Sorge is a great man!" … Would you like to die with Sorge?'

Hanako replied that she was scared of dying.

'Well, everybody is afraid of dying,' he replied as he fell sleep, his disjointed stream of consciousness recorded by Hanako in her memoir. 'But Sorge is a strong man,' he continued, 'I shan't forget you, but now I can do without you … I will write many good books. You will find out later … Sorge is great! … I will die soon…. Something is very wrong with me today.'[58]

Sorge's final gift to the most long-standing – some might say long-suffering – mistress of his life would be to fix her problems with the police. About a week after her second interrogation, Sorge invited Hanako to a swanky restaurant in Nihonbashi. She wore a silk kimono for the occasion. To her surprise they were not alone. Mr Tsunajima, an interpreter from the German embassy, appeared, smartly dressed, and then both officer Aoyama and his boss. 'Miyake-san, you are very attractive in a kimono,' the older policeman commented. 'Aoyama can't talk about anything but "Miyake-san, Miyake-san".'

Aoyama himself had removed his moustache. 'I shaved it off after Mr Sorge hit me, to make a new man of myself,' he explained with a smile. Sorge, in his most charming mode, set about convincing the police to forget the dossier they had compiled on Hanako. The formal dinner – and perhaps some other persuasion of which Hanako was not aware – did the trick. Days later, the police chief appeared at Nagasaki Street and set fire to Hanako's file in one of Sorge's iron incense-burning pots.[59]

Sorge took Hanako to Lohmeyer's, the scene of their first dinner, to break the news that she would have to move out. He spoke once more about her finding herself a nice Japanese husband. 'I don't like Japanese men,' Hanako retorted. Back home, after their date, Sorge extracted a bottle of vermouth from his liquor stock and put Edwin Fischer's recording of Beethoven's Fantasia on the record player. In this last conversation, according to Hanako, Sorge came close to revealing the truth about his life. 'You will find out later what Sorge has done,' he told her, the exaltation of the music and the booze seizing him. 'Sorge is wise, strong, he doesn't worry about danger ... Sorge is ready to die for the cause.' He then asked Hanako what she wished for most in life.

'I want Sorge,' she replied.

'You can't have Sorge. Sorge is going to die.' Then the drink abruptly filled him with a more optimistic vision and he changed tack. 'I want to live! It would be wonderful if both of us could go back to Russia together ... You would like to go to Russia with Sorge?'

'Yes, I would like to.'

'If you and I return to Russia, Japan will be in bad shape. Everyone will die. I know it. The United States is very strong. Japan can't win. Russia won't fight the United States. I told Stalin that Russia could not fight against America. Do you know who Stalin is?'

Hanako said that she did.

'You please write what Sorge has said and what Sorge has done. Sorge is a big man. He does good things all the time. Do you know what Sorge is? Sorge is a God ... God is always a man. People need more Gods. Sorge will become a God. Do you know what Sorge has done? I have arranged that the Japanese government will be defeated soon. The Japanese people are a little weak. French and American men are not strong, but Russian men are strong … Let's drink together, then let's sleep together.'[60]

Hanako had heard the last, and most honest, of her lover's drunken rants. The next day Sorge suggested that the time had come for her to take her things to her mother's. He also insisted that she accept $2,000. And this time Hanako made no objection.

Breaking Point

'I am a Nazi!'[1]

Richard Sorge to his interrogators, 19 October 1941

Mid-August 1941, with hundreds of thousands of Japanese troops entraining for northern Manchuria and workers of the Mantetsu busy building railway sidings for a possible advance on Siberia, was the moment of maximum peril for the Soviet Union. A Japanese attack hung poised on news of the success of the Wehrmacht in the west. Konoe's attempts to make peace with America were faltering.

It was also the moment of greatest danger for Sorge. At least five deadly threats hung over the spy ring. Harutsugu Saito, the sharp young agent of the foreign section of the Tokko political police, had just returned from an assignment in China and resumed his surveillance of Sorge. The Japanese Ministry of Communications were also closing in on the location of the coded short-wave transmissions they had been chasing since 1936. The local policeman, Aoyama, had a tantalising lead on Clausen as the possible operator of an illegal radio. Hanako had also come to the police's attention, and though she knew little about the specifics of Sorge's work, it was clear that if the police chose to arrest and interrogate her violently she could reveal plenty of suspicious details about her lover's activities. And of course Meisinger of the Gestapo, despite his good reports on Sorge, remained a menacing and unpredictable threat.

Unbeknown to Sorge yet another jeopardy was heading his way from a sixth, and entirely unexpected, direction. In June 1941 the Tokko remembered the little Japanese-American lady with a suspiciously communist past who was now earning her living as a seamstress in Wakayama province – Tomo Kitabayashi, Miyagi's old landlady from California. Officer Mitsusaburo Tamazawa of the Tokko's Thought Section was asked to authorise a warrant for her interrogation, along with her husband. Mitsusaburo reviewed the evidence against her and found it insubstantial. He recommended that the 'old lady' (Kitabayashi was fifty-six at the time) be spared interrogation during the hot summer months and recommended that her questioning be postponed until September. Thus the spy ring received a stay of execution thanks to one policeman's curiously old-world chivalry.[2]

The delay would be vital for Sorge's most important task: to get Moscow some kind of firm confirmation that Plan North had been abandoned. In the course of August, hard evidence began finally to come conclusively together. Wenneker returned from an inspection tour of Manchuria and told Sorge that the units being assembled for possible use on the Russian front were inexperienced and second-class; the best troops were being sent south to fight in China. Ozaki obtained more details of the looming oil crisis, which was fast becoming the main argument for Japan's southward expansion. But what truly counted were reports from Wenneker that the Japanese Navy had successfully opposed opening a war on two fronts, north and south, and had won approval to occupy Thailand by the end of the year.[3]

This information was quickly followed by a similar report from Ozaki. In a three-day meeting between the commanders of the Kwangtung Army, the Imperial General Staff and the civilian government, it was decided to postpone an attack on Russia until the following year. The army, especially the radical nationalists who styled themselves the Young Officers, was 'absolutely dissatisfied with the decision', Ozaki reported. But the generals could not totally ignore both the navy and the government. A full-scale assault northwards required massive logistical support and thousands of tons of fuel – which was by now mostly controlled by the navy. Miyagi, too, chimed in with the welcome news that troops called up in a second wave of mobilisation were being issued with tropical shorts, not overcoats. On 24 August, Prince Saionji, dropping in on Ozaki at the South Manchuria Railway building, confirmed that the 'army and government have already made their decision not to go to war' with Russia.[4]

Reporting the news to Sorge, Ozaki added some caveats. The Kwangtung Army would still attack if its own strength was three times that of the Red Army in Siberia, or if the Soviet Union was defeated and 'signs of internal collapse in the Red Army in Siberia become clear ... if such a situation does not occur by the middle of September at the latest, the Russian problem will be left over definitely until next spring's snow-melting ... at the earliest'.[5] Despite Ozaki's caution, Sorge 'looked as happy as if he had been released from a heavy burden'.[6] He was at last able to compose the message that Moscow had been waiting for so anxiously. 'Green Bottle [the Japanese Navy] and the government have decided not to launch a war [against Russia] in the course of this year,' he wrote on 22 August, and handed the message to Clausen.

The radio man failed to send it.

By now Clausen was motivated by far more than just resentment of Sorge and fear of discovery. By his own account, he was actively sabotaging the ring's work. 'My way of thinking was changing at that time. It was unbearable for me to send such information to Moscow,' Clausen told the Japanese police after his arrest. But this apparent confession may not be the whole truth. In prison, Clausen was bargaining for his life. Of his decision to scrap sections of an earlier transmission pertaining to oil, Clausen told his captors that 'the portion reported that the stock of petroleum of the Japanese Army was decreasing very much. This was very important to Japan and nobody else knew that sort of thing except us.'[7] In other words, Clausen was attempting to claim that he was really on the Japanese side.

In fact, Clausen did get around to transmitting the gist of Sorge's fateful message – but three weeks later, on 14 September. 'INVEST [Ozaki] ... says that Jap government has decided not to attack USSR this year, but the armed forces will remain in Manchuria in case of a possible attack next spring in the case of a defeat of the USSR by then. INVEST remarked that the USSR can be absolutely free after 15th Sept. INTERI [Miyagi] says that one of the battalions of 14th infantry divisions destined for North has been stopped in the barracks of the guards division in Tokyo.'[8] So perhaps Clausen was more coward than traitor after all.

The radio man even decided to add Sorge's vital news that 'PAUL [Centre's bizarrely insecure codename for Wenneker – whose first name actually was Paul] told me that the next German advance will be on the Caucasus via the Dniepr. PAUL believes that if the Germans do not obtain oil soon they will lose the war. That is why the attacks on Leningrad and Moscow are all more or less feints, main attack will be on Caucasus.'[9]

Sorge had given the Kremlin its first, absolutely accurate warning that Hitler was preparing an attack on Stalingrad. For good measure, Sorge also passed on Wenneker's equally spot-on prediction that Japan would soon be at war with America. 'Navy friends of PAUL say that war against USSR is no longer being discussed. The sailors no longer believe in the possibility of success of talks between Konoe and Roosevelt. Preparing for attack on Thailand and Borneo he thinks that Manila must be taken [as a staging post]. That means war with America.'[10] Few dispatches in the history of intelligence have nailed so much prophetic information in so few words. Sorge did not, as would later be claimed, explicitly warn Stalin of the Pearl Harbor attack. But he signalled the inevitability of war between America and Japan three months before it happened.

Sorge, happily ignorant of the delay in his vital message, was elated. Eta moved into her own apartment on 1 September. He brought flowers and drank whisky as she played Scarlatti and even shouted a cheery 'good night' to the policemen lurking outside. A few days later he visited again, in triumphant mood. 'The draft is finished,' he bellowed – presumably of the cable Clausen eventually sent on 14 September. 'Ott can go to hell. I have beaten them.' He took Eta on a wild, drunken drive through the streets of Tokyo, the speed and the whisky surging into an adrenaline-fuelled simulacrum of his coming, imagined flight from the city.

Ozaki travelled to Manchuria to gather further confirmation. When he returned to Tokyo on 19 September he was able to report just how close the USSR had been to danger. From the statistics director of the Mantetsu's Ho-t'ien branch, Ozaki had learned that back in July the Kwangtung Army had suddenly ordered the railway to be prepared to handle 100,000 tons of military freight per day for forty days, summoning 3,000 freight cars to be brought from northern China.[11] By the time Ozaki visited, most of the rolling stock had been returned. The 3,000 trained railwaymen drafted in to take over the Trans-Siberian had also been dispersed, with only ten or so remaining.[12] Though the Kwangtung Army had prepared contingency plans for a possible attack the following spring – including a plan for a new road to be constructed to Khabarovsk – Plan North had well and truly been stood down.

Exactly what role Sorge's information played in Stalin's decision making has been hotly debated by Russian historians. But it is clear from the wide circulation that Sorge's reports received that the Fourth Department, the top members of the Politburo and Soviet Army, had finally begun to trust Sorge's information. Towards the end of September, troops began moving from the Far Eastern Military District in large numbers to fight the Germans on the plains of European Russia. By December, fifteen infantry divisions, three cavalry divisions, 1,500 tanks and some 1,700 aircraft were redeployed.[13] In all, Stalin would shift over half the available troops in Siberia to the defence of Moscow.[14] Though this left the Soviet Far East desperately vulnerable to a possible Japanese assault in 1942, it was clear – as Sorge had repeatedly warned – that the best way to protect Russia's east was to beat off the Germans in the west.

Around 27 September, when the typhoon-season atmospherics made it difficult to transmit, Clausen also received an intriguing message from Centre asking a series of questions about potential bombing targets in Japan. 'What is the location of the petroleum storage facilities and docks on the islands around Kobe? Where is the Air Defence command of Tokyo located? Also where are anti-aircraft bases to be established?'[15] And so on. The mood in Moscow, even though Leningrad was now besieged and Kiev had fallen, had clearly switched from defensive to offensive. 'Around that time,' Sorge claimed to his captors, 'they sent me a special telegram of their appreciation' – though there is no trace of such a message in the Soviet archives.[16] In accordance with Centre's request, Sorge sent Miyagi to reconnoitre the anti-aircraft emplacements that were springing up in Tokyo's parks and gardens. It would be the young Okinawan's final mission.

While Miyagi was busy scouting the capital for air defences, Ozaki met up with his old friend Prince Saionji at the Kuwana house of assignation – not quite as sleazy as it sounds, as these establishments were a cross between a modern love hotel and a private dining establishment. Saionji was expecting guests, but hurriedly showed Ozaki a long handwritten note on the latest status of Japan's negotiations with the US. The document revealed that Konoe was fast running out of time to strike a deal with Washington. The navy was pressing for a full-scale offensive against Singapore, the Dutch East Indies and the Philippines to begin no later than the beginning of October. Though Konoe was ready to offer Roosevelt a partial withdrawal from central China and southern Indochina, the reality was that with both the Japanese public and military against such a compromise, the chances of a peace deal had shrunk to next to nothing. 'Although the United States, of course, desires to reach agreement in the negotiations, there is a great gap between her and Japan in the conditions and enthusiasm for the negotiations,' Saionji warned Ozaki.[17]

Meanwhile at least one member of Sorge's spy ring had decided that it was time to get away. Vukelić's ex-wife, Edith, had had enough of the deprivations of wartime Japan – not to mention the constant fear of living in a house with a secret radar antenna installed in the attic. Edith pleaded with Sorge to give her the money to join her younger sister in Australia. The *rezident* may have been relieved to see her go, despite the loss of a valuable transmission station. Since her divorce Edith had been a volatile security risk to the group. American intelligence even claimed after the war that Sorge had seduced her after her separation from Vukelić as a means of keeping her loyal and quiet, though this assertion is not supported by any extant testimony. In any case, Sorge extracted $400 from Centre for her travel expenses – amended to $500 in pen by Clausen in the draft of the message subsequently found by Japanese police – and on 25 September, Edith and her son Paul sailed to Perth.[18]

Vukelić, like Clausen, was also having his doubts about working for the ring. In autumn of 1940 he and Yoshiko had their first baby, a boy christened Kiyoshi Jaroslav Yamasaki-Voukelitch. They called the child Yo for short.[19] Vukelić 'had a good wife and child and loved them from the bottom of his heart', recalled Clausen. 'So it was natural for him to turn away from this adventurous and dangerous life.'[20] Vukelić had also established a name for himself as a foreign correspondent – and evidently preferred journalism to spying. Sorge wrote in his prison memoir that he had gone to Japan 'for the purpose of this spy activity, and was a journalist to disguise my true work', and found his 'work as a journalist was rather bothersome to me ... As for Vukelić, however, journalism came to be as if it were his true profession and doing spy activity as if it were his part-time work.'[21]

Vukelić's enthusiasm for communism was fading as fast as his appetite for the thankless risks of espionage. 'Communism will be defeated anyway and that therefore it would be useless to work for the principle any longer,' he confided to Clausen in the mid-summer of 1941 – though the radio man dared not, by his own account, return the confidence and admit that he strongly agreed. Vukelić was also becoming more reluctant to fulfil the orders of a boss who had 'a very strong personality and demanded absolute obedience from his men'.[22] When Clausen brought a document to be photographed, Vukelić claimed to be too busy – but actually 'stayed at home another two hours and read a book he liked'.[23] He would avoid his colleagues for a week at a time. The imperious Sorge – who had only recently discovered that his best agent Ozaki was married, despite working with him closely for nine years – was equally tone-deaf to the signs of Vukelić's disaffection.

Edith Vukelić would be the only member of the group to escape in time. On 28 September the Tokko's Thought Section renewed its postponed request to arrest Miyagi's old Californian landlords, the Kitabayashis. This time investigator Tamazawa made no objection. The couple were arrested at their home in Wakayama province for possible violation of the National Defence Security Law and transferred to Roppongi police station in Tokyo – by coincidence, the closest precinct to Miyagi's home.[24] The questioning of the hapless Kitabayashis about their communist past and their current associates began.

October brought chilly winds and sudden storms to Tokyo Bay. On 4 October, Sorge celebrated his forty-sixth birthday with Hanako at Lohmeyer's restaurant, six years to the day after they had first met. Hanako recalled in her memoir that she wore a Western skirt and jacket for the occasion. He only had time for a drink. They sat at a table in the middle of the restaurant. Sorge remarked on how many police seemed to be following him these days. The coming war with America was on his mind; he believed that Japan would inevitably lose. 'America is strong, she is big, she produces many good things,' Sorge said in his simple Japanese. 'If Japan fights with America, Japan will never win. She will be defeated over and over.'[25] Hanako remembered trying to lighten the mood with a joke. 'Perhaps Japan will imitate Germany and try a blitzkrieg,'[26] she ventured. Sorge smiled.

They parted on the pavement at half past six. 'I don't think you should come home with me tonight because the secret police are following me,' Sorge told her. 'I think you should stay at your mother's tonight. And when things look bright, I'll send you a telegram.'

'You won't be lonely?' Hanako asked.

'Even if I am, it will be all right,' Sorge replied. 'You had better go home now. Please remember me to your mother.'

Sorge turned into the gathering dusk towards Shimbashi station. He never had been one for walking his girlfriends home. As Hanako walked in the opposite direction she turned to catch a glimpse of him but he had already disappeared in the crowd.[27]

A birthday party had been arranged in Sorge's honour at economic attaché Erich Kordt's house. The Otts and the Mohrs came to toast their incorrigible friend. But Sorge quickly became drunk and sarcastic, and Kordt was thoroughly relieved when he abruptly left his own birthday celebration at around nine. Alone, Sorge made his way to Weise's apartment, where he drank with the DNB bureau chief until morning.[28]

That evening Clausen was also busy with a radio transmission. Nervous of sending from home, he had set up his apparatus at Vukelić's house. 'In light of the fact that there will be no war against the USSR this year, a small number of troops are being returned to the Islands [Japan],' Clausen telegraphed. Sorge passed on Ozaki's warning that the Kwangtung Army was still a danger, readying rail lines 'for a possible attack next March, if the progress of the German-Russian war gives the Japanese such an opportunity'.[29] He ended with the reassuring news that 'no troops have been transferred from Northern China to Manchuria'. Clausen packed up his remarkable, home-made transmitter and drove home, doubtless with a sense of relief. The next person to open the well-used suitcase would be an officer of the Tokko.

Two days later Sorge met Ozaki at their favourite restaurant, the Asia in the Mantetsu building. The boss seemed distracted and irritable and seemed to be coming down with a cold. Ozaki passed on the latest reassuring – to Stalin at least – news that Konoe had given up on talks with the US and that the whole government was considering resigning, for good this time. The navy had won.

'War with the United States will begin in the near future, this month or next,' Sorge wrote in a draft dispatch that was later discovered among his papers. As they parted, the last two faithful members left in the

Sorge spy ring agreed to meet the following Monday at the same place. It was the last Sorge and Ozaki would see of each other as free men.

The Tokko's questioning of the Kitabayashis proceeded slowly. After ten days of desultory interrogation the elderly (to the young policemen) couple appeared to be minnows with little to say. There was one item, though, that interested the Tokko. Where had Tomo Kitabayashi got the sum of dollars that had been discovered on her arrest? Truthfully, she answered that her old lodger Yotoku Miyagi sometimes gave her money. The young interrogator, hearing the name Miyagi for the first time, decided to try the oldest interrogator's ruse. 'Miyagi didn't say that. Don't tell lies!' he snapped, according to the later account of prosecutor Mitsusada Yoshikawa.[30] Resignedly concluding that Miyagi had already talked, Tomo immediately told the full story as she knew it. She and Miyagi had been members of the American Communist Party, she admitted, and though she denied having engaged in any communist activity since her return to Japan she told them that Miyagi was engaged in spying.[31]

This was an unexpected lead. A few enquiries revealed that Miyagi was already a person of interest to the Tokko First Section's Cultural Department, in charge of keeping tabs on the theatrical and artistic world. The morning after Tomo had first mentioned Miyagi's name, the chief of the Cultural Department himself set out with two detectives from Roppongi police station to arrest him.[32] They knocked on his door at around 7 a.m. on 10 October. His landlady answered, one of the detectives later recalled, and quaked at the sight of their Tokko identity cards. When they asked for her artist lodger she exclaimed, 'Miyagi is not a bad person!'[33] They found their suspect still asleep in his room. On his table were sheaves of papers, including a detailed and absolutely incriminating study of Japan's oil stock levels in Manchuria. Such information – holding as it did the key to whether Japan would go to war with Russia or America – counted among the most closely guarded military secrets in the country. Even more damningly, the papers were written not only in Japanese but also in a typed English translation. 'We thought it strange that an artist had such a kind of document,' one of the officers later testified, an example of the Japanese habit of boasting through understatement. It was immediately clear to the Tokko officers that this man was no minnow but a very significant shark.[34]

Miyagi went quietly, with no sign of inner turmoil or alarm.[35] After a night in Roppongi police station it was decided to transfer Miyagi to Tsukiji station, where he would be unable to communicate with his accuser, Mrs Kitabayashi, between interrogations. The Tokko questioned Miyagi hard for hours, but though he admitted that the documents were his, he refused to speak when asked about his espionage activities. The detectives decided not to torture him, not because they were unwilling to do so but because they judged that it would not work. 'Miyagi was not the type to break under torture,' said Yoshikawa, who would become the leading prosecutor in the Sorge trials. He would not confess 'unless he wanted to'.[36] The tubercular young artist was turning out to be tougher than his captors had anticipated.

The policemen conferred over lunch about their extraordinary suspect. Among the papers found in Miyagi's room was a collection of love letters written to him by a thirty-year-old divorcee, Kimiko Suzuki, who worked as an interpreter in the American–European Division of the Tokko. Had Miyagi penetrated the political police itself? the interrogators wondered. (It turned out he had not; Suzuki was exonerated of any involvement in Miyagi's spying.) As the interrogators opened the door of the interview room for a long afternoon of questioning, the two guards posted to watch Miyagi reflexively turned towards the new arrivals. At that moment Miyagi sprang up and dived, head first, out of the second-floor window and fell towards an approaching tram.[37]

The first thought to flash through the mind of chief interrogator Tamotsu Sakai was, he told an interviewer twenty years later, 'I must not let Miyagi get away. He is our star witness.' Shouting a command to surround the building, Sakai himself jumped out of the window in hot pursuit. What he did not realise until he was already hurtling through the air was that Miyagi did not intend to escape. He intended to die – as the English reporter Jimmy Cox had died falling, or perhaps being thrown, from a Tokyo police station window the previous year.

Both men landed in shrubbery. The tram rumbled by harmlessly a few feet in front of them. Struggling to rise, Sakai found that his body would not obey him. Miyagi was less badly injured. He was helped to his feet by police, shaken but lame in one leg.[38] Chivalrously Miyagi insisted on seeing Sakai put safely into a police car before getting in himself. They were both taken to a nearby naval hospital for treatment.

Sakai would be back at work within three weeks. His spine had been bruised, but not broken. Miyagi, though physically unhurt, had gone through a profound psychological transformation. He had attempted *seppuku* – ritual suicide – to avoid shame, in the traditional manner of an ancient samurai. But death had refused his sacrifice. 'He had crossed the barrier of death and had come back to life,' as Prosecutor Yoshikawa expressed it in 1965. 'Miyagi had experienced no less than a resurrection, and what life remained to him he must live with clean hands. He must make a general confession and start over with an unmarked slate.'[39]

Miyagi told his interrogators repeatedly how impressed he had been that one of their number had risked his life to bring him to justice. And so he talked, at great length and detail. He told the Tokko of his work for the Comintern – whom Miyagi still believed he was serving – and of his association with Hotsumi Ozaki and Richard Sorge.

Miyagi's revelations were so shocking that they verged on the unbelievable. The involvement of Sorge, prominent journalist and confidant of the German ambassador, was astonishing. But it was the information about Ozaki that caused the deepest shockwaves. Ozaki had, in fact, been under surveillance by the Tokko for over a year, as they scoured his writings for signs of leftist sympathies. Miyagi's evidence that a member of Konoe's Breakfast Group was a paid-up Soviet spy was 'a terrific revelation', Yoshikawa recalled. 'The arrest of a group of underground communists was a routine business in Japan at the time, but the discovery of such a high-level spy ring was an altogether different matter.'[40]

The case was clearly far above the pay grade of the Tokko officers who scribbled down Miyagi's confession. Yoshikawa, as Senior Prosecutor of the Tokyo District Criminal Court, was hastily summoned to take over the case. Questioning Miyagi in person the day after his suicide attempt, he learned the names of Clausen, Vukelić, Kawai and other lesser collaborators in the ring. He also ordered the arrests of Akiyama, the ring's translator, and of Miyagi's informant, Mrs Kuzumi.

Akiyama immediately talked. A quantity of documents on the South Manchuria Railway as well as military information was found in his home, all material from Ozaki and Miyagi awaiting translation into English.[41] Kuzumi's evidence also confirmed Miyagi's confession. Yoshikawa was left in the uncomfortable position of having to believe his prisoner's extraordinary allegations that two of the most powerfully connected men in Tokyo were Soviet spies.

Ozaki had not been particularly worried when Miyagi failed to show up at his house to give his daughter Yoko her weekly painting lesson on Sunday, 12 October. He had also not been unduly perturbed when Sorge, too, failed to make their agreed rendezvous the following evening at the Asia Restaurant (Sorge, confused by a rising fever, mistook the date and arrived on Tuesday instead). But when he walked into the Asia for lunch on Tuesday, Ozaki found three senior policemen – including the chief of the Security Section of the Home Affairs Ministry and a division chief of the Tokko – apparently waiting for him. Ozaki, who knew the men slightly, greeted them courteously and walked on by. They made no attempt to arrest him. It was only the following morning, when Ozaki was in his library reading the morning papers, that a black car full of plain-clothes Tokko men pulled up outside his house, and politely presented business cards and a warrant for his arrest. He left the house quietly, with great dignity.

In custody at Meguro police station, Ozaki still believed that he was under investigation for the liberal slant of his writings rather than for spying. Miyashita Hiroshi, one of the Tokko's most experienced interrogators, quickly disabused him. 'We're not examining you as a Japanese but as a spy for the Comintern or the Soviet Union,' Miyashita told his prisoner. 'When Japan is at war, spies can't expect any mercy.'[42] For the first time 'inner unrest clearly manifested itself on [Ozaki's] face'.[43]

Detaining a senior Japanese government insider and respected scholar – 'one of the most brilliant advisers of Konoe', as Yoshikawa put it – was already a bold move by the Tokko. Arresting a prominent foreigner like Sorge, one who enjoyed the confidence of the German ambassador, Japan's closest ally, was a problem of even greater magnitude. The diplomatic ramifications of a mistake could damage Japan's delicate relationship with Berlin. But if Miyagi's story was true, the political consequences could be, if anything, even worse.

Formally, Japan was committed to a non-aggression pact with the Soviet Union. The discovery of a Soviet espionage ring at the heart of the Japanese government could disturb those already tense relations with Moscow at a time when Japan was about to commit the bulk of its troops to an invasion of Southeast Asia and was also heading towards war with the United States. And then there was a third possibility: that Sorge could in fact be a senior German agent, posing as a communist as a false flag to collect intelligence for the Reich. In short, the investigators believed Sorge to be doubly protected, by his position with the Germans if innocent and his relationship with Moscow if guilty. A mistake about such a man could leave Yoshikawa and his colleagues facing professional and personal ruin.[44]

The Foreign Section of the Tokko balked at such a risk. They needed Ozaki's confession to make a move on such prominent foreigners as Sorge and Clausen. Inspector Miyashita also knew that he was working against time; Ozaki's powerful friends might arrange for him to be released at any moment. News of his arrest had reached the Breakfast Group while it was in session that very morning, thanks to frantic phone calls from Ozaki's wife.[45]

It took Miyashita the best part of a day of relentless questioning to break him. Ozaki finally capitulated at midnight. 'I will tell all the facts,' he said, as if released from unbearable tension that was also shared by his questioners. 'So let me take a rest today and let me think a little.'[46]

Sorge, still unaware of the arrests of Miyagi or Ozaki, chose this moment finally to make the decisive move he had hinted at about to Eta and Hanako. On 15 October, while Ozaki was undergoing his first day of questioning, Sorge summoned Clausen to his house. He handed his radio man a sheaf of messages for Moscow requesting new instructions for the members of the *rezidentura*, and asking whether he was to return to Russia or start new activity in Germany.[47] After seven years, and precisely a week too late, Sorge had decided to wind up the Tokyo spy ring whether Centre liked it or not. Clausen, after reading the messages, handed them back to his boss in his first ever act of open defiance. 'It is a little too early to send these,' Clausen said. 'So I want you to keep them for a while.'[48]

For Clausen, of course, a return to Moscow was out of the question. Quite apart from his private loss of communist faith and his thriving business, Clausen knew that his two years of quiet sabotage of the ring's communications would be discovered as soon as Sorge returned to Centre. His open revolt at Sorge's plan to wind down the ring was a matter of life or death for them both – in opposite directions. Sorge no longer frightened Clausen; the spell of his chief's imperiousness was broken. The boss was clearly feverish and exhausted (Miyagi, on his last visit, had found Sorge so ill that he urged him to go to hospital). He was also increasingly uneasy about the unexpected disappearance of his Japanese agents. Sorge had attempted to find Ozaki's telephone number, Clausen recalled, but failed to locate it in the chaos of his study.

'Let's wait for a couple of days anyway, and if [Ozaki] does not show up, I will call him on the telephone,' Sorge said resignedly. As he left the house Clausen felt 'that the time of arrest was approaching'.[49] His departure was observed by the Tokko agent Saito, who had rented a second-floor apartment opposite Sorge's front door and was now keeping a permanent watch on all comings and goings lest the suspect attempt escape.[50] Vukelić, too, had been placed under close surveillance with a policeman outside his door and a hard-pressed team of Tokko men struggling to keep up with him as he made his way around town via a succession of trolleybuses and trams.[51]

In Meguro police station, Prosecutor Yoshikawa decided that frankness would be the quickest route to getting a full confession out of Ozaki. He gave his prisoner a full account of Miyagi's confession, not bothering to try to catch Ozaki out on possible contradictions in their testimony. Ozaki listened gravely without interrupting. When the prosecutor had finished, Ozaki bowed his head politely and said: '*Wakarimashita* – I understand.' By that evening Ozaki had outlined his entire espionage career, from his beginnings with Agnes Smedley in Shanghai to his collaboration with 'Mr Johnson', his recruitment at Nara and his long relationship with Miyagi.

His captors allowed him, for the first time since his arrest, to smoke. They gave Ozaki a box of matches decorated with spy warnings, which prompted him to share the wry recollection that he had always felt nervous using such matches at his meetings with Sorge.[52] By the end of the third day of questioning – 17 October, the day after Konoe resigned for the last time as prime minister in favour of the war-mongering General Tojo – Ozaki was relaxed enough to crack another joke. 'This cabinet is the one which is going to war against the United States,' he told his captors. But 'if they adopt my idea, the China Incident will be solved in three days. If the Chinese Communist Party takes over China and the Japanese Communist Party takes over Japan, then Japan, Russia, and China could cooperate with each other.'[53]

Clausen returned to Sorge's house the following day. The pair set out for the local garage, where Sorge's much-battered Datsun had been undergoing repairs. The previous week Clausen had borrowed the car to fetch medicine for Sorge from a local chemist's, lost control driving down a steep hill and turned the car on its roof. Uninjured, Clausen had crawled out of the window and righted the car with the help of a passing policeman. The damage had now been fixed, and Sorge and Clausen drove to the Minoru restaurant for lunch. They lingered over their meal until 4 p.m. Neither elaborated in their prison testimonies on what was said.

It seems likely that Sorge, at least, was planning to make a run for it. After lunch Clausen walked into Ginza to do some shopping, watched a movie, then returned to the bar of the Minoru to drink some more. Sorge headed back home, then drove the Datsun back to the garage where it was usually parked. The police were waiting, but did not pounce. They searched the car and discovered a large sum of cash stuffed into envelopes and casually hidden inside the vehicle – presumably Sorge's escape fund. The constable took the money to Torizawa police station, counted and photographed it. Then, with impeccable Japanese courtesy, he returned the cash-filled envelopes to the garage owner with instructions to hand them back to Sorge.[54]

Vukelić was also nervous. He phoned Sorge in the early evening from a call box near Shimbashi station. His watchers overheard him say: 'Boss, can I come and see you?' and followed him onto a tram bound for Azabu-ku. Sorge summoned Clausen to the emergency meeting. Clausen arrived with a half-gallon bottle of sake. As the three spies drank, there was a knock on the door that doubtless made them freeze with fear. However, it was just the garage owner returning the money he claimed he had found in the car, for which he received polite thanks and a cash reward from Sorge. The man scuttled back to the police station to report that three foreigners were in the house.

Settling back down to his sake, Sorge admitted to his colleagues that it was by now clear that 'Joe' and 'Otto' – or Ozaki, as he referred to him, the first time that Clausen had ever heard the star agent's real name – had been arrested.[55] It was likely from the garage owner's mysterious visit that the police had Sorge's Datsun under surveillance. Even driving off into the night was no longer an option. The arrests of their Japanese comrades made no difference, Sorge morosely told his guests, 'our destiny would be the same'.[56]

Clausen, filled with 'an inexpressible uneasiness', left the glum gathering and drove home.[57] As Anna slept upstairs, he took stock of the incriminating evidence that filled his study: original and coded copies of telegrams already sent and those still awaiting transmission; his well-thumbed code book, and of course his trusty transmitter. He considered burning the papers, but flames in the garden at night would attract the attention of fire-wary Tokyo residents. He also thought of burying the transmitter, but again the darkness defeated him. A kind of terrified paralysis had settled over him. In the end, Clausen simply went to bed, where he spent a sleepless night.[58]

Vukelić left the boss's house not long after Clausen but did not immediately return home, as his watchers saw him stumbling home drunk at around midnight. Saito, monitoring Sorge's front door from across the street, observed one more visitor that night: an official from the German embassy whom he logged as 'Third Secretary Embritch' (though it is not clear who this might be, as no one of that name is listed on the 1941 diplomatic register). Sorge's visitor sat on the windowsill of his first-floor study rather than on the sofa. It is possible that Sorge wished to signal his links to the embassy to the police he suspected were outside. Saito, sitting by his darkened window, felt a twinge of sympathy for his quarry. 'Those poor men, talking so loudly and not knowing that I am watching them,' he told an interviewer in 1965.[59] By 10 p.m. the diplomat left. Sorge's light went out an hour later.

With the confessions of Ozaki and Miyagi in hand, Prosecutor Yoshikawa and his colleague Tamazawa Mitsusaburo had spent the afternoon at the Ministry of Justice obtaining permission to issue warrants for the arrest of Sorge and Clausen. Their case, while extraordinary, was watertight. 'If you have proof, I will take the responsibility,' Minister of Justice Michiyo Imawura told them.[60]

Before dawn on 19 October, three ten-man squads of Tokko agents met at the official residence of their Foreign Section chief, Shinichi Ogata, for a briefing. They were instructed not to harm the suspects, and to make a careful search of their homes. The first team headed to Vukelić's house, knocking on the door shortly after six. A maid opened it and the policemen pushed past her, running up the stairs and burst into the bedroom where Branko Vukelić and his wife Yoshiko slept with their one-year-old son. Inspector Suzuki shook Vukelić awake, while Yoshiko huddled under the covers in horror. Suzuki would later recall that she seemed utterly shocked by the revelation of her husband's espionage. The policeman was convinced – quite wrongly – that she knew nothing about it. Yoshiko Vukelić's excellent acting would save her life.

The police watched carefully as their prisoner dressed, wary that he might try to swallow a suicide pill. Three Tokko agents drove him to Sugamo prison, while the rest stayed to embark on a detailed search of the house. They found the darkroom filled with developed negatives of confidential documents and Japanese military installations.[61]

Aoyama, the officer who had first suspected Clausen of possible espionage, led the raid on the Clausens' home. The radio man had just fallen asleep after an anxious night. He woke to find Aoyama standing over his bed. 'I would like to ask you something about an automobile accident that happened the other day,' the policeman said with perfect politeness, by Clausen's later account. 'So I would like you to come over to the police station.' Max had little doubt that 'this was not just a problem of an automobile accident'.[62] The police allowed him to dress and eat breakfast before driving him to Mita police station. Standing on a desk in the living room, in plain view, was the suitcase containing his home-made radio set.

The team sent to arrest Sorge sat anxiously in their cars waiting for Aoyama to join them. It had been decided that the presence of a policeman that Sorge knew would reduce the risk of Sorge attempting suicide. In any case, the Tokko men found a German embassy car parked outside Sorge's house when they arrived, so had to wait for the official visitor – who has been variously identified as journalist Wilhelm Schulz of the DNB, or possibly a second secretary of the embassy – to leave.[63] One of the squad was Saito, the Tokko agent who had been watching Sorge from afar but had never met his target face to face. Saito's biggest worry, he told an interviewer twenty years later, was that Sorge's housekeeper would try to resist the police and cry out, giving him a chance to end his life. In the event, the woman emerged from the house soon after the embassy car departed, carrying a single large shoe and evidently bound for a cobbler's shop.

Aoyama, speeding from his arrest of Clausen, eventually joined the waiting posse. He and Saito led the group, gingerly trying the door and, as with Aoyama's last visit, finding it unlocked.

The officer's reflexive politeness got the better of his need for stealth. 'Excuse me,' Saito called out. 'Good morning!' Sorge, in his pyjamas but shaven, appeared at the top of the stairs. He invited his unexpected guests into his study and waited – in another moment of exquisitely Japanese courtesy on the part of the Tokko agents – while they removed their shoes. Saito recalled that Sorge's face was expressionless. The three men sat down on the sofa, with Sorge in the middle. As the arresting officers composed themselves for an embarrassing conversation, their commander, Hideo Ohashi, bounded in. The spell of awkwardness broken, the policemen seized Sorge by his arms. Someone found a coat and draped it over the suspect's shoulders as they marched him out of the house and into a waiting car. Ohashi remained behind to begin the search. Surveying the piles of papers, the thousand-book library, and very un-Japanese mountains of clutter in Sorge's study, the Tokko chief picked up the phone to summon a two-ton truck to collect the mountain of evidence.[64]

By the time Prosecutor Yoshikawa arrived at Toriizaka police station, he found Sorge properly dressed in slacks and a shirt brought from his home. He had also had time to compose himself for the duel of his life.

Sorge went on the offensive immediately. 'Why have you arrested me?' he demanded. Yoshikawa showed his prisoner the warrant he had signed.

'We are holding you on the basis of the National Public Security Preservation Law on suspicion of espionage,' the prosecutor replied formally. 'Have you not been guilty of spying for the Comintern?'[65]

'No!' roared Sorge, banging his fist on the table. 'I am a Nazi! Inform the German ambassador at once! This arrest will be a reflection on the good relations between Japan and Germany! I am a correspondent for the *Frankfurter Zeitung* and an information officer in the German embassy!' Sorge refused to speak unless Ambassador Ott was present. As he bluffed for his life, perhaps Sorge regretted his refusal of Ott's offer of a staff position at the embassy that could have conferred him diplomatic immunity.

Yoshikawa remained calm in the face of Sorge's storm of imperious bluster. 'There are also communists in the German Nazi Party,' the prosecutor observed, quite accurately. He sent his prisoner down to the cells to cool off before being transferred to Sugamo prison. The prosecutor's subordinates were more cowed. As the police attempted to search him, Sorge bellowed for Aoyama and raised his fists at the terrified guards. The policeman duly came running and ordered the body search to be abandoned. Pacified, Sorge entered his cell. 'This is the end,' he told the young policeman that he had once knocked down. 'I shall leave all my possessions to you, Mr. Aoyama. Please discuss this with my lawyer.'[66]

Vukelić was the first of the foreigners to break. Inspector Suzuki, speaking to his prisoner through a French interpreter, used the oldest ruse in the interrogator's book: he claimed that Sorge had already confessed. Vukelić, asking constantly after the well-being of his wife and son, told all. He explained the uses for the cameras found at his house, including the high-speed telescopic lens, the microfilms, the photographic plates and all the rest. He also revealed that his copy of the 1933 German Statistical Yearbook was the spy ring's code book. Only an empty electric phonograph cabinet found at his house baffled Vukelić (it later emerged that this was where Wendt had once kept his short-wave set, now at the bottom of Yamanaka Lake). Occasionally during his testimony Vukelić would pause to ask: 'Has Sorge told you this?'[67]

As a reward for his confession Vukelić was allowed to receive Yoshiko's daily letters, and also to wear socks against the damp and cold of Sugamo prison in winter. Suzuki developed a fondness for the suspect, though he noted immediately the difference between the gentle, uxorious Yugoslav and his steely boss. 'Sorge was top-flight, Vukelić second-rate,' Suzuki recalled.[68]

Clausen held out a little longer. His main concern seems to have been for Anna. While she was still free, he refused to say a word to his interrogators, Taiji Hasebe and Tonekichi Horie, chief of the Asian department of the Tokko. Though he maintained stoic silence, it was clear to his questioners that Clausen was deeply upset. On 20 October, they tried the obvious lie, telling Clausen that his wife was now in Sugamo prison (in fact she would remain at liberty for nearly another month). They also told him – quite truthfully – that they knew from Vukelić that Anna Clausen had acted as a secret courier between Tokyo and Shanghai.[69] What finally broke him were the Japanese transcripts of the draft messages in English that Clausen had carelessly left lying about his study. Ogata, chief of the Tokko's Foreign Section, stayed up all night reading the translations as they were produced. Among

Clausen's papers was a ten-page typescript detailing top-secret details gleaned by Ozaki of the recent Japanese–American peace negotiations in Washington – something so deeply classified that even the Tokko department head had never heard of them. Leaving the unencoded messages to be found by police 'was Clausen's fatal error', recalled Ogata.[70]

This final disaster did the trick. Clausen began to talk, spilling the secrets of the Statistical Yearbook code. The Tokko men had already identified the book as the key to the ring's communications because they had found the 1933 edition on Clausen's shelf well-thumbed, but all other years untouched. The cipher key was swiftly passed to the Japanese Telecommunications Ministry, who began decrypting the pile of messages they had been intercepting since 1936 which lay in a thick file known as 'Dal X'. They even reunited Clausen with his radio set, with which the Japanese engineers had been tinkering in vain. Clausen's professional pride kicked in and he set them right. 'We Japanese had tried to reach Harbin with it,' said Yoshikawa, 'but we had no luck. But once we called Clausen in, he made a few rapid adjustments, turned a few knobs, and he got Harbin in about a minute.'[71]

Clausen's decade of silence broke like a dam, and with it all his unspoken resentment of Sorge. He sat down to write a lengthy confession in clear but clunky English – the only language he had in common with his interrogators. One of the first things he admitted was that he and Sorge were officers of the Red Army and worked directly for Soviet military intelligence.

This presented his captors with an immediate problem. Miyagi and Ozaki had admitted spying for the Comintern – still notionally an international organisation independent of the Kremlin. The 1925 Public Security Preservation Law, under which all the suspects were being held, had been drafted as an anti-Comintern statute, aimed at the Japanese Communist Party and other socialist groups. If the spy ring was in fact working on behalf of a foreign power, then the case would fall within the purview of the War Ministry and its own intelligence agency, the Kempeitai. To the Tokko and the Justice Ministry prosecutors who were running the case the choice was clear. There was no way they were going to surrender their prize spy case to a rival agency. The Sorge spy ring would go to trial as the last and greatest – albeit fictitiously attributed – Comintern espionage case.[72]

Sorge was proving an altogether tougher nut. The German embassy, as Sorge calculated, reacted with alarm and disbelief at his arrest. Sorge's colleagues in the German press corps presented the embassy with 'a declaration signed by all of them attesting to Sorge's human and political reliability',[73] as Ott duly reported to Berlin. Helma Ott was furious, and her husband was convinced that the police had made a terrible mistake. Ott ventured an explanation to the German Foreign Ministry – that Sorge had been set up by the police in order to embarrass ex-Prime Minister Konoe by implying that one of his advisers had been leaking material about the US–Japanese talks.

The local Nazi Party organisation, including Meisinger himself, protested against 'the obvious blunder of the overzealous Japanese secret police'.[74] Ott lodged an official complaint with the Foreign Ministry, along with an urgent request to see the prisoner. The new prime minister, General Tojo, nervous of the political implications of the case, passed the buck to his Minister of Justice, who bounced it to the chief prosecutor, who laid the request at the door of Prosecutor Yoshikawa. If no confession was forthcoming from Sorge within a week, the prosecutor knew, then the pressure from the Germans to release Sorge could become critical.

Sorge knew it too. Far smarter than Clausen, he realised that it would be useless to pretend that he had not been collecting sensitive intelligence. But he also understood that his best chance of survival was to pretend to be working for the Reich – or more precisely, to admit to the work he had been doing for German military intelligence, the Abwehr, while concealing his ties to Moscow.[75] In the meantime he stalled while they waited for Ott to be given permission to visit. Sorge claimed not to understand the interpreter's German. His interrogators switched to English.[76] They questioned him in relays, bombarding him with new information gleaned from Ozaki, Miyagi, Clausen, Vukelić and – now – Kawai, who had been arrested on 22 October. The incriminating papers found on Sorge's desk, including seven pages of a report from Ozaki, were quoted to him as soon as they were translated. Still he refused to talk, and demanded Ott.[77]

Few who read this can claim really to know what goes on in the minds of captive, tortured men. We have just the dry written record, and some interviews with Sorge's questioners, to tell us what happened in his head between the fifth and the sixth days of his interrogation. The prison was bitterly cold. The prisoner was exhausted by continuous questioning and sleep deprivation – a method that the Soviet NKVD called 'the conveyor'. He was probably still feverish. Certainly he knew that he stood alone in his silence. To his captors he was 'most contemptuous' when he learned Clausen had become an 'informant' and grimly joked that even if Clausen 'escaped the noose in Japan if he ever got back to the USSR he would be taken care of'.[78] But the knowledge that even his closest collaborators had abandoned him, and the cause, must have been devastating – all the more so because he had come so close to abandoning the cause and the job himself.

In any case, exactly why Sorge broke at around 10.45 a.m. on the sixth day after his arrest will always remain a mystery. Cold logic dictated that his chances of survival through rescue by the German embassy would be greater if he remained silent. And yet, he talked. It was Inspector Ohashi's shift. The policeman had brought some of his own precious charcoal from home to dispel some of the chill of the interview room. Ohashi began with his often-repeated point that his confederates had confessed and that Sorge had no reason to continue to lie. 'You have engaged in spying activities,' Ohashi told his prisoner. 'Your answer must be yes.'

To Ohashi's surprise, Sorge said exactly that. 'Yes.'

'You have been active for the Comintern?'

Sorge again replied, 'Yes.'[79]

Perhaps it was Sorge's unbending pride that drove him. Prosecutor Yoshikawa was, by chance, in the prison that day, though he had decided to give up his interrogation for a couple of days. 'I did not wish to question Sorge anymore that week,' Yoshikawa recalled, 'and yet for some reason I went out to Sugamo. Perhaps this would be the day, I thought.'[80] When Ohashi summoned the prosecutor to take over after this incredible breakthrough, he brought with him a gaggle of senior officials – the Tokko's Ogata and his deputy, Prosecutor Tamazawa, and Judge Nakamura Toneo. The cell was too small for them to all sit in, but finally Sorge had his audience. He stood politely as the grandees filed in. Tamazawa had the impression that Sorge was 'very polite, very well brought up'.[81] Yoshikawa restarted the questioning where Ohashi had left off. As if in a dream Sorge returned to his earlier position of complete denial.

'All your colleagues have confessed,' Yoshikawa pressed on. 'We have your radio, your codes, and we know everything about you. In order to lessen the sentence on your assistants and on yourself, don't you think it is time for you to confess?' Another change came over Sorge. He seemed to stiffen and go pale, and asked for paper. On it he wrote, in German: 'I have been an international communist since 1925.' Yoshikawa read it out loud to his colleagues. 'You have been spying for the Comintern,'[82] he said to Sorge.

Abruptly the prisoner sprang from his chair, drew himself up to attention, threw his prison coat on the floor and began pacing up and down the cramped cell, hands in his pockets. 'Indeed, I am a communist and have been doing espionage. I am defeated!' Sorge shouted. 'I have never been defeated since I became an international communist. But now I am beaten by the Japanese police.'[83] He sat down again, buried his face in his hands, and wept bitterly. It was, Yoshikawa recalled, 'obvious that he was emotionally very disturbed … we were all surprised and aghast at Sorge's behaviour. He completely broke down before us. He was a pathetic picture of a caught, defeated, and emotionally defeated person.'[84]

'I will confess everything,' Sorge said finally. 'If I can have a rest.'[85]

'The Greatest Man I Have Ever Met'

'A devastating example of a brilliant success of espionage'[1]
General Douglas MacArthur on Sorge

Ambassador Ott came to visit his old friend at Sugamo prison some days after Sorge's breakdown and admission of guilt. Having earlier insisted on seeing Ott, Sorge now shrank from a confrontation with the man whom he had deceived so thoroughly for so many years.

'I have betrayed the ambassador, and therefore I do not want to see him,' Sorge told Yoshikawa. 'You may be politically of different minds,' the prosecutor replied. 'Yet you ought to say good-bye to him as a friend.'[2]

Ott had not yet been informed that Sorge had confessed. Still convinced of his friend's innocence, he was 'proud, stern, angry, and very serious as he walked into the big conference room', accompanied by several senior embassy officials, recalled Yoshikawa. Sorge was brought in with his hands cuffed and a bamboo basket over his head – the usual practice in Sugamo for preventing prisoners from communicating while outside their cells. Ott 'had a very pained expression on his face. [Sorge] and Ott looked intently at one another, and then the questions began.'[3] By prior arrangement, all the questions had been agreed in advance and avoided any talk of the charges facing the accused.

'How are you?' Ott began, according to Yoshikawa's account.

'I am well,' Sorge replied.

'How is the food you are receiving?'

'It is satisfactory.'

'Are you being well treated?'

'Yes, I am.'

Within ten minutes the prepared questions were over. Ott asked his friend if he had anything to say. There was moment of tense silence. 'Mr Ambassador, this is our final farewell,' Sorge said in a low voice.[4] 'When Sorge uttered these words Ott's face suddenly became pale and weak,' Yoshikawa remembered. 'It seemed to me as though he had now for the first time caught the true meaning of things and that he understood the significance of what Sorge had said. Sorge's words provided an emotional and dramatic climax to their close friendship.'[5] In that moment Ott realised that his trusted friend and confidant, the man with whom he had shared not only his personal and professional secrets but also his wife, was a traitor. Yoshikawa ordered Sorge to be taken back to his cell. 'He rose quietly from his chair, made a slight bow to the ambassador, and walked slowly out of the room.'[6]

Ott, clearly shaken, took his leave, thanking the prosecutor for his cooperation. 'For the good of our two countries, investigate this case thoroughly,' Ott told the prosecutor. 'Get to the bottom of it!'[7] Ott would publicly maintain, until at least Christmas 1941, that Sorge was a 'martyr to Japanese suspicion and spy mania' and claimed that he expected his friend to be freed.[8] After the war, Ott continued to insist that: 'No, it is impossible, I still don't believe that [Sorge] was a spy.'[9] But the truth was that Ott's own position was severely compromised by his association with Sorge. The ambassador, with fading hope that the whole espionage nightmare would somehow prove an unfortunate mistake, held off for as long as possible before reporting the grim truth to Berlin.

His painful confrontation with Ott out of the way, Sorge's mood changed. Recovering some of his former confidence, he set about charming those around him. Both Inspector Ohashi of the Tokko and Yoshikawa would recall their prisoner with admiration and fondness. 'Sorge had a wonderful personality,' Yoshikawa told an interviewer in 1965. 'He was open and warm-hearted … In my whole life, I have never met anyone as great as he was.'[10]

Sorge asked for his old typewriter and offered to draft a memoir of his life in espionage. Prosecutor Yoshikawa, shrewdly suspecting that his prisoner would be unable to resist the temptation to boast about his own exploits, agreed. Sorge set to writing his confession in the same spirit that he approached everything in life – energetic, didactic, convinced of his own righteousness. It is clear from the tone of his prison memoir that Sorge expected eventually to be freed. Unlike Clausen, who did his utmost to convince his captors that he was no longer a communist, Sorge implicitly addressed his memoir over the heads of his Japanese captors to his own superiors in the Fourth Department. His chief message was that he was not only an extraordinary and devoted spy, but also a great newsman, scholar and expert on all things Japanese. 'When necessary, I performed my duties with speed, resolution, courage and resourcefulness,' he wrote of himself. 'My research was likewise of importance to my position as a journalist. It enabled me to gain recognition as the best reporter in Japan.'[11]

Protecting the women in his life – particularly Hanako – was part of Sorge's motivation in cooperating so freely. He struck a deal with Yoshikawa that Hanako would not be harmed, and never mentioned her in his official testimony. He also, with considerable chivalry, refused to speak about any of his other Tokyo affairs, which the Japanese police estimated at around thirty women.[12]

The prosecutor kept his word. On the day of Sorge's arrest, Hanako's old tormentor from Toriizaka police station paid her a call at her mother's house. The police inspector, whom she knew only as 'Mr M', was polite. He told Hanako that her lover was under arrest for 'currency speculation'. He also speculated that the charges might be 'justified' as 'they say that he is a Jew'. Certainly, Mr M told a bewildered Hanako, the prisoner Sorge was not a Christian as he had been observed praying to the rising sun (perhaps a watcher's misinterpretation of Sorge's early morning callisthenics). 'No, he never prays to the sun,' Hanako assured the policeman, quite accurately. 'He doesn't pray to anything.'[13]

A week later the inspector returned and broke the news that Sorge was a Russian spy. 'He will be shot,' Mr M said bluntly. 'There is no hope for him to survive.' Only wives could visit suspects in jail, so there was no way for Hanako to see him. Christmas 1941 passed with no present or letter, only another brief visit from Mr M to assure Hanako that 'Sorge-san is worried about you'.[14]

Sorge could clearly expect no help from the Germans. But he certainly believed he could count on the Russians, still officially bound in a friendship pact to Japan, to come to his rescue. A few days after his arrest he waited for a moment when he was alone with Ohashi and asked him to inform 'Zaitsev of the Soviet embassy' of his arrest. Viktor Sergeyevich Zaitsev was the embassy's second secretary – and the NKVD courier whom Clausen and Sorge had known as 'Serge'. But Ohashi never made contact with the Soviet embassy.[15]

Sorge would doubtless have remembered the extraordinary efforts to which Moscow had gone to rescue even such lowly agents as the Noulens from Chinese captivity – the money freely spent, the international press campaigns, the reckless mobilisation of all the USSR's intelligence assets, including himself – and taken heart. Surely Moscow would be frantically working to rescue its greatest (in his own opinion at least) and longest-serving spy? Sorge told his interrogators that he was sure that his old Comintern patron, Solomon Lozovsky, one of the delegates to the conference in Frankfurt where Sorge was first headhunted by the Soviets and now deputy foreign minister, would intervene in his case.

He was mistaken. Unfortunately, Sorge no longer worked for the Comintern in peacetime but for the Red Army in the midst of a world war. The Fourth Department may have come to warily trust Sorge's information. But the idea of making an effort to rescue an agent with a chequered ideological past, a man associated with so many recently purged Comintern bigwigs and self-confessed traitors, a *rezident* who might be working for the Nazis and a German national to boot, did not rank high on their list of priorities. In August, General Kolganov had essentially labelled Sorge a double agent in his report into Agent Ramsay's background. Though Kolganov was himself ousted from the Fourth Department in October 1941, just before Sorge's arrest, the doubts had stuck. The truth was that Sorge could expect no rescue from Moscow.

In the wake of Sorge's arrest, Centre sent a pair of diplomats from the Soviet embassy to speak to Anna Clausen, who confirmed that something disastrous had happened. But Sorge and his agents had been the USSR's eyes and ears in Japan for so long that without him Moscow was blind. Without Sorge's excellent contacts neither Centre nor the NKGB's separate *rezidentura* in the Tokyo embassy had any way of knowing the true facts of the case. 'We have information that five days ago INSON [Sorge] and GIGOLO [Vukelić] were arrested for espionage – for whom we do not know,' someone from the Soviet embassy in Tokyo cabled the Fourth Department in an unsigned message on 30 October (Clausen was not even mentioned).[16] In other words the NKVD* was not sure which side the Japanese thought Sorge and Vukelić were spying for – the Germans or the Soviets. Nor, of course, was Soviet military intelligence sure itself.

By January the NKVD got wind that Sorge had confessed. The NKVD's Zaitsev and his sidekick Butkevich – the Soviet 'legals' under diplomatic cover who had been ordered to act as couriers to the ring in the final dangerous months – had managed to glean some information from their few Japanese sources. It is not clear whether it was they or their NKVD bosses who garbled the message, but by the time the intelligence had worked its way to the top levels of the party even Sorge's name had become mangled. 'It has come to our attention that one of the arrested Germans in Tokyo, one ZORGE or KHORGE, confessed that he has been a member of the Communist Party since 1919, joined the Party in Hamburg ... and worked in the information department of IKKI (Comintern),' wrote NKVD deputy chief Pavel Fitin to Comintern chief Dmitrov on 7 January 1942. 'In Tokyo he was in touch with our workers ... I ask you to inform me how accurate this information is.'17

In other words, the NKVD in Moscow was completely unaware of Sorge's importance as a spy – and apparently had forgotten the connection between him and the military intelligence Agent Ramsay/ Inson reported by their own *rezidentura* in Tokyo in October. Moreover, it is clear that the NKVD's main interest in the Sorge case was to protect their agents Zaitsev and Butkevich from exposure.

Sorge's old handler Boris Gudz, who had by now left the Fourth Department and was working as a bus driver in Moscow, speculated that Stalin had been angered by Sorge's confession and therefore did not wish to exchange him.18 More likely, as Sorge froze in his cell, tapping out his account of his intelligence triumphs on his trusty typewriter, Moscow simply ignored him. The NKVD's own file on Sorge erroneously listed him as having been shot in 1942. The Fourth Department simply appeared to forget about his existence.

Centre did not even bother to immediately inform Katya of her husband's arrest. She continued writing him letters well into the autumn of 1941 and sending them to the headquarters at Bolshoi Znamensky

*Confusingly, the People's Commissariat for State Security (NKGB) reverted back to its old title, People's Commissariat for Internal Affairs (NKVD), between July 1941 and 1943.

Lane. 'Dear Ika, I have had no news for such time that I don't know what to think,' she wrote in an undated letter included in a 1965 Soviet collection of documents on Sorge which is described as having been sent after his arrest. 'I have lost hope that you exist. All this time was very hard and difficult. Very hard because I repeat I do not know what is happening with you and how you are. I am coming to the thought that it is unlikely that we will meet again in this life. I do not believe it any more and I am tired of solitude. What can I say about myself? I am getting older slowly. I work a lot and lose hope of seeing you ever. I hug you tightly. Your K.'[19] Fourth Department clerks simply inserted her letter into Sorge's file, never to be transmitted.

Prosecutor Yoshikawa conducted some fifty interrogations of Sorge over a period of four months. Some of the sessions lasted until ten at night. The prisoner was not mistreated. The Sugamo authorities allowed Sorge to spend the money that had been found in his house – 1,000 yen, plus a black leather wallet containing $1,782 in American currency. Ohashi observed that his prisoner regularly bought copies of the *Economist* which, curiously, were available in the prison shop, and bought five-yen lunches, which the policeman himself could not afford. Sorge also sought two audiences with the prison governor, both times to ask about the progress of the war. He lived in a three-tatami-mat cell with a toilet-cum-chair and washbasin with a wooden cover that became a small table where he typed.[20]

Ozaki, less ascetic and psychologically tough than Sorge, had a harder time of it. The prison governor found him a man of quick intelligence and much charm, but Ozaki was clearly profoundly shaken by his enforced separation from his family. From Sugamo Ozaki wrote a series of exquisite love letters to his wife Eiko, a selection of which were published after his death under the title *Love Was Like a Falling Star*, which became a bestseller after the war and are now considered a classic of Japanese love poetry.[21] He also penned two volumes of lyric poems, *The White Cloud Report*, which Ozaki entrusted to the governor for safekeeping but which were lost in the firebombing of Tokyo in 1945.

The Tokko were also busy rounding up all those mentioned in the confessions of the members of the spy ring. They eventually arrested eleven people in connection with the case. Among them were Anna Clausen and Kawai; two of Sorge's collaborators from his Shanghai days; a number of Miyagi's humble helpers and the grandees Prince Saionji and Takeru Inukai (also known by his pen name Ken Inukai), a Breakfast Group colleague of Ozaki's.[22]

The Sorge spy trials began in a closed session of the Tokyo District Court in May 1942. Sorge himself was defended by a prominent lawyer known for representing communists. His defence was that he had done nothing illegal and never forced anyone to divulge information. But now that the Tokko had the keys to the ring's code they were able to finally decrypt the reams of radio intercepts that they had been gathering for years. Soon, after a titanic amount of legwork, the Japanese had a near-complete record of every message Clausen had ever sent to Centre.

The evidence of the scale of Sorge's espionage was so overwhelming that the verdict was never in doubt. Curiously, one of the things the Japanese found especially damning was the contents of a case of personal papers that Sorge had left with his friend Paul Wenneker for safekeeping. After Sorge's arrest Wenneker had turned the papers over to the Japanese authorities (it is not clear whether he did this on his own initiative or because ordered to do so by Ott). It contained old love letters from both Sorge's former German wife Christiane and his current wife Katya. Sorge was not only proven to be a spy, but also the secret husband of a Soviet citizen.[23]

The Japanese authorities also chose the start of the trials to finally make Sorge's arrest public knowledge. If Schellenberg's memoirs are to be believed, it was only now, eight months after Sorge's arrest, that his Gestapo agent Meisinger sheepishly reported the outline of the case to his superiors. Unsurprisingly, Meisinger chose to pile as much blame as possible on Ott's indiscretion and bad judgement.[24]

The repercussions in Berlin were profound. 'In a long and uncomfortable session with Himmler, I had to justify our collaboration with Sorge,' Schellenberg wrote. 'As far as Ambassador Ott was concerned, Meisinger did his best to ruin him. After a careful examination of the evidence, however, it became quite clear that, while Ott had been thoroughly exploited by Sorge, he had never been guilty of knowing complicity in espionage activities.'[25]

Himmler, who had always had doubts about Sorge, informed the Führer that their valued informant in Tokyo was in fact a Soviet spy. 'In a confidential discussion between Hitler and Himmler, Hitler agreed that no blame could be placed on the German Secret Service in this affair.'[26] Hitler however took a dim view of Ott's weakness. 'Hitler held to the opinion that a man in Ott's position should never allow trust and friendship to carry him so far as to reveal confidential political information. It was lucky for Ott that Hitler took such an objective view of the matter. He was recalled from his post as ambassador, and, although Meisinger received secret instructions to look out for additional evidence, nothing was ever found and no further measures were taken against him.'[27] The unfortunate Ott attempted to redeem himself by requesting a transfer to the front line. This was refused, and he was instead ordered to a remote posting in the German consulate in Peiping, China. It was there, in late 1942, that he learned that his only son Podwick had keen killed at Stalingrad.

It was not until 15 December 1942 that both Ozaki and Sorge were convicted of violations of the Peace Preservation Law and the National Defence Security Law. The case, as a capital crime, was automatically referred to the Supreme Court for sentencing. The official Soviet news agency TASS announced that 'no member of the Soviet Government or the Soviet embassy is directly connected with the case'.[28] Unofficially, one Soviet embassy official called the trial 'a plot engineered by the fifth column of Hitler's Elite Guards and Special Police. Moscow knows nothing about it.'[29]

It is not clear whether Moscow ever knew about the courtroom revelations of Sorge's relationship with Katya. Sorge's Russian wife was not mentioned in any of the press reports. But in any case it is likely that the ruthless logic of the secret police simply demanded that loose ends of the Sorge case be cleaned up. Katya's personal file notes that she was placed under surveillance from October 1941. In November 1942, Katya was fired from her job at the factory and arrested. Her official workbook for June of that year noted 'criticism with a formal warning for irresponsibility and unpunctuality'. The official cause of her dismissal was listed as Item 47(D) of the Labour Code – 'criminal activity' – though of what kind is not recorded.

Katya Maximova was sentenced to five years of internal exile in the village of Bolshaya Murta, 120 kilometres from Krasnoyarsk in central Siberia. In spring 1943 she wrote two letters to her sister in Moscow complaining that she was freezing, hungry and very weak. That summer Katya fell seriously ill and was admitted to the local hospital. She was nursed by Lyubov Ivanovna Kozhymakina, who recalled in 2011 that her patient's 'eyes were large and grey ... Who she was I didn't know, but she caught something in my soul, lying in bed all pale and tortured. "Do you want some water?" I asked, but she didn't answer, just looked at me with her big and grey eyes and a tear on her cheek.'[30] The only two doctors in the village had left for the front two years before. There was nobody to treat her properly. The following day Kozhymakina returned for her shift and found Katya's cot bed empty. The patient had died and been taken to the local cemetery. The graveyard where Katya was buried was destroyed after the war. Sorge would never learn of his wife's fate, nor of the vicious ingratitude of the Soviet state towards the woman who had waited for him for so long.

Japanese justice, surprisingly for an authoritarian state, turned out to be both thorough and scrupulous. The three volumes of investigative documents prepared by the Tokko are exhaustive, far more professional than the cursory evidence which the NKVD assembled to convict hundreds of thousands of suspected spies in the 1930s. Ozaki spent weeks preparing a moving personal statement to the court explaining that he was motivated by a species of patriotism and had not, in fact, offended against the sacrosanct principle of *kokutai* – the natural bond that every Japanese owes to his homeland and emperor, soil and ancestral spirits. Ozaki did not deny his communist convictions, but argued that he had acted in the interests of his country.

Sorge, for his part, told the court that he 'had absolutely no thought or plan to start a communist revolution in Japan or spread communism in Japan whatsoever ... I take full responsibility, however, so please treat my Japanese colleagues as lightly as possible'.[31] It did not help. On 29 September 1943, both Ozaki and Sorge were sentenced to death by hanging. The verdict took Ozaki, at least, completely by surprise.

Sorge was calmer. A German embassy translator sent to take down his last will and testament found him looking well. The lines in his face had smoothed out after two years of enforced sobriety. He gave the impression of 'a man who is proud to have accomplished a great work and is now ready to leave the scene of his accomplishments'. Sorge asked for his eighty-year-old mother, still living in Berlin, to be spared repercussions, and asked for more history books to read.[32] Kawai, also imprisoned at Sugamo, caught a glimpse of Sorge dancing with joy and banging a guard jovially on the back when word went around the prison of the German defeat at Stalingrad.[33]

Perhaps Sorge was so calm because he still, up to the very last, expected the USSR to save him. Early in his interrogation Sorge said that the Soviet government would exchange him for Japanese prisoners – though since the two countries were not at war it is not clear what prisoners he had in mind. It is possible that the Japanese approached Moscow with such an offer. Sorge's old comrade Leopold Trepper, the famous Soviet spy who served time in the Gulag alongside a Japanese general after the war, reported that his fellow prisoner confided that the Japanese government had made three attempts to arrange an exchange for Sorge and had been told every time that Moscow had no knowledge of him. Trepper, an unreliable narrator, is the only source for this story.[34] There is no trace of such an offer in the Japanese archives.

Later, largely fictionalised Soviet accounts have Japanese foreign minister Mamoru Shigemitsu unexpectedly showing up to the Soviet embassy for a reception on the eve of Revolution Day, 6 November 1943, to offer Soviet ambassador Yakov Malik a last chance to save its agent. But Mikhail Ivanov, then a military attaché at the Soviet embassy in Tokyo, gives the lie to that story. Ivanov confirmed that Shigemitsu did indeed speak to Malik that night – but it was to urge continued friendly relations between Japan and the USSR as the tide of the war turned against Germany. Sorge was not mentioned.[35]

The day after Malik and Shigumitsu's talk at the Soviet embassy was the thirty-fourth anniversary of the Great October Revolution, a day of celebration for communists all over the world. The Japanese authorities deemed it an appropriate moment for Sorge and Ozaki's executions. Ichijima Seiichi, the governor of Sugamo prison, wore his full dress uniform with epaulettes, brass buttons, white gloves and police sword. Other officials were in formal morning dress, and the prison chaplain wore Buddhist robes. Ozaki was woken as usual as six, breakfasted on rice, bean soup, and pickles, and wrote a last postcard to his wife Eiko.

'It is gradually getting colder,' he wrote. 'I am going to fight the cold bravely.'[36]

Ozaki refused the ceremonial tea and cakes, but did kneel to pray in front of an image of the Buddha while the priest intoned the mantra

'The Three Promises of the Great Sutra of Constant Life'.[37] He was led to the large execution chamber where the charges were read and he was hooded and placed on a trapdoor. Five prison officers operated the release mechanism so that no one of them would feel the guilt of having killed a man.

Sorge was led in next. It was only when he saw the formally dressed officials that he realised that the moment of his execution had come. 'It is today?' he enquired. 'Yes, today,' the governor answered. Sorge wore dark trousers, an open shirt and a loose jacket. He seemed calm and self-possessed. Asked about his property, he replied that he would like it left to Anna Clausen, doubtless to protect Hanako from further involvement with the police. Sorge left his Leica camera and dictionaries to his executioners, and requested that letters he had prepared be sent to his mother and sister though the German embassy. He politely refused the priest's tea and cakes, but asked for a cigarette. The governor told him it was against the rules. Yuda Tamon, the official Tokko witness to the execution, spoke up impulsively. 'Oh, let him have a cigarette!' he urged. 'I know it is against the rules, but it is his last wish. You can say you let him have some medicine at the last minute.'[38] The governor still refused, and Sorge was led to the trapdoor.

As his arms and legs were bound and the noose put around his neck, Sorge spoke three phrases in loud, clear Japanese. 'Sakigun [the Red Army]! Kokusai Kyosanto [the International Communist Party]! Soviet Kyosanto [the Soviet Communist Party]!' The door opened beneath his feet and Sorge dropped into oblivion.[39] Governor Ichijima said he had 'never seen anyone act as nobly as Ozaki and Sorge at their deaths'.[40]

Other members of the ring died less gloriously. Miyagi succumbed to pneumonia halfway though his own trial in 1943, his weak lungs unable to bear the damp and cold of the prison. Vukelić was sentenced to life imprisonment and in July 1944 was transferred from Sugamo to the Abashiri prison on the freezing northern island of Hokkaido where he perished from starvation. Vukelić weighed only thirty-two kilos – five stone – when he died. Yoshiko was informed of his death on 15 January 1945.

Clausen and Anna were luckier. They survived the war and were liberated by the Americans in August 1945. Both returned to Germany, where Max – the admirer of Hitler and lapsed communist – was feted as a socialist hero by the new East German regime.

Ozaki's remains were handed over to his wife and cremated at Ochiai cemetery in Shinjiku-ku, Tokyo. 'There is nothing before me, not even colours,' she wrote. 'All that exists is a weary, endless amount of empty hours and empty space. I walked through the dark road in the rain holding the still-warm ashes of my husband in my arms. I said to the ashes of my husband, "This is the home to which you wanted to come so much. Now you have your study." I put the ashes on the table in his study with tears in my eyes. Outside, it was pouring rain.'[41]

Neither the Germans nor the Russians had any interest in giving Sorge a proper burial, so he was interred in Zoshigaya cemetery near Sugamo prison, a wooden board marking his final resting place.[42] In July 1945 the prison was destroyed by Allied bombing. Sorge's house burned too, together with his extensive library, which his defence lawyer had donated to the prosecutor's office.[43] Hanako only learned of Sorge's execution in October 1945, two months after the Japanese capitulation, when the Allied occupation authorities published details of the case in the local press. The full story caused a sensation, not least because Ozaki came to be seen by many Japanese leftists as a hero and patriot, resisting militarism while so many of their countrymen had remained shamefully silent. The Ozaki case inspired several films and plays, including the 1962 play *A Japanese Called Otto*, by Junji Kinoshita. Over a hundred books have been written in Japanese about the Sorge spy ring, and a thriving Tokyo-based Sorge Society holds well-attended annual conferences.

In 1948, Kawai, who had been liberated from prison by the Allies, and Ozaki's half-brother Hotsuki encouraged Hanako to write a memoir. They published it in a leftist magazine they had founded, the *Junken News*. Hanako also painstakingly researched the possible site of her dead lover's grave. With the proceeds of her memoir, Hanako was able to finance an exhumation, and identified Sorge's body from his shrapnel-wounded legs and the gold bridgework in his skull, which she had made into a ring. She also bought a grave plot at Tama cemetery, where Sorge lies today among the dignified graves of Japanese notables under a granite stone with the Japanese inscription: 'Here lies a hero who sacrificed his life fighting against war and for world peace.'[44] Hanako died in Tokyo in 2000 at the age of eighty-nine and her ashes were interred alongside his.[45]

After the war the American occupation authorities in Japan took a keen interest in the surviving judicial records of the Sorge ring, largely because they feared the Soviets might have mounted a similarly successful penetration operation on their own soil. General Douglas MacArthur, the US viceroy in post-war Tokyo, called Sorge's achievement 'a devastating example of a brilliant success of espionage'. US Army General Charles Willoughby was tasked with preparing a detailed report on the case for MacArthur. His findings were extensively cited during August 1951 sessions of the US House of Representatives Un-American Activities Committee chaired by Senator Joseph McCarthy as it searched for possible Sorges in America – and for possible Soviet involvement in encouraging Japan to attack Pearl Harbor.

During his testimony to Congress Willoughby gave the impression that Sorge had warned the Soviets of the planned Japanese attack on America. 'Stalin did get the information,' he told McCarthy on 22 August 1951. The next day Willoughby explained, more accurately, that 'Pearl Harbor is a fixed date and did not appear in the Sorge message. But that was not important – the important thing was that the Japanese were aiming south into a collision with the United States and Britain'.[46] But the myth that the Soviets knew of Japan's plans for a surprise attack and failed to warn their allies in Washington of the danger was off and running. Senator Adlai Stevenson spoke of Stalin's 'duplicity' over Pearl Harbor. Several books were written claiming that the Japanese attack on the US was a plot orchestrated by the Kremlin to defuse the danger to Siberia.[47] Even Sorge's German embassy colleague, Third Secretary Hans-Otto Meissner (not to be confused with Gestapo Colonel Joseph Meisinger), made the Pearl Harbor story the culmination of his bizarre 1955 book *The Man with Three Faces*. In this confection of memoir and invention, Meissner has Sorge sending a message to Centre 'JAPANESE CARRIER AIR FORCE ATTACKING UNITED STATES NAVY AT PEARL HARBOR PROBABLY DAWN NOVEMBER SIX STOP SOURCE RELIABLE STOP JOE'.[48] The telegram was entirely a figment of Meissner's imagination (not least because JOE was Miyagi's codename, not Sorge's).

It took the Soviets much longer to exhume Sorge's memory from among the millions of Stalin's victims. In 1956, Katya Maximova was officially rehabilitated, along with Sorge's Comintern and Fourth Department colleagues who had perished in the Purge. But it was only in 1964, when a Franco-German film about the life of Sorge was premiered at the Moscow Film Festival, that the case caught the eye of Stalin's successor, Nikita Khrushchev. French director Yves Ciampi's 1961 *Qui êtes-vous, Monsieur Sorge?* (released in the US as *Who Are You, Doctor Sorge?*) was largely based on Meissner's highly fantastical account of the case. Meissner even played himself in the film. But when Khrushchev saw the movie – Zhukov and Golikov also attended the screening – he demanded to have his own answer to the question posed by the title of Ciampi's film. An official commission was formed to collect documents and testimony from the surviving Soviet intelligence officers who had worked with Sorge, and the results – including surprisingly extensive extracts from the top-secret Fourth Department cable traffic with Tokyo – were published as a book.

The Soviet leadership decided that Sorge should join the official pantheon of Soviet saints. The Berlin Wall had recently gone up and the East German people needed a pro-Soviet, anti-fascist hero – a good German who was also a Soviet patriot. Sorge was made a posthumous Hero of the Soviet Union, and a bulky stone gravestone decorated with an image of the medal joined Hanako's original, more dignified monument over his grave in Tokyo. The Soviet press swung into action, with a series of adulatory full-page articles in *Sovietskaya Rossiya* based on Sorge's personnel files. A street in Moscow was named after him, complete with a statue of a commanding figure in a flowing trench coat stepping out of a curtain of bronze shadow. A ship was also christened with his name, and a 10-kopek stamp was produced bearing Sorge's rugged face. One such stamp was bought by the author's father, then a visiting academic at Moscow University, at the request of William Deakin, head of St Antony's College, Oxford. Deakin was working on the first Western scholarly account of the case and the stamp featured as the cover illustration of the first edition of *The Case of Richard Sorge* in 1966. In the same year the first novel based on Sorge's career was published in the USSR, spawning a curious literary tradition that by 2017 included at least half a dozen fictionalised biographies of the famous spy in Russian.

Sorge enjoyed another burst of officially sanctioned fame in the late 1970s. Again, the story of Sorge became a canvas on which the Kremlin's power struggles could be projected. The KGB, and its director Yury Andropov, were rising in power and prestige and they needed a hero-spy – a dashing Soviet version of James Bond – to glamorise the image of the KGB. A new series of books and articles was commissioned. The Soviet writer Yulian Semyonov penned a series of novels called 'Seventeen Moments of Spring' that followed the adventures of a fictional Soviet mole in the Nazi intelligence apparatus in Berlin, which was made into a cult television serial in 1979. Semyonov said that his fictional hero, Max Otto von Stierlitz, was closely modelled on Sorge. In 1982 a new monument went up in Sorge's native Baku. It is a bizarre piece of sculpture – a monumental bronze wall pierced by a pair of giant staring eyes intended to represent the all-seeing eye of Soviet espionage.

The Soviet Union had officially canonised Sorge as a hero. Yet all the statues and the books could never quite efface the USSR's actual suspicion, indifference and ultimate betrayal of its greatest spy. No other Soviet agent served Moscow so well or for so long. The spy network Sorge created was unique in the history of modern espionage in its access to the inner circles of power in both Germany and Japan. Yet at the moment of greatest danger for his adopted country, the atmosphere of paranoia that Stalin had created meant that the intelligence gold that he dutifully cabled to Moscow was ignored. Sorge was a flawed individual, but an impeccable spy – brave, brilliant and relentless. It was Sorge's tragedy that his masters were venal cowards who placed their own careers before the vital interests of the country that he laid down his life to serve.

Notes

Abbreviations used in the Notes

PADAA: German Foreign Office Political Archive (Politisches Archiv des Auswärtigen Amts), Berlin

RGASPI (known as RTsKhIDNI, 1991–99): Russian State Archive of Social and Political History, Moscow (former Archive of the Central Committee of the Communist Party of the USSR, incorporating the Archive of the Comintern)

TNA: The National Archives, London

TsAMO RF: Central Archives of the Ministry of Defence of the Russian Federation, Podolsk

INTRODUCTION

1 F. W. Deakin and G. R. Storrey, *The Case of Richard Sorge*, London, 1966.
2 John le Carré, *Progress* magazine, November 1966.

CHAPTER I

1 John le Carré, interview, *New York Times*, 17 August 2017.
2 Stalin, *Works*, Vol. 2, p. 188; Vol. 8, pp. 174–5, quoted in Simon Sebag Montefiore, *Young Stalin*, London, 2008, p. 237.
3 Anastas Mikoyan, *Tak bylo*, pp. 347–8, and Anastas Mikoyan, *Memoirs*, pp. 72–4, quoted in Montefiore, *Young Stalin*, Chapter One.
4 Jörg Baberowski, *Der Feind*, pp. 62–7, quoted in Montefiore, *Young Stalin*, Chapter One.

5 Russia's first engineering university, the Bauman Institute in Moscow, had been founded only in 1830.

6 Mikhail Alekseyev, *Your Ramsay: Richard Sorge and Soviet Military Intelligence in China 1930–1933*, Moscow, 2010, p. 18.

7 Deakin and Storrey, *Case of Richard Sorge*, p. 22.

8 Deakin and Storrey, *Case of Richard Sorge*, p. 23.

9 Montefiore, *Young Stalin*, p. 188.

10 Anna Alliluyeva, *The Alliluyev Memoirs*, pp. 52–5, 84–6, quoted in Montefiore, *Young Stalin*, Chapter One.

11 Tom Reiss, *The Orientalist*, pp. 9–15, quoted in Montefiore, *Young Stalin*, Chapter One.

12 Julius Mader, Gerhard Stucklik, and Horst Pehnert, *Dr Sorge funkt aus Tokyo: Ein Dokumentarbericht über Kundschafter des Friedens mil auggewählten Artikeln von Richard Sorge*, Berlin, 1968, p. 40.

13 'Richard Sorge did not know any Russian then; they spoke only German in his family': Dorothea von During letter to General Willoughby, 2 July 1951, in Charles Andrew Willoughby, *Shanghai Conspiracy: The Sorge Spy Ring*, New York, 1952. p. 133.

14 'Partial Memoirs of Richard Sorge' (hereafter 'Sorge Memoir'); Sorge typed this autobiographical material while in Sugamo prison. Unfortunately, it is incomplete, the rest lost when the Ministry of Justice burned in the bombing of Tokyo during the Second World War. The English translation quoted here is reproduced in Willoughby, *Shanghai Conspiracy*, pp. 90–230. Another version appears in 'A Partial Documentation of the Sorge Espionage Case', Military Intelligence Section, US Far East Command, US Congress House Committee on Un-American Activities, Tokyo, 1950.

15 Barry Moreno, 'Sorge, Friedrich Adolf', in *Encyclopedia of New Jersey*, New Brunswick, NJ, 2004, p. 302.

16 F. A. Sorge, 'Report of the North American Federal Council to the Hague Congress', in *Documents of the First International: The Hague Congress … Minutes and Documents*, Madison: University of Wisconsin Press, 1958, p. 224.

17 Willoughby, *Shanghai Conspiracy*, p. 133.

18 Obi Toshito (ed.), *Gendai-shi Shiryo, Zoruge jiken* ('Materials on Modern History: The Sorge Incident'), Tokyo, 1962, Vol. 1, p. 320.

19 Willoughby, *Shanghai Conspiracy*, p. 142.

20 Gordon W. Prange, Donald M. Goldstein, and Katherine V. Dillon, *Target Tokyo*, New York, 1985, see chapter 2.

21 Prange et al., *Target Tokyo*, chapter 2.

22 Prange et al., *Target Tokyo*, chapter 2.

23 Sorge Memoir, Pt 1, 'My past history as a German Communist', pp. 91–8.

24 Deakin and Storrey, *Case of Richard Sorge*, p. 24.

25 Sorge Memoir, Pt 1, 'My past history as a German Communist', pp. 91–8.

26 Sorge Memoir, Pt 1, 'My past history as a German Communist', pp. 91–8.

27 Sorge Memoir, Pt 1, 'My past history as a German Communist', pp. 91–8.

28 Sorge Memoir, Pt 1, 'My past history as a German Communist', pp. 91–8.

29 Bundesarchiv, Bild 183-Z0519-022/ CC-BY-SA 3.0 ADN-ZB/19.5.1981/ Berlin. In an interview on WBA 6 radio on 6 April 1981, Correns said that Sorge 'did an outstanding reconnaissance job for the Soviet Union … During the First World War and afterwards, we often discussed the future and shared our thoughts of what could be, once this terrible mass-murder is over … If my friend Richard Sorge could witness here today what the power of the people achieved after 1945, how proud would he be to have contributed to this.'

30 Sorge Memoir, Pt 1, 'My past history as a German Communist', pp. 91–8.

31 Sorge Memoir, Pt 1, 'My past history as a German Communist', pp. 91–8.

32 Sorge Memoir, Pt 1, 'My past history as a German Communist', pp. 91–8.

33 Sorge Memoir, Pt 1, 'My past history as a German Communist', pp. 91–8.

34 Sorge Memoir, Pt 1, 'My past history as a German Communist', pp. 91–8.

35 Prange et al., *Target Tokyo*, chapter 2.

36 Sorge Memoir, Pt 1, 'My past history as a German Communist', pp. 91–8.

37 Deakin and Storrey, *Case of Richard Sorge*, p. 25.

38 Sorge Memoir, Pt 1, 'My past history as a German Communist', pp. 91–8.

39 Sorge Memoir, Pt 1, 'My past history as a German Communist', pp. 91–8.

40 Sorge Memoir, Pt 1, 'My past history as a German Communist', pp. 91–8.

41 Sorge Memoir, Pt 1, 'My past history as a German Communist', pp. 91–8.

42 Sorge Memoir, Pt 1, 'My past history as a German Communist', pp. 91–8.

43 Sorge Memoir, Pt 1, 'My past history as a German Communist', pp. 91–8.

44 Murray Sayle, 'Spying doesn't get any better than this', *London Review of Books*, Vol. 19, No. 10, 22 May 1997. Sayle tracked down Philby in 1967, four years after his defection, by hanging about at Moscow bookshops and theatres where the spy might show up. 'After a few days, I forget how many exactly, I saw a man looking like an intellectual of the 1930s, all leather patches on the elbows of his tweed jacket.' Sayle found Philby 'a charming, entertaining man with a great sense of humour', Jessica Mitford, 'Old School Spies', *Washington Post*, 26 March 1989.

CHAPTER 2

1 Murray Sayle, *Daily Telegraph*, 21 September 2010.

2 Karl Marx to the editor of the *Otechestvenniye Zapisky*, November 1877, see http://www.marxists.org/archive/marx/works/1877/11/russia.htm.

3 Friedrich Engels to Georgi Plekhanov, 26 February 1895, *Marx–Engels Collected Works*, Vol. 50, New York, 2004, pp. 449–51.

4 David Howarth, *The Dreadnoughts*, Amsterdam, 1980, pp. 158–9.

5 Sorge Memoir, Pt 1, 'My past history as a German Communist', pp. 91–8.

6 Sorge Memoir, Pt 1, 'My past history as a German Communist', pp. 91–8.

7 Hauptkrankenbuch Festungslazarett Kiel, Nr 15918, Krankenbuchlager Berlin, quoted in Dirk Dähnhardt, *Revolution in Kiel*, Neumünster, 1978, p. 66.

8 Dähnhardt, *Revolution in Kiel*, p. 83.

9 Prinz Max von Baden, *Erinnerungen und Dokumente (Reihe Deutsches Reich – Schriften und Diskurse: Reichskanzler)*, Hamburg, 2011 p. 599 f.

10 Christiane Sorge, 'Mein Mann – Dr. R. Sorge', *Die Weltwoche*, 11 December 1964. According to *Weltwoche*, Christiane Sorge's article was written ten years earlier.

11 Heinrich August Winkler, *Der lange Weg nach Westen*, Munich, 2000, p. 55.

12 Carlos Caballero Jurado and Ramiro Bujeiro, *The German Freikorps 1918–23*, Oxford, 2001.

13 Heinrich August Winkler, *Weimar 1918–33*, Taschenbuch, 2005, p. 58.

14 Sorge Memoir, Pt 1, 'My past history as a German Communist', pp. 91–8.

15 Hagan Schulze, *Weimar: Germany 1917–1933*, Severin und Siedler, 1982, p. 158.

16 Sorge Memoir, Pt 1, 'My past history as a German Communist', pp. 91–8.

17 C. Sorge, 'Mein Mann', *Die Weltwoche*.

18 Elisabeth K. Poretsky, *Our Own People*, quoted in Robert Whymant, *Stalin's Spy: Richard Sorge and the Tokyo Espionage Ring*, London, 1996, p. 325n.

19 Stephen Koch, *Double Lives: Stalin, Willi Münzenberg and the Seduction of the Intellectuals*, New York, 2004, p. 11.

20 Sayle, *London Review of Books*, 22 May 1997.

21 Poretsky quoted in Whymant, *Stalin's Spy*, p. 325n.

22 Stéphane Courtois, Nicolas Werth, and Andrzej Paczkowski, *The Black Book of Communism*, Cambridge, MA, 1997, p. 282; Marxist Internet Archive.

23 'Der Märzaufstand 1920', Deutsches Historisches Museum: https://www.dhm.de/lemo/kapitel/weimarer-republik/innenpolitik/maerzaufstand.

24 Prange et al., *Target Tokyo*, chapter 2.

25 Mader, *Dr Sorge-Report*, Berlin, 1985, p. 45.

26 Erich Correns, 29 October 1919, quoted in Whymant, *Stalin's Spy*, p. 22.

27 Sorge Memoir, Pt 2, p. 32.

28 Sorge Memoir, Pt 2, p. 33.

29 Toshito (ed.), *Gendai-shi Shiryo*, Vol. 3, p. 5.

30 Gerlach never formally took up the post, dying suddenly of diabetes in October 1922. See Rolf Wiggershaus, *The Frankfurt School: Its History, Theories, and Political Significance* (Studies in Contemporary German Social Thought), Cambridge, MA, 1995.

31 Prange et al., *Target Tokyo*, p. 33.

32 Hede Massing, *This Deception: KBG Targets America*, New York, 1951, p. 71.

33 'I read about the Russian Revolution, about Lenin and Vera Figner, who became my idol; and I learned to love the idea of socialism the idea of a better life for everyone. True, I never faced the reality of everyday work within the movement,' she wrote (Massing, *This Deception*, p. 29).

34 Unlike Sorge, Massing was able to escape from the secret world. After the Second World War she defected from the Soviet underground and came to prominence by testifying in the second case of Alger Hiss in 1949; later, she published sensational accounts about her life as a Soviet intelligence operative.

35 Sorge Memoir, Pt 1, 'My past history as a German Communist', pp. 91–8.

36 David North and Joe Kishore, *The Historical and International Foundations of the Socialist Equality Party*, World Socialist Website (wsw.org), 2008, p. 13.

37 Robert Service, *Lenin: A Biography*, London, 2010, p. 262.

38 See William Henry Chamberlin, *Soviet Russia: A Living Record and a History*, London, 1931, chapter 11; Max Shachtman 'For the Fourth International!' *New International*, Vol. 1, No.1, July 1934; Walter Kendall, 'Lenin and the Myth of World Revolution', *Revolutionary History*, Vol. 3 (3), 1991.

39 Koch, *Double Lives*, p. 16.

40 Koch, *Double Lives*, p. 11.

41 Koch, *Double Lives*, p. 17 note 20.

42 Koch, *Double Lives*, p. 17.

43 P. Broue, *The German Revolution: 1917–1923*, Chicago, 2006, p. 516.

44 Courtois et al., *Black Book of Communism*, pp. 277–8.

45 Sorge Memoir, Pt 1, 'My past history as a German Communist', pp. 91–8.

46 Viktor Suvorov, *Spetsnaz: The Story Behind the Soviet SAS*, trans. David Floyd, London, 1987, chapter 3.

47 'Sorge Memoir', Pt. 2, p. 23.

48 As also detailed by Nikolai Bukharin in his brochure *Can We Build Socialism in One Country in the Absence of the Victory of the West-European Proletariat?*, April 1925. The position was finalised as the state policy after Stalin's January 1926 article 'On the Issues of Leninism' (David Priestland, *The Red Flag: A History of Communism*, New York, 2009, p. 124).

49 Sorge Memoir, Pt 3, 'The Comintern and the Soviet Communist Party', pp. 102–17.
50 Sorge, *Die Weltwoche*, 11 December 1964.
51 'Sorge Memoir', Pt. 2, p. 28.
52 Sorge, *Die Weltwoche*, 11 December 1964.
53 'Sorge Memoir', Pt 1, p. 55.

CHAPTER 3

1 John le Carré, *Progress* magazine, 1966.
2 Renamed after the writer Maxim Gorky in 1935.
3 Alexander Cammann, 'Müde Kalauer im roten Bunker', *Die Zeit*, 23 October 2011.
4 *Comrade Sorge: Documents and Memoirs*, Moscow, 1965, p. 8, written by journalists from *Sovietskaya Rossiya*, this was the book on Sorge published in Russia.
5 Agnes Smedley, quoted by J. R. and S. R. MacKinnon, *The Life and Times of an American Radical*, Berkeley, 1988.
6 Krivitsky, *I Was Stalin's Agent*, London, 1940, p. 78.
7 Sorge Memoir, Pt 3, 'The Comintern and the Soviet Communist Party', pp. 102–117.
8 Whymant, *Stalin's Spy*, p. 23.
9 Whymant, *Stalin's Spy*, p. 43.
10 The Soviets did not seem to be in a hurry to bring her to Russia. Sorge wrote to the party apparatus in Germany from Moscow on 6 October 1924, worrying that he had heard nothing about Christiane's transfer to the USSR despite having put in an official request in mid-August (1924) for the German party's permission to allow her to work in Moscow. Sorge noted that Ryazanov of the Institute of Marxist–Leninism had expressed a desire for Christiane to reorganise his library as 'she knows the latest techniques', A. G. Fesyun, *Delo Rikharda Zorge: Neisvestnye Dokumenty*, Moscow, 2000, (henceforth, Fesyun, *Documents*), 'The Unknown Sorge', Doc. 5.
11 Sorge, *Die Weltwoche*, 11 December 1964.
12 Sorge, *Die Weltwoche*, 11 December 1964.
13 Massing, *This Deception*, p. 74.
14 Deakin and Storrey, *Case of Richard Sorge*, p. 43.
15 Whymant, *Stalin's Spy*, p. 44.
16 *Comrade Sorge: Documents and Memoirs*, p. 12.
17 Kollontai was the most prominent woman in the Soviet administration and was best known for founding the Zhenotdel or 'Women's Department' in 1919. In 1923 the Soviet authorities, perhaps finding her philosophy of

free love a little too much even for their liberated sensibilities, appointed her ambassador to Norway.

18 *Der Spiegel*, 27 June 1951, p. 25. From 13 June to 3 October 1951, this West German magazine ran a series of articles entitled '*Herr Sorge sass mit zu Tische: Porträt eines Spions*'.

19 Sorge reported delightedly to his mother and sisters in Berlin with news that the old acacia tree in the garden was still standing (*Comrade Sorge: Documents and Memoirs*, p. 13).

20 Sorge, *Die Weltwoche*, 11 December 1964. Nevertheless, Christiane kept a soft spot for Sorge. Eventually she emigrated to the United States, but she did not marry again and maintained a warm correspondence with him. Although there is no evidence of a divorce, Sorge considered himself a bachelor and wrote-off family life as 'not for him' (see Alain Guerin and Nicole Chatel, *Camarade Sorge*, Paris, 1965, pp. 16, 274).

21 *Comrade Sorge: Documents and Memoirs*, p. 3.

22 A list of works by Richard Sorge in the Communist International journal for 'Sonder R' 1926–29 reviews and articles 'the material situation of the German proletariat at the end of 1927' shows eight reviews and twelve learned articles (see Fesyun, *Documents*).

23 'While in Moscow, I published The Economic Provisions of the Versailles Peace Treaty and the International Labour Class, and in 1927 I published German Imperialism. I believe that these were competent pieces of work. Both were read widely in Germany and translated into Russian,' Sorge Memoir, Pt 2, p. 42.

24 Deakin and Storrey, *Case of Richard Sorge*, p. 40.

25 *Comrade Sorge: Documents and Memoirs*, p. 12.

26 In 1925 he also published a brochure in Germany 1925 under the name I. K. Sorge, 'The Dawes Plan and Its Consequences', Fesyun, *Documents*, p. 24.

27 RGASPI, Fond 495, opis. 165, doc. 23, pp. 48–9.

28 RGASPI, Fond 495, opis. 166, doc. 15, p. 9.

29 RGASPI, Fond 495, opis. 25, doc. 107, pp. 166, 206.

30 Fesyun, *Documents*, 25.10.26, 06.04.27, p. 25.

31 Fesyun, *Documents*, 27.09.27, p. 25.

32 Massing, *This Deception*, p. 95.

33 Fesyun, *Documents*, Doc. 12, 22.04.27, p. 26.

34 Deakin and Storrey, *Case of Richard Sorge*, p. 47.

35 'I remember Sorge as if it were yesterday – now I know that he and Johann were one and the same,' recalled Richard Jensen, a member of the Danish Communist Party. Danish CP leaders at the time seemed to think Sorge's mission was from Berlin, but 'when he had carried out his assignment in this country [Denmark] we travelled together to Moscow at the end of

1928 or the beginning of 1929'. Jensen says that Sorge advised the party to switch from small street cells to factory cells. Sorge was 'a tall slender and very intelligent man'. Jensen took him on a tour of the port and seamen's clubs of Copenhagen ('I Saw Sorge Last', *Politiken*, 27 December 1964).

36 Fesyun, *Documents,* Doc. 13, 19.12.27, p. 27.

37 Fesyun, *Documents*, Doc. 13.

38 'Where the master spy drank beer in Copenhagen': Jensen, 'I Saw Sorge Last'.

39 Massing, *This Deception*, p. 96.

40 Sorge Memoir, Pt 3, 'The Comintern and the Soviet Communist Party', pp. 102–17.

41 Yury Georgiyev, 'Rikhard Sorge, Biografichesky Ocherk' in *Yaponiya Segodnya*, 2002, p. 91.

42 Fesyun, *Documents*, No. 17. On 10 October 1928, Sorge sent a cable justifying to unidentified colleagues in the Comintern why he had spent over $500 in six weeks; he explained that his ticket from Moscow to Berlin alone cost $100.

43 Sorge Memoir, Pt 2, p. 44.

44 Fesyun, *Documents*, No. 20, p. 30.

45 Fesyun, *Documents*, No. 19, p. 30.

46 Sorge Memoir, Pt 2, p. 44.

47 The phrase was the poet Osip Mandelstam's – he would pay for it with his life.

48 *Comrade Sorge: Documents and Memoirs*, p. 5.

49 *Comrade Sorge: Documents and Memoirs*, p. 6.

50 *Comrade Sorge: Documents and Memoirs*, p. 6.

51 *Comrade Sorge: Documents and Memoirs*, p. 7.

52 *Comrade Sorge: Documents and Memoirs*, p. 13.

53 General Charles Willougby, the resolute cold war warrior who investigated Sorge as a case study in the making of a Soviet spy, took a less charitable view of these Moscow days. He found Sorge's prison confession 'a rare opportunity to see the development of a patriotically inclined young man into a tool of the Kremlin' and claimed that in Moscow 'the open, good-hearted youth learned to hate', Willoughby, *Shanghai Conspiracy*, p. 18. See also *Comrade Sorge: Documents and Memoirs*, p. 9.

54 *Comrade Sorge: Documents and Memoirs*, p. 7.

55 *Comrade Sorge: Documents and Memoirs*, p. 15.

56 Deakin and Storrey, *Case of Richard Sorge*, p. 47.

57 Sorge Memoir, Pt 3, 'The Comintern and the Soviet Communist Party', pp. 102–17.

58 Sorge Memoir, Pt 2, p. 47.

59 Sorge Memoir, Pt 3, 'The Comintern and the Soviet Communist Party',
    pp. 102–17.

60 Jane Degras, *The Communist International, Selected Documents*, Oxford,
    1960, p. 367.

61 Vladimir Mikhailovich Chunikhin, *Richard Sorge: Notes on the Margins of
    a Legend*, Moscow, 2008, p. 34.

62 RGASPI, Fond 508, opis. 1, doc. 79, p. 1; Fond 495, opis. 7, doc. 8, p. 1.

63 Sorge Memoir, Pt 2, p. 47.

64 Deakin and Storrey, *Case of Richard Sorge*, p. 52.

65 Deakin and Storrey, *Case of Richard Sorge*, p. 50.

66 Gill Bennett, *'A Most Extraordinary and Mysterious Business': The Zinoviev
    Letter of 1924*, series: 'Historians LRD', No. 14, London, January 1999, p. 1.

67 TNA: KV 2/770 PRO KV, Records of the Security Service KV 2, the
    Security Service: Personal (PF Series) Files Subseries within KV 2 –
    Communists and Suspected Communists, including Russian and
    Communist Sympathisers.

68 Deakin and Storrey, *Case of Richard Sorge*, p. 49.

69 Geoff Layton, *Access to History: From Kaiser to Führer: Germany 1900–45*,
    London, 2009, p. 98.

70 Sorge, *Die Weltwoche*, 11 December 1964.

71 In Wright's book *Spycatcher* he describes how Ellis fell under
    suspicion: 'Within a year of [Kim] Philby's falling under suspicion
    Ellis took early retirement, pleading ill-health. He travelled to
    Australia, and took up a job as a consultant to ASIS, the Australian
    overseas intelligence-gathering organisation. While there he was
    briefed by the Australians on the impending defection of Vladimir
    Petrov, an [NKVD] henchman who opted to stay in the West rather
    than take his chances in Moscow. Almost immediately Ellis returned
    to Britain and contacted Kim Philby, despite being specifically
    warned against doing so by [MI6 chief] Maurice Oldfield ... The
    reasons for Ellis's hasty flight from Australia have never been clear,
    but I have always assumed that he thought that Petrov, who was about
    to defect, was the same "Von Petrov" with whom [Ellis] had been
    involved in the 1920s, and who must have known the secret of his
    treachery' (Peter Wright, *Spycatcher*, New York, 1988, p. 325). Wright
    seems to be referring to the Comintern agent David Petrovsky, alias
    A. J. Bennett, who served as Soviet consul in London and was the
    official liaison between the British Communist Party and Moscow.
    See Dr Sharman Kadish, *Bolsheviks and British Jews: The Anglo-
    Jewish Community, Britain and the Russian Revolution*, London, 21
    August 2013.

72 James Dalrymple has claimed that Ellis sold 'vast quantities of information' about the British secret service to the Germans during the Second World War. However, Ellis's biographer, Frank Cain, has argued that he was not guilty of spying: 'Experts have dismissed these claims, if only because important information held by Ellis was known not to have been transmitted to the Soviet Union.' Ernest Cuneo, who worked for Ellis during the Second World War argues: 'If the charge against Ellis is true … it would mean that the OSS, and to some extent its successor the CIA, in effect was a branch of the Soviet KGB.' Benjamin de Forest Bayly worked with Ellis at British Security Coordination. 'Dickey Ellis was MI6 and the only professional … in the office. He had been for years and years in MI6. He's the one they thought must be a Russian or German agent, I regard as entirely unproved, because I had known him quite well. He visited us in our apartment in New York quite often. He was a musician and he just didn't ever give an indication that he was that way concerned.' William Stephenson was convinced that Ellis was not a spy and offered to sue the journalists who were writing these articles about him. See article by John Simkin at spartacus-educational.com (September 1997).

73 Wright, *Spycatcher*, p. 326.

74 Fesyun, *Documents*, No. 22.

75 Though the apparat does not seem to have taken the arrest too seriously. When Sorge's personal files were examined for signs of treachery – including personally by Stalin – there was no suggestion that he may have been recruited after his arrest by British intelligence, a classic charge for any foreign communists who had been detained by the authorities.

76 Fesyun, *Documents*, No. 24, Protocol No. 18, Delegation of the VKPb in IKKI 16 August 1929, 'One copy sent to comrade Stalin, present: Molotov, Manuilsky, Pyatnitsky, Vasiliyev, Lovitsky'.

77 RGASPI, Fond 508, opis. 1, doc. 31, p. 2.

78 RGASPI, Fond 495, opis. 18, doc. 666, p. 59.

79 Paul R. Gregory, *Politics, Murder, and Love in Stalin's Kremlin: The Story of Nikolai Bukharin and Anna Larina*, Stanford, CA, 2010, chapter 17.

80 Deakin and Storrey, *Case of Richard Sorge*, p. 51.

81 Deakin and Storrey, *Case of Richard Sorge*, p. 51.

82 Chunikhin, *Richard Sorge: Notes*, Doc. 25, Pismo v Tsentr reddotsenta K. Basova ot 16 September 1929 г. (sent from Berlin).

83 Chunikhin, *Richard Sorge: Notes*, Doc. 27, Pismo v Tsentr reddotsenta K. Basova ot 16 September 1929.

84 The Bolshevik Party – and particularly the secret police – was dominated by members of the Russian Empire's ethnic minorities such as Latvians, Jews, Poles and Georgians.

85 Boris Volodarsky, *Stalin's Agent: The Life and Death of Alexander Orlov*, Oxford, 2015, p. 528.

86 Fesyun, *Documents*, No. 23.

87 Chunikhin, *Richard Sorge: Notes*, Doc. 25.

88 Chunikhin, *Richard Sorge: Notes*, Chunikhin, Doc. 25.

89 RGASPI, Fond 546, Opis. 1, Doc. 112, l54, 60–3.

90 RGASPI, Fond 546, Opis. 1, Doc. 112, l54, 60–3.

91 Sorge's own account in his prison confession gives some clues about why he needed 'no introduction' from Basov. 'General Berzin, who was at that time head of the Fourth Department, and also a close friend of Pyatnitsky, knew me from my time in the Comintern.' But Sorge's telling of his transition from the Comintern to the Fourth Department – apparently a civilised handover from one boss to another – doesn't track with the trail of telegrams between Basov and Moscow Centre describing Sorge's desperation and abandonment in Berlin. It seems that, even fifteen years later, Sorge still smarted from his humiliating expulsion from the Comintern. 'On my return from England, discussing with Pyatnitsky my future work in the Comintern, I told him that I wished to expand my sphere of activity, but it was unlikely to be possible as long as I remained in the Comintern. Pyatnitsky told Berzin about this conversation. In Berzin's opinion, such a plan could be realised through the Fourth Department. A few days later Berzin invited me to see him and we had an extensive discussion of the problems of intelligence work in Asia,' Chunikhin, *Richard Sorge: Notes*, Doc. 26.

CHAPTER 4

1 According to Berzin's former subordinate, Walter Krivitsky (Krivitsky, *I Was Stalin's Agent*, p. 115).

2 Deakin and Storrey, *Case of Richard Sorge*, p. 58.

3 Viktor Suvorov, *Inside Soviet Military Intelligence*, New York, 1984.

4 Koch, *Double Lives*, p. 9.

5 *Comrade Sorge: Documents and Memoirs*, p. 13.

6 Massing, *This Deception*, p. 333.

7 *Comrade Sorge: Documents and Memoirs*, p. 14.

8 Fesyun, *Documents*, No. 28.

9 Fesyun, *Documents*, No. 29.

10 Deakin and Storrey, *Case of Richard Sorge*, p. 58.

11 Frederic Wakeman Jr, *Policing Shanghai*, 1927–1937, Berkeley and Los Angeles, CA, 1996, pp. 145–50.

12 Other agents in Germany, Western Poland, Italy, Turkey, Persia, Afghanistan and Japan had no radios and still had to work through official embassy channels (Alekseyev, *Your Ramsay*, p. 159).

13 Jonathan Haslam, *Near and Distant Neighbours: A New History of Soviet Intelligence*, Oxford, 2015, p. 28.

14 Alekseyev, *Your Ramsay*, p. 160.

15 Alekseyev, *Your Ramsay*, p. 166.

16 Alekseyev, *Your Ramsay*, p. 168.

17 Despite the rushed and imperfect nature of the team's preparation, Basov seemed to consider the latest Shanghai team unusually well furnished with legal cover. Basov reported to Centre in February 1930 that 'we understand legalisation to be the existence of a good cover story alone without supporting proper documents, military docs, birth certificates. But the conditions of work demand that our agents need to have these documents – it is expensive but necessary and will set them up for productive work in future,' Chunikhin, *Richard Sorge: Notes*, Doc. 28

18 Wakeman Jr, *Policing Shanghai*, p. 98. A private survey in 1929 of the gambling houses of the French Concession alone estimated that $150,000 changed hands every day in the average casino, which boasted between 1,000 and 5,000 clients in a 3 p.m. to 3 a.m. shift.

19 Harriet Sergeant, *Shanghai: Collision Point of Cultures, 1918–1939*, New York, 1990, p. 14.

20 Wakeman Jr, *Policing Shanghai*, pp. 145–50.

21 Alekseyev, *Your Ramsay*, p. 142.

22 Sorge Memoir, Pt 5, 'My espionage group in China 1930–33', pp. 124–33.

23 E. Prudnikova, and O. Gorchakov, *Legendy GRU*, St Petersburg, 2005, p. 53.

24 Alekseyev, *Your Ramsay*, p. 182.

25 Alekseyev, *Your Ramsay*, p. 181.

26 Alekseyev, *Your Ramsay*, p. 182.

27 Alekseyev, *Your Ramsay*, p. 196.

28 Alekseyev, *Your Ramsay*, p. 194.

29 Ruth Price, *The Lives of Agnes Smedley*, Oxford, 2004, pp. 86–8.

30 Whymant, *Stalin's Spy*, p. 32.

31 Price, *Lives of Agnes Smedley*, p. 194.

32 See Werner, *Sonja's Rapport*, chapter 3.

33 Price, *Lives of Agnes Smedley*, p. 200.

34 Price, *Lives of Agnes Smedley*, p. 203.

35 Price, *Lives of Agnes Smedley*, p. 204.

36 Agnes Smedley, 'The Social Revolutionary Struggle in China' and 'The Revolutionary Peasant Movement in China', Lewis Gannett Papers.

37 Chen Hansheg, 'Shi MoTe Lai zai shanghai', trans. courtesy of Robert Farnsworth, quoted in Price, *Lives of Agnes Smedley*, p. 466.

38 Julius Mader, *Dr Sorge-Report*, 3rd extended edition, Berlin, 1986, p. 119.

39 Whymant, *Stalin's Spy*, p. 33.

40 Price, *Lives of Agnes Smedley*, p. 203.

41 Agnes Smedley to Karin Michaelis, 23 July 1930, Karin Michaelis papers quoted in Price, *Lives of Agnes Smedley*, p. 201.

42 Price, *Lives of Agnes Smedley*, p. 205.

43 Willoughby, *Shanghai Conspiracy*, p. 28.

44 Curiously, he was not able to connect with Weingarten's transmitter in Shanghai.

45 State Department passport (130) pile, Agnes Smedley, 4 July 1930; Douglas Jenkins to the Honorable Secretary of State, August 1930, 800.00b, Smedley, Agnes/9 RG 59, quoted in Price, *Lives of Agnes Smedley*, p. 458.

46 Alekseyev, *Your Ramsay*, p. 182.

47 Alekseyev, *Your Ramsay*, p. 188.

48 Alekseyev, *Your Ramsay*, p. 198.

49 'The Revolution in China, and the Menace of Imperialistic Intervention', *Izvestia*, 216, 7 August 1930.

50 Price, *Lives of Agnes Smedley*, p. 200.

CHAPTER 5

1 Haslam, *Near and Distant Neighbours*, chapter 2.

2 Alekseyev, *Your Ramsay*, p. 211.

3 Alekseyev, *Your Ramsay*, p. 216.

4 After his failed attempt to extract money from Ulanovsky, Pik's next project was another extortion operation. Pik approached a local businessman and huckster, one Israilevich, alias 'Bomont', posing as a Belgian. Pik had got wind of a blackmail scheme that Bomont was attempting against an American woman who ran a Shanghai brothel. Pik had learned of the scheme from one of the prostitutes, a Russian woman named Anna Zalewsky. Zalewsky had demanded $18,000 from her madame, which she proposed to divide with Bomont. Pik demanded a cut of this blackmail operation, threatening to expose Bomont to the American consul. When Bomont refused to include Pik in the deal he made good on his threat to expose Bomont – but got nowhere as it turned out that Bomont was not, as Pik had believed, an American citizen after all. Pik then attempted to blackmail a member of the American consular staff with homosexual revelations, which again backfired after the man committed suicide. At this point Pik turned to literature, letting it be known that he was

writing a sensational book about the private lives of many prominent citizens, including members of the Shanghai Municipal Council. The work was never published, presumably because some of the subjects of the scandalous memoir paid Pik some hush money. At the same time Pik also attempted to expand his circle of spying clients by peddling information to the Shanghai departments of the German Gestapo political police, as well as to Japanese naval intelligence. One of his associates at this time was the extravagant and scandalous Shanghai society hostess who styled herself 'Princess Sumeyer', who claimed to be the daughter of the Indian Maharajah of Patiala. The princess was also a Japanese agent. In the summer of 1941, Pik seems to have turned his hand to contract murder. An anonymous brochure published in Russian in Shanghai, entitled 'Who are you, Evgeny Hovants?', exposed the eponymous Hovants, a prominent member of the local Russian community, as a Soviet police agent. The author, an émigré named Mamontov-Ryabchenko, was shot some months later – and before he died named Pik as the organiser of his murder. For this mis-step Pik was tried in a British Settlement court, found guilty and sentenced to fifteen years in prison. He was, however, released after the Japanese occupied Shanghai and was used once again as an intelligence agent. Pik prepared lists of foreigners he counted as enemies of Japan or linked to foreign espionage services, who should be interned for Japanese naval intelligence. Before the end of the war Pik fled to Japan, but his ship hit a mine. His incredible luck held, however: his leg broken, he was rescued from the sea and delivered safely to Japan. There, posing as a German citizen called 'K. Kluge', he spent several months recovering in hospital in Kyoto. After the Americans occupied Japan, Pik was arrested and imprisoned in Sugamo prison in Tokyo as a war criminal, but was released after a few months. It is likely that he was recruited by American intelligence and worked for them for some years after the war. See Alekseyev, *Your Ramsay*, pp. 218–19; Viktor Usov, *Sovietskaya Razvedka v Kitae 20–iye gody XX veka*, Moscow, 2007, pp. 356–7.

5 Alekseyev, *Your Ramsay*, p. 227.
6 Price, *Lives of Agnes Smedley*, p. 211.
7 Ruth Werner, *Sonja's Rapport*, Berlin, 1977, p. 44.
8 Alekseyev, *Your Ramsay*, p. 307.
9 Alekseyev, *Your Ramsay*, p. 313.
10 Werner, *Sonja's Rapport*, p. 55.
11 Sorge Memoir, Pt 7, 'General remarks on Efficiency', p. 146.
12 Paul Monk, 'Christopher Andrew and the Strange Case of Roger Hollis', *Quadrant* magazine, 1 April 2010.

13 http://fbistudies.com/wp-content/uploads/2015/04/20150417_
ReportandChronologyHollis.pdf.

14 The evidence seems compelling that MI5 had kept tabs on Ursula Kuczynski
and her husband and fellow Soviet agent, Len Beurton, in Oxford;
knew they were active and dangerous communists, and had reasons to
at least suspect that they were in fact agents working for the Fourth
Department. 'Sonja' was already a known communist before she moved to
Oxford in 1940. Hollis was expressly warned about the couple by his staff.
Yet Hollis chose in every case to set aside such warnings and do nothing
about them. He was personally responsible for preparing and sending
reports to the US intelligence services about dangerous communists in
Britain who might be of possible concern to the United States – yet he
omitted all mention of Kuczynski in every such report. Hollis cleared the
Soviet atomic spy Klaus Fuchs and others, whose 'controller' or courier
was 'Sonja' herself.

On two separate occasions Hollis refused permission for US
intelligence officers to interview 'Mrs Beurton', arguing that this would
serve no useful purpose and that she was merely a harmless housewife. He
arranged for himself and Kim Philby to be the recipients of reports from
the Radio Security Service and then, according to two key and credible
wit-nesses, consistently marked their reports that there was an illegal
wireless transmitter operating in the Oxford area: 'No Further Action'.
Years later, while Hollis was under investigation by Peter Wright and
other British counter-intelligence officers, it was learned that his Peking
roommate – the retired British Army officer, Captain Anthony Staples –
recalled that Hollis had been visited there both by an American woman
and a German man: Agnes Smedley and Arthur Ewert. Ewert was the
Comintern's chief secret agent in China. Could he have been Hollis's
recruiter? Many in British counter-intelligence believed so. That Hollis
knew Karl and Luise Rimm (GRU operatives who joined the Shanghai
rezidentura after Sorge's departure for Tokyo), likewise came out only
much later. There is also evidence that Luise Rimm had a love affair with
Roger Hollis lasting three years, until the Rimms were recalled to Moscow.
For many years, Hollis also obfuscated that he had travelled via Moscow
to and from England in the 1930s, immediately before applying for a job
at MI5. He also said nothing about who he met while he was there. His
contacts with Comintern officers in Shanghai, the fact of Hollis's 1934
and 1936 visits to Moscow, and a fortnight's visit to Paris in November
1937, have led to the suspicion that Hollis was recruited by the GRU. For
example, his visit to Paris was made immediately after he had been offered
a job at MI5 to start the following year. Paris was the epicentre of Soviet

intelligence operations in Western Europe, including Britain. 'Sonja' also visited London in 1938, the year Hollis began work at MI5; she was posted to Oxford by the GRU immediately after Hollis's job at MI5 required him to move to nearby Blenheim Palace, from late 1940 until 1943. 'Sonja' then became the courier and controller of Klaus Fuchs, whom Hollis cleared; and he insistently shielded her from all surveillance or interference throughout the 1940s. Writing from behind the Iron Curtain as Ruth Werner, 'Sonja' declared coyly that she often felt she had had a protective hand within MI5 during the 1940s. The record is clear that Hollis was that protective hand, for reasons that make no apparent sense unless he was the agent 'Elli' and was working, like Sonja, for the GRU. See Paul Monk, PhD, and John L. Wilhelm, 'British Patriot or Soviet Spy? Clarifying a Major Cold War Mystery. An Analysis of Chapman Pincher's Indictment of Sir Roger Hollis', presented at the Institute of World Politics, Washington, DC, 10 April 2015.

15 This story is based on the testimony of Einar Sanden, which remains to be corroborated. It comes very late in Pincher's account of the case and depends upon alleged tape recordings of interviews with Luise Rimm in her old age. If it could be authenticated, it would certainly add to the many threads of evidence suggesting that Hollis was recruited by the GRU and that those soundings began in China in the early 1930s. See Chapman Pincher, *Their Trade is Treachery*, London, 1981, chapter 11.

16 'Extracts', Police interrogation, Hotsumi Ozaki, 5 March and 21 July 1942, ID 923289, RG 319. For more on Ozaki and Smedley see Chalmers Johnson, *An Instance of Treason: Ozaki Hotsumi and the Sorge Spy Ring*, Stanford, CA, 1990.

17 'Extracts', Police Interrogation, Hotsumi Ozaki, 5 March and 21 July 1942.

18 'Extracts', Police Interrogation, Hotsumi Ozaki, 8 March 1942.

19 Whymant, *Stalin's Spy*, p. 36.

20 Toshito (ed.), *Gendai-shi Shiryo*, Vol. 2, p. 8.

21 Price, *Lives of Agnes Smedley*, p. 217.

22 Werner, *Sonja's Rapport*, p. 55.

23 Deakin and Storrey, *Case of Richard Sorge*, p. 87.

24 Alekseyev, *Your Ramsay*, p. 355.

25 Frederick S. Litten, 'The Noulens Affair', *China Quarterly*, No. 138, June 1994, pp. 492–512.

26 Sorge reported that an intermediary had suggested a $50,000 bribe to the Chinese judges to release his wife Tatiana Moyesenko in December 1931. In May 1932, Centre actually sent a $20,000 bribe in an attempt to commute the Noulens' life sentence passed by a Chinese court in Nanking the previous August.

27 Alekseyev, *Your Ramsay*, p. 401.

28 Historian James Weland has concluded that senior commanders had tacitly allowed field operatives to proceed on their own initiative, then endorsed the result after a positive outcome was assured (James Weland, 'Misguided Intelligence: Japanese Military Intelligence Officers in the Manchurian Incident, September 1931', *Journal of Military History*, 58 (3), 1994, pp. 445–60).

29 Each year at 10 a.m. on 18 September, air-raid sirens sound for several minutes in numerous major cities across China in commemoration.

30 Deakin and Storrey, *Case of Richard Sorge*, p. 64.

31 Robert H. Ferrell, 'The Mukden Incident: September 18–19, 1931', *Journal of Modern History* 27 (1), 1955, pp. 66–72.

32 Jay Taylor, *The Generalissimo: Chiang Kai-shek and the Struggle for Modern China*, Cambridge, MA, 2009, p. 93.

33 Prange interview with Teikichi Kawai, 13 January 1965, *Target Tokyo*; Toshito (ed.), *Gendai-shi Shiryo*, Vol. 2, p. 208; Johnson, *Instance of Treason*, p. 80.

34 Price, *Lives of Agnes Smedley*, p. 218.

35 Alekseyev, *Your Ramsay*, p. 407.

36 Alekseyev, *Your Ramsay*, p. 407.

37 See Jamie Bisher, *White Terror: Cossack Warlords of the Trans-Siberian*, London, 2009.

38 Alekseyev, *Your Ramsay*, p. 412.

39 'Extracts', Police Interrogation, Teikichi Kawai, 31 March 1949.

40 Deakin and Storrey, *Case of Richard Sorge*, p. 76.

41 Toshito (ed.), *Gendai-shi Shiryo*, Vol. 2, p. 105.

42 'Extracts', Police Interrogation, Teikichi Kawai, March 1949–1 April 1949.

43 Deakin and Storrey, *Case of Richard Sorge*, p. 81.

44 Wakeman Jr, *Policing Shanghai*, p. 160.

45 Alekseyev, *Your Ramsay*, p. 632.

CHAPTER 6

1 Sorge Memoir, Pt 6, 'Espionage of my group in Japan', p. 134.

2 Sorge Memoir, Pt 6, 'Espionage of my group in Japan', p. 135.

3 'Extracts', Examination No. 10 by Preliminary Judge, 28 July 1942; Deakin and Storrey, *Case of Richard Sorge*, p. 95.

4 Sorge Memoir, Pt 6, 'Espionage of my group in Japan', p. 136.

5 Raymond W. Leonard, *Secret Soldiers of the Revolution: Soviet Military Intelligence*, 1918–1933, Westport, Conn. and London, 1999, p. 17.

6 N. S. Cherushev, and J. N. Cherushev, *Rasstrelenaya Elita PKKA* (*Komandiry 1ogo i 2ogo rangov, Komkory, Komdivy, i im ravniye*): *1937–41*, Moscow, 2012, pp. 322–496.

7 Prange et al., *Target Tokyo*, p. 96.

8 Alekseyev, *Your Ramsay*, p. 279.

9 Volodarsky, *Stalin's Agent*, p. 206.

10 Ya Gorev, 'Ya Znal Sorge', *Pravda*, 1964, p. 13.

11 Deakin and Storrey, *Case of Richard Sorge*, p. 101.

12 Massing, *This Deception*, p. 69.

13 Toshito (ed.), *Gendai-shi Shiryo*, Vol. 1, p. 228.

14 Curt Reiss, *Total Espionage*, New York, 1941, pp. 88–9, 219; *Democratic Idea: The Myth and Reality* is perhaps Haushofer's best-known work.

15 Evgeny Sergeev, *Russian Military Intelligence in the War with Japan*, 1904–05, London, 2012, p. 28.

16 Reiss, *Total Espionage*, p. 219.

17 Toshito (ed.), *Gendai-shi Shiryo*, Vol. 1, p. 228.

18 Toshito (ed.), *Gendai-shi Shiryo*, Vol. 1, p. 229.

19 Deakin and Storrey, *Case of Richard Sorge*, p. 100.

20 Hede Massing, 'The Almost Perfect Russian Spy', *True*, December 1951, p. 96.

21 Toshito (ed.), *Gendai-shi Shiryo*, Vol. 1, p. 348.

22 Toshito (ed.), *Gendai-shi Shiryo*, Vol. 1, p. 334.

23 Toshito (ed.), *Gendai-shi Shiryo*, Vol. 3, p. 315.

24 Toshito (ed.), *Gendai-shi Shiryo*, Vol. 3, p. 315.

25 Ralph de Toledano, *Spies, Dupes, and Diplomats*, New York, 1952, pp. 70–1.

CHAPTER 7

1 Quoted in Michael Yudell (ed.), *Richard Sorge: A Chronology*, richardsorge.com, 1996.

2 Toshito (ed.), *Gendai-shi Shiryo*, Vol. 1, pp. 228, 359.

3 Toshito (ed.), *Gendai-shi Shiryo*, Vol. 1, p. 229.

4 Deakin and Storrey, *Case of Richard Sorge*, p. 108.

5 Deakin and Storrey, *Case of Richard Sorge*, p. 109.

6 Whymant, *Stalin's Spy*, p. 49.

7 Whymant, *Stalin's Spy*, p. 51.

8 Deakin and Storrey, *Case of Richard Sorge*, p. 110.

9 See Edward Behr, *Hirohito: Behind the Myth*, New York, 1989, chapter 5.

10 Saionji, who had spent time in republican Paris during the Commune in the 1870s, distrusted the role of military men in politics. He admired England and likened the role of the emperor to that of the British

monarchy, aloof from politics except in exceptional circumstances; that is a constitutional monarch as well as a theocratic sovereign. Deakin and Storrey, *Case of Richard Sorge*, p. 104.

11 Deakin and Storrey, *Case of Richard Sorge*, p. 113.

12 Prange interview with Araki, 6 January 1965, *Target Tokyo*.

13 Toshito (ed.), *Gendai-shi Shiryo*, Vol. 1, p. 230.

14 *Der Spiegel*, 20 June 1951, p. 29.

15 John Wheeler-Bennett, *The Nemesis of Power*, London, 1967, pp. 127–8.

16 *Der Spiegel*, 20 June 1951, p. 28; Reiss, *Total Espionage*, p. 9; Dirksen, *Moscow, Tokyo, London*, p. 143.

17 Toshito (ed.), *Gendai-shi Shiryo*, Vol. 3, p. 163; 'Sorge's Notes', and 'Extracts', Interrogation of Richard Sorge, 22 December 1941, p. 27, Record Group 319, File ID923289, Pt 47, Box 7484, Pt XV, p. 192.

18 'Extracts', Preliminary Judge Examination of Sorge No. 10, 28 July 1942.

19 Article IV in Kinjiro Nakamura, *Zoruge, Ozaki Hotzumi Supai Jiken No Zenbo: Soren Wa Subete o Shitte Ita* ('The Entire Picture of the Sorge-Ozaki Hotzumi Spy Incident' – hereafter *Entire Picture*), Osaka, 1949, p. 17.

20 Toshito (ed.), *Gendai-shi Shiryo*, Vol. 1, p. 267.

21 Review of Dusan Cvetic, 'Who Was Branko Vukelić?', *Yugoslav Monthly Review*, October 1964, p. 38.

22 *Yugoslavia Monthly Review*, October 1964, p. 38; Toshito (ed.), *Gendai-shi Shiryo*, Vol. 3, p. 635.

23 *Comrade Sorge: Documents and Memoirs*, p. 14.

24 Toshito (ed.), *Gendai-shi Shiryo*, Vol. 3, pp. 66–7.

25 Hugo Klein went on to become a well-known Zagreb psychoanalyst; Milo Budak was later an extreme right-wing Croat politician and minister of education in Pavelic's independent state of Croatia. Deakin and Storrey, *Case of Richard Sorge*, p. 119.

26 Toshito (ed.), *Gendai-shi Shiryo*, Vol. 1, p. 345.

27 His reluctance was shared even by many committed French communist intellectuals of the time, who did not see spying as an acceptable task. For example, Henri Barbé, a leading figure in the French Communist Party, indignantly refused Jan Berzin's proposal in Moscow in 1931 (Deakin and Storrey, *Case of Richard Sorge*, p. 121).

28 Stahl is one of the fascinating characters to have walk-on parts in the Sorge story. According to one encyclopedia of Soviet intelligence, she was born in 1885 in Rostov-on-Don and went on to marry and have children with a wealthy nobleman. The family moved to New York after the revolution and Stahl studied for a degree at Colombia University. After the death of her son in 1918 she lived in Paris and moved in Bolshevik circles. She ran a photography shop where she copied documents for Soviet intelligence.

After a spell back in New York she returned to Paris from 1931–33, when she was arrested for espionage and jailed for five years. See Robert K. Baker, *Rezident: The Espionage Odyssey of Soviet General Vasily Zarubin*, Bloomington, 2015, chapter 5.

29 Deakin and Storrey, *Case of Richard Sorge*, p. 123.

30 Toshito (ed.), *Gendai-shi Shiryo*, Vol. 3, p. 623.

31 Toshito (ed.), *Gendai-shi Shiryo*, Vol. 1, p. 347

32 Toshito (ed.), *Gendai-shi Shiryo*, Vol. 1, p. 348.

33 Whittaker Chambers, *Witness*, New York, 1952, p. 87. See also David J. Dallin, Soviet Espionage, New Haven, 1955, pp. 60–6.

34 Toshito (ed.), *Gendai-shi Shiryo*, Vol. 3, p. 624; introduction to Vol. 3, p. xiii; Prange interview with Vukelić's interrogator, Ken Fuse, 22 January 1965, *Target Tokyo*.

35 Toshito (ed.), *Gendai-shi Shiryo*, Vol. 3, p. 628.

36 Toshito (ed.), *Gendai-shi Shiryo*, Vol. 1, p. 351.

37 Toshito (ed.), *Gendai-shi Shiryo*, Vol. 1, p. 350; Vol. 3, pp. 628–9; 'Extracts', Interrogation of Richard Sorge, 22 December 1941, p. 27.

38 Prange et al., *Target Tokyo*, p. 94.

39 Toshito (ed.), *Gendai-shi Shiryo*, Vol. 3, p. 637; Sorge Memoir, Pt 2, p. 7.

40 Toshito (ed.), *Gendai-shi Shiryo*, Vol. 3, p. 162; Vukelić did not use his home as a sending site until May 1938.

41 'Police Bureau Report of Sorge Case', cited in Prange et al., *Target Tokyo*, p. 34.

42 Toshito (ed.), *Gendai-shi Shiryo*, Vol. 3, pp. 308–09, 636; *Japan Advertiser*, 6–9 December 1933.

43 Prange et al., *Target Tokyo*, p. 94.

44 Toshito (ed.), *Gendai-shi Shiryo*, Vol. 3, p. 313.

45 Toshito (ed.), *Gendai-shi Shiryo*, Vol. 3, p. 311.

46 Toshito (ed.), *Gendai-shi Shiryo*, Vol. 3, p. 315.

47 'The Sorge Spy Ring: A Case Study in International Espionage in the Far East', in *US Congressional Record, 81st Congress, First Session*, Vol. 95, Part 12, Appendix, 9 February 1949, p. A711.

48 Toshito (ed.), *Gendai-shi Shiryo*, Vol. 3, pp. 308, 311.

49 It is also conceivable, though unlikely, that Roy was Manebendra Nath Roy, an Indian member of the Comintern who also used the name Roy – or so General Willoughby suggests (*Shanghai Conspiracy*, p. 54). Chalmers Johnson points out that Roy was in prison at the time (*Instance of Treason*, p. 94n.); also, it seems odd for a recruiter to use his real name in such a conspiratorial situation.

50 Toshito (ed.), *Gendai-shi Shiryo*, Vol. 3, pp. 308, 311.

51 Toshito (ed.), *Gendai-shi Shiryo*, Vol. 3, p. 312; 'Sorge Spy Ring', p. A716.

52 Toshito (ed.), *Gendai-shi Shiryo*, Vol. 3, pp. 308–09, 636; according to the case summary in Vol. I, p. 29, Wendt made the initial contact with both Miyagi and Vukelić. But both Miyagi's and Sorge's testimony (Vol. I, p. 349) indicate that the go-between with Miyagi was Vukelić.

53 Whymant, *Stalin's Spy*, p. 53.

CHAPTER 8

1 *New York Times*, 25 August 2017.

2 Sorge Memoir, Pt 6, 'Espionage of my group in Japan', p. 137.

3 Toshito (ed.), *Gendai-shi Shiryo*, Vol. I, p. 230.

4 Herbert von Dirksen, *Moscow, Tokyo, London*, London, 1951, pp. 135, 142.

5 Dirksen, *Moscow, Tokyo, London*, p. 154.

6 Sorge Memoir, p. 54.

7 Toshito (ed.), *Gendai-shi Shiryo*, Vol. I, p. 227.

8 Whymant, *Stalin's Spy*, p. 57.

9 Prange interviews with Araki, 6 and 11 January 1965, *Target Tokyo*.

10 Whymant, *Stalin's Spy*, p. 61.

11 Deakin and Storrey, *Case of Richard Sorge*, p. 140.

12 Toshito (ed.), *Gendai-shi Shiryo*, Vol. I, pp. 234–5.

13 Prange interviews with Araki, 6 and 11 January 1965, *Target Tokyo*.

14 Dirksen, *Moscow, Tokyo, London*, p. 143.

15 Toshito (ed.), *Gendai-shi Shiryo*, Vol. I, pp. 236–7.

16 Prange et al., *Target Tokyo*, p. 110.

17 Founded in 1903, now the Tsingtao Brewery; Deakin and Storrey, *Case of Richard Sorge*, p. 142.

18 The Japanese, in stark contrast to their treatment of Allied prisoners during the Second World War, treated their First World War German prisoners of war with conspicuous respect.

19 *Comrade Sorge: Documents and Memoirs*, p. 16.

20 Deakin and Storrey, *Case of Richard Sorge*, p. 137.

21 Whymant, *Stalin's Spy*, p. 69.

22 Whymant, *Stalin's Spy*, p. 69.

23 Prange et al., *Target Tokyo*, p. 119.

24 Prange interview with Hanako, 11 January 1965, *Target Tokyo*. Sorge's house succumbed to the fire bombings late in the Second World War.

25 *Der Spiegel*, 3 August 1951, p. 28.

26 Toshito (ed.), *Gendai-shi Shiryo*, Vol. I, p. 231; V. Kudriatsev, 'I Meet Richard Sorge', *Izvestia*, 1–7 November 1964; Deakin and Storrey, *Case of Richard Sorge*, p. 141.

27 See Hans-Otto Meissner, *The Man with Three Faces*, New York, 1956, p. vi.

28 Sorge Memoir, Pt 2, p. 19.

29 Whymant, *Stalin's Spy*, p. 62.

30 Toshito (ed.), *Gendai-shi Shiryo*, Vol. 1, p. 230.

31 Sorge Memoir, Pt 2, pp. 19–20.

32 Deakin and Storrey, *Case of Richard Sorge*, p. 125.

33 *Comrade Sorge: Documents and Memoirs*, p. 18.

34 Toshito (ed.), *Gendai-shi Shiryo*, Vol. 1, pp. 246–7.

35 Toshito (ed.), *Gendai-shi Shiryo*, Vol. 3, pp. 61–2.

36 Toshito (ed.), *Gendai-shi Shiryo*, Vol. 3, p. 308.

37 Toshito (ed.), *Gendai-shi Shiryo*, Vol. 3, p. 317.

38 Toshito (ed.), *Gendai-shi Shiryo*, Vol. 3, p. 311.

39 Toshito (ed.), *Gendai-shi Shiryo*, Vol. 1, p. 28; Vol. 2, p. 211; Vol. 3, p. 308. Miyagi recalled his initial meeting with Ozaki as being in late spring, probably May 1934.

40 Toshito (ed.), *Gendai-shi Shiryo*, Vol. 2, p. 211.

41 See Johnson, *Instance of Treason*, p. 98.

42 See English translation by Lawrence Rogers published in J. Thomas Rimer, (ed.), *Patriots and Traitors, Sorge and Ozaki: A Japanese Cultural Casebook*, Maine, 2009.

43 Toshito (ed.), *Gendai-shi Shiryo*, Vol. 2, pp. 131–2.

44 Toshito (ed.), *Gendai-shi Shiryo*, Vol. 2, pp. 106–08; Johnson, *Instance of Treason*, pp. 99–100.

45 Toshito (ed.), *Gendai-shi Shiryo*, Vol. 2, p. 126; Johnson, *Instance of Treason*, pp. 99–100. In 1951 and 1958, uncensored editions were published with Ozaki's true byline.

46 Prange et al., *Target Tokyo*, p. 108.

47 Toshito (ed.), *Gendai-shi Shiryo*, Vol. 2, pp. 219–20; Vol. 1, p. 236.

48 Prange interview with Mitsusada Yoshikawa, 16 January 1965, *Target Tokyo*.

49 Prange et al., *Target Tokyo*, p. 108.

50 Dirksen, *Moscow, Tokyo, London*, pp. 144–5.

51 Toshito (ed.), *Gendai-shi Shiryo*, Vol. 1, p. 237.

52 Dirksen, *Moscow, Tokyo, London*, pp. 145–6.

53 Young, *Japan's Total Empire*, pp. 31–2.

54 'Provisional Convention ... concerning the junction of the Japanese and Russian Railways in Manchuria', 13 June 1907, *Carnegie Endowment for International Peace, Manchuria: Treaties and Agreements*, Reprint Biblio Bazaar, 2009, p. 108.

55 Toshito (ed.), *Gendai-shi Shiryo*, Vol. 1, pp. 237, 232. In the summer of 1938 Thomas was involved in a plot with several other disaffected German

generals to capture Hitler and proclaim Germany under a military dictatorship, in an attempt to save the country from the Nazis. Later Thomas was associated with the abortive, disastrous attempt on Hitler's life (Wheeler-Bennett, *Nemesis of Power*, pp. 414–27, 560).

56 *Der Spiegel*, 20 June 1951, p. 29.

57 Prange interviews with Araki, 6 and 11 January 1965, *Target Tokyo*.

58 *Der Spiegel*, 27 June 1951, p. 23.

59 See Deutsche Architechtur Museum, 'Ernst May 1886–1970: New Cities on Three Continents', 2011.

60 May's plans for the city were never realised. He left the USSR in 1933, disillusioned with the socialist paradise, and went to British East Africa – now Kenya – where he created many modernist buildings.

61 Guerin and Chatel, *Camarade Sorge*, p. 86.

62 Hanako Ishii, *Ningen Zoruge, Aijin Miyake Hanako no Shuki* ('The Man Sorge, Memoirs of His Mistress Miyake Hanako'), Tokyo, 1956, pp. 52–3; Prange interview with Hanako, 7 February 1965, *Target Tokyo*.

63 Toshito (ed.), *Gendai-shi Shiryo*, Vol. 1, p. 235.

64 Aino Kuusinen, *God Throws Down His Angels: Memoirs for the Years 1919–1965*, Helsinki, 1972, p. 77.

65 Whymant, *Stalin's Spy*, p. 79.

66 Toshito (ed.), *Gendai-shi Shiryo*, Vol. 2, p. 212; 'Extracts', Kawai Statement, p. 11, Record Group 319, File ID 923289, Pt 46, Box 7384.

67 Sorge Memoir, Pt 2, p. 15.

68 Toshito (ed.), *Gendai-shi Shiryo*, Vol. 2, p. 212; 'Extracts', Kawai Statement, p. 12.

69 Sorge Memoir, Pt 7, 'General remarks on efficiency', p. 145.

70 Toshito (ed.), *Gendai-shi Shiryo*, Vol. 1, p. 349; Vol. 2, pp. 137, 276; also Johnson, *Instance of Treason*, pp. 100, 238.

CHAPTER 9

1 Massing, *This Deception*, p. 68.

2 'Extracts', Pt XV, Sorge's Notes, pp. 201–03, Record Group 319, File ID 923289, Pt 37, Box 7482.

3 'Extracts', Pt XV, Sorge's Notes, p. 202; Prange et al., *Target Tokyo*, p. 125.

4 Sorge Memoir, Pt 2, p. 5.

5 The Norwegian photographer Eirik Sundvor memorialised 1935 Soviet Moscow. Many of his photographs have been preserved in the municipal archives in Trondheim, Norway.

6 *Comrade Sorge: Documents and Memoirs*, pp. 20, 21.

7   *Comrade Sorge: Documents and Memoirs*, p. 21.

8   *Comrade Sorge: Documents and Memoirs*, p. 27.

9   *Comrade Sorge: Documents and Memoirs*, p. 21.

10 Jan Valtin, *Out of the Night*, London, 1941, p. 276.

11 Mink was tried together with another American, Nicholas Sherman, and condemned to eighteen months' imprisonment for espionage on behalf of a foreign power (*New York Times*, 31 July 1935). After serving his sentence Mink returned to Moscow, from where he was sent to Barcelona. Under the name of Alfred Herz he was at that time publicly charged by the anarchists as the organiser of two political murders. Having successfully fulfilled his mission in Spain, Mink was next reported, sometime in April 1938, as being on his way to Mexico. He was suspected of also playing a leading role in organising the assassination of Leon Trotsky – but if he was in Mexico at the time he managed to keep completely under cover. See A. I. Kolpakidi, and D. P. Prokhorov, *Imperiya GRU*, Moscow, 1999, chapter 8.

12 TNA, HW 17/18, Radio Telegram London–Moscow, 18 May 1935.

13 Volodarsky, *Stalin's Agent*, p. 22.

14 D. P. Prokhorov, *Skolko Stoit Prodat' Rodinu?*, St Petersburg, 2005.

15 Yu Geller, 'On the 70th Anniversary of the Birth of S. P. Uritskii', *Krasnaya Zveda*, 2 March 1965. Uritskii was killed in the Stalinist purges.

16 Kolpakidi, and Prokhorov, *Imperiya GRU*, p. 87.

17 Toshito (ed.), *Gendai-shi Shiryo*, Vol. 1, p. 358.

18 Sorge Memoir, Pt 2, p. 27; Toshito (ed.), *Gendai-shi Shiryo*, Vol. 1, p. 356; 'Extracts', Interrogation of Richard Sorge, 22 December 1941, p. 28.

19 Sorge Memoir, Pt 2, p. 27; Toshito (ed.), *Gendai-shi Shiryo*, Vol. 1, pp. 236, 361.

20 Sorge Memoir, Pt 2, p. 27; 'Extracts', Interrogation of Richard Sorge, 22 December 1941, p. 28.

21 Toshito (ed.), *Gendai-shi Shiryo*, Vol. 3, p. 61.

22 'Extracts', Pt XVI, Clausen Notes, p. 246, Record Group 319, File ID 923289, Pt 37, Box 7482; 'Extracts,' Interrogation of Richard Sorge, 20 December 1941; Deakin and Storrey, *Case of Richard Sorge*, p. 156.

23 'Sorge Spy Ring', p. A709.

24 Toshito (ed.), *Gendai-shi Shiryo*, Vol. 3, pp. 55–6, 437, 455–6.

25 Toshito (ed.), *Gendai-shi Shiryo*, Vol. 3, pp. 55–6, 437, 455–6; ibid., pp. 36, 458.

26 Toshito (ed.), *Gendai-shi Shiryo*, Vol. 3, pp. 57–8.

27 Toshito (ed.), *Gendai-shi Shiryo*, Vol. 3, p. 58.

28 Clausen says April but Berzin had already resigned by that time, so either his conversation was with Berzin earlier than he remembered or indeed in

April, but with Uritsky. It is much more likely that Max confused the date than the identity of his interlocutor at this life-changing confrontation.

29 'Extracts', Pt XVI, Clausen testimony, original p. 560, Record Group 319, File ID 923289, Box 5 F8–18.

30 Toshito (ed.), *Gendai-shi Shiryo*, Vol. 3, p. 59.

31 Toshito (ed.), *Gendai-shi Shiryo*, Vol. 3, p. 62.

32 *Comrade Sorge: Documents and Memoirs*, p. 32.

33 Whymant, *Stalin's Spy*, p. 72.

34 Whymant, *Stalin's Spy*, p. 73.

35 *Comrade Sorge: Documents and Memoirs*, p. 29.

36 Toshito (ed.), *Gendai-shi Shiryo*, Vol. 1, pp. 352–3. Sorge kept this to himself until sure his case would not be turned over to the Kempeitai.

37 *Comrade Sorge: Documents and Memoirs*, p. 32.

38 *Comrade Sorge: Documents and Memoirs*, p. 29.

39 'Extracts', Pt XV, Sorge's Notes, p. 201.

40 'Extracts', Pt XV, Sorge's Notes, p. 202.

41 Massing, *This Deception*, pp. 67–8.

CHAPTER 10

1 Meissner, *Man with Three Faces*, p. vi.

2 Toshito (ed.), *Gendai-shi Shiryo*, Vol. 3, p. 298; Vol. 2, p. 212.

3 Prange interview with Kawai, 13 January 1965, *Target Tokyo*.

4 Prange interview with Kawai, 13 January 1965, *Target Tokyo*.

5 Toshito (ed.), *Gendai-shi Shiryo*, Vol. 3, p. 398.

6 Toshito (ed.), *Gendai-shi Shiryo*, Vol. 3, p. 250.

7 Toshito (ed.), *Gendai-shi Shiryo*, Vol. 2, p. 265.

8 Sorge Memoir, Pt 2, p. 14. Chalmers Johnson wrote that Shinotsuka 'was dropped before he learned too much' (*Instance of Treason*, p. 110). Yet Shinotsuka testified that he met with Ozaki and Miyagi from around autumn 1935 to February 1941 (Toshito, ed., *Gendai-shi Shiryo*, Vol. 2, p. 265).

9 Toshito (ed.), *Gendai-shi Shiryo*, Vol. 3, p. 398.

10 Prange interviews with Hanako, 9 and 11 January 1965; interview with Karl Keitel, son of Helmut ('Papa') Keitel, on Prange's behalf, 23 March 1965, *Target Tokyo*.

11 Hanako Ishii, *Ningen Zoruge*, pp. 1–10. Interviews with Hanako, 7 and 9 January 1965, *Target Tokyo*.

12 Prange interviews with Hanako, 7 and 11 January 1965, *Target Tokyo*.

13 Hanako Ishii, *Ningen Zoruge*, p. 12.

14 Hanako Ishii, *Ningen Zoruge*, p. 13.

15 Hanako Ishii, *Ningen Zoruge*, p. 91.

16 Hanako Ishii, *Ningen Zoruge,* p. 13.

17 Prange interview with Hanako, 9 January 1965, *Target Tokyo.*

18 Hanako Ishii, *Ningen Zoruge*, pp. 14, 15.

19 Hanako Ishii, *Ningen Zoruge*, p. 48.

20 Toshito (ed.), *Gendai-shi Shiryo*, Vol. 3, pp. 64, 234.

21 'Extracts', Pt XVI, Clausen testimony, original p. 566.

22 Prange et al., *Target Tokyo*, p. 146.

23 Guerin and Chatel, *Camarade Sorge*, p. 82.

24 Sorge Memoir, Pt 2, p. 7.

25 'Extracts', Pt XI, Summary of Radio Communications Facilities, p. 156.

26 Prange interview with Procurator Mitsusada Yoshikawa, 16 January 1965, *Target Tokyo.*

27 'Extracts', interrogation of Kawai; Toshito (ed.), *Gendai-shi Shiryo*, p. 104; Johnson, *Instance of Treason*, p. 110.

28 'Extracts', interrogation of Kawai; Toshito (ed.), *Gendai-shi Shiryo*, p. 105.

29 'Extracts', Pt XI, Summary of Radio Communications Facilities, p. 156.

30 'Extracts', Interrogation of Richard Sorge, 22 December 1941, p. 28; Police Report, p. 22; Johnson, *Instance of Treason*, p. 107.

31 Toshito (ed.), *Gendai-shi Shiryo*, Vol. 3, p. 162; 'Extracts', Clausen testimony, p. 9; Guerin and Chatel, *Camarade Sorge*, pp. 84–5.

32 Toshito (ed.), *Gendai-shi Shiryo*, Vol. 3, pp. 3, 103.

33 'Extracts', Pt XI, Summary of Radio Communications Facilities, p. 156. Clausen correctly guessed that 'Wiesbaden' was Vladivostok, but he also suggested to his interrogators that it may have been Khabarovsk or Komsomolsk-na-Amure.

34 Hugh Byas, *Government by Assassination*, New York, 1942; 2017 edition, pp. 120–1.

35 Byas, *Government by Assassination*, pp. 123–4.

36 Dirksen, *Moscow, Tokyo, London*, pp. 150–52.

37 Toshito (ed.), *Gendai-shi Shiryo*, Vol. 1, p. 253.

38 Byas, *Government by Assassination*, p. 122.

39 Byas, *Government by Assassination*, pp. 124–5.

40 *Japan Times*, 28 February 1936.

41 Joseph C. Grew, *Ten Years in Japan*, New York, 1944, pp. 188–9.

42 Kita's book, *A Reconstruction Programme for Japan* (1919), had Marxist overtones and had long been banned. Possibly the Kita connection plus Ozaki's hints that the uprising had an agrarian background may account for Sorge's telling Urach that the Japanese communists might have been

connected with the incident (Deakin and Storrey, *Case of Richard Sorge*, p. 174).

43 Toshito (ed.), *Gendai-shi Shiryo*, Vol. 3, p. 253.

44 Toshito (ed.), *Gendai-shi Shiryo*, Vol. 3, pp. 253, 251.

45 Toshito (ed.), *Gendai-shi Shiryo*, Vol. 1, p. 253. Unbeknown to Sorge, the Fourth Department *rezident* in Copenhagen, Walter Krivitsky, had also obtained a Japanese diplomatic code cipher book, allowing Soviet signals intelligence to read all the confidential telegrams that passed between Oshima and Tokyo (see Jeffery T. Richelson, *A Century of Spies: Intelligence in the Twentieth Century*, Oxford, 1997, p. 89).

46 Toshito (ed.), *Gendai-shi Shiryo*, Vol. 3, p. 241.

47 Prange et al., *Target Tokyo*, p. 179.

48 Toshito (ed.), *Gendai-shi Shiryo*, Vol. 1, p. 255.

49 Toshito (ed.), *Gendai-shi Shiryo*, Vol. 1, p. 256.

50 John W. M. Chapman, 'A Dance on Eggs: Intelligence and the "Anti-Comintern"', *Journal of Contemporary History*, Vol. 22, No. 2, Intelligence Services during the Second World War, April 1987, pp. 333–72.

51 Sorge Memoir, Pt 2, p. 25.

52 Dirksen, *Moscow, Tokyo, London*, p. 156.

53 Dirksen, *Moscow, Tokyo, London*, p. 153.

54 Chapman, 'A Dance on Eggs', *JCH*. 'In 1933, in a power struggle between Hermann Göring and Heinrich Himmler against Ribbentrop, the people around Ribbentrop were also closely investigated by Heydrich's security service. The results of this investigation have not survived archival destruction. One of these individuals was Dr Friedrich Wilhelm Hack, who was arrested, interrogated, and so frightened that he left at the earliest opportunity for exile in Switzerland, where he was installed as an informant of the Japanese Navy's intelligence service up to the end of the war in Europe. According to one Japanese source, it was discovered that he was non-Aryan; according to General Oshima, he was accused of being a homosexual, a crime under Article 175 of the German Penal Code.

55 Toshito (ed.), *Gendai-shi Shiryo*, Vol. 1, pp. 248, 255.

56 'Letters between Sorge and his wife Katya', *Ogonek* magazine, April 1965, p. 25.

57 Hanako Ishii, *Ningen Zoruge*, pp. 18–19.

58 *Der Spiegel*, 8 August 1951, pp. 25–6.

59 This letter was probably one of the items Sorge carried when he made a courier-run to Peking in August 1936 (see Toshito (ed.), *Gendai-shi Shiryo*, Vol. 1, pp. 305–06; Sorge Memoir, Pt 2, p. 5).

60 *Comrade Sorge: Documents and Memoirs*, p. 27.

61 Alekseyev, *Your Ramsay*, p. 313.

62 *Der Spiegel*, 8 August 1951, p. 28.

63 Meissner, *Man with Three Faces*, p. vi.

64 Toshito (ed.), *Gendai-shi Shiryo*, Vol. 2, p. 451.

65 Toshito (ed.), *Gendai-shi Shiryo*, Vol. 3, p. 3.

66 Toshito (ed.), *Gendai-shi Shiryo*, Vol. 3, pp. 425–6; Guerin and Chatel, *Camarade Sorge*, p. 84.

67 Johnson, *Instance of Treason*, pp. iii, 113.

68 Toshito (ed.), *Gendai-shi Shiryo*, Vol. 2, pp. 222, 224.

69 Toshito (ed.), *Gendai-shi Shiryo*, Vol. 2, p. 279.

70 Toshito (ed.), *Gendai-shi Shiryo*, Vol. 2, p. 279.

71 Toshito (ed.), *Gendai-shi Shiryo*, Vol. 2, p. 224. Even when Ozaki's treason was revealed, Saionji remained a firm friend, attempting to intercede to save Ozaki from execution and insisting that his betrayal was undertaken for patriotic motives. (See Johnson, *Instance of Treason*, p. 113.) Saionji was among the suspected communist sympathisers arrested in the Sorge case, but he escaped with a three-year suspended sentence ('Sorge Spy Ring', p. A722).

72 Aino Kuusinen, *Before and After Stalin: A Personal Account of Soviet Russia from the 1920s to the 1960s*, London, 1974, p. 117.

73 Dirksen, *Moscow, Tokyo, London*, pp. 173–4.

74 Chapman, 'A Dance on Eggs', *JCH*.

75 The full text of the Anti-Comintern Pact, the accessory protocol, and the secret agreement which accompanied it appear, among other sources, in Tokyo Judgments, Vol. II, 'Sorge Memoir' in Willoughby, *Shanghai Conspiracy*, pp. 832–3.

76 Grew, *Ten Years in Japan*, p. 191.

77 Alekseyev, *Your Ramsay*, p. 313.

78 Kuusinen, *Before and After Stalin*, pp. 119–20.

CHAPTER 11

1 John le Carré in *Encounter* magazine, November 1966.

2 Richard Pipes, *Communism: A History*, New York, p. 67.

3 Marc Jansen, and Nikolai Petrov, *Stalin's Loyal Executioner: People's Commissar Nikolai Ezhov, 1895–1940*, Stanford, CA, 2002, p. 42.

4 Vadim Rogovin, *1937: Stalin's Year of Terror*, Oak Park, MI, 1998, pp. 36–8.

5 Jansen and Petrov, *Stalin's Loyal Executioner*, p. 45.

6 Courtois et al., *Black Book of Communism*, pp. 298–301.

7 Smedley saw him for the last time in Moscow in 1934. After his execution she wrote of Chattopadhyaya: 'He embodied the tragedy of a whole race.

Had he been born in England or America, I thought, his ability would
have placed him among the great leaders of his age ... He was at last
growing old, his body thin and frail, his hair rapidly turning white. The
desire to return to India obsessed him, but the British would trust him only
if he were dust on a funeral pyre.' (Agnes Smedley, *China Correspondent*,
London and Boston, 1943, reprint edition, 1984, p. 99).

8 Edvard Radzinski, *Stalin*, London, 1997, p. 171.
9 Leonard, *Secret Soldiers of the Revolution*, p. 152.
10 Igor Lukes, *Czechoslovakia Between Stalin and Hitler: The Diplomacy of Edvard Beneš in the 1930s*, Oxford, 1996.
11 Volodarsky, *Stalin's Agent*, p. 231.
12 Christina Shelton, *Alger Hiss: Why He Chose Treason*, New York, pp. 47–50.
13 Alexander Barmine, *One Who Survived*, New York, 1945, pp. xi–xii.
14 Chambers, *Witness*, p. 36.
15 Boris Gudz interview, ORT television, Razvedchik, September 1999.
16 Gudz interview, ORT, 1999.
17 Gudz interview, ORT, 1999.
18 Gudz interview, ORT, 1999.
19 An exhibition on Shalamov, featuring a photograph of Gudz's denunciation, was held at the Museum of Moscow in May 2017.
20 Excerpts from an article by Catherine Moore, based on letters from her father, Honor Guard Howard Wills (June 1945–January 1946) http://generalmacarthurshonorguard.com.
21 Prange interview with Hanako, 9 January 1965, *Target Tokyo*.
22 Robert Whymant interview with Hanako, *Stalin's Spy*, p. 89.
23 Robert Whymant interview with Hanako, *Stalin's Spy*, p. 90.
24 *Comrade Sorge: Documents and Memoirs*, p. 29.
25 Almost certainly number 22 – the only large apartment house on that embankment.
26 *Comrade Sorge: Documents and Memoirs*, p. 27.
27 Installed for the benefit of blind passengers.
28 *Comrade Sorge: Documents and Memoirs*, p. 30.
29 *Comrade Sorge: Documents and Memoirs*, p. 31.
30 British embassy report: Viscount Chilston to Mr Eden, 6 February 1937, British Foreign Office Correspondence, 1937, Reel 4, Vol. 21099, p. 206.
31 Chiefs of Soviet Military intelligence:

   • Jan Berzin, 1924–April 1935
   • Semyon Uritsky, April 1935–July 1937
   • Jan Berzin, July 1937–August 1937
   • Alexander Nikonov, August 1937–August 1937

- Semyon Gendin, September 1937–October 1938
- Alexander Orlov, October 1938–April 1939
- Ivan Proskurov, April 1939–July 1940
- Filipp Golikov, July 1940–October 1941
- Alexei Panfilov, October 1941–November 1942

(source: Owen A. Lock, 'Chiefs of the GRU 1918–46', in Hayden B. Peake and Samuel Halpern (eds.), *In the Name of Intelligence: Essays in Honor of Walter Pforzheimer*, Washington, DC, 1994, pp. 353–78.)

32 Fesyun, *Documents*, 'The Unknown Sorge', p. 139.

33 Fesyun, *Documents*, 'The Unknown Sorge', p. 140.

34 Chambers, *Witness*, p. 36.

35 Whymant, *Stalin's Spy*, p. 62.

36 *Der Spiegel*, 27 June 1951, pp. 23–4.

37 'Sorge Spy Ring', p. A716.

38 Sorge Memoir, Pt 2, pp. 14–15.

39 Sorge Memoir, Pt 2, p. 15.

40 Toshito (ed.), *Gendai-shi Shiryo*, Vol. 3, p. 310.

41 Nikolai Dolgopolov, 'Why Stalin Didn't Exchange Sorge', *Rossiyskaya Gazeta*, 1 October 2015; Gudz interview, ORT.

42 Jay Taylor, The Generalissimo: Chiang Kai-shek and the Struggle for Modern China, Cambridge, MA, 2009, especially pp. 124–37.

43 Steve Tsang, 'Chiang Kai-shek's "secret deal" at Xian and the start of the Sino-Japanese War', *Palgrave Communications*, Vol. 1, 2015.

44 Wang Bingyang.

45 John W. Garver, 'The Soviet Union and the Xi'an Incident [Arrest Of Chiang Kaishek, 1936]', *Australian Journal of Chinese Affairs*, No. 26, July 1991, pp. 145–75.

46 Edgar Snow, *Random Notes on China*, Cambridge, MA, 1957, pp. x, 21.

47 Toshito (ed.), *Gendai-shi Shiryo*, Vol. 2, p. 220.

48 Sir Robert Craigie, *Behind the Japanese Mask*, London, 1945, p. 69.

49 Toshito (ed.), *Gendai-shi Shiryo*, Vol. 2, p. 161.

50 Bob Tadashi Wakabayashi, 'Emperor Hirohito on Localised Aggression in China', *Sino-Japanese Studies* 4 (1), 1991, p. 15.

CHAPTER 12

1 Sayle, *London Review of Books*, 22 May 1997.

2 *Der Spiegel*, 1 August 1941, p. 31.

3 Prange interview with Hanako, 7 January 1965, *Target Tokyo*.

4 Deakin and Storrey, *Case of Richard Sorge*, p. 198.

5 Toshito (ed.), *Gendai-shi Shiryo*, Vol. 3, pp. 5, 181.

6 Toshito (ed.), *Gendai-shi Shiryo*, Vol. 1, pp. 374, 259–60.

7 Meissner, *Man with Three Faces*, p. 159.

8 Deakin and Storrey, *Case of Richard Sorge*, pp. 198–9.

9 Whymant, *Stalin's Spy*, p. 99.

10 Whymant, *Stalin's Spy*, p. 102.

11 Lt Col. Philip R. Faymonville, US military attaché, Moscow, 'Comments on Statements of Fugitive Generals', to Assistant Chief of Staff, G-2, War Department, 1 August 1938 (1282319.1), quoted in Willoughby, *Shanghai Conspiracy*.

12 Alvin D. Coox, ' "The lesser of two hells": NKVD general G. S. Lyushkov's defection to Japan, 1938–1945, part I', *The Journal of Slavic Military Studies*, 11 (3), 1998, pp. 145–86.

13 Anton Antonov-Ovseyenko, *The Time of Stalin: Portrait of a Tyranny*, New York, 1981, p. 162; *Asahi Shimbun*, 2 July 1938; *Tokyo Nichi-Nichi Shimbun*, 2 July 1938

14 *Asahi Shimbun* (*Extra*), 2 July 1938.

15 Cipher officer Vladimir Petrov, who would later follow Lyushkov's lead and himself defect.

16 Petrov does not identify the bullying officer by name but it is clear from his description that it is Lyushkov, then commander of the Black Sea region NKVD (see Vladimir and Evdokia Petrov, *Empire of Fear*, London, 1956, pp. 74–5).

17 Coox, 'Lesser of two hells', *JSMS*.

18 Blyukher, despite his German name, was in fact was born into a Russian peasant family named Gurov in the village of Barschinka in Yaroslavl Governorate. In the nineteenth century a landlord had given his father the nickname Blyukher because he resembled the famous Prussian marshal, Gebhard Leberecht von Blücher (1742–1819). Vasily Gurov – a factory worker before the First World War – formally assumed Blyukher as his surname. He joined the army of the Russian Empire in 1914 and served as a corporal until discharged in 1915 after being seriously wounded (see W. Bruce Lincoln, *Red Victory: A History of the Russian Civil War*, New York, 1999; reprint 1989, p. 443).

19 Alvin Coox, interviews with Nishimura Ko and Yabe Chuta, 'Lesser of two hells', *JSMS*.

20 In the event, Lyushkov's family sent the telegram but did not escape. Ina Lyushkova was interrogated so brutally in the Lubyanka prison that she was brought back to her cell on a stretcher. 'They simply tore her apart. Then they liquidated [Lyushkov's] parents in Odessa. And all his relatives,' a source told NKVD defector Antonov Ovseyenko (see Anton

Antonov-Ovseyenko, *The Time of Stalin: Portrait of a Tyranny*, New York, 1981, p. 162 n. 2). Also Coox interview with Yabe Chuta, 'Lesser of two hells', *JSMS*.

21 Coox, 'Lesser of two hells', *JSMS*.

22 Toshito (ed.), *Gendai-shi Shiryo*, Vol. 2, p. 265.

23 Based on Tokyo Asahi, 14 July 1938 (a.m. ed.), p. 2; *New York Times*, 14 July 1938, p. 13; Tokyo 13 July. Quoted in Coox, 'Lesser of two hells', *JSMS*.

24 Coox, 'Lesser of two hells', *JSMS*.

25 Coox interview with Kohtani Etsuo, 'Lesser of two hells', *JSMS*.

26 'The Battle of Lake Khasan Reconsidered', *Journal of Slavic Military Studies*, Vol. 29, No. 1, 2016, 99–109.

27 Alvin Coox, *Nomonhan*, Stanford, 2003, p. 124.

28 Quoted in Dmitri Volkogonov, *Triumph and Tragedy*, ('Triumf i tragediia: politicheskii portret I.V. Stalina'), Moscow, 1989, pp. 272–3. See Hiroaki Kuromiya, 'The Mystery of Nomonhan, 1939', *Journal of Slavic Military Studies*, 24 (4), 2011, pp. 659–77.

29 Stuart D. Goldman, *Nomonhan, 1939: The Red Army's Victory that Shaped World War II*, Annapolis, MD, 2012.

30 Coox, *Nomonhan*, 2003, p. 135.

31 'O sobytiyakh v raione ozera Khasan', *Izvestiya*, No. 187, 6654, 12 August 1938, p. 1.

32 A. A. Koshkin, 'Kantokuen – the Japanese Barbarossa. Why Japan did not attack the USSR', *Veche*, 2011. pp. 51–7.

33 Volkogonov, *Triumph and Tragedy*, p. 242.

34 Jansen, and Petrov, *Stalin's Loyal Executioner*, p. 145.

CHAPTER 13

1   Guerin and Chatel, *Camarade Sorge*, pp. 37–8.

2   *Comrade Sorge: Documents and Memoirs*, p. 22.

3   *Der Spiegel*, 8 August 1951, p. 27.

4   Toshito (ed.), *Gendai-shi Shiryo*, Vol. 2, p. 167.

5   Guerin and Chatel, *Camarade Sorge*, pp. 37–8.

6   Toshito (ed.), *Gendai-shi Shiryo*, Vol. 2, p. 168.

7   Prange et al., *Target Tokyo*, chapter 23.

8   Toshito (ed.), *Gendai-shi Shiryo*, Vol. 2, p. 220.

9   Toshito (ed.), *Gendai-shi Shiryo*, Vol. 2, pp. 140, 164–5.

10 For a list of Ozaki's published works, see Johnson, *Instance of Treason*, pp. 259–62.

11 More properly called the Toa Kyodo Tai, or 'East Asian Cooperative Body' – but better known as 'The Greater East Asia Co-Prosperity Sphere' in the West.

12 Johnson, *Instance of Treason*, p. 119.

13 Toshito (ed.), *Gendai-shi Shiryo*, Vol. 2, p. 227.

14 Interestingly, the South Manchuria Railway was deeply infiltrated by communists – though its not clear whether this was a factor in Ozaki being hired, since he was careful to avoid any public association with known party members. Out of approximately one thousand Investigation Department employees, about thirty were communists, overt or covert. They had organised an efficient little investigation department of their own within the official department. Among them were two former associates of Ozaki's from Shanghai days, Ko Nakanishi and Kuraji Anzai. The aim of the department had been to collect source data for the Kwangtung Army and the General Staff in the furtherance of Japan's expansionism. Yet the means whereby the information was gathered and evaluated came close to academic freedom. Hence the company was able to employ a number of intellectuals either blind to the dichotomy or else able to rationalise that the means justified the ends. When one Suehiro Okami joined the department, he espoused the Marxist economic theory, a decision that played an important part in forming the organisation's policies – and presumably its recruitment of personnel. See Kodama Daizo, 'A Secret Record: The Mantetsu Chosabu', *Chuo Koron*, December 1960, pp. 192–6.

15 Toshito (ed.), *Gendai-shi Shiryo*, Vol. 3, p. 175.

16 'Sorge Spy Ring', pp. A715–16.

17 'Sorge Spy Ring', pp. A715–16.

18 Sorge Memoir, Pt 1, p. 8; Toshito (ed.), *Gendai-shi Shiryo*, Vol. 1, pp. 441, 452; 'Sorge Spy Ring', p. A716.

19 Toshito (ed.), *Gendai-shi Shiryo*, Vol. 2, p. 440.

20 Toshito (ed.), *Gendai-shi Shiryo*, Vol. 2, pp. 433–34.

21 Toshito (ed.), *Gendai-shi Shiryo*, Vol. 2, pp. 440, 435, 462.

22 Toshito (ed.), *Gendai-shi Shiryo*, Vol. 3, pp. 156, 221–2. At this time, Sorge paid himself between 600–800 yen a month and gave 300–400 yen a month to Miyagi. Ozaki had no regular wages, although Sorge helped defray transportation and social expenses. According to Sorge, Moscow allowed him $10,000 a year, with a maximum expenditure of $1,000 each month (Toshito, ed., *Gendai-shi Shiryo*, Vol. 1, pp. 478–9; Vol. 2, pp. 116–17).

23 Robert J. C. Butow, *Tojo and the Coming of the War*, Princeton, 1961, pp. 33, 74, 115.

24 Office of US Chief of Council for Prosecution of Axis Criminals, Nazi Conspiracy and Aggression, VII, pp. 753–4, quoted in David J. Dallin, *Soviet Russia and the Far East*, New Haven, 1948, p. 150.

25 Coox, *Nomonhan*, 2003, pp. 191–2.

26 Timothy Neeno, *Nomonhan: The Second Russo-Japanese War*, www.militaryhistoryonline.com, 2005.

27 Toshito (ed.), *Gendai-shi Shiryo*, Vol. 1, p. 381.

28 Toshito (ed.), *Gendai-shi Shiryo*, Vol. 2, p. 169.

29 Neeno, *Nomonhan*.

30 H. Ogi, *Shihyo Nomonhan*, Tokyo, 1986, pp. 318–20.

31 I. Hata (ed.), *Nihon Riku kaigun sogo jiten*, Tokyo, 1991, p. 59.

32 This testimony was published by Russian historians Teodor Gladkov and N. G. Zaitsev in 1983.

33 Around 1960, when a Japanese specialist of Hungarian and Uralic languages visited Estonia to attend an academic meeting, a Soviet woman came to his hotel to enquire about Komatsubara, with whom she said she had been 'intimate' when he was a military attaché 'in Estonia' (see I. Matsumoto, *Ota Kakumin to nichiro koryu Tokyo*, Minerva, 2006, pp. 214–17, quoted in Kuromiya, 'Mystery of Nomonhan, 1939', *JSMS*).

34 T. K. Gladkov and N. G. Zaitsev, *I ia emu ne mogu ne verit ...*, Moscow, 1986, pp. 215–16. Komatsubara is misspelled as Kamatsubara. Gladkov repeated this in his subsequent publications: *Nagrada za vernost'– kazn*, pp. 247–78 (Moscow, 2000), and *Artuzov Moscow: Molodaia gvardiia*, Moscow, 2008, p. 399.

35 *Vechernaya Moskva*, 26 February 1929, p. 2.

36 Kuromiya, 'Mystery of Nomonhan, 1939', *JSMS*.

37 Dimitar Nedialkov, *In the Skies of Nomonhan, Japan vs Russia, May–September 1939*, 2011, Manchester, p. 144.

38 G. F. Krivosheeva (ed.), *Grif sekretnosti sniat: poteri Vooruzhennykh Sil SSSR v voynakh, boevykh deystviyakh i voennykh konfliktakh*, Moscow, 1993, pp. 77–85.

CHAPTER 14

1 Office of US Chief of Council, quoted in Dallin, *Soviet Russia*, p. 150.

2 Otto Friedrich, *City of Nets: A Portrait of Hollywood in the 1940s*, Berkeley, CA, 1997, p. 24.

3 Office of US Chief of Council, quoted in Dallin, *Soviet Russia*, p. 150.

4 Hermann Rauschning, *Hitler Speaks: A Series of Political Conversations with Adolf Hitler on His Real Aims*, London, 2006, pp. 136–7.

5 F. I. Chuev, V. H. Molotov, and Albert Resis, *Molotov Remembers, Inside Kremlin Politics, Conversations with Felix Chuev*, Chicago, 1991, p. 23.

6 William L. Shirer, *The Rise and Fall of the Third Reich: A History of Nazi Germany*, New York, 1990, p. 668.

7 Chuev et al., *Molotov Remembers*, p. 24.

8 Aleksandr Moiseevich Nekrich et al., *Pariahs, Partners, Predators: German–Soviet Relations, 1922–1941*, New York, p. 123.

9 Nekrich et al., *Pariahs, Partners, Predators*, pp. 128–9.

10 Steven J. Zaloga, and Howard Gerrard, *Poland 1939: The Birth of Blitzkrieg*, Oxford, 2002, p. 8

11 Bundesarchiv, Bild 101I-121-0011A-22, Polen, Siegesparade, Guderian, Kriwoschein.

12 Toshito (ed.), *Gendai-shi Shiryo*, Vol. 1, p. 384.

13 Toshito (ed.), *Gendai-shi Shiryo*, Vol. 1, pp. 267–8.

14 General Ivan Proskurov, director April 1939–July 1940.

15 Fesyun, *Documents*, Doc. 38, pp. 55–6, pp. 48–9.

16 Toshito (ed.), *Gendai-shi Shiryo*, Vol. 3, p. 176.

17 Whymant, *Stalin's Spy*, p. 110.

18 Prange et al., *Target Tokyo*, p. 332.

19 *Tokyo Advertiser*, 3 February 1938.

20 Joseph Newman, *Goodbye Japan*, New York, 1942, pp. 161, 163.

21 Prange interview with Saito, 23 January 1965, *Target Tokyo*.

22 Prange interview with Saito, 23 January 1965, *Target Tokyo*.

23 Prange interview with Saito, 23 January 1965, *Target Tokyo*.

24 Prange interview with Hanako, 7 January 1965, *Target Tokyo*.

25 Interview with Shigeru Aoyama conducted on behalf of Prange by Ms Chi Harada, 1965, *Target Tokyo*.

26 Hanako Ishii, *Ningen Zoruge*, pp. 60–1.

27 Toshito (ed.), *Gendai-shi Shiryo*, Vol. 3, p. 5.

28 Toshito (ed.), *Gendai-shi Shiryo*, Vol. 3, p. viii.

29 Guerin and Chatel, *Camarade Sorge*, p. 268.

30 Whymant, *Stalin's Spy*, p. 132.

31 Prange interview with Suzuki, 18 January 1965, *Target Tokyo*.

32 Prange interview with Hanako, 7 January 1965, *Target Tokyo*.

33 Guerin and Chatel, *Camarade Sorge*, p. 268.

34 'Extracts', Clausen testimony, p. 10.

35 'Extracts', Clausen testimony, p. 10.

36 Toshito (ed.), *Gendai-shi Shiryo*, Vol. 3, pp. 159, 227.

37 Whymant, *Stalin's Spy*, p. 135.

38 'Extracts', Clausen testimony, p. 41.

39 Toshito (ed.), *Gendai-shi Shiryo*, Vol. 3, p. 108.

40 'Extracts', Clausen testimony, p. 41.

41 Toshito (ed.), *Gendai-shi Shiryo*, Vol. 3, pp. 226–8, 65.

42 Deakin and Storrey, *Case of Richard Sorge*, p. 135.

43 'Extracts', Clausen testimony, p. 561; Toshito (ed.), *Gendai-shi Shiryo*, Vol. 3, p. 64–5.

44 Prange interview with Hanako, 7 January 1965, *Target Tokyo*.

45 Toshito (ed.), *Gendai-shi Shiryo*, Vol. 3, pp. 8, 234.

CHAPTER 15

1 Sorge, *Die Weltwoche*, 11 December 1964.

2 Whymant, *Stalin's Spy*, p. 119.

3 Toshito (ed.), *Gendai-shi Shiryo*, Vol. 1, p. 242.

4 Toshito (ed.), *Gendai-shi Shiryo*, Vol. 1, p. 243.

5 Toshito (ed.), *Gendai-shi Shiryo*, Vol. 1, p. 243.

6 Toshito (ed.), *Gendai-shi Shiryo*, Vol. 1, p. 243.

7 *Der Spiegel*, 15 August 1951, p. 31.

8 Toshito (ed.), *Gendai-shi Shiryo*, Vol. 1, pp. 260, 435.

9 Prange et al., *Target Tokyo*, p. 355.

10 Deakin and Storrey, *Case of Richard Sorge*, pp. 204–06.

11 Sorge Memoir, Pt 2, p. 23.

12 Toshito (ed.), *Gendai-shi Shiryo*, Vol. 1, pp. 390, 403.

13 Toshito (ed.), *Gendai-shi Shiryo*, Vol. 1, p. 452.

14 Toshito (ed.), *Gendai-shi Shiryo*, Vol. 3, p. 182; Vol. 1, p. 452.

15 David E. Murphy, *What Stalin Knew: The Enigma of Barbarossa*, New Haven and London, 2005, p. 141.

16 Murphy, *What Stalin Knew*, p. 138.

17 Article II in Kinjiro Nakamura, *Entire Picture*, p. 24.

18 Article II in Kinjiro Nakamura, *Entire Picture*, p. 24.

19 Toshito (ed.), *Gendai-shi Shiryo*, Vol. 1, p. 177.

20 Toshito (ed.), *Gendai-shi Shiryo*, Vol. 1, p. 232.

21 Guerin and Chatel, *Camarade Sorge*, p. 92.

22 Toshito (ed.), *Gendai-shi Shiryo*, Vol. 1, p. 176.

23 Herbert Feis, *Road to Pearl Harbor: The Coming of the War Between the United States and Japan*, Princeton, NJ, 1971, 2015, p. 78.

24 Prange et al., *Target Tokyo*, p. 367.

25 Feis, *Road to Pearl Harbor*, p. 113.

26 Toshito (ed.), *Gendai-shi Shiryo*, Vol. 3, p. 173.

27 Cornelia Schmitz-Berning, *Vokabular des Nationalsozialismus*, Berlin, 2007, p. 745.

28 Feis, *Road to Pearl Harbor*, p. 116.

29 'Three-Power Pact Between Germany, Italy, and Japan, Signed at Berlin, September 27, 1940', Yale Law School, Lillian Goldman Law Library, Avalon Law Project.

30 Fesyun, *Documents*, p. 144.

31 Fesyun, *Documents*, p. 145.

32 Fesyun, *Documents*, p. 145.

33 In notable contrast to the various tragicomically inept commercial ventures that Moscow had financed as cover operations in Shanghai that had included a cannery, and a tyre import business.

34 'Extracts,' Clausen Testimony, p. 566; Toshito (ed.), *Gendai-shi Shiryo*, Vol. 3, pp. 160, 195, 224.

35 Toshito (ed.), *Gendai-shi Shiryo*, Vol. 3, p. 234.

36 Prange interview with Hanako, 7 January 1965, *Target Tokyo*.

37 Geoffrey Regan, *Book of Military Anecdotes*, London, 1992, p. 210.

38 Admiral Karl Dönitz, *Memoirs*, London, 1958; 1997, p. 114.

39 Gordon Wright, *The Ordeal of Total War: 1939–1945*, New York, 1968, p. 32. There is some debate about whether Hitler actually ever intended to invade Britain. Reichsmarschall Hermann Göring, commander-in-chief of the Luftwaffe, believed the invasion could not succeed and doubted whether the German air force would be able to win control of the skies; nevertheless he hoped that an early victory in the Battle of Britain would force the British government to negotiate, without any need for an invasion. Adolf Galland, commander of Luftwaffe fighters at the time, claimed invasion plans were not serious and that there was a palpable sense of relief in the Wehrmacht when it was finally called off. Generalfeldmarschall Gerd von Rundstedt also took this view and thought that Hitler never seriously intended to invade Britain and the whole thing was a bluff to put pressure on the British government to come to terms following the Fall of France (see David Shears on the German invasion plans in Richard Cox (ed.), *Operation Sea Lion*, London, 1975, p. 158, and Richard Overy, *The Battle of Britain: Myth and Reality*, London, 2010).

40 Stephen Bungay, *The Most Dangerous Enemy: A History of the Battle of Britain*, London, 2009, p. 337.

41 John Lukacs, *The Duel: Hitler vs. Churchill 10 May–31 July 1940*, London, 2000, chapter 7.

42 Stephen Fritz, *Ostkrieg: Hitler's War of Extermination in the East*, Lexington, 2011, p. 51.

43 Toshito (ed.), *Gendai-shi Shiryo*, Vol. 1, p. 271.

44 James P. Duffy, *Hitler's Secret Pirate Fleet: The Deadliest Ships of World War II*, Lincoln, Nebraska, 2005, pp. 22–4.

45 James Rusbridger, and Eric Nave, *Betrayal at Pearl Harbor*, New York, 1991, p. 311.

46 For his feat, after the fall of Singapore in 1942, Captain Rogge received from the Emperor of Japan a samurai sword of honour, that been given to only two other Germans, Hermann Göring and Erwin Rommel.

47 John W. M. Chapman, *The Price of Admiralty: The War Diary of the German Attaché in Japan 1939–1943*, Lewes, Sussex, 1989, chapter 5.

48 Ken Kotani, *Japanese Intelligence in World War II*, Osprey, Oxford, 2009, p. 102.

49 Wenneker's diary recalls: '[Vice-Admiral] Kondo repeatedly expressed to me how valuable the information in the [British] War Cabinet memorandum was for the [Japanese] Navy. Such a significant weakening of the British Empire could not have been identified from outward appearances.' Rusbridger and Nave, *Betrayal at Pearl Harbor*, p. 212.

50 Reiss, *Total Espionage*, pp. 203–04.

51 Toshito (ed.), *Gendai-shi Shiryo*, Vol. 1, p. 277.

52 Toshito (ed.), *Gendai-shi Shiryo*, Vol. 3, p. 272.

53 Sorge Memoir, Pt 2, p. 18.

54 Hanako Ishii, *Ningen Zoruge*, pp. 100–01; Prange interview with Hanako, 7 January 1965, *Target Tokyo*.

55 Viktor Anfilov, *Doroga k Tragedii Sorok Pervogo Goda*, Moscow, 1997, p. 195.

56 Ovidy Gorchakov, 'Nakanune ili Tragedia Kassandry', *Gorizont*, No. 6, 1988, p. 31.

57 Fesyun, *Documents*, No. 11.

CHAPTER 16

1 Walter Schellenberg, *The Schellenberg Memoirs*, London, 1956, p. 177 (known in later editions as *The Labyrinth*).

2 Schellenberg, *Memoirs*, p. 160.

3 Schellenberg, *Memoirs*, p. 161.

4 Schellenberg was sentenced to six years in jail and died in Italy in 1952.

5 Chunikhin, *Richard Sorge: Notes*, p. 121.

6 John W. M. Chapman, 'A Dance on Eggs: Intelligence and the "Anti-Comintern"', *Journal of Contemporary History*, Vol. 22, No. 2, Intelligence Services during the Second World War, April 1987, pp. 333–72.

7 Eta Harich-Schneider, *Charaktere und Katastrophen*, Berlin, 1978, p. 203.

8 Michael Wildt, *Generation des Unbedingten*, Hamburg, 2003, p. 478.

9 'Swiss Neutral Claims Nazis are Still on the Loose in Japan', *Spartanburg Herald-Journal*, 12 May 1946, p. A5.

10 Schellenberg, *Memoirs*, p. 160.

11 Schellenberg, *Memoirs*, p. 161.

12 Harich-Schneider, *Charaktere und Katastrophen*, p. 206.

13 Whymant, *Stalin's Spy*, p. 152.

14 Toshito (ed.), *Gendai-shi Shiryo*, Vol. 1, pp. 270–72.

15 Feis, *Road to Pearl Harbor*, pp. 146–7.

16 Toshito (ed.), *Gendai-shi Shiryo*, Vol. 2, p. 272.

17 Winston S. Churchill, *The Grand Alliance*, Boston, 1950, pp. 162–63, 361.

18 Chuev et al., *Molotov Remembers*, pp. 44–6.

19 Deakin and Storrey, *Case of Richard Sorge*, p. 226.

20 Toshito (ed.), *Gendai-shi Shiryo*, Vol. 1, p. 272.

21 Toshito (ed.), *Gendai-shi Shiryo*, Vol. 1, p. 392.

22 Toshito (ed.), *Gendai-shi Shiryo*, Vol. 1, p. 391.

23 Deakin and Storrey, *Case of Richard Sorge*, p. 227.

24 Toshito (ed.), *Gendai-shi Shiryo*, Vol. 2, p. 345.

25 Toshito (ed.), *Gendai-shi Shiryo*, Vol. 1, p. 349.

26 Document Nr. 103202/06. After Georgy Zhukov became Chief of the General Staff in February 1941, the plan was renamed 'MP 41' (Mobilisatsyonni Plan 41). ZAMO, f. 15A, op. 2154, d.4,l. 199–287. See Igor Bunich, *Operatsia Groza*, 3 vols, 1994–2004.

27 Meretskov was a remarkable survivor. He was arrested by the NKVD as a member of an alleged anti-Soviet military conspiracy on 23 July 1941. After being subjected to two months of torture, including being beaten with rubber truncheons, in the Lubyanka, Meretskov signed a written confession that was used against other commanders arrested in May–July 1941, who were executed on the order of NKVD chief Lavrenty Beria near Kuybyshev on 28 October 1941. Meretskov was released in September 1941, presented to Stalin in full army uniform, and given command of the 7th Army. He helped to break the Siege of Leningrad, and in April 1945 led a Soviet invasion of Japanese Manchuria. He died, a decorated Hero of the Soviet Union, in 1968.

28 See Bunich, *Operatsia Groza*.

29 See 'Unquestionable Facts of the War's Beginning', in *Voenno-istorichesky Zhournal*, the official military-historical journal of the Russian forces, February 1992,

30 Toshito (ed.), *Gendai-shi Shiryo*, Vol. 2, p. 175; Vol. 1, pp. 247–9.

31 Toshito (ed.), *Gendai-shi Shiryo*, Vol. 2, p. 175; Vol. 1, pp. 247–9.

32 Wheeler-Bennett, *Nemesis of Power*, pp. 127–29, 611–12 n.

33 Toshito (ed.), *Gendai-shi Shiryo*, Vol. 1, p. 274.

34 Murphy, *What Stalin Knew*, p. 144.

35 Murphy, *What Stalin Knew*, p 145.

36 Murphy, *What Stalin Knew*, pp. 146–7.

37 Murphy, *What Stalin Knew*, p. 147.

38 Anne Nelson, *Red Orchestra: The Story of the Berlin Underground and the Circle of Friends Who Resisted Hitler*, New York, 2009 pp. 189–92.

39 Nelson, *Red Orchestra*, pp. 189–92.

40 Nelson, *Red Orchestra*, pp. 189–92.

41 Konstantin Umansky.

42 Murphy, *What Stalin Knew*, pp. 147–8.

43 Murphy, *What Stalin Knew*, p. 149.

44 Herrnstadt had been working for the Soviets since the early 1930s, and after his expulsion from the USSR, along with most other German correspondents, he moved to Warsaw, where he developed a Sorge-like relationship with the German ambassador Hans-Adolf von Moltke, who frequently sought his advice and through whom he was able to meet, assess, and recruit several individuals who would produce outstanding intelligence reports.

45 Murphy, *What Stalin Knew*, p. 147, 'Proskurov Sets Stalin Straight', chapter 3.

46 When the invasion actually came, Leeb commanded Army Group North (Leningrad), Bock Army Group Centre (Moscow), and Rundstedt Army Group South (Kiev).

47 Murphy, *What Stalin Knew*, p. 147, chapter 3.

48 Rodric Braithwaite, *Moscow 1941: A City and its People at War*, London, 2007, p. 58.

CHAPTER 17

1 Harich-Schneider, *Charaktere und Katastrophen*, p. 245.

2 Toshito (ed.), *Gendai-shi Shiryo*, Vol. 3, pp. 109, 164.

3 Toshito (ed.), *Gendai-shi Shiryo*, Vol. 3, p. 190.

4 Fesyun, *Documents*, No. 148, Decoded Telegram No. 8298 to the Chief of the Intelligence Directorate of the Red Army General Staff, Tokyo, 19 May 1941.

5 Ovidy Gorchakov, 'Nakanune ili Tragedia Kassandry', *Gorizont*, No. 6, 1988, pp. 31, 43.

6 Toshito (ed.), *Gendai-shi Shiryo*, Vol. 3, pp. 164, 197.

7 Toshito (ed.), *Gendai-shi Shiryo*, Vol. 3, pp. 164, 197, 109, 164, 178.

8 Erich Kordt, *Nicht aus den Akten*, Stuttgart, 1950, p. 426.

9 Spy Week lasted from 11–17 May, placing Sorge's conversation with Kordt just after his meeting with Scholl.

10 Kordt, *Nicht aus den Akten*, p. 427.

11 Guerin and Chatel, *Camarade Sorge*, pp. 87–8.

12 Whymant, *Stalin's Spy*, p. 184.

13 Hanako Ishii, *Ningen Zoruge*, p. 109.

14 Hanako Ishii, *Ningen Zoruge*, p. 109; Prange Interview with Hanako, 7 January 1965, *Target Tokyo*.

15 Whymant, *Stalin's Spy*, p. 153.

16 Schellenberg, *Memoirs*, p. 177.

17 Hanako Ishii, *Ningen Zoruge*, p. 112.

18 *Der Spiegel*, 5 September 1951.

19 Hanako Ishii, *Ningen Zoruge*, p. 125.

20 *Der Spiegel*, 5 September 1951.

21 *Der Spiegel*, 5 September 1951.

22 Robert Whymant interview with Harich-Schneider, *Stalin's Spy*, p. 158; also Harich-Schneider, *Charaktere und Katastrophen*, p. 228.

23 Sorge was not present at the welcome dinner held at the embassy in honour of Lt Col. Erwin Scholl on 20 May, which he would surely have attended if he had still been in Tokyo. Sorge's absence suggests that the two old friends just missed each other, and that their reunion occurred after Sorge's return from Shanghai. See Whymant, *Stalin's Spy*, p. 164.

24 Erwin Wickert, *Mut und Übermut: Geschichten aus meinem Leben Gebundene Ausgabe*, Stuttgart, 1992, pp. 177–8.

25 Toshito (ed.), *Gendai-shi Shiryo*, Vol. 1, p. 278.

26 Whymant, *Stalin's Spy*, p. 337 n. 27; also Wickert, *Mut und Übermut*, p. 178.

27 Harich-Schneider, *Charaktere und Katastrophen*, p. 243.

28 Harich-Schneider, *Charaktere und Katastrophen*, p. 245.

29 Harich-Schneider, *Charaktere und Katastrophen*, p. 246.

30 Harich-Schneider, *Charaktere und Katastrophen*, p. 247.

31 Harich-Schneider, *Charaktere und Katastrophen*, p. 248.

32 Whymant, *Stalin's Spy*, p. 163.

33 Fesyun, *Documents*, No. 151, Decoded Telegrams Nos 8914, 8915.

34 Toshito (ed.), *Gendai-shi Shiryo*, Vol. 1, pp. 249, 274.

35 Toshito (ed.), *Gendai-shi Shiryo*, Vol. 3, pp. 164, 197.

36 The dish consists of a beaten sirloin steak marinated in grated onion. Whymant, *Stalin's Spy*, p. 166.

37 Fesyun, *Documents*, No. 151, Decoded Telegrams Nos 8914, 8915.

CHAPTER 18

1 Whymant, *Stalin's Spy*, p. 170.

2 Whymant, *Stalin's Spy*, p. 170.

3 Harich-Schneider, *Charaktere und Katastrophen*, p. 255.

4 Harich-Schneider, *Charaktere und Katastrophen*, p. 256.

5 Harich-Schneider, *Charaktere und Katastrophen*, p. 257.

6 Harich-Schneider, *Charaktere und Katastrophen*, p. 258.

7 Harich-Schneider, *Charaktere und Katastrophen*, p. 258.

8 Whymant, *Stalin's Spy*, p. 173.

9 Whymant, *Stalin's Spy*, p. 174.

10 Fesyun, *Documents*, No. 152.

11 Fesyun, *Documents*, No. 153, Decoded Telegram No. 9917 to the Chief of the Intelligence Directorate, Red Army General Staff, Tokyo, 15 June 1941.

12 Whymant, *Stalin's Spy*, p. 174.

13 Whymant, *Stalin's Spy*, p. 174.

14 Fesyun, *Documents*, No. 154, Decoded Telegram No. 10216. Tokyo, 20 June 1941.

15 A collection of interviews which would later be published as Chuev et al., *Molotov Remembers: Inside Kremlin Politics*.

16 Murphy, *What Stalin Knew*, p. 186.

17 Major General M. Ivanov of the central apparat of military intelligence confirmed that Poskrybyshev ordered up Sorge's file 'one night in 1940' for Stalin to examine, *Asia and Africa Today*, No. 2, 2000, p. 48.

18 Chuev et al., *Molotov Remembers*, pp. 34, 66, 69.

19 Chuev et al., *Molotov Remembers*, pp. 34, 66, 69.

20 Fesyun, *Documents*, Decoded Telegram No. 9917, Tokyo, 15 June 1941.

21 Murphy, *What Stalin Knew*, p. 186.

22 Murphy, *What Stalin Knew*, p. 186.

23 Murphy, *What Stalin Knew*, p. 186.

24 Murphy, *What Stalin Knew*, p. 186.

25 Murphy, *What Stalin Knew*, p. 179.

26 In a 1969 article entitled 'The Lessons of War', Golikov insisted that the most important of all reports was 'Report No. 5' of 15 June 1941, which gave precise figures for the German troops facing each of our border regions – Baltic, Western, and Kiev – from 400 kilometres deep into German territory. 'We also knew the strength of the German troops in Romania and Finland,' Golikov continued: 'From the RU intelligence reports we knew the date of the invasion, and every time Hitler put it off (mainly because his troops were not ready), we reported this to our leaders. We found out and reported all the strategic blueprints for the attack against the USSR drafted by the German General Staff, the main one being the notorious Barbarossa plan.' As there is no archival reference to 'Report No. 5', it seems probable that it is a creature of Golikov's imagination.

Likewise, his claim for its handling, given his usual treatment of Fourth Department reporting (see Murphy, *What Stalin Knew*, p. 210).

27 Murphy, *What Stalin Knew*, p. 88.

28 Whymant, *Stalin's Spy*, p. 178.

29 Harich-Schneider, *Charaktere und Katastrophen*, p. 263.

30 Lloyd Clark, *Kursk: The Greatest Battle: Eastern Front 1943*, London, 2012, p. 70.

31 Braithwaite, *Moscow 1941*, p. 74.

32 Christer Bergstrom, *Barbarossa the Air Battle, July–December 1941*, Hersham, 2007, p. 21.

33 Robert Kirchubel, *Operation Barbarossa 1941*: Army Group Centre, Oxford, 2007, p. 34.

34 David Glantz, *Operation Barbarossa: Hitler's invasion of Russia* 1941, The History Press, 2012, p. 33.

35 Harich-Schneider, *Charaktere und Katastrophen*, p. 91.

36 Wickert, *Mut und Übermut*, p. 69.

37 Wickert, *Mut und Übermut*, p. 69.

38 *Der Spiegel*, 5 September 1951, p. 24.

39 Kordt, *Nicht aus den Akten*, p. 429.

40 Fesyun, *Documents*, No. 156, Telegrams Nos 6058/6897, Moscow to Tokyo, 23 June 1941.

CHAPTER 19

1 Hanako Ishii, *Ningen Zoruge*, p. 145.

2 Toshito (ed.), *Gendai-shi Shiryo*, Vol. 1, p. 284.

3 Toshito (ed.), *Gendai-shi Shiryo*, Vol. 2, p. 229.

4 Toshito (ed.), *Gendai-shi Shiryo*, Vol. 2, pp. 258, 187.

5 Toshito (ed.), *Gendai-shi Shiryo*, Vol. 2, p. 280.

6 Sorge Memoir, Pt 2, p. 24.

7 Sorge Memoir, Pt 2, p. 24.

8 Prange interview with Matsumoto, 8 January 1965, *Target Tokyo*.

9 Toshito (ed.), *Gendai-shi Shiryo*, Vol. 2, p. 258.

10 Toshito (ed.), *Gendai-shi Shiryo*, Vol. 2, p. 187.

11 Toshito (ed.), *Gendai-shi Shiryo*, Vol. 2, p. 192.

12 Toshito (ed.), *Gendai-shi Shiryo*, Vol. 1, p. 292; Vol. 2, p. 178.

13 Toshito (ed.), *Gendai-shi Shiryo*, Vol. 3, pp. 6, 110.

14 Toshito (ed.), *Gendai-shi Shiryo*, Vol. 3, p. 110.

15 Whymant, *Stalin's Spy*, p. 195.

16 Toshito (ed.), *Gendai-shi Shiryo*, Vol. 3, p. 495.

17 Hisaya Shirai, *Kokusai supai Zoruge no sekai senso to kakumei/ Shirai Hisaya hencho*, Tokyo, 2003, chapter 11.
18 Toshito (ed.), *Gendai-shi Shiryo*, Vol. 2, p. 347.
19 Sorge, when Ott reported this conversation, blithely contradicted the ambassador and said that in fact the Russians had far larger air forces than the Germans were aware of – without elaborating on how he might have known such sensitive information.
20 Fesyun, *Documents*, No. 163, Decoded Telegrams Nos 12316, 12310, 12318, 12317 to the Chief of the Intelligence Directorate of the Red Army General Staff, Tokyo, 10 July 1941.
21 Fesyun, *Documents*, No. 163, Decoded Telegrams Nos 12316, 12310, 12318.
22 Toshito (ed.), *Gendai-shi Shiryo*, Vol. 2, p. 275.
23 Fesyun, *Documents*, No. 163, Decoded Telegrams Nos 12316, 12310, 12318, 12317.
24 Fesyun, *Documents*, No. 163, Decoded Telegrams Nos 12316, 12310, 12318, 12317.
25 Fesyun, *Documents*, No. 161, Decoded Telegram Bx., Nos 11583, 11575, 11578, 11581, 11574 to the Chief of the Intelligence Directorate of the Red Army General Staff Tokyo, 3 July 1941.
26 Toshito (ed.), *Gendai-shi Shiryo*, Vol. 1, p. 274.
27 Yury Rubtsov, 'Command is my calling' in *Voyenno-promyshlenny Kuryer*, 13 June 2005.
28 Fesyun, *Documents*, No. 38, Report: 11 August 1941.
29 Prange interview with Kawai, 14 January 1965, *Target Tokyo*.
30 Whymant, *Stalin's Spy*, p. 229.
31 Whymant, *Stalin's Spy*, p. 190, interview with Kawai.
32 Whymant, *Stalin's Spy*, p. 191.
33 Toshito (ed.), *Gendai-shi Shiryo*, Vol. 2, p. 239.
34 Toshito (ed.), *Gendai-shi Shiryo*, Vol. 1, p. 283.
35 Whymant, *Stalin's Spy*, p. 231.
36 Whymant, *Stalin's Spy*, p. 233.
37 Fesyun, *Documents*, Decoded Telegram No. 15374, Tokyo, 12 August 1941.
38 Fesyun, *Documents*, Decoded Telegram No. 15374.
39 Fesyun, *Documents*, Decoded Telegram No. 15374.
40 Toshito (ed.), *Gendai-shi Shiryo*, Vol. 2, p. 253.
41 Whymant, *Stalin's Spy*, p. 241.
42 Whymant, *Stalin's Spy*, p. 241.
43 Harich-Schneider, *Charaktere und Katastrophen*, p. 155.
44 Harich-Schneider, *Charaktere und Katastrophen*, p. 155.
45 Toshito (ed.), *Gendai-shi Shiryo*, Vol. 3, p. 6.
46 Prange interview with Aoyama/Harada, *Target Tokyo*.

47 Prange interview with Aoyama/Harada, *Target Tokyo*.

48 Hanako Ishii, *Ningen Zoruge*, p. 128.

49 Hanako Ishii, *Ningen Zoruge*, p. 113. Interview with Hanako, 14 January 1965, *Target Tokyo*. In this interview, Hanako dated this incident as late July 1941, but in *Ningen Zoruge* she placed it in August.

50 Hanako Ishii, *Ningen Zoruge*, pp. 113–14; Prange interview with Hanako, 14 January 1965, *Target Tokyo*.

51 Prange interviews with Hanako, 11 and 14 January 1965, *Target Tokyo*.

52 Prange interview with Hanako, 14 January 1965, *Target Tokyo*; Hanako Ishii, *Ningen Zoruge*, p. 128.

53 Prange interview with Hanako, 14 January 1965, *Target Tokyo*; Hanako Ishii, *Ningen Zoruge*, p. 129.

54 Prange interview with Hanako, 14 January 1965, *Target Tokyo*; Hanako Ishii, *Ningen Zoruge*, p. 131.

55 Massing, *This Deception*, p. 75.

56 Hanako Ishii, *Ningen Zoruge*, pp. 120–1.

57 Prange interview with Hanako, 14 January 1965, *Target Tokyo*; Hanako Ishii, *Ningen Zoruge*, p. 128.

58 Hanako Ishii, *Ningen Zoruge*, p. 148.

59 Whymant, *Stalin's Spy*, p. 255.

60 Hanako Ishii, *Ningen Zoruge*, p. 145.

CHAPTER 20

1 Prange interviews with Ogata, 20 January 1965, Yoshikawa, 14 January 1965, and Saito, 23 January 1965, *Target Tokyo*.

2 Prange interview with Tamazawa, 21 January 1965, *Target Tokyo*.

3 Toshito (ed.), *Gendai-shi Shiryo*, Vol. 2, pp. 182, 238.

4 Toshito (ed.), *Gendai-shi Shiryo*, Vol. 2, pp. 182–3.

5 Toshito (ed.), *Gendai-shi Shiryo*, Vol. 2, p. 183.

6 Toshito (ed.), *Gendai-shi Shiryo*, Vol. 2, p. 239.

7 'Extracts', Clausen testimony, p. 41.

8 Fesyun, *Documents*, No. 175, Telegram No. 18054, Doc. 176, Telegram No. 180058.

9 Fesyun, *Documents*, No. 177, Telegram No. 18063, Doc. 178, Telegram No. 18068.

10 Fesyun, *Documents*, No. 177, Telegram No. 18063, Doc. 178, Telegram No. 18068.

11 Toshito (ed.), *Gendai-shi Shiryo*, Vol. 2, p. 240.

12 Toshito (ed.), *Gendai-shi Shiryo*, Vol. 2, pp. 184, 240.

13 The Americans noted this redeployment with remarkable accuracy. On 27 November 1941, the US War Department G-2 advised in a memorandum for the chief of staff: '1. It has been reported on good authority, that between 18 and 24 Infantry Divisions and 8 Armored Brigades from the Russian Far Eastern Army have been identified on the Western front. If this is true, between 24 and 18 Divisions and 2 Armored Brigades remain in Eastern Siberia…', FDR Papers, PSF Box 85.

14 'Study of Strategical and Tactical Peculiarities of Far Eastern Russia and Soviet Far East Forces', *Japanese Special Studies on Manchuria*, Vol. XII, Tokyo, 1955, pp. 64–6.

15 Article II in Kinjiro Nakamura, *Entire Picture*, p. 25; Toshito (ed.), *Gendai-shi Shiryo*, Vol. 1, p. 473. Sorge always maintained that he spied to keep the peace and that the Soviet Union would never attack Japan. He barely admitted that Russia might defend itself if Japan attacked (*Gendai-shi Shiryo*, Vol. 1, p. 480). This message, with its emphasis upon potential bombing targets, makes Sorge's pose somewhat shaky.

16 Toshito (ed.), *Gendai-shi Shiryo*, Vol. 1, p. 276.

17 Toshito (ed.), *Gendai-shi Shiryo*, Vol. 3, pp. 213–14, 226, 297, 300; Vol. 1, p. 445.

18 Toshito (ed.), *Gendai-shi Shiryo*, Vol. 3, pp. 185, 230. Edith joined her sister and brother-in-law, Mr and Ms G. Pederson, in a suburb of Perth. Letter, D. R. Anderson to Prange, 26 September 1967, Prange p.829.

19 Guerin and Chatel, *Camarade Sorge*, p. 268.

20 Toshito (ed.), *Gendai-shi Shiryo*, Vol. 3, pp. 66–7.

21 Toshito (ed.), *Gendai-shi Shiryo*, Vol. 1, p. 431.

22 Toshito (ed.), *Gendai-shi Shiryo*, Vol. 3, pp. 66–7, p. 157.

23 Toshito (ed.), *Gendai-shi Shiryo*, Vol. 3, pp. 66–7, p. 157.

24 Prange interview with Yoshikawa, 14 January 1965, *Target Tokyo*; Article I, Kinjiro Nakamura, *Entire Picture*, pp. 21–2.

25 Prange interview with Hanako, 11 January 1965, *Target Tokyo*; Hanako Ishii, *Ningen Zoruge*, pp. 146–7.

26 Prange interview with Hanako, 11 January 1965, *Target Tokyo*; Hanako Ishii, *Ningen Zoruge*, pp. 146–7.

27 Prange interview with Hanako, 11 January 1965, *Target Tokyo*; Hanako Ishii, *Ningen Zoruge*, pp. 146–7.

28 *Der Spiegel*, 5 September 1951, p. 24.

29 Fesyun, *Documents*, No. 179, Decrypted Telegram Nos 10682, 19681.

30 Prange interviews with Yoshikawa, 14 January 1965; Tamazawa, 21 June 1965; Kawai, 14 January 1965, *Target Tokyo*.

31 Prange interview with Tamazawa, 21 January 1965, *Target Tokyo*; Hearings on the Un-American Aspects of the Richard Sorge Spy Case, US Government Printing Office, Washington DC, 1951, p. 1135. At the trials, Yoshisaburo Kitabayashi was found innocent. Tomo received a five-year sentence and was released with time off for good behaviour (see 'Sorge Spy Ring', p. A716).

32 Chief Noboru Takagi and two of his best detectives, Sakai Tamotsu and Tsuge Jimpei (Prange et al., *Target Tokyo*, p. 542).

33 Prange interview with Sakai, 31 January 1965, *Target Tokyo*.

34 Prange interview with Tamazawa, 21 January 1965, *Target Tokyo*; Hearings on the Un-American Aspects of the Richard Sorge Spy Case, US Government Printing Office, Washington DC, 1951, p. 1136; Article 1, Kinjiro Nakamura, *Entire Picture*, p. 22.

35 Prange interview with Sakai, 31 January 1965, *Target Tokyo*.

36 Prange interview with Yoshikawa, 16 January 1965, *Target Tokyo*.

37 Prange interview with Sakai, 31 January 1965, *Target Tokyo*.

38 Prange interview with Sakai, 31 January 1965, *Target Tokyo*. Taiji Hasebe, who worked on Clausen's case, told Prange in an interview of 19 January 1965 that Miyagi fractured a leg in his fall. But according to Yoshikawa, Miyagi injured his thigh (Prange interview of 14 January 1965). Sakai confirmed that the hospital found nothing wrong with Miyagi (Prange interview of 31 January 1965).

39 Prange interview with Yoshikawa, 16 January 1965, *Target Tokyo*.

40 Prange interview with Yoshikawa, 14 January 1965, *Target Tokyo*.

41 Prange interviews with Yoshikawa, 14 and 16 January 1965, *Target Tokyo*; Hearings on the Un-American Aspects of the Richard Sorge Spy Case, US Government Printing Office, Washington DC, 1951, p. 1136.

42 Hirosbi Miyashita, *Tokko no Koiso* ('*Reminiscences of the Tokko*'), Tokyo, 1978, p. 212; Article 1, Kinjiro Nakamura, *Entire Picture*, p. 24.

43 Article 1, Kinjiro Nakamura, *Entire Picture*, p. 24.

44 Prange interview with Yoshikawa, 14 January 1965, *Target Tokyo*.

45 Prange interview with Matsumoto, 8 January 1965, *Target Tokyo*.

46 Article 1, Kinjiro Nakamura, *Entire Picture*, p. 25.

47 Toshito (ed.), *Gendai-shi Shiryo*, Vol. 1, pp. 465, 480; Vol. 3, p. 229.

48 'Extracts', Clausen testimony, p. 41.

49 Toshito (ed.), *Gendai-shi Shiryo*, Vol. 1, p. 479, Vol. 3, p. 229.

50 Prange interview with Saito, 23 January 1965, *Target Tokyo*.

51 Prange interview with chief of the American–European Division of the Tokko's Foreign Section Suzuki Tomiki, 18 January 1965, *Target Tokyo*.

52 Prange interviews with Yoshikawa, 14 and 16 January 1965, *Target Tokyo*.

53 Article 1, Kinjiro Nakamura, *Entire Picture*, p. 25.

54 Toshito (ed.), *Gendai-shi Shiryo*, Vol. 3, pp. 230, 227, 230.

55 Toshito (ed.), *Gendai-shi Shiryo*, Vol. 3, pp. 230, 7, 104.

56 Toshito (ed.), *Gendai-shi Shiryo*, Vol. 3, pp. 7, 230.

57 Toshito (ed.), *Gendai-shi Shiryo*, Vol. 3, pp. 7, 230.

58 Toshito (ed.), *Gendai-shi Shiryo*, Vol. 3, pp. 7, 230.

59 Prange interview with Saito, 23 January 1965; with Saito/Harada interview, *Target Tokyo*.

60 Prange interviews with Yoshikawa, 14 January 1965, and Suzuki, 18 January 1965, *Target Tokyo*.

61 Prange interview with Suzuki, 18 January 1965, *Target Tokyo*.

62 Prange interviews with Vukelić prosecutor, Fuse Ken, 22 January 1965, and Suzuki, 18 January 1965, *Target Tokyo*.

63 Testimony on this individual's identity is conflicting. Suzuki claimed that it was Ms Ott and that the police held off because they anticipated enough trouble with the German embassy without involving the ambassador's wife (see Prange et al., *Target Tokyo*, chapter 59, n. 28). Saito emphatically denied this (see Prange Saito/Harada interview, May 1965). On the basis of an article by Ohashi, Deakin identified the caller as Wilhelm Schulz of the DNB (Deakin and Storrey, *Case of Richard Sorge*, p. 254n). Yet Ohashi told Prange that the visitor was the embassy's second secretary (interview with Ohashi, 21 January 1965, *Target Tokyo*). Yoshikawa only stated that someone was there; he did not know who (Prange interview with Yoshikawa, 14 January 1965, *Target Tokyo*; also Hearings on the Un-American Aspects of the Richard Sorge Spy Case, US Government Printing Office, Washington DC, 1951, p. 1137).

64 Prange interviews with Aoyama/Harada; Saito, 23 January 1965; Saito/Harada; Ohashi, 21 January 1965, *Target Tokyo*.

65 Prange interviews with Ogata, 20 January 1965; Yoshikawa, 14 January 1965; Saito, 23 January 1965, *Target Tokyo*.

66 Prange interview with Aoyama/Harada, *Target Tokyo*. Aoyama was never able to take up Sorge's generous offer – he was drafted into the army, where he remained throughout Sorge's trial and its grim aftermath.

67 'Extracts', Clausen testimony, original p. 482.

68 Prange interview with Suzuki, 18 January 1965, *Target Tokyo*.

69 Prange interview with Hasebe, 19 January 1965, *Target Tokyo*; 'Sorge Spy Ring', p. A721.

70 Prange interviews with Ogata, 20 January 1965 and Yoshikawa, 14 January 1965, *Target Tokyo*; 'Extracts', Clausen testimony, pp. 481–2.

71 Prange interviews with Ogata, 20 January 1965; Hasebe, 19 January 1965; Yoshikawa, 16 January 1965, *Target Tokyo*.

72 Johnson, *Instance of Treason*, pp. 183–6.

73 Message, Ott to Berlin, 23 October 1941, German Foreign Ministry Archives. German Foreign Office Political Archive (PADAA – Politisches Archiv des Auswärtigen Amts), Berlin: State Security File, Japan (1941–44): file on Sorge Case, p. 578.

74 Prange interviews with Yoshikawa, 16 January 1965, and Araki, 6 January 1965, *Target Tokyo*.

75 Prange interview with Yoshikawa, 16 January 1965, *Target Tokyo*.

76 Prange interviews with Hasebe, 19 January 1965, and Yoshikawa, 16 January 1965, *Target Tokyo*.

77 Prange interview with Ohashi, 21 January 1965, *Target Tokyo*; 'Extracts', Clausen testimony, original p. 481.

78 'Sorge Spy Ring', pp. A722–3.

79 Prange interview with Ohashi, 21 January 1965, *Target Tokyo*.

80 Prange interviews with Yoshikawa, 16 January 1965, Ohashi, 21 January 1965, and Tamazawa, 21 January 1965, *Target Tokyo*; Hearings on the Un-American Aspects of the Richard Sorge Spy Case, US Government Printing Office, Washington DC, 1951, p. 1144; Article 1, Kinjiro Nakamura, *Entire Picture*, p. 26.

81 Prange interviews with Yoshikawa, 16 January 1965, Ohashi, 21 January 1965, and Tamazawa, 21 January 1965, *Target Tokyo*.

82 Prange interviews with Yoshikawa, 16 January 1965, Ohashi, 21 January 1965, and Tamazawa, 21 January 1965, *Target Tokyo*.

83 Prange interviews with Yoshikawa, 16 January 1965, Ohashi, 21 January 1965, and Tamazawa, 21 January 1965, *Target Tokyo*.

84 Prange interviews with Yoshikawa, 16 January 1965, Ohashi, 21 January 1965, and Tamazawa, 21 January 1965, *Target Tokyo*.

85 Prange interviews with Yoshikawa, 16 January 1965, Ohashi, 21 January 1965, and Tamazawa, 21 January 1965, *Target Tokyo*.

CHAPTER 21

1 Willoughby, *Shanghai Conspiracy*, Preface by General Douglas MacArthur, p. 7.

2 Prange interview with Yoshikawa, 16 January 1965, *Target Tokyo*; Hearings on the Un-American Aspects of the Richard Sorge Spy Case, US Government Printing Office, Washington DC, 1951, p. 1142.

3 Prange interview with Yoshikawa, 16 January 1965, *Target Tokyo*.

4 Prange interviews with Yoshikawa, 16 January 1965, and Ohashi, 21 January 1965, *Target Tokyo*. Kordt, who claimed to have been present, wrote that

this interview lasted only three minutes (*Nicht aus den Akten*, p. 430), but Yoshikawa's estimate of at least ten minutes seems more likely.

5 Prange interviews with Yoshikawa, 16 January 1965, Ohashi, 21 January 1965, and Tamazawa, 21 January 1965, *Target Tokyo*.

6 Prange interviews with Yoshikawa, 16 January 1965, Ohashi, 21 January 1965, and Tamazawa, 21 January 1965, *Target Tokyo*.

7 Prange interview with Yoshikawa, 16 January 1965, *Target Tokyo*.

8 *Der Spiegel*, 19 September 1951, p. 24.

9 Ott quoted in a newspaper interview in 1959, cited in Prange et al., *Target Tokyo*, p. 592.

10 Prange interview with Yoshikawa, 16 January 1965, *Target Tokyo*.

11 Sorge Memoir, Pt 2, pp. 23, 31.

12 Prange interview with Ohashi, 21 January 1965, *Target Tokyo*; 'Sorge Spy Ring', p. A706.

13 Hanako Ishii, *Ningen Zoruge*, p. 154. Interview with Hanako, 16 January 1965, Prange, *Target Tokyo*.

14 Hanako Ishii, *Ningen Zoruge*, p. 154. Interview with Hanako, 16 January 1965, Prange, *Target Tokyo*.

15 Whymant, *Stalin's Spy*, p. 299.

16 Fesyun, *Documents*, Nos 180, 21102.

17 Fesyun, *Documents*, No. 181; RTsKhIDNI: f 495 op 73 d 188, list 7.

18 Gudz interview, ORT, 1999.

19 *Comrade Sorge: Documents and Memoirs*, p. 16.

20 Interview which Ms Harada conducted on behalf of Prange with Seiichi Ichijima, February 1965, *Target Tokyo*.

21 Johnson, *Instance of Treason*, pp. 2, 36.

22 'Sorge Spy Ring', pp. A717, 721.

23 Toshito (ed.), *Gendai-shi Shiryo*, p. 135.

24 Schellenberg, *Memoirs*, p. 162.

25 Schellenberg, *Memoirs*, pp. 163–4.

26 Schellenberg, *Memoirs*, pp. 163–4.

27 Schellenberg, *Memoirs*, pp. 164–5.

28 'Extracts', Pt XIV, Effect of Public Announcement of Case.

29 'Extracts', Pt XIV.

30 Nikolai Dolgopolov and Nadezhda Stolarchuk, 'Delo 3947. To Find the Grave of Katya Maximova', *Rossiyskaya Gazeta*, 20 October 2011.

31 *Der Spiegel*, 3 October 1951.

32 *Der Spiegel*, 3 October 1951.

33 'Extracts', Interrogation of Kawai.

34 Chunikhin, Vladimir Mikhailovich, *Richard Sorge: Notes*, p. 120.

35 Chunikhin, *Richard Sorge: Notes*, the evidence of V. T. Roshchupkin, p. 122.

36 Prange interview with Yuda, 18 January 1965, *Target Tokyo*.

37 Prange interview with Yuda Tamon, official Tokko witness to the execution, May 1965, *Target Tokyo*.

38 Prange interview with Yuda, 18 January 1965, *Target Tokyo*.

39 Prange interview with Yuda, 18 January 1965, *Target Tokyo*.

40 Interview which Ms Harada conducted on behalf of Prange, with Seiichi Ichijima, February 1965, *Target Tokyo*.

41 Answers to undated questionnaire submitted to Hotsuki Ozaki by Ms Harada on behalf of Prange, *Target Tokyo*; Toshito (ed.), *Gendai-shi Shiryo*, p. 6.

42 Prange interview with Yuda, 18 January 1965, *Target Tokyo*.

43 Prange interviews with Asanuma/Harada, and with Hanako, 7 January 1965, *Target Tokyo*.

44 Johnson, *Instance of Treason*, p. 254; Deakin and Storrey, *Case of Richard Sorge*, p. 345; Prange interview with Hanako, 9 January 1965, *Target Tokyo*.

45 https://www.findagrave.com/memorial/7284385/hanako-ishii.

46 *Washington Evening Star*, 23 and 24 August 1951.

47 *Washington Post*, 8 October 1952.

48 Meissner, *Man with Three Faces*, p. 218.

Select Bibliography

ARCHIVE SOURCES

Bundesarchiv: German Federal Archives, Koblenz: Bild 101I-121-0011A-22;
Bild 183-Z0519-022
Central Archives of the Ministry of Defence of the Russian Federation
(TsAMO RF), Podolsk: Fond 15, 15A, 17, 18, 39, 40, 47, 55, 58
FDR Papers at Franklin D. Roosevelt Presidential Library and Museum,
Hyde Park, NY, PSF Box 85
German Foreign Office Political Archive (PADAA – Politisches Archiv des
Auswärtigen Amts), Berlin: State Security File, Japan (1941–44): file on
Sorge Case
Library of Congress, Washington, DC: US Congress, 79th Congress,
Joint Committee on the Investigation of the Pearl Harbor Attack;
Hearings Before the Joint Committee on the Investigation of the
Pearl Harbor Attack, US Government Printing Office, Washington,
DC, 1945–46; US House of Representatives, 82nd Congress,
First Session: Un-American Activities Committee; Hearings on
Un-American Aspects of the Richard Sorge Spy Case, US Government
Printing Office, Washington, DC, 1951
The National Archives (TNA), London: HW 17/18, Radio Telegrams from
FO London–Moscow Embassy, 1935
Russian State Archive of Social and Political History, Moscow (RGASPI –
known as RTsKhIDNI, 1991–99): (former Archive of the Central
Committee of the Communist Party of the USSR, incorporating the
Archive of the Comintern): Fond 495, 496, 498, 508, 509, 510, 511.

PUBLISHED PRIMARY SOURCES

Antonov-Ovseyenko, Anton, *The Time of Stalin: Portrait of a Tyranny*,
    New York, 1981
Barmine, Alexander, *One Who Survived*, New York, 1945
Bukharin, Nikolai, 'Can We Build Socialism in One Country in the Absence
    of the Victory of the West-European Proletariat?', *Izvestiya*, April 1925
Chambers, Whittaker, *Witness*, New York, 1952
Comrade Sorge: Documents and Memoirs, Moscow, 1965 (written by
    journalists from *Sovietskaya Rossiya*, this was the first book on Sorge
    published in Russia)
Degras, Jane, *The Communist International, Selected Documents*,
    Oxford, 1960
Dirksen, Herbert von, *Moscow, Tokyo, London*, Norman, 1952
Dönitz, Admiral Karl, *Memoirs*, London, 1958, reprinted 1997
Fesyun, A. G., *Delo Rikharda Zorge: Neisvestnye Dokumenty*, Moscow, 2000
Gorev, Ya, 'Ya Znal Sorge', *Pravda*, 1964
Grew, Joseph C., *Ten Years in Japan*, New York, 1944
Harich-Schneider, Eta, *Charaktere und Katastrophen*, Berlin, 1978
Ishii, Hanako, *Ningen Zoruge, Aijin Miyake Hanako no Shuki* ('The Man
    Sorge, Memoirs of His Mistress Miyake Hanako'), Tokyo, 1956
Jensen, Richard, 'I Saw Sorge Last', *Politiken*, 27 December 1964
Kawai, Teikichi, *Am Kakumeika No Kaiso* ('Memoirs of a Revolutionary'),
    Tokyo, 1953
Kordt, Erich, *Nicht aus den Akten*, Union, Stuttgart, 1950
Krivitsky, Walter, *I Was Stalin's Agent*, London, 1940
Kudriatsev, V., 'I Meet Richard Sorge', *Izvestia*, 1–7 November 1964
Kuusinen, Aino, *Der Gott stürzt Seine Engel: Memoiren 1917–1965*, trans.
    A. Vuoristo. Helsinki, 1972 (*God Throws Down His Angels: Memoirs for
    the Years 1919–1965*); also published as *Before and After Stalin: A Personal
    Account of Soviet Russia from the 1920s to the 1960s*, London, 1974
'Letters between Sorge and his wife Katya', *Ogonek* magazine, April 1965
Marx–Engels Collected Works, Vol. 50, New York, 2004 (Friedrich Engels to
    Georgi Plekhanov, 26 February 1895)
Massing, Hede, *This Deception: KBG Targets America*, New York, 1951
Miyashita, Hiroshi, *Tokko no Kaiso* ('Reminiscences of the Tokko'),
    Tokyo, 1978
Newman, Joseph, *Goodbye Japan*, New York, 1942
'A Partial Documentation of the Sorge Espionage Case', Military Intelligence
    Section, United States Far East Command, US Congress House
    Committee on Un-American Activities, Tokyo, 1950

'Partial Memoirs of Richard Sorge' ('Sorge Memoir'), the English translation quoted here is reproduced in C. A. Willoughby, *Shanghai Conspiracy: The Sorge Spy Ring*, New York, 1952

Poretsky, Elizabeth, *Our Own People: A Memoir of Ignace Reiss and His Friends*, Oxford, 1969

Schellenberg, Walter, *The Schellenberg Memoirs*, London, 1956 (known in later editions as *The Labyrinth*)

Smedley, Agnes, 'The Social Revolutionary Struggle in China', and 'The Revolutionary Peasant Movement in China', Lewis Gannett Papers, Houghton Library, Harvard College Library, Cambridge, MA, c.1930–33

———'The Tokyo Martyrs', *Far East Spotlight*, March 1949

———*China Correspondent*, London and Boston, 1943, reprint edition, 1984

———*Daughter of Earth*, New York, 2011

Sorge, Christiane, 'Mein Mann – Dr R. Sorge', *Die Weltwoche*, 11 December 1964

'The Sorge Spy Ring: A Case Study in International Espionage in the Far East', in *US Congressional Record, 81st Congress, First Session*, Vol. 95, Part 12, Appendix, 9 February 1949

Toshito, Obi, (ed.), *Gendai-shi Shiryo, Zoruge jiken* ('Materials on Modern History: The Sorge Incident'), Tokyo, 1962, 3 Vols

Valtin, Jan, *Out of the Night*, London, 1941

Werner, Ruth, *Sonja's Rapport*, Berlin, 1977

Wickert, Erwin, *Mut und Übermut: Geschichten aus meinem Leben Gebundene Ausgabe*, Stuttgart, 1992

Zhukov, G. K., *The Memoirs of Marshal Zhukov*, New York, 1971

NEWSPAPERS

Asahi Shimbun, 2 July 1938

Japan Advertiser, 6–9 December 1933

Japan Times, 28 February 1936

New York Times: 31 July 1935; 14 July 1938

Spartanburg Herald-Journal, 12 May 1946

Der Spiegel, 20 June 1951; 27 June 1951; 8 August 1951; 3 October 1951

Tokyo Advertiser, 3 February 1938

Tokyo Asahi, 14 July 1938 (a.m. edition)

Tokyo Nichi Nichi Shimbun, 2 July 1938

Washington Evening Star, 23 and 24 August 1951

Washington Post, 8 October 1952

PUBLISHED SECONDARY SOURCES

GENERAL WORKS

Alekseyev, Mikhail, '*Vash Ramzai*' – *Your Ramsay: Richard Sorge and Soviet Military Intelligence in China 1930–1933*, Moscow, 2010

Braithwaite, Rodric, *Moscow 1941: A City and its People at War*, London, 2007

Chunikhin, Vladimir Mikhailovich, *Richard Sorge: Notes on the Margins of a Legend*, Moscow, 2008

Churchill, Winston S., *The Grand Alliance*, Boston, 1950

de Toledano, Ralph, *Spies, Dupes, and Diplomats*, New York, 1952

Deakin, F. W., and Storrey, G. R., *The Case of Richard Sorge*, London, 1966

Georgiyev, Yury, *Rikhard Sorge: Biografichesky Ocherk*, Moscow, 2002

Guerin, Alain, and Chatel, Nicole, *Camarade Sorge*, Paris, 1965

Howarth, David, *The Dreadnoughts*, Amsterdam, 1980

Johnson, Chalmers, *An Instance of Treason: Ozaki Hotsumi and the Sorge Spy Ring*, Stanford, CA, 1990

le Carré, John, *Progress* magazine, November 1966

————interview in *New York Times*, 17 August 2017

Mader, Julius, *Dr Sorge-Report*, 3rd extended edition, Berlin, 1985

Mader, Julius, Stucklik, Gerhard, and Pehnert, Horst, *Dr Sorge funkt aus Tokyo: Ein Dokumentarbericht über Kundschafter des Friedens mil auggewählten Artikeln von Richard Sorge*, Berlin, 1968

Massing, Hede, 'The Almost Perfect Russian Spy', *True* magazine, December 1951

Meissner, Hans-Otto, *The Man with Three Faces*, New York, 1956

Monk, Paul, 'Christopher Andrew and the Strange Case of Roger Hollis', *Quadrant* magazine, 1 April 2010

Montefiore, Simon Sebag, *Young Stalin*, London, 2008

Pincher, Chapman, *Their Trade is Treachery*, London, 1981

Prange, Gordon W., Goldstein, Donald M., and Dillon, Katherine V., *Target Tokyo*, New York, 1985

Richelson, Jeffery T., *A Century of Spies: Intelligence in the Twentieth Century*, Oxford, 1997

Rimer, J. Thomas, (ed.), *Patriots and Traitors, Sorge and Ozaki: A Japanese Cultural Casebook*, Maine, 2009

Shelton, Christina, *Alger Hiss: Why He Chose Treason*, New York, 2013

Whymant, Robert, *Stalin's Spy: Richard Sorge and the Tokyo Espionage Ring*, London, 1996

Willoughby, Charles Andrew, *Shanghai Conspiracy: The Sorge Spy Ring*, New York, 1952

Wright, Peter, *Spycatcher*, New York, 1988

Yudell, Michael, (ed.), *Richard Sorge: A Chronology*, www.richardsorge. com, 1996

SECOND WORLD WAR

Anfilov, Viktor, *Doroga k Tragedii Sorok Pervogo Goda*, Moscow, 1997

Bergstrom, Christer, *Barbarossa the Air Battle*, July–December 1941, Hersham, 2007

Bungay, Stephen, *The Most Dangerous Enemy: A History of the Battle of Britain*, London, 2009

Chapman, John W. M., *The Price of Admiralty: The War Diary of the German Attaché in Japan 1939–1943*, Lewes, Sussex, 1989

Cox, Richard, (ed.), *Operation Sea Lion*, London, 1975

Duffy, James P., *Hitler's Secret Pirate Fleet: The Deadliest Ships of World War II*, Lincoln, Nebraska, 2005

Feis, Herbert, *Road to Pearl Harbor: The Coming of the War Between the United States and Japan*, Princeton, NJ, 1971, 2015

Fritz, Stephen, *Ostkrieg: Hitler's War of Extermination in the East*, Lexington, 2011

Glantz, David, *Operation Barbarossa: Hitler's invasion of Russia 1941*, Stroud, 2012

Gorchakov, Ovidii, 'Nakanune, ili Tragedia Kassandry', *Gorizont*, No. 6, 1988

Gorodetsky, Gabriel, 'Was Stalin planning to attack Hitler in June 1941?', *RUSI Journal*, 1986, Vol. 131 (2)

Herman, John, 'Soviet Peace Efforts on the Eve of World War Two: A Review of the Soviet Documents', *Journal of Contemporary History*, 1 July 1980, Vol. 15 (3)

Kirchubel, Robert, *Operation Barbarossa 1941: Army Group Centre*, Oxford, 2007

Kotani, Ken, *Japanese Intelligence in World War II*, Oxford, 2009

Lukacs, John, *The Duel: Hitler vs. Churchill 10 May–31 July 1940*, London, 2000

Murphy, David E., *What Stalin Knew: The Enigma of Barbarossa*, New Haven and London, 2005

Overy, Richard, *The Battle of Britain: Myth and Reality*, London, 2010

Rusbridger, James, and Nave, Eric, *Betrayal at Pearl Harbor*, New York, 1991

Theobald, Robert A., *The Final Secret of Pearl Harbor*, New York, 1954

Wright, Gordon, *The Ordeal of Total War: 1939–1945*, New York, 1968

Zaloga, Steven J., and Howard, Gerrard, *Poland 1939: The Birth of Blitzkrieg*, London, 2002

CHINA

Garver, John W., *The Soviet Union and The Xi'an Incident [Arrest of Chiang Kaishek, 1936]*, Australian Journal of Chinese Affairs, No. 26, July 1991

MacKinnon, J. R., and MacKinnon, S. R., *Agnes Smedley: The Life and Times of an American Radical*, Berkeley, CA, 1968

Price, Ruth, *The Lives of Agnes Smedley*, Oxford, 2004

'The revolution in China, and the Menace of Imperialistic Intervention', *Izvestia*, 216, 7 August 1930

Sergeant, Harriet, *Shanghai: Collision Point of Cultures, 1918–1939*, New York, 1990

Snow, Edgar, *Random Notes on China*, Cambridge, MA, 1957

Taylor, Jay, *The Generalissimo: Chiang Kai-shek and the Struggle for Modern China*, Cambridge, MA, 2009

Tsang, Steve, 'Chiang Kai-shek's "secret deal" at Xian and the start of the Sino-Japanese War', *Palgrave Communications*, Vol. 1, 2015

Wakeman Jr, Frederic, *Policing Shanghai, 1927–37*, Berkeley and Los Angeles, CA, 1996

GERMANY

Broue, P., *The German Revolution: 1917–1923*, Chicago, 2006

Bullock, Alan, *Hitler: A Study in Tyranny*, New York, 1962

Dähnhardt, Dirk, *Revolution in Kiel*, Neumünster, 1978

Jurado, Carlos Caballero, and Bujeiro, Ramiro, *The German Freikorps 1918–23*, Oxford, 2001

Layton, Geoff, *Access to History: From Kaiser to Führer: Germany 1900–1945*, London, 2009

Lukes, Igor, *Czechoslovakia Between Stalin and Hitler: The Diplomacy of Edvard Beneš in the 1930s*, Oxford, 1996

Moreno, Barry, 'Sorge, Friedrich Adolf', in *Encyclopedia of New Jersey*, New Brunswick, NJ, 2004

Nekrich, Aleksandr Moiseevich, Ulam, Adam Bruno, and Freeze, Gregory L., *Pariahs, Partners, Predators: German–Soviet Relations, 1922–1941*, New York, 1997

Nelson, Anne, *Red Orchestra: The Story of the Berlin Underground and the Circle of Friends Who Resisted Hitler*, New York, 2009

Rauschning, Hermann, *Hitler Speaks: A Series of Political Conversations with Adolf Hitler on His Real Aims*, London, 2006

Reiss, Curt, *Total Espionage*, 1941, reprinted New York, 2016

Schmitz-Berning, Cornelia, *Vokabular des Nationalsozialismus*, Berlin, 2007

Shirer, William L., *The Rise and Fall of the Third Reich: A History of Nazi Germany*, 1960; reprinted New York, 1990

Wheeler-Bennett, Sir John W., *Nemesis of Power*, London, 1953

Wiggershaus, Rolf, *The Frankfurt School: Its History, Theories, and Political Significance* (Studies in Contemporary German Social Thought), Cambridge, MA, 1995

Winkler, Heinrich August, *Der lange Weg nach Westen*, Munich, 2000

————*Weimar 1918–33*, Munich, 2005

JAPAN

Behr, Edward, *Hirohito: Behind the Myth*, New York, 1989

Butow, Robert J. C., *Tojo and the Coming of the War*, Princeton, 1961

Byas, Hugh, *Government by Assassination*, 1942; reprinted New York, 2017

Coox, Alvin, *Nomonhan*, Stanford, 2003

Craigie, Sir Robert, *Behind the Japanese Mask*, London, 1945

Daizo, Kodama, *A Secret Record: The Mantetsu Chosabu*, Tokyo, 1960

Elphick, Peter, *Far Eastern File: The Intelligence War in the Far East, 1930–45*, London, 1997

Robert H. Ferrell, 'The Mukden Incident: September 18–19, 1931', *Journal of Modern History* 27 (1), 1955

Goldman, Stuart D., *Nomonhan, 1939: The Red Army's Victory that Shaped World War II*, Annapolis, MD, 2012

Hata, I., (ed.), *Nihon Riku kaigun sogo jiten*, Tokyo, 1991

Nakamura, Kinjiro, *Zoruge, Ozaki Hotzumi Supai Jiken No Zenbo: Soren Wa Subete o Shitte Ita* ('The Entire Picture of the Sorge-Ozaki Hotzumi Spy Incident'), Osaka, 1949

Koshkin, A. A., 'Kantokuen – the Japanese Barbarossa. Why Japan did not attack the USSR', Moscow, 2011

Kuromiya, Hiroaki, 'The Mystery of Nomonhan, 1939', *Journal of Slavic Military Studies*, Vol. 24, No. 4. 2011

————'Stalin's Great Terror and International Espionage', *Journal of Slavic Military Studies*, Vol. 24, No. 2, 2011

————'The Battle of Lake Khasan Reconsidered', *Journal of Slavic Military Studies*, Vol. 29, No. 1, 2016

Mitamura, Takeo, *Senso to Kyosanshugi, Showa Seiji Hiroku* ('War and Communism, Secret Records of Showa Politics'), Tokyo, 1950

Nedialkov, Dimitar, *In the Skies of Nomonhan, Japan vs Russia, May– September 1939*, Manchester, 2011

Neeno, Timothy, *Nomonhan: The Second Russo-Japanese War*, www. militaryhistoryonline.com, 2005

Ogi, H., *Shihyo Nomonhan*, Tokyo, 1986

Presseisen, Ernst L., *Germany and Japan: A Study in Totalitarian Diplomacy, 1933–1941*, The Hague, 1958

'Study of Strategical and Tactical Peculiarities of Far Eastern Russia and Soviet Far East Forces', *Japanese Special Studies on Manchuria*, Vol. XII, Tokyo, 1955

Wakabayashi, Bob Tadashi, 'Emperor Hirohito on Localised Aggression in China', *Sino-Japanese Studies* 4 (1), 1991

Weland, James, 'Misguided Intelligence: Japanese Military Intelligence Officers in the Manchurian Incident, September 1931', *Journal of Military History*, 58 (3), 1994

Young, John, *The Research Activities of the South Manchurian Railway Company, 1907–1945: A History and Bibliography*, New York, 1966

Young, Louise, *Japan's Total Empire*, Berkeley, CA, 1999

SOVIET UNION

Agaiants, Nikolail, and Yakovlev, Egor, *Tovarishch Zorge: dokumenty, vospominaniya, intervyu o podvige sovetskogo razvedchika Dementyeva, Irina, (1928–)*, Sovetskaya Rossiya, Moscow, 1965

Baker, Robert K., *Rezident: The Espionage Odyssey of Soviet General Vasily Zarubin*, Bloomington, IN, 2015

Bisher, Jamie, *White Terror: Cossack Warlords of the Trans-Siberian*, London, 2009

Brook-Shepherd, Gordon, *The Iron Maze: The Western Secret Services and the Bolsheviks, 1918–2004*, London, 1999

Bruce, Lincoln W., *Red Victory: A History of the Russian Civil War*, New York, 1989

Budkevich, Serge Leonidovich, *'Delo Zorge': sledstvie i sudebnyĭ protsess: lyudi, sobytiya, dokumenty, fakty*, Moscow, 1969

Bunich, Igor, *Operatsia Groza*, 3 Vols, 1994–2004, Moscow, 1998

Chamberlin, William Henry, *Soviet Russia: A Living Record and a History*, London, 1931

Chekhonin, B., 'Heroes Do Not Die', *Izvestia*, 8 September 1964

Cherayavsky, V., 'Richard Sorge's Exploit', *Pravda*, 6 November 1964

Cherushev, N. S., and Cherushev J. N., *Rasstrelenaya Elita PKKA (Komandiry 1ogo i 2ogo rangov, Komkory, Komdivy, i im ravniye): 1937–41*, Moscow, 2012

Clark, Lloyd, *Kursk: The Greatest Battle: Eastern Front 1943*, London, 2012

Coox, Alvin D., '"The lesser of two hells": NKVD general G. S. Lyushkov's defection to Japan, 1938–1945, part I', *Journal of Slavic Military Studies*, 11 (3), 1998

Dallin, David J., *Soviet Russia and the Far East*, New Haven, 1948

———*Soviet Espionage*, New Haven, 1955

Dolgopolov, Nikolai, 'Why Stalin Didn't Exchange Sorge?', *Rossiyskaya Gazeta*, 1 October 2015

Dolgopolov, Nikolai, and Stolarchuk, Nadezhda, 'Delo 3947: To Find the Grave of Katya Maximova', *Rossiyskaya Gazeta*, 20 October 2011

Gavrilov, Viktor, *Voennaya razvedka informiruet: dokumenty razvedupravleniya Krasnoĭ Armii, yanvar 1939–iyun 1941*, Moscow, 2008

Gavrilov, Viktor, and Gorbunov, Evgeniy, *Operatsiya 'Ramzaĭ': triumf i tragediya Rikharda Zorge*, Moscow, 2014

Geller, Yu, 'On the 70th Anniversary of the Birth of S. P. Uritskii', *Krasnaya Zveda*, 2 March 1965

Gladkov, T. K., *Nagrada za vernost' – kazn'*, Moscow, 2000

———*Artuzov Moscow: Molodaia gvardiia*, Moscow, 2008

Gladkov, T. K., and Zaitsev, N. G., *I ia emu ne mogu ne verit …*, Moscow, 1986

Goliakov, Sergei Mikhailovich, and Ilinskiy, Mikhail Mikhailovich, *Zorge: podvig i tragediya razvedchika*, Moscow, 2001

Gorbunov, Evgeniy, *Stalin i, GRU*, Moscow, 2010

Gorchakov, Ovidii, *Ian Berzin-komandarm GRU*, St Petersburg, 2014

Gregory, Paul R., *Politics, Murder, and Love in Stalin's Kremlin: The Story of Nikolai Bukharin and Anna Larina*, Stanford, CA, 2010

Haslam, Jonathan, *Near and Distant Neighbours: A New History of Soviet Intelligence*, Oxford, 2015

Jansen, Marc, and Petrov, Nikolai, *Stalin's Loyal Executioner: People's Commissar Nikolai Ezhov, 1895–1940*, Stanford, CA, 2002

Kochik, Valerii, *GRU: dela i lyudi*, Moscow, 2002

Kolpakidi, A. I., and Prokhorov, D. P., *Imperiya GRU, ocherki rossiskoi voyennoi razvedki*, Moscow, 1999

Krivosheeva, G. F., (ed.), *Grif sekretnosti sniat: poteri Vooruzhennykh Sil SSSR v voynakh, boevykh deystviyakh i voennykh konfliktakh*, Moscow, 1993

Kuznetsov, Viktor, *Protivostoianie: sovetskaya razvedka v gody vtoroy mirovoy voyny*, St Petersburg, 2006

Leonard, Raymond W., *Secret Soldiers of the Revolution: Soviet Military Intelligence*, 1918–1933, Westport, Conn. and London, 1999

Lock, Owen A., 'Chiefs of the GRU 1918–46', in Hayden B. Peake and Samuel Halpern (eds), *In the Name of Intelligence: Essays in Honor of Walter Pforzheimer*, Washington, DC, 1994

Lota, Vladimir, *GRU: ispytanie voĭnoĭ: voennaya razvedka Rossii nakanune i v gody Velikoi Otechestvennoi voiny 1941–1945*, Moscow, 2010

Marich, N., and Dzhuvarevich, M., 'Sorge's Assistant', *Krasnaya Zvezda*, 17 October 1964

Martirosyan, Arutyun, *Stalin i razvedka nakanune voiny*, Moscow, 2014

Mayevsky, Viktor, 'Comrade Richard Sorge', *Pravda*, 4 September 1964

Moore, Harriet L., *Soviet Far Eastern Policy, 1931–1945*, Princeton, 1945

Orlov, B., 'Centre Listens in to Ramsay', *Izvestia*, 28 October 1964

Pekelnik, N., 'The Exploits of Richard Sorge: The Story of a Soviet Spy's Heroism', *Izvestia*, 4 September 1964

Petrov, Vladimir, and Petrov, Evdokia, *Empire of Fear*, London, 1956

Prokhorov, D. P., *Skolko Stoit Prodat' Rodinu?*, St Petersburg, 2005

Prudnikova, Elena, *Rikhard Zorge – razvedchik No. 1*, St Petersburg, 2004

Prudnikova, E., and Gorchakov, O., *Legendy GRU*, St Petersburg, 2005

Radzinski, Edvard, *Stalin*, London, 1997

Chuev, F. I, Molotov, V. H., and Resis, Albert, *Molotov Remembers: Inside Kremlin Politics: Conversations with Felix Chuev*, Chicago, 1991 (also '*Sto Sotok Besed s Molotvym*', Chicago, 1993)

Rogovin, Vadim, *1937: Stalin's Year of Terror*, Oak Park, MI, 1998

Rubtsov, Yury, 'Command is my calling', in Voyenno-promyshlenny Kuryer, 13 June 2005

Semichastny, Vladimir, 'Soviet Chekists in the Great Patriotic War', *Pravda*, 7 May 1945

Sergeev, Evgeny, *Russian Military Intelligence in the War with Japan, 1904–05*, London, 2012

Service, Robert, *Lenin: A Biography*, London, reprints edition, 2010

Sever, Aleksandr, and Kolpakidi, Aleksandr Ivanovich, *GRU: unikalnaya entsiklopediya*, Moscow, 2009

Sokolov, Gennady, *Shpion nomer raz*, St Petersburg, 2013

Sokolov, Vladimir, *Voennaya agenturnaya razvedka: istoriya vne ideologii i politiki*, Moscow, 2013

Suvorov, Viktor, *Inside Soviet Military Intelligence*, New York, 1984

——*Spetsnaz: The Story Behind the Soviet SAS*, trans. David Floyd, London, 1987

——*The Chief Culprit: Stalin's Grand Design to Start World War II*, Annapolis, MD, 2008

'Unquestionable Facts of the War's Beginning', *Voenno-istorichesky Zhournal*, the official military-historical journal of the Russian forces, February 1992

Usov, Viktor, *Sovietskaya Razvedka v Kitae 20 – iye gody XX veka*, Moscow, 2007

Volkogonov, Dmitri, *Triumph and Tragedy* ('Triumf i tragediia: politicheskii portret I.V. Stalina'), Moscow, 1989

Volodarsky, Boris, *Stalin's Agent: The Life and Death of Alexander Orlov*, Oxford, 2015

COMMUNISM AND THE COMINTERN

Bennett, Gill, *'A Most Extraordinary and Mysterious Business': The Zinoviev Letter of 1924*, series: 'Historians LRD', No. 14, London, January 1999

Chapman, John W. M., 'A Dance on Eggs: Intelligence and the "Anti-Comintern"', *Journal of Contemporary History*, Vol. 22, No. 2 (Intelligence Services during the Second World War), April 1987

Courtois, Stéphane, Werth, Nicolas, and Paczkowski, Andrzej, *The Black Book of Communism*, Cambridge, MA, 1997

Kadish, Sharman, *Bolsheviks and British Jews: The Anglo-Jewish Community, Britain and the Russian Revolution*, London, 2013

Kendall, Walter, Review of Piero Melograni, 'Lenin and the Myth of World Revolution', *Revolutionary History*, Vol. 3 (3), 1991

Koch, Stephen, *Double Lives: Stalin, Willi Münzenberg and the Seduction of the Intellectuals*, New York, 2004

Litten, Frederick S., 'The Noulens Affair', *China Quarterly*, No. 138, June 1994

North, David, and Kishore, Joe, *The Historical and International Foundations of the Socialist Equality Party*, Oak Park, MI, 2008

Pipes, Richard, *Communism: A History*, New York, 2003

Priestland, David, *The Red Flag: A History of Communism*, New York, 2009

Shachtman, Max, 'For the Fourth International!' *New International*, Vol. 1, No.1, July 1934

Acknowledgements

In writing this book on Richard Sorge I am deeply in the debt of many scholars who have explored the subject before me, in conditions far more challenging than I myself have faced. Frederick William Deakin, former Warden of St Antony's College Oxford, was the first to bring the story to a Western readership and his 1965 book *The Case of Richard Sorge* was all the more remarkable for having extremely limited access to Soviet sources. My father, Mervyn Matthews, was a fellow of St Antony's at the time and I was touched to see his name in Deakin's own acknowledgements – in thanks for translation work, and for obtaining a Soviet four-kopeck stamp with Sorge's face on it, which illustrated the cover of the first edition. In Tokyo, Professor Gordon Prange could hardly have been more exhaustive in his research on the Japanese career of Sorge. Prange spent thirty years on his great work, *Target Tokyo*, and his interviews with many people who knew Sorge personally, from his mistress to the policemen who watched him tirelessly, is invaluable. Robert Whymant, a fellow journalist and former Tokyo bureau chief for *The Times*, also interviewed several of the principals in the 1980s for his *Stalin's Spy*, the most recent English-language work on the subject.

I must also acknowledge my deep gratitude and admiration for the work of modern Russian scholars Vladimir Chunikhin, Alexander Fesyun and Mikhail Alekseyev, who have done so much to unearth the tragic story of Moscow Centre's indifference to its star agent in Tokyo.

In the summer of 2016 I was privileged to have been invited to attend the annual conference of Japan's Sorge society at Tokyo's Meiji University. I am extremely grateful to Professor Tetsuro Kato of Waseda University, and to Tsutomu Shinozaki for taking the time to meet me and talk on matters Sorge related over sandwiches and tea. I am also grateful to Professor Jeffrey Burds for sharing archival material and for pointing me in the right direction on untapped Soviet sources on Sorge. Professor Hiroaki Kuromiya was also kind enough to share his groundbreaking work on the Nomonhan incident.

In Moscow I am also very thankful to the staff of RGASPI – the former Central Committee Archive – as well as to the librarians at the Central Defence Ministry Archives in Podolsk. In Baku I was able to find Sorge's house after an afternoon of tireless questioning of the locals of Sabunchi by Fareed Ismailov – who drove me around in a London black taxi, a bizarrely common sight on the streets of Azerbaijan's capital. I am also grateful to my old university friend Nikolaus Twickel for his translations of German sources. My friend and colleague Alexei Kazakov in Moscow also helped me see the dramatic potential of the Sorge story, and helped me enormously in framing the human story in the sweep of history.

I am also deeply thankful to my agent Natasha Fairweather for her enthusiasm and energy, and to Michael Fishwick, my long suffering editor at Bloomsbury, and to his excellent team.

My wife Ksenia and children Nikita and Theodore have lived with Sorge as a virtual family member for four years, traveling with me to his various haunts and putting up with dinner-table stories of a long-dead spy. I could not have written this book without their support.

Picture Credits

'From the schoolroom to the slaughterhouse' – Richard Sorge, aged 20, after being wounded, 1916: © ullstein bild Dtl./Getty Images

Baku days – the oil engineer Wilhelm Sorge and his Russian wife Nina with their children (Richard in white): © Sputnik/Bridgeman Images

The Sorge's house in the once-affluent Baku suburb of Sabunchi today: © Private Collection

Sorge and his cousin, Erich Correns: © ullstein bild Dtl./Getty Images

Osip Pyatnitsky, the Comintern commissar who recruited Sorge in Frankfurt in 1924: © History and Art Collection / Alamy Stock Photo

Sorge's official Comintern identity photograph, Moscow, 1924: © Private Collection

General Jan Karlovich Berzin, the founder of Red Army Intelligence who headhunted Sorge from the disintegrating Comintern: © Archive PL / Alamy Stock Photo

Sorge's signature in the Comintern files in Moscow, 1924: © Private Collection

Konstantin Basov, the brilliant Berlin spymaster who launched Sorge for his Fouth Department career: Courtesy of the Sakharov Center

Katya Maximova and her two sisters around the time she met Sorge: © Private Collection

Fourth Department officer Boris Gudz: © Svetlana and Serguey Zlobin private archive

The only surviving photograph of Katya and Sorge together: © ullstein bild Dtl./Getty Images

The Shanghai Bund, 1930: © Gibson Green / Alamy Stock Photo

Alexander Ulanovsky, Sorge's charming but indiscreet boss in Shanghai: Courtesy of Alexander Yakobson, Grandson of Alexander Ulanovsky.

Swindler, spy and former secret policeman Evgeny Kozhevnikov, aka Captain Pik: © NARA II/Washington DC

Humanitarian, journalist and spy Agnes Smedley, in Chinese uniform. Sorge unchivalrously called his lover 'a mannish woman': © Historic Images / Alamy Stock Photo

Ursula Kuczynski, alias Ruth Werner: Courtesy of cia.gov

Hede Massing: © akg-images / TT News Agency / SVT

Hotsumi Ozaki, the idealistic Japanese journalist who worked with Sorge in Shanghai and became his most valuable agent in Japan: © Kyodo News/Getty Images

Yotoku Miyagi, the consumptive painter who became the spy ring's most indefatigable leg-man: © Kyodo News/Getty Images

Branko Vukelić, the failed Croatian journalist recruited in Paris as the ring's photographer, with his Japanese wife Yoshiko Yamasaki: © SVF2/Getty Images

Max Clausen, Sorge's trusty radio man in Shanghai who followed him to Tokyo: © TopFoto

Max's wife Anna Clausen: © SVF2/Getty Images

Ambassador Major General Eugen Ott, whose unshakeable trust in his friend Sorge enabled a great espionage career: © SZ Photo / Knorr + Hirth / Bridgeman Images

Helma Ott, wife of Eugen and lover of Sorge: © Private Collection

The German Embassy in Tokyo: © Chronicle / Alamy Stock Photo

Eugen and Helma visit the palace, Tokyo, 1938: © Hawaii Times Photo Archives Foundation

Hanako Miyake, Sorge's longstanding Japanese mistress: © Private Collection

Rear-Admiral Paul 'Paulchen' Wenneker, one of Sorge's most devoted bottle-mates and informants: © Hawaii Times Photo Archives Foundation

Prince Albrecht von Urach, Tokyo correspondent of the rabidly anti-semitic *Völkischer Beobachter*, also joined Sorge on his late night drinking binges in Ginza: © ullstein bild Dtl./Getty Images

'A face like a ravaged robber baron' – Sorge after drunkenly crashing his motorcycle: © SZ Photo / Bridgeman Images

Sorge in Japanese clothes at home on Nagasaki street: © ullstein bild Dtl./Getty Images

Sorge at the German Embassy dacha: © Pictures from History / Bridgeman Images

Sorge on one of his regular tours across Japan: © INTERFOTO / Alamy Stock Photo

Eta Harich-Schneider, the celebrated harpsichordist who was Sorge's last lover: © Max Ehlert/ullstein bild Dtl./Getty Images

Anita Mohr, the glamorous blonde who was best friend to Helma Ott, Eugen Ott's love object – and Sorge's mistress: © Private Collection

Aino Kuusinen, the Comintern princess sent to summon Sorge back to Moscow in 1937: Courtesy of Hannes Hólmsteinn Gissurarson

Prince Fumimaro Konoye, three times prime minister of Japan, who brought Ozaki into his inner circle of advisers: © Bettmann/Getty Images

General Hideki Tojo, who masterminded Japan's invasion of China as well as the attack on Pearl Harbor: ©AFP/Getty Images

The South Manchurian Railway, or Mantetsu, also controlled its own intelligence agency and the army: © Chronicle of World History / Alamy Stock Photo

Gestapo Colonel Joseph Meisinger, the 'Butcher of Warsaw' sent to investigate Sorge: Courtesy of Instytut Pamięci Narodowej (GK 166/251)

SS-Brigadeführer and spymaster Walter Schellenberg, who suspected Sorge of being a Soviet agent: ©Bundesarchiv/Bild 101III-Alber-178-04A/Kurt Alber

Joseph Stalin looks on as Soviet and German Foreign Ministers Vyacheslav Molotov and Joachim von Ribbentrop sign the non-aggression pact that secretly divided Eastern Europe between Berlin and Moscow: © Universal images Group/Getty Images

Stalin greets Japanese Foreign Minister Yosuke Matsuoka in Moscow in 1939. By the time of his departure Matsuoka was so drunk that he and Stalin sang folk songs together on the platform: © The Asahi Shimbun /Getty Images

General Filip Golikov, whose six predecessors as heads of the Fourth Department had all been executed. Golikov suppressed Sorge's urgent reports of an imminent German invasion: © Sovfoto/Getty Images

Sorge's police photograph after his arrest: © SPUTNIK / Alamy Stock Photo

A Soviet four-kopeck stamp produced after Sorge's official rehabilitation in 1961: © Sputnik / Bridgeman Images

Sorge's grave in Tokyo, the original humble gravestone paid for by his mistress swamped by the hulking Soviet monument featuring his posthumous Hero of the Soviet Union star: © Sputnik/Topfoto.co.uk

Monument to Sorge in his native Baku: © Private Collection

All reasonable attempts have been made to contact the copyright holders of all images. You are invited to contact the publisher if your image was used without identification or acknowledgement

Index

A Note on the Author

Owen Matthews studied Modern History at Oxford University before beginning his career as a journalist in Bosnia. He has written for the *Moscow Times*, *The Times*, the *Spectator* and the *Independent*. In 1997, he became a correspondent at *Newsweek* magazine in Moscow where he covered the second Chechen war, Afghanistan, Iraq and the conflict in Eastern Ukraine. His first book on Russian history, *Stalin's Children*, was translated into twenty-eight languages and shortlisted for the *Guardian* First Book Award and France's Prix Médicis.

A Note on the Type

The text of this book is set Adobe Garamond. It is one of several versions of Garamond based on the designs of Claude Garamond. It is thought that Garamond based his font on Bembo, cut in 1495 by Francesco Griffo in collaboration with the Italian printer Aldus Manutius. Garamond types were first used in books printed in Paris around 1532. Many of the present-day versions of this type are based on the *Typi Academiae* of Jean Jannon cut in Sedan in 1615.

Claude Garamond was born in Paris in 1480. He learned how to cut type from his father and by the age of fifteen he was able to fashion steel punches the size of a pica with great precision. At the age of sixty he was commissioned by King Francis I to design a Greek alphabet, and for this he was given the honourable title of royal type founder. He died in 1561.